Conservatism is UNAMERICAN
& Other Self-Evident Truths

The second edition of the book that looks at America's socialist genesis
and the right's historic hostility to liberty, equality, and democracy

JEROME NICOLAS

Copyright 2014 © by Jerome Nicolas
All rights reserved,
Including the right of reproduction
in whole or in part in any form

ISBN-13: 978-1500314637
ISBN-10: 1500314633

Acknowledgements

I want to thank, in alphabetical order, Mike Males, James H. Miller, Gary B. Nash, and Rachel Rosen for looking over my early, unwieldy manuscript and making so many insightful suggestions. It helped make this work far more focused and approachable. Then I wrote more and spoiled it.

So, I would like to add thanks to Robin Harris who proofread the ugly result and rescued me from myself.

Then I wrote more and spoiled it again.

Also, please accept my apologies for the improper pagination: I know these preliminary pages should not have page numbers. Unfortunately, the morons at Microsoft who wrote this latest version of Word do not know this and accordingly removed the tools I need to format this manuscript correctly. I did not have this particular difficulty with the first edition in 2014.

Contents

The More Things Change 9
Introduction: Dinosaur Bones 15
1: The Three Legs of the Tripod 25
2: The Skinny on Liberty 54
3: Liberté, Egalité, and Rock & Roll 77
4: Why the Right is Wrong on Property 100
5: Why I am Not a Libertarian 129
6: Three Different Libertarians 158
7: Participatory Democracy 187
8: Springtime for Goldberg 206
9: Liberty, Equality, & Empathy 238
10: The Tory's Phony Loyalty 272
Notes 292

"The long memory is the most radical thing in America."

– Utah Phillips

The More Things Change
Preface to the "Second" Edition

This is not *quite* a second edition. Let me explain exactly why.

This book took over a decade to write. I started typing it on 9-11 and finally self-published it in the middle of President Barack Obama's second term in 2014. By that point, George W. Bush's administration seemed like a bad dream. Optimism ran high and I thought people would see my book as a quaint and antiquated autopsy of conservatism.

So, in the original introduction, I cautioned against overconfidence. Conservatism would return: The empire would strike back. Of course, the loss of Congress and so many state governors and legislatures had already suggested that. The presidency is not everything, but it is so symbolically potent that many people cannot think beyond it.

Today, under Donald Trump, my warning seems as dated as it was prescient, so I probably look irrelevant for being right. But, I am leaving the warning in because it will eventually become relevant again. Optimism shall surely return – and stupid hubris with it.

You will probably notice numerous dated references in this book. At the particular political moment that I finished this thing, the fight for gay marriage had not quite reached the Supreme Court and the GOP was still trying to repeal Obamacare. I am leaving most old references in "as is" because time capsules are cool, but also for another more important reason.

You see, most of those dated references were deliberate to begin with. One of my main points is that conservatism does not change much across time. As Corey Robin explained in *The Reactionary Mind: Conservatism from Edmund Burke to Sarah Palin*, conservatism may make cosmetic changes to adapt (including theft of the left's rhetoric and tactics); but otherwise, it basically remains the same mindset. In the original edition of this book, I provided ample examples from both distant and recent history to prove that point. The rhetoric and policies of Richard Nixon, Ronald Reagan, and both George Bushes got plenty of attention. To those I added the Tea Party's racist antics as the Obama era unfolded.

I could now add examples from the current Trump era. But why bother? Anything I could say about Trump or Trumpism would be redundant. Nearly everything Donald Trump has said or done has a precedent among conservative presidents, even if it was to a lesser extent.

Even "Grab them by the pussy"? Hell, yes. Remember when George W. Bush tried to give German Chancellor Angela Merkel a sudden unwanted shoulder rub? It did not entail genitalia, but the incident was still pretty creepy – and committed in a room full of world leaders and journalists and therefore on video. Donald Trump's language was certainly more brazen, but his verified behavior less so. At least until the rumored pee tape drops.

"But what about the Nazi stuff?" you may ask. "Old hat," I can still answer. Ronald Reagan hired Pat Buchanan as White House Director of Communications before Donald Trump hired Steve Bannon to handle his messaging. Why? Because both Buchanan and O'Bannon understood the Republican Party's virulently racist base. This is GOP SOP.

And Buchanan was Trump before Trump became a significant political figure. Trump straight-up stole Buchanan's Mexican border wall idea along with the rest of his rhetoric. Despite their clashing egos, they share the same paleoconservative base.

Fun fact: Trump once called Buchanan a "Hitler-lover" in 1999 when they were fighting over the dying remains of Ross Perot's Reform Party. But Trump is hardly a recent convert to this mindset, as his old newspaper ads against the Central Park Five vividly illustrate.

Moreover, Donald Trump did not invent the Southern Strategy. Those infamous Willie Horton campaign ads ran in 1988 and were the work of Reagan/Bush strategist Lee Atwater, who famously explained how you could mobilize racist whites without using the N-word. How could anyone forget or ignore that the GOP became the party of Strom Thurmond and David Duke long ago? They started using their ancient racist dog whistles with Barry Goldwater's 1964 failed presidential bid.

Ditto with Donald Trump's vicious anti-immigrant policies. I mentioned that his border wall was originally Buchanan's idea, but that nativist attitude did not go underground in the interim. It metastasized in the meantime. Anyone who watched Fox News (or CNN, for that matter) during the Bush and Obama years saw conservative frothing on immigration steadily mount. In my original text, I gave several ugly examples from Bill O'Reilly to Lou Dobbs. Remember Arizona's draconian "papers please" legislation? I wrote a lot about the Tea Party's bigotry. Of course, there was a lot to write about.

In short, Trump is just an old boil bursting so we can see the putrid puss inside. The content is not novel unless your memory has the lifespan of a mayfly. I mean, Spoiler Alert: If this book's title did not already clue you in, I have no intention of letting conservatism off the hook to nail the villain of the minute – especially when he exemplifies a longstanding problem.

And again, this long view was built into the original edition right from the start. When I began work on this book right after 9-11, the idea that conservatism is un-American was already pretty fixed in my head. Once you connect fun and freedom in your brain, the battle lines are pretty clearly drawn. Moral scolds do not appreciate individual liberty. And once you notice conservatism's overt hostility toward equality, it becomes even clearer. But repeatedly reading pundits insist we must give up our freedoms in order to preserve them was what finally got me typing.

The establishment's rationale was that this dangerous new world required unusual (but permanent) sacrifices of civil liberties. It was exactly the sort of cowardly and pompous response you would expect from servile stenographers posing as objective reporters.

But their story was already a pretty moldy. It was used to set up the national security state during the Cold War. After the Berlin Wall fell, the War on Drugs became the new reason for stepped up surveillance. The War on Terror kicked it up another notch but its function was just the same. Stoking fear to control people is nothing new.

I knew my book would quickly become dated. After all, *all* political books do. This forward is already collecting dust as I type it.

But I am not arguing that history repeats itself (or stutters, as Mark Twain famously quipped). What I *am* arguing is that conservatism is a predictable constant. It is consistently authoritarian and therefore anti-freedom, anti-egalitarian, and anti-democratic. This is inherently un-American in every single aspect. Specific examples will come and go, but they play out roughly the same way.

This is not as contradictory as it sounds. People are creatures of habit: Sometimes that helps them, but sometimes it backfires. But the political terrain is always shifting. And although it helps to know your opponent's habits, assuming the landscape remains the same is a grave mistake. People frequently play to their strengths, but the situation does not always compliment those strengths. On the other hand, we can also change the terrain ourselves. A little grassroots landscaping goes a long way.

So, not much has really changed. I made a few stylistic tweaks to this book, but the content is largely untouched. There were some portions that I thought were clunky or redundant, so I dropped them. But I did this on a case-by-case basis and in some instances I decided things needed repeating.

I also approached the content on a case-by-case basis. It is not my intent to hide my mistakes, but I do not want to circulate incorrect information either, so I have an obligation to edit. So I note the change either in the text or in an endnote, depending on things like reading flow or the significance of the change. Mostly, this was a matter of celebrity references that have not aged very well and I do not want to promote those people anymore.

For example, I am a democratic socialist (or social democrat – I go back and forth), yet I used to enjoy libertarian comedian Bill Maher despite our differences. But my familiarity with him was apparently pretty limited. I do not have cable, so my exposure was and remains sporadic secondhand clips on social media of the "Bill Maher destroys fundamentalist hypocrites again" ilk. So what I saw was filtered. Maybe the misogyny and Islamophobia have grown over the years. Maybe I did not notice the extent before. Maybe I was less "woke" before. In any case, the incidents are no longer isolated or arguable anymore. The jury is in: He is a dick. And I confess I was late to get the memo.

Bill Maher is, to be sure, far better than most libertarians are now. He supported Barack Hussein Obama to the tune of a million dollars, so I suppose Obama's middle name was not a deal-breaker for him. And Maher is pro-choice; whereas the "Libertarian" Party ran its first anti-choice presidential candidate, Ron Paul, back in 1988 so that betrayal is ancient news. I mainly used Maher to show how very un-libertarian many libertarians have increasingly become. And if Maher is the best they can produce, that says a lot about them – hence his continued inclusion in this book, even though my opinion of him has dimmed considerably.

One last caveat: Since finishing this book in 2014, the 2016 election happened and I took a side in the Democratic primaries. This was ludicrously stupid of me from a sales standpoint. After all, why alienate half my potential audience?

Well, the title of this book is *Conservatism is Un-American*, so I am openly hostile to conservatism and all its apologists who suggest Republicans "have some good ideas." No, they do not. And my argument that some of our founding fathers had inspired a lot of subsequent socialist thought should also have been a humongous clue as to where I stood.

For what it's worth, I voted "blue no matter who" as Bernie Sanders, Elizabeth Warren, and Noam Chomsky had urged.

If any of that grates, take comfort in the fact that I finished my book in the spring of 2014, so there should be minimal offensive content. In one original endnote, I had professed my profound hope that Elizabeth Warren would run and give us a progressive alternative to Hillary Clinton. (Bernie Sanders did not declare his candidacy for the presidency until the spring of 2015 – nearly a year after this book went live.) And while I was grousing about conservative outrages, I often had to admit that Democrats had done similar things. I was very unhappy to do so, but accuracy compelled it.

Otherwise, nothing in these pages should annoy any honest opponent of conservatism. And what does annoy should spur reflection instead of prickly defensiveness.

So, a lot of horror has occurred in the intervening years between finishing this book and now. And yet, none of it suggests that I should rethink my thesis. On the contrary, these things were as predictable are they were terrible and only prove my points. Trump is indeed utterly un-American in every facet, yet conservatives have been caricaturing themselves with increasing grotesqueness for decades on end. Seriously, the "Spitting Image" puppets seem almost genteel by comparison.

But Trump is just the ultimate result. He personifies this longtime trend. He is the symptom – not the disease. The problem is conservatism itself and it always has been.

Look, if placing Trump's face on this reactionary mentality helps you conceptualize it better, go for it. Just know that you will see his face repeatedly the further back you go – in 80s Reaganism, 60s Goldwaterism, and 50s McCarthyism. If you have even the slightest historical literacy, this makes perfect sense and requires no additional explanation.

After all, does not Donald Trump personify the status-mongering gold-painted egoism of the 80s? His hilarious hair alone embodies it.

So many television shows of that decade were about tacky, callous rich people. Think of "Dallas," "Dynasty" (with a Henry Kissinger cameo), and "Lifestyles of the Rich and Famous."

This was the decade of "greed is good," executive excess, copious hairspray, and the general celebration of dickish materialism. It was a boorish and buffoonish decade that rewarded all of Donald Trump's worst acting out with additional attention. You cannot honestly ignore these influences. Trump defined the 80s as much as Reagan did.

Sixties conservatism might seem pretty different at first blush, but remember that Ronald Reagan gave the official nomination for Barry Goldwater at the 1964 GOP convention.

And how was Reagan's rhetoric that different a decade and a half later? Goldwater's slogan was "In your heart, you know he's right." The Democrats' accurate rejoinder was "In your guts, you know he's nuts."

Yes, Goldwater often made unhinged open mic gaffes – as did Reagan, G.W. Bush, and Trump. Underlying them was a Paleolithic conservative paranoia slathered with *volkish* nostalgia for an America that never was and that mentality long predated Joe McCarthy.

One day, one way or another, Trump will eventually be gone, Yet the problem will still remain. Maybe he will have one too many well-done steaks smothered in ketchup. Perhaps he will choke on a pretzel.

Then what?

Will we forgive and forget his crimes as we have Richard Nixon's, Ronald Reagan's, and George W. Bush's as conservatism's next grotesque incarnation inevitably emerges?

Perhaps that has already happened by the time you read this and the monster of the moment has softened you on Donald Trump making you almost nostalgic for that vulgar clown. Should we not, at long last, honestly confront this chronic problem and examine its root causes to stop it?

I am not actually taunting you – the problem is. It is brazen and obvious. To put it plainly, the problem is being something of a cocky asshole. You can banish this constant, recurrent discomfort. It is within your power to do so. But alas, a temporary spike in your discomfort is the price you must pay. It may seem too steep, but inaction is ultimately steeper.

I do not entirely relish your discomfort since, compassion aside, it makes my job far harder and I am pretty damn lazy for an obsessive-compulsive. If you thought this forward ran long, you may be the cause.

So, adult-up. Step outside your comfort zone – because nothing of any historic importance was ever accomplished inside anyone's comfort zone.

Jerome Nicolas, 2019

Introduction: Dinosaur Bones
The Political Fossil Record

Way back in 1981, the true nature of American conservatism was laid bare on the air. In a moment of reactionary candor, California state senator John G. Schmitz told a television interviewer that if Ronald Reagan's economic policies fail, "the best we could probably hope for is a military coup or something like that."[1] Schmidt quickly clarified that he meant "a good military coup, not a bad military coup." Nice save.

Granted, everyone knew that the man from Orange County was crazy. After all, he represented Orange County. John Schmitz had been National Director of the right wing John Birch Society. He once joked that he had joined, "to get the middle-of-the-road vote in Orange County."[2] It may not have been a joke: In 1982, the Society finally expelled him for his frequent extremist remarks, but his district kept reelecting him.[3]

Schmitz was a political curio who reporters often sought for colorful quotes. He was a United States Congressman in 1972 when he had famously quipped, "I have no objection to President Nixon going to China. I just object to his coming back."[4] The California Republican Party subsequently blocked him from running for national office ever again.

Today, such voices are no anomaly. They are promoted, rather than demoted. This reversal occurred shortly after John G. Schmitz's fall from grace. In 1987, Conservative Caucus leader Howard Phillips called President Ronald Reagan a "useful idiot for Kremlin propaganda." It was comparable to John Birch Society founder Robert Welch calling President Dwight Eisenhower a "communist dupe" in the 1950s.

Yet instead of placing Phillips outside the realm of respectable political discourse, the comment was his ticket into mainstream media outlets like the opinion page of the *New York Times*.[5] Since then, pundits such as Pat Buchanan and Ann Coulter flaunt their authoritarian enthusiasms in print and on the air fairly regularly.

Of course, those two are crazy too, but they represent a far larger population than Orange County and they have countless copycats. Indeed, between talk radio, the Internet, and cable TV, such punditry has become a cottage industry. And many of these opinion-slingers considered President George W. Bush to be a secret liberal. Imagine that.

This has had a profound impact on the electoral process. Nowadays, any display of sanity is the kiss of death in the Republican Party. Conservative purists have declared open season on "RINOs" – "Republicans In Name

Only." So, moderate Republicans are politically endangered, if not extinct. They must tack far right to survive the primaries. And if the party faithful remain suspicious, their lack of zeal will show at the polls. There are no more Eisenhower Republicans in Washington, let alone Rockefeller Republicans. Party leaders from Jeb Bush to Mike Huckabee have admitted that not even Ronald Reagan could pass the Tea Party's yardstick of conservative purity.[6] Ironically, it is often called the "Reagan Test."

What is conservatism? Forget all their small government rhetoric because each of their recent presidents had swelled police powers and the debt. Libertarian bombast cannot camouflage their mile-wide authoritarian streak. Their real ideology is actually less an ideology than an attitude which ultimately boils down to the late Robert Bork's hostility to liberty and equality (and to democracy by extension). Conservatives practice a paradoxical form of patriotism that resists all America represents.

For example, when France refused to support George W. Bush's invasion of Iraq, conservatives said we should return the Statue of Liberty. Remember that? This went beyond France-bashing because there was zero ambivalence. The right has never liked anything that statue stands for, neither liberty nor immigration. Consider its inscription: "Give me your tired, your poor/Your huddled masses yearning to breathe free/The wretched refuse of your teeming shore." Try wedging that plank into the Republican platform sometime.

Conservatives hate everything America stands for. They hate the separation of church and state and see upholding the rights of the accused as being "soft on crime." Indeed, they loathe everything that the American Civil Liberties Union (ACLU) stands for – in sum, the Constitution.

Their contempt is chronic. According to lore, former Secretary of State Henry Kissinger had once joked, "The illegal we do immediately. The unconstitutional takes a little longer."[7] But they invariably get around to it. His joke would have been funnier if this predilection was limited to the Nixon Administration. But after Watergate, we had Ronald Reagan's Iran-Contra scandal followed by a host of constitutional abuses by George W. Bush. It is an inexorable reflex for those who scorn the democratic process and the rule of law. In short, Enlightenment principles of government inconvenience their vigilante tendencies. Conservatives think that consensus and consistency are for sissies.

There was a phrase that Ronald Reagan was awfully fond of: "The law of the land." It has a familiar majesty. It should – it is in the Constitution. It is the part which declares that ratified treaties are U.S. law. Yet few conservatives know or honor this. They often treat international law as an optional inconvenience, thus George W. Bush's administration dismissing the Geneva

Conventions' ban against torturing prisoners as "quaint." Of course, the Constitution bans "cruel and unusual punishment" too.

Conservatives have also historically opposed most American art forms such as jazz, the comic book, rock and roll, and rap. They have banned or burned each for the same reasons: Because minorities invented them and these forms all expressed freedom and rebellion.

Of course, that is precisely what makes American pop culture *American –* and so popular worldwide. (It buys us a lot of international good will, which we subsequently squander on stupid wars.) Thus, conservatism's hatred of America is cultural as well as procedural. And, as my Statue of Liberty example illustrates, they are ultimately related.

Social conservatives are not wrong when they say that policy and culture are two sides of the same coin. That is why they are wrong on both policy and culture. Their failure as Americans is total because their mindset loathes America's every ethos. They are temperamentally un-American.

Look at any rightist pundit, either in print or on the air. All their ideas, ideals, and desires are antithetical to America.

Consider Dinesh D'Souza's book, *The Enemy at Home: The Cultural Left and Its Responsibility for 9/11*, for example. His thesis is essentially that our secular society provoked those of traditional faith. He thinks our modern society is a great mistake:

Yes, I would rather go to a baseball game or have a drink with Michael Moore than with the grand mufti of Egypt. But when it comes to core beliefs, I'd have to confess that I'm closer to the dignified fellow in the long robe and prayer beads than to the slovenly fellow with the baseball cap.[8]

There, in two sentences, is the inherent tension of being a reactionary in a free society. American conservatives do not often acknowledge this dilemma even though it defines them.

And just what was Dinesh D'Souza's brilliant solution to this identity crisis and the War on Terror as well? He proposed forming a global alliance of Christian and Muslim fundamentalists against secularism. In short, he said we should beat Osama bin Laden by stealing his issues.

Such thinking is as predictable as it is sickening. Indeed, as Andrew Sullivan noted in his book review:

It is crucial to remember that, for all the conservative criticism of The Enemy at Home, *this argument is just as central to the base of the current Republican Party as it is to this book. In this respect,* The Enemy at Home *is an utterly unremarkable exploration of what theoconservatism really requires.*[9]

Of course, economic conservatives have noisily distanced themselves from Dinesh D'Souza's thesis. Pay it no mind; they do this all the time. At the end of the day, they will still vote their pocketbook rather than their rights – or yours. Republican electoral success depends on it just as it depends on the religious right. As I elaborate on later on, most libertarians are not terribly libertarian. As long as the rich get their tax cuts, econ cons will collude with loons like D'Souza and Pat Robertson. After all, they always have in the past. Why should they stop now?

This is not just a question of political bedfellows. Economic conservatives have their own unpatriotic behavior to account for. Apart from exporting jobs, they have also totally distorted the founding fathers' concepts on property. America's architects frequently expressed their fear that a "moneyed aristocracy" would take root and saw great wealth as a threat to everyone's liberty. Thomas Jefferson, Benjamin Franklin, and Thomas Paine were especially concerned.

Moreover, these three men all thought that property was the creation of society and thus subject to society's needs. Accordingly, they advocated using government to help the poor and unfortunate. For example, Thomas Jefferson once suggested a system of progressive taxation. Benjamin Franklin called for a federal jobs program for freed slaves. (This was arguably our first affirmative action proposal.) And Thomas Paine devised a Social Security system over a century and a half before Franklin D. Roosevelt realized his. All of these things are detailed later in this book.

These three men were not the only founding fathers who felt this way, and I am certainly not the only person who has noticed this. Historians from Gary B. Nash to Larry E. Tise have written on the surprisingly progressive character of our country's origins at great length. As Stephanie Coontz noted in *The Way We Never Were: American Families and the Nostalgia Trap,* this sentiment was quite widespread in that era. "Most urban craftsmen, rural farmers, and republican political leaders agreed with Noah Webster that 'equality of property' is 'the very soul of a republic.' Thomas Jefferson, for example, devised numerous schemes to preserve small farmers; James Madison desired to 'reduce extreme wealth towards a state of mediocrity' and remove 'unnecessary opportunities' for accumulation."[10]

You are going to see a lot of this. The fact that the Pledge of Allegiance was originally written by a socialist is not an ironic accident. Rather, it is just the tip of the iceberg and it encapsulates how much America's identity has been twisted beyond recognition in the interim.

It seems economic conservatives have not been quite honest about that epoch's ideas on property. Just look at who they have in their camp. It is a mishmash of misrepresented figures. For example, there is the aristocratic-minded Alexander Hamilton who felt that the rich should rule, but who could hardly be called an advocate of "small government." Then there is the pseudonymous Cato who had warned in his famous *Letters* that, "In every country and under every government, particular men may be too rich."[11] I doubt that the libertarian Cato Institute will adopt that as their motto too soon, but Benjamin Franklin and many others echoed that notion repeatedly. Indeed, it was a recurrent theme in Enlightenment political thought. Their rhetoric of equality had an economic component.

Conservatism is counterrevolutionary by its inherent nature and that applies to the American Revolution as well. As William Kristol had once admitted, "[W]e conservatives are on the side of the lords and barons."[12] After grousing that there has been "too much concern and attention for, quote, the people," the man who was "Dan Quayle's brain" proclaimed, "We at the *Weekly Standard* are pulling up the drawbridge against the peasants." What could I possibly add to that? Between Dinesh D'Souza and William Kristol, you have conservatism encapsulated.

The distinction between economic and cultural conservatives is ultimately a pretty trivial one. For econ cons, freedom begins and ends with greed. They have often proven their willingness to push all other forms of freedom in front of a bus if it will put some extra coin in their pocket – thus their longstanding alliance with religious zealots who oppose almost every single personal freedom. Speaking of which, cult cons have given Christian charity a similar shove, joining in a war on the poor to get jurisdiction over the contents of other people's pants.

Despite appearances, the gulf between D'Souza and Kristol is not very wide. After all, the lords and barons have always sought to keep their peasants in hair shirts and prayer beads. Karl Marx got a lot of flak for saying religion was the "opium of the masses," but many of our founding fathers essentially said it first. This is why.

Finally, cult and econ cons only have each other. They literally have nowhere else to go. Granted, they talk the walk, but it is always for naught. Libertarians had once planned a mass migration to New Hampshire.[13] (Not some Caribbean tax haven?) And "Christian Constitutionalists" had similarly called for a "Christian Exodus" to South Carolina followed by another attempt at secession.[14] But they did not leave. Instead, they invented the Tea Party movement which pledged to focus only on economic issues. But once their candidates took the House in 2010, they dropped all libertarian pretense and resumed trying to legislate their morality.

But why should they part when they have always been so effective together? They are stuck with each other and we are stuck with them as well. They are not going anywhere, literally or figuratively.

In short, our country was founded on liberal traditions that conservatives have always sought to destroy. While I have frequently heard conservatives called un-American on specific issues, I have never heard it directed against their ideology as a whole. Yes, advocating censorship and opposing immigration are both un-American, ditto for torture. But they are also part of a far larger pattern that conservatives can only hide by questioning *other* people's patriotism as they routinely do.

And it is no secret that conservatives reflexively question their opponents' patriotism. In the final days of the 2008 election, Alaska governor and GOP vice-presidential candidate Sarah Palin spoke of her supporters as the "pro-America areas of this great nation."[15] Likewise, Rep. Michele Bachmann (R-MN) called for the press to investigate other members of Congress to "find out if they are pro-America or anti-America."[16] It is old hat. Ronald Reagan's Secretary of the Interior, James Watt, said, "I never use the words Democrats and Republicans. It's liberals and Americans."[17] This tactic actually predates McCarthyism.

Some timid liberals will insist we should not stoop to their level, but there is more here than name-calling. I am not so much proposing that we adopt it as a tactic, but I think we should examine it as fact. Psychologists call it "projection." The right's entire platform stands *against* everything America is supposed to stand *for*, so small wonder they constantly challenge others' patriotism. Obviously, no moratorium on doing so will ever hold because this hair-trigger contradiction is hardwired into their ideology. Thus, no serious discussion of America's identity can ever be honest or complete without finally acknowledging this built-in mechanism and directly addressing it.

I can also anticipate other objections. I quote the founding fathers a lot in this book, and anyone who does that is going to be accused of cherry-picking. But, unlike so many conservatives, I recognize that the founders had fought amongst themselves and did not speak with one voice. They did not have a hive mind, nor were they prophets taking dictation from God. To repurpose that famous line in *Amadeus* (1984), the founders were not actually, "people so lofty they sound as if they shit marble."

I also recognize that the founders often changed their minds. Thomas Jefferson originally thought our nation should remain an agricultural republic of yeoman farmers and avoid manufacturing. Then the War of 1812 convinced him we needed to have our own factories. Perhaps once conservatives grasp this, they will cease facilitating the export of our industries overseas.

Obviously, many of the founders were men of property, but some were not. And many of those who were deeply distrusted their own class. It is not cherry-picking to say there was a debate. Today, many founders would be considered "limousine liberals" and join billionaires William Buffet and Bill Gates in demanding that the rich pay more in taxes. Long before Barack Obama and Elizabeth Warren, Benjamin Franklin and Thomas Paine said, "You didn't build that." What these founders said about property's origin would unquestionably get them called socialists today. Indeed, their ideas influenced later socialist thought. Thus, the notion that socialism is un-American is utter bunk. On the contrary, these founders' proto-socialist theories are interwoven into many of their concepts on liberty, equality, and democracy (which conservatives also loathe). And while conservatives can find quotes of their own, they can no longer ignore that there was a debate.

There are other predictable criticisms. Parts of my book may seem dated. Ronald Reagan was president when I was in high school and I still listen to my Dead Kennedys albums. References to the constitutional abuses of George W. Bush's "War on Terror" may seem quite stale by the time this sees print. That is okay because I am establishing that a pattern of behavior exists. Conservatism is a predictable constant. Treat these bits as you would a reference to the Nativist movement of the 1840s. The Tea Party is only warmed-over Goldwaterism; and as Richard Hofstadter wrote in his 1964 essay, "The Paranoid Style in American Politics," we have seen such movements before. As a student of history, I know I am writing during a particular political moment. The Tea Party may very well evaporate in to obscurity by the time you read this and seem as irrelevant as the Tea Pot Dome Scandal of the 1920s. But something quite like it will be back shortly – make no mistake about that.

Yes, many people say Rush Limbaugh's geriatric demographic is dying off and we just need to wait. But Limbaugh's audience is made up of Baby Boomers. In their youth, *they* were supposed to bury conservatism with their idealistic activism but, alas, that prediction fizzled pretty spectacularly. Barry Goldwater's dramatic 1964 landslide defeat was also supposed to be conservatism's swan song, but instead it paved the way for the Reagan Revolution. Richard Nixon got elected twice in the interim and his ignominious resignation was another occasion to predict conservatism's "inevitable" demise. Obviously, that did not happen.

Yes, America is getting browner. But old immigrants can be played off against new immigrants. Think of all the Irish and Italian names on Fox News attacking immigrants. Shit, think of Dinesh D'Souza.

Moreover, it is not terribly likely that human greed will soon disappear.

And almost half of Americans score over .75 on a 0 to 1 scale of authoritarian attitudes.[18] Do you think they are going to stop voting or become more tolerant and permissive? Not most.

I am not denying that tangible progress has been made, but we cannot take progress for granted. Conservatism will always regroup under the same repeatedly discredited, reactionary banners. What we have is a window of opportunity, and we must make the most of the moment.

Those I have shown early versions of this book to asked me two annoying questions: "Who's your audience?" and "What's your goal?" Of course, these are standard editor questions. And although I have made some changes, these standard questions still perplex me because the answers always seemed obvious:

My audience is *an audience*. I am standing on a soapbox at a street corner before a crowd that contains both hostile and friendly elements. From time to time, I will address my likely hecklers directly. I try to anticipate their arguments as any piece of persuasive writing should. My middle school English teacher Ms. Barnett taught me that.

But more importantly, the crowd contains the undecided. Even a broken clock is right twice a day and conservatives are right on just two things. The gun issue is (partially) one and I will discuss it at the top of chapters two and five. The other is that politics is *not* the art of converting your opponents – it is the art of ridiculing them to entertain and sway the undecided.

So my audience is everybody. One person's "preaching to the choir" is another's "rallying the troops," but I am actually addressing a far larger crowd – as are all political writers.

If I convert a conservative, that is a bonus but I am not banking on it. I am somewhat brusque and I expect they will react to my evidence the same way Creationists react to dinosaur bones. This is not a "reach across the aisle" sort of book. The title effectively prevents that.

Moreover, as Chris Mooney and many others have already noted, disproving conservatives' arguments only hardens their positions. I think they see each defeat in debate as a test of faith and believe that *feeling harder* salves every embarrassment. It at least reaffirms their victim script, which is certainly a large part of their worldview. That is assuming they have grasped that they have lost the debate. The Dunning-Kruger Effect is a wonder.

But, they are still part of the audience, so I acknowledge them. Is this writing style so unusual today?

And, tactics aside, this book actually is for everybody. People across the political spectrum accept a lot of the same debate-restricting shibboleths about patriotism and history. Since so many erroneous notions enjoy disastrous consensus, I am correcting everybody – centrists, libertarians, liberals, and leftists too. It is both amazing and maddening how many stupid conservative premises everyone accepts.

I also want to say that, despite appearances, I am more interested in ideologies than personalities. I may mock famous people, but my focus is on ideology. This is not some polite way of saying "nothing personal." It is just that I am writing from a historical perspective and personalities are transitory. This has been especially true lately since the right's icons have been dropping off like flies – Strom Thurmond, Ronald Reagan, Jesse Helms, Charlton Heston, Rev. Jerry Falwell, Paul Weyrich, William F. Buckley, and Robert Bork have all kicked the bucket since I had started writing this thing. I suppose it means I write too slowly.

Some see this as an occasion for rosy-eyed *schadenfreude*, but I know these folks get replaced. If Rush Limbaugh has a coronary today, his successor would have a loyal following by tomorrow morning.

In fact, I had watched Limbaugh get eclipsed by Bill O'Reilly, who in turn got eclipsed by Glenn Beck. There is always another understudy in the wings because their demagogue reservoir is enormous, and they are all constantly trying to out-crazy each another. I cannot keep up with all the new blowhards on Fox News, let alone all the Ted Nugent and Alex Jones clones out there now. In fact, as Adam Meyerson, former editor of the Heritage Foundation's *Policy Review*, had admitted:

Journalism today is very different from what it was 10 to 20 years ago. Today, op-ed pages are dominated by conservatives. We have a tremendous amount of conservative opinion, but this creates a problem for those who are interested in a career in journalism after college. If Bill Buckley were to come out of Yale today, nobody would pay much attention to him. He would not be that unusual because there are probably hundreds of people with those ideas [and] they have already got syndicated columns.[19]

The kicker is that Meyerson said this way back in *1988*. So much for the myth of the "liberal media."

Whether in office or the media, there is always another rising star on the right. Had you ever heard of Sarah Palin before 2008? Me neither. It was the same with George W. Bush before 2000. Nationally, his name recognition came second-hand from his father. And yet he was quickly hailed as the second coming. Watch the documentary *Jesus Camp* (2006) if you need your memory jogged on his idolatry-courting adoration. New faces constantly appear in the political arena.

Of course, this holds true across the political spectrum – Barack Obama's rise was pretty rapid as well. The difference is conservative candidates often implode once the public gets to know them. Witness Michelle Bachman, Herman Cain, Rick Perry, and all the right's other shooting stars. And lest you blame the "liberal media" for this, Reverend Pat Robertson told these Tea

Party favorites to tone down their rhetoric and be less overt about their goals if they wished to win in the general election.[20]

Conservatism is not going to change or go away. The volume on their crazy may go up or down. (It is currently cranked to eleven.) But it is always the same song. Instead, we see a parade of new faces necessitating a slew of new books and articles asking, "Who *are* these nuts and exactly how crazy are they?" But, this was always the routine: Like housework, it never stays done. So, I focus more on ideology than personality.

This brings us to my goal, which I think is even more obvious. I am trying to initiate a national debate on America's true identity. Thus, conservatives are part of the process. I expect to do well since my side consists almost entirely of reminding. The socialist parts might surprise. But other than that, my book is, to tweak Andrew Sullivan, an utterly unremarkable exploration of what true patriotism really requires. You already know most of this stuff – you just need to hear someone else say it.

Of course, I do not think that I can stop conservatives from questioning other people's patriotism forever – or even briefly. But I want to put the clarifying history on the table and always keep it within reach. I want to make it a fixture, like those pens chained to the counter at the post office.

Yes, they often get stolen and repeatedly need to be replaced. But at least their bead chains remain to hint that something is missing.

And that's at least a start.

1: The Three Legs of the Tripod
Liberty, Equality, & Democracy

"Why do you hate freedom? Why do you hate democracy?"

That was what conservatives asked those who opposed the Iraq War in 2003. Ann Coulter was particularly fond of these talking points.

It was ironic considering conservatives' historic opposition to these ideals. After all, they have mocked democracy for over two centuries. Throughout the Cold War, they had installed or supported despots the world over. They told us that various brown populations were "not yet ready for democracy" while weak-willed liberals often went along, fearing being called "soft on communism." Of course, Iraq's dictator Saddam Hussein was one of these many U.S.-backed butchers.

But the 9-11 attacks caused a stunning ideological somersault. For one long odd political moment, conservative Christians claimed they were spreading secular democracy. Rightwing talk show hosts who routinely denigrated feminists were suddenly upset about how the Taliban treated women in Afghanistan. (Of course, there was zero outrage over how women were treated in Saudi Arabia.) No, these were not oils wars in Afghanistan and Iraq, they defensively insisted: They were about *burqas*.

Of course, George W. Bush's supporters resumed democracy-bashing soon after he left office and the Arab Spring started toppling despots without the use of U.S. troops. Ann Coulter and Glenn Beck did an instant reversal on the desirability of Arab democracy. But until then, they continued to accuse liberals of hating liberal ideals while absurdly co-opting the same.

Had the Iraq invasion's advocates been consciously ironic? Were they relishing their phony role-reversal the same way many conservatives like to say "Liberals are the *real* racists"? Or were they militantly oblivious to any inconsistency? Probably both: It likely varied by the individual conservative.

But either way, the right's hostility to liberty, equality, and democracy is beyond doubt. In fact, it is so overt that we almost do not notice it anymore. It has become such a familiar odor that only a particularly acrid waft can catch our attention – one like Reverends Jerry Falwell and Pat Robertson's totally bonkers assessment of 9-11.

Remember the American Taliban's reaction? Two days after the attacks, they said we got "probably what we deserved" because they thought our free, tolerant society had angered God. Falwell charged, "The ACLU's got to take the blame for this," and elaborated:

"I really believe that the pagans, and the abortionists, and the feminists, and the gays and the lesbians who are actively trying to make that an alternative lifestyle, the ACLU, People for the American Way – all of them who have tried to secularize America – I point the finger in their face and say **you helped this happen!**[21]

That definitive instant sparked a firestorm of indignation across the nation. Everyone had acknowledged that the comments were staggeringly callous; but more importantly, we all saw that they were unquestionably un-American. President Bush had *just* said that the terrorists struck because they "hate freedom" and Falwell's vocalization of conservative thought was rhetorically inconvenient. Talk about impolitic timing.

And yet, Falwell's comments did and did not shock us. Yes, they were abominable; but they were hardly an anomaly. After all, when *haven't* these two televangelists tried to tie personal liberty to national tragedy? Only three years before, Robertson had threatened us with terrorist attacks if we did not follow his interpretation of scripture:

If the widespread practice of homosexuality will bring about the destruction of your nation, if it will bring about terrorist bombs, if it'll bring about earthquakes, tornadoes and possibly a meteor, it isn't necessarily something we ought to open our arms to.[22]

And naturally, it is not just gays who they say are inviting disaster, but our entire free society. Robertson's repeated assaults on American culture are on par with the rhetoric of any terrorist cleric:

[God] has little obligation at the present time to spare America, because we are polluting the world with our television programs, our movies and so forth, our books. We are polluting the whole world. We've made the world drunk, if you will, with the wine of our fornication. The whole world has been affected by Hollywood.[23]

Such conservatives despise our free society and actively seek to destroy it. Their harangues against secularism are indistinguishable from Osama bin Laden's and always have been. For some conservatives, the step from un-American to anti-American is a short one. Countless self-identified conservatives are liberty's manifest enemies and many explicitly admit their antipathy toward America as well.

For example, the Reverend Sun Myung Moon says, "The country that represents Satan's harvest is America, the kingdom of extreme individuality, of free sex."[24] Along these lines, he also calls American women "worse than prostitutes."[25] To call Reverend Moon a character would be something of an understatement. The self-proclaimed Messiah has performed several mass marriages. The newlyweds are usually perfect strangers and often do not share a common language.

But Reverend Moon is no lone loon – he has both dollars and followers at his disposal. He once saved Jerry Falwell's "Liberty University" from bankruptcy.[26] Moon also owns the *Washington Times*, the daily newspaper that the right trusts for "Fair and Balanced" coverage, the Fox News of the newsstand. It was President Ronald Reagan's favorite paper.

Of course, the *Times*' apologists insist it enjoys total editorial independence from Moon's Unification Church. Unfortunately, former employees tell a different story. Actually, *Reverend Moon* tells a different story. At its 20th anniversary celebration in 2002, he ordained that, "*The Washington Times* will become the instrument in spreading the truth about God to the world."[27] Presumably, without sounding too much like Osama bin Laden – or Sun Myung Moon, for that matter.

Fundamentalists of all faiths are fundamentally alike, but this hostility to liberty is not just limited to politically ambitious clergy. In his 2002 book, *The Death of the West*, Pat Buchanan had described America as, "a moral sewer and a cultural wasteland that is not worth living in and not worth fighting for."[28] Of course, Buchanan believes America can be saved, provided we jettison our rights and end immigration. Robert Bork's books also claimed we have too much freedom.

Most conservative books do. From William Bennett to "Dr. Laura," vilifying liberty is primarily why conservatives write books. We all know this is true, so there is no point in being cute about it. Conservatives may occasionally pay lip service to liberty, but ultimately their message is that we have too much of a good thing and must drastically cut back.

Conservatives are consistently, if not instinctually, anti-American in both temperament and action and always have been. Indeed, any Republican who telegraphs respect for anything America stands for is instantly considered "too liberal."

Take the late Senator John McCain (R-AZ). The "Maverick" went off message on only two issues, campaign finance reform and torture. But these were unpardonable betrayals in the eyes of conservative orthodoxy. So, in 2008, Ann Coulter said she would sooner vote for Hillary Clinton than John McCain. The vocal pundit revolt included Rush Limbaugh.[29]

Yes, freedom may be conservatives' most conspicuous pet peeve, but they also loathe America as a whole. They are not exactly fond of equality or democracy either. This is a rare area of consistency since liberty, equality, and democracy are interdependent and supposed to be the three pillars of America's identity. Indeed, they form a tripod: Each leg supports the other two and thus the structure as a whole. That and the fact that conservatism has always subverted all three is essentially my thesis in this book.

This interdependence between the three is undeniable. They are all built into each other's definitions. As Thomas Jefferson said, "Rightful liberty is unobstructed action, according to our will, within limits drawn around us by the equal rights of others."[30]

Yes, Jefferson was a slaveholder and therefore a hypocrite. But he was at fault, not the logic. The principle still holds despite his failure to apply it. His personal behavior ironically becomes an object lesson and cautionary example. He predicted titanic disaster if we kicked that can down the road and did not address this iniquity. Well, he did exactly that himself and civil war was the collective result of our national negligence.

But you cannot quite define freedom without equality and *vice versa*. For example, freedom is about being able to *do* things – often the *same* things as everybody else, like drink from any public water fountain regardless of your skin color or marry regardless of your sexual orientation. Not enjoying the same rights as others is a stark mark of lesser status just as lesser status frequently means exercising fewer rights. Again, they define each other.

The mechanics are manifest. In the wild, predators pounce on the already weak or wounded because they are easier targets. It is no different in politics, so demagogues frequently demonize the same favorite scapegoats. It is a vicious cycle which vividly illustrates the interdependence of liberty and equality. This is all obvious to anyone who bothers to think about it. In fact, it is so obvious that just writing this feels like a tautology and I imagine reading it does too. Well, just imagine living it.

Voting proves this inherent interdependence too. Democracy is the embodiment of political equality – my vote counts as much as yours. Thus, it is a badge of equality as well as citizenship. And democracy cannot function without freedom of speech, freedom of association, freedom of assembly, freedom of the press, etc. Thus, democracy is also about civic participation – casting your ballot, voicing your consent. So freedom and democracy are *both* about *doing*. Both ideals are about political agency *and* expression.

But voting not only expresses liberty and equality: It helps protect them too. Since a minority voting block can swing a close election, most politicians have become more wary of overtly violating their rights too often. Bullying minorities is a lot harder than it was before. Other minorities might identify with the victims' plight (and/or realize that they are next) and then join forces. And justice-loving members of the majority might defect in disgust. Checks and balances operate at the ballot box as well.

In fact, in Federalist #10, James Madison had explained how a greater diversity of factions makes oppressing minorities more difficult. This is because it is harder to cobble together a stable majority coalition. But disenfranchise the margins and the plurality becomes the *de facto* majority – and therefore more cocky and abusive (more on this later). It's a numbers game, or more precisely, a proportions game.

In sum, spreading freedom spreads both the incentive and capacity to defend it. But few will lift a finger if "freedom" sounds like a hollow joke. It may sound like another tautology, but if we defend everyone's freedom then everyone's freedom is more secure. That is the inherent interdependence that I mentioned. It is a snowball effect and things either roll toward more freedom or less freedom. Therefore, more equality means more freedom for everyone. But exclusive privilege has fewer partisans.

Moreover, historically, each expansion of the vote has lessened social tumult. When the vote was limited to white male property holders, rioting was called "voting out of doors" and a common occurrence because the working poor had no other way to voice their dissent or influence politics. Colonial Era rioting made the anti-war protests of the 1960s and 70s look pretty sleepy by comparison. Back then, angry mobs actually pulled down rich people's houses or utterly gutted them.[31] So I do not think conservatives realistically grasp the practical consequences of their reactionary nostalgia. Indeed, this is one of the anarchist left's biggest critiques of democracy – that it tames protest. Old elites often said that only those who have "a stake in society" should be allowed to vote. But having a vote is a stake in society too. Take that away (or render it ridiculously meaningless) and you may one day see the true security of your gated communities tested in earnest.

Acknowledging this is just competent citizenship. But some conservatives routinely pit liberty and equality against each other in a zero-sum game. They say a gain for one is a loss for the other. And yet, the late Robert Bork claimed that both had grown totally out of control – which is an obvious impossibility in a zero-sum game.

Amusingly, Robert Bork had actually made the zero-sum argument himself,[32] but he claimed that rampant liberty and equality had not clashed because they operated in separate spheres of society. Bork believed that individualism reveled in the realm of idle pleasure while egalitarianism wreaked havoc in the realm of achievement. Like Siamese fighting fish, Bork thought liberty and equality swam in separate tanks.

But then Robert Bork undermined his argument by saying that they ally against traditional morality. Indeed, his whole point in *Slouching Toward Gomorrah* is that both have lost their boundaries, so how does *that* work? For better or worse, when people like an idea, they apply it everywhere. This human tendency is well-known. So, if liberty and equality are both unfettered and spreading, how can they possibly be kept separate? Unlike a fish tank, there are no glass walls between them.

And, again, these two ideals are inherently related. For example, among feminism's demands is ending the double-standard that shames women for being as sexual as men. That demand obviously invokes both liberty and equality. Most social issues do. Again, this is totally obvious to anyone who bothers to think about it, even briefly.

To switch metaphors in midstream, Robert Bork's destructive genies are simultaneously both in and out of their bottles: They are everywhere, but they do not clash because they are supposedly kept separate – except, of course, when they cooperate which is always.

Moreover, Robert Bork thought this cooperation was the central threat to civilization in contemporary society, so his exception was really his rule. Indeed, it was his thesis, so there goes his zero-sum argument.

Robert Bork was correct that liberty and equality are growing and cooperating; but, like most conservatives, he thought this was a bad thing. I say it is a good one and how America was meant to function all along. Conservatives have always sabotaged and delayed that promise, thus causing America's every hypocritical embarrassment. But the ultimate liberal thrust of our national ethos is both obvious and unquestionable.

Let us look at conservatives' historic hostility to equality and democracy a little closer. They have sneered at "egalitarian schemes" for over 200 years. Never mind that "The American Experiment" is itself an egalitarian scheme. In his Gettysburg Address, Abraham Lincoln reminded us that America was, "conceived in liberty and dedicated to the proposition that 'all men are created equal.'" We needed reminding, so Lincoln mentioned a *"new birth* of freedom" because the founders had failed to end slavery.

Lincoln was quoting the Declaration of Independence, which his political adversaries had blasted as "self-evident lies." Plantation owners did not appreciate abolitionists quoting any of Thomas Jefferson's anti-slavery writings at them, however hypocritical they may have been for Jefferson.

Likewise, Robert Bork had bemoaned Thomas Jefferson's "rhetorical flourishes."[33] In *Slouching Towards Gomorrah*, he wrote that he found the power of America's egalitarian ethos "profoundly unfortunate" even though "it verges on heresy to say so."[34] But when have conservatives *not* said so? After all, it's what they do. It's what makes them conservatives.

Robert Bork's books are bizarre. Like most conservative best sellers, they are stunningly un-American. But *unlike* such books, they are slightly more historically informed and most folks who know this stuff have the opposite politics. Bork was a rare self-aware conservative who said what most other conservatives cannot acknowledge – not even to themselves. His candor is therefore quite valuable.

After quoting Irving Kristol on the "rot and decadence germinating within American society," Robert Bork noted, "I would add only that current liberalism's rot and decadence is merely what liberalism has been moving towards for better than two centuries."[35] In other words, since our nation's founding. It almost sounds as if Bork was mocking Kristol, but he was not – he was *agreeing* with him.

And what is liberalism exactly? Bork wrote, "Liberalism does not vary; it is always the twin thrusts of liberty and equality, and they never change."[36] That is two of the three main things our nation is supposed to stand for.

Again, Bork's whole point was that both had been pushed too far. But how far is too far? Conservative columnist George Will wrote that a return to things as they were in 1900 would be "a serviceable summation of the conservative's goal."[37] I am more used to hearing 1920, but since Ann Coulter has bemoaned women getting the vote, this must be their latest revision. They keep pushing the goalpost further back in time. (Start to expect this.) Of course, both dates precede the Civil Rights Movement. But Robert Bork thought things were botched from the beginning:

Jefferson was a man of the Enlightenment and the Declaration of Independence is an Enlightenment document. That means not only faith in the power of reason to build a just and stable social order, but also emphasis on the individual as the building block of society. The Enlightenment optimists made a serious mistake about the nature of the individual human in whom they placed so much faith.[38]

Robert Bork believed, "[T]hey would have done better had they remembered original sin."[39] So much for individual liberty.

He was no friendlier toward equality. For Bork, "The idea of equality began to undergo considerable and worrisome change soon after its enshrinement in the Declaration."[40]

Um, yeah, people started thinking about applying it.

And that was exactly what disturbed Bork about it. He thought all that pretty stuff about liberty and equality should not be taken seriously:

It is indeed stirring rhetoric, entirely appropriate for the purpose of rallying the colonists and justifying their rebellion to the world. But some caution is in order. The ringing phrases are hardly useful, indeed may be pernicious, if taken, as they commonly are as a guide to action, governmental or private. Then the words press eventually towards extremes of liberty and the pursuit of happiness that court personal license and social disorder. The necessary qualifications assumed by Jefferson and the signers of the Declaration were not expressed in the document. It would rather have spoiled the effect to have added "up to a point" or "within reason" to Jefferson's resounding generalities.[41]

Abraham Lincoln had a decidedly different take:

The principles of Jefferson are the definitions and axioms of free society and yet they are denied and evaded, with no small show of success. One dashingly calls them "glittering generalities." Another bluntly calls them "self-evident lies" and others insidiously argue that they apply to "superior races." These expressions, differing in form, are identical in object and effect – the supplanting the principles of free government, and restoring those of classification, caste, and legitimacy. They would delight a convocation of crowned heads plotting against the people. They are the vanguard, the miners and sappers of returning despotism. We must repulse them, or they will subjugate us.[42]

Abraham Lincoln was not anticipating Robert Bork's argument but accusing his own contemporaries. But this similarity only shows how little conservatism has changed, which is predictable given its temperamental resistance to change.

People often hate and fear what they do not understand, and some conservatives do not quite understand our form of government. The Reverend Sun Myung Moon does not like American democracy any more than he likes American women. Moon calls "American-style democracy" a "good nursery for the growth of Communism."[43] And Pat Buchanan has a huge soft spot for fascist dictators like Francisco Franco and Augusto Pinochet.[44] In fact, Pat Buchanan had fondly called both "soldier-patriots."[45] In his book *A Republic, Not an Empire,* he says democracy should not be an important consideration in forming foreign policy. "Whether a nation is democratic should be of less concern to us than how it views America. In the Cold War, autocratic Pakistan was a better friend than democratic India, which sided with Moscow in the Afghan war."[46] Perhaps democratic India was concerned about those Afghan fundamentalists we were funding. You know – the ones who later attacked us on 9-11?

Yeah, Pat does not want democracy for other countries; but to be fair, he does not want it here either. Both at home and abroad, Buchanan's biggest bugaboo is "the worship of democracy as a form of governance." He thinks, "Like all idolatries, democratism substitutes a false god for the real, a love of process for a love of country."[47] In other words, love your country, but never mind how it is run.

Along these lines, Pat Buchanan had actually suggested that "quasi-dictatorial rule" could solve the problems that beset our nation's big cities: "If the people are corrupt, the more democracy, the worse the government."[48] Notice how he conflates corrupt officials with the public. And if officials are corrupt, just how is the public supposed to remove them under "quasi-dictatorial rule"? Moreover, the overt corruption of crown-appointed officials was one the colonists' original grievances against England. Honestly, how un-American can you get?

Unfortunately, Pat Buchanan is not alone. On MSNBC, Ann Coulter remarked, "My libertarian friends are probably getting a little upset now but I think that's because they never appreciate the benefits of local fascism."[49]

Coulter's libertarian friends may object, but I suppose her conservative ones do not. Otherwise, she probably would have mentioned them.

The right as a whole has never been fond of democracy. This is why they so often snarl, "This is a republic, not a democracy!" It was a favorite refrain of the John Birch Society.

Actually, we are *both* a republic and a democracy. Of course, which form of government is a subcategory of the other depends on which founding father you consult. James Madison said a republic was a form of democracy, whereas John Adams said a democracy was a form of republic. And Thomas Jefferson used these two terms interchangeably as late as 1816 when he called direct democracy a pure republic.

I will elaborate in a later chapter; but either way, we are obviously a democracy and the Constitution's authors repeatedly stressed that.

For example, James Madison had argued that his new compact was, "[T]he only defence *[sic]* against the inconveniences of democracy, consistent with the democratic form of government."[50] Thus, we have a democratic form of government, albeit a modified one.

And shortly before becoming our first Chief Supreme Court Justice, John Marshal defended his fellow Federalists against the charge that they were closet monarchists by saying, "We, sir, idolize democracy."[51] Well, there's that democratic idolatry already.

Suffice to say that many conservatives do not really know what a republic is, but they are damn sure it is not a democracy and that is all they need to know. Despite their "Federalist" rhetoric, they apparently reject James Madison's concept that a republic is a democracy with safeguards to protect individual liberty and minority rights. After all, they do not really like those other things either. They just like saying we are not a democracy.

But, whatever they think a republic is, they seem to believe it permits "quasi-dictatorial rule" and "local fascism." Ponder that.

Incidentally, those quotes show their deep-rooted antipathy toward liberty and equality as well. Again, these three ideals tie together. Their hostility to democracy is also rooted in their hostility to equality. Referring to the Warren Court's upholding the voting rights of blacks, Pat Buchanan has repeatedly heaped scorn on the "one man, one vote Earl Warren system."[52] And Rev. Pat Robertson considered such a system unsuitable for post-Apartheid South Africa. "I think one man, one vote, just unrestricted democracy, would not be a wise idea."[53]

Wait. "One man, one vote" is "unrestricted democracy"? Perhaps Pat would have preferred a three-fifths compromise.

Now, I suppose I should probably clarify something at this point. I realize that there are all different sorts of conservatives. There are social conservatives and there are economic conservatives. There are Neo-Cons and Nativists. Hell, there are even "Crunchy Cons," i.e. right wing hippies. Yes, I get this. And yet, social and economic conservatives are not just an odd couple, *they're an old one*. Politics makes strange bedfellows, but they sure are not strangers. They have been together forever and have seldom strayed. Griping aside, their wedding anniversaries have used up every metal on the Periodic Table of Elements.

This is because plutocrats and moralists have always joined forces. We the People, their workforce, are a sinful, unruly lot so social control is their common goal. In the pre-New Deal era they seek to return to, you could not buy a drink or go on strike. Then Franklin D. Roosevelt gets elected in 1932 and we get the Wagner Act, booze, *and* Social Security. Everyone then gets uppity for the next forty years. As we shall see, this was what the founding fathers had always intended – those like Jefferson, Franklin, and Paine at any rate. But both social and economic conservatives were horrified. They still are, and this basis for their alliance will always remain.

And therein lays the key. Conservatism is less a cohesive ideology than a grab bag of likes and dislikes (almost entirely dislikes). Social and economic conservatives are both called "conservatives" because their dislikes overlap so thoroughly that we have to make this conscious effort to tell them apart.

Granted, there are both sex-positive libertarians and populist moralists in the mix, but most are both social *and* economic conservatives who embraced the Reagan Revolution without reservation or turning a blind eye to either side of the party. Indeed, they have merged together even further. A 2011 quadrennial Pew Research Center study had discovered that this was "the most visible shift in the political landscape since 2005." "The long-standing divide between economic, pro-business conservatives and social conservatives has blurred."[54]

This can be seen in the Tea Party, a strange marriage of libertarian rhetoric and fundamentalist Christian theology. Try to imagine pro-choice atheist Ayn Rand as an anti-abortion Evangelical. It is nothing that *she* could have conceived of ever happening as she lived; but when it is too late for a deathbed conversion, a graveside one must suffice. I suppose Mormons are not the only religious sect that practices post-mortem baptisms.

Of course, I am actually talking about *committed* conservatives rather than those who occasionally vote so. I am referring to the typical Rush Limbaugh listener and that ilk. If they say guys like Robert Bork also speak for them, then I can safely say that they hate America whether they want to acknowledge it or not. As John Adams said, "Facts are stubborn things."

And conservatives do indeed hate America. They despise liberty, equality, and democracy. These ideals make our nation great. They *define* America. And yet, most conservatives are either woefully unclear on these concepts or rabidly hostile to them. Conservatives are conspicuously contemptuous of America's most cherished civic and judicial institutions. They have always wanted to gut the Bill of Rights and the War on Terror was a platinum opportunity for them. Pundits had insisted we must give up some freedom in wartime. But they had also promised this war will last forever. This is an unacceptable combination to those who really love freedom, but conservatives seemed disconcertingly unconcerned. They were either too comfy with the concept or incapable of putting two and two together. James Madison had warned that, "No nation could preserve its freedom in the midst of continual warfare,"[55] yet, Dick Cheney matter-of-factly suggested the War on Terror was a permanent fixture. "It is different than the Gulf War, in the sense that it may never end. At least, not in our lifetime."[56] You can almost hear him licking his chops between the lines.

Deep down, conservatives know what they will not openly acknowledge: They cannot be happy in a free society. This explains their constant and paradoxical assaults on freedom's safeguards as "un-American." Psychologists call this "projection." Most of us figured out projection once we realized that the first kid to ask, "Who farted?" was the probable culprit. In other words, "He who smelt it dealt it."

Conservatives make a great show of their patriotism so that no one will ever ask exactly *what* makes them feel patriotic. Of course, the answer to that question is Pat Buchanan's love of place over process. But even this sense of attachment is fraught with awkward contradictions. Apart from Native Americans, we are a nation of immigrants and the descendants of slaves so "Blood and Soil" notions of belonging do not work here. So, conservatives grope for some other mystical bond and religion becomes their default attachment to the land. They say this is "God's Country" and claim he gave it to them – like the story of Moses, only with the Declaration of Independence standing in for stone tablets. Of course, the slaying and enslaving of the native population remains faithful to the original.

This, in part, explains the intensity of conservatives' religious politics. Without it, they have no sense of belonging because they have closed off most other options to themselves. After they reject liberty, equality, and democracy, i.e. the "love of process," what is left to inspire them? Religion is not only a convenient vehicle for bull dozing over individual liberty: It is the only remaining basis for their claim to be authentic Americans.

Prior to Donald Trump, overtly invoking whiteness was no longer okay. When politicos did, they had to use subtle racist dog whistles to do it. Another, safer, tactic is to cloak whatever oppression they sought to impose in the rhetoric of "religious liberty." For example, the anti-abortion movement sprang from Evangelical universities like Bob Jones trying to stay white-only. When they failed, they needed a new rallying cry.

Conservatives' identity feels under constant assault. They are not only philosophically opposed to the secular ideals of the Enlightenment: They feel *personally threatened* by them. It is not just a matter of faith, but one of *self*. On top of existential dread, there is the terror of confronting their contradictory identity. They just do not fit in the land of the free.

Trump proved that blatant racism is not dead. But there were plenty of previous warning signs. Barack Obama's election was a bracing milestone, but hate crimes spiked after his election,[57] as did racist rhetoric in political discourse. The use of coded language rose, along with language that was not coded at all. Tea Party protestors made signs showing President Obama as a primitive witch doctor with a bone in his nose.

Who could forget any of that?

Moreover, Fox News's immigration debate coverage was just what you would expect from Fox News. Bill O'Reilly claimed that Mexicans were trying to take back the Southwest. In fact, when interviewing then presidential candidate John McCain in late May of 2007, O'Reilly put more of his cards down on the table:

But do you understand what The New York Times wants and the far-left want? They want to break down the white Christian male power structure of which you are a part, and so am I. And they want to bring in millions of foreign nationals to basically break down the structure that we have. In that regard, Pat Buchanan is right.[58]

McCain did not challenge anything O'Reilly said. Indeed, he spent much of the televised "interview" pathetically playing yes-man.

Similarly, in an infamous anti-immigration tirade, Fox News host John Gibson actually told his audience, "Do your duty. Make more babies."[59] And during the 2009 swine flu outbreak, conservative pundits like Glenn Beck, Michael Savage, and Michele Malkin all accused Mexican immigrants of being vehicles for Islamic bio-terrorism. Savage called them "perfect mules for bringing the strain into America." It was a new twist on the claim that immigrants were spreading leprosy, made by CNN's Lou Dobbs.[60] Not that CNN's xenophobic coverage was limited to Dobbs.[61]

But for the most part, the official face of social conservatism remains politicized religiosity. Case in point, when John Gibson later insisted he was not racist, he retreated to religion. "Fifty years from now, Europe will be brown and Muslim and America will be brown and Christian. I am fine with that, America, and I've said so many times. I'd rather live with the Christians here than live ... under Sharia law in Europe."

Then why urge non-Hispanics to make more babies? Why raise an alarm if you have already made peace with the projected outcome?

In his original broadcast, Gibson framed this as Hispanics already doing "their part." But given the fact that a Muslim takeover of Europe is a longstanding white supremacist trope, it is hard to take his framing at face value. He is also on Fox, whose other hosts have repeatedly made clear that they are NOT fine with the browning of America. So, there is that.

John Gibson's Sharia crack was equally misleading. Surely he knows that many fundamentalist Christians want to run the country according to "Biblical Law." This, according to Operation Rescue founder Randal Terry, includes the execution of homosexuals, doctors who perform abortions, and kids who curse their parents.

Yes, sassy kids too. As Terry put it, "I think that we would have a heck of a lot fewer rebellious teenagers if a law like that existed in America."[62] And such conservatives demand the subjugation of women as well. This is not the inherent nature of Islam – it is the inherent nature of fundamentalism.

The misinformed notion that "we are a Christian nation" is a tenacious one. It is still around, despite having been refuted by many founders in one document after another. In Article 11 of the Treaty of Peace and Friendship between the U.S. and the Bey and Subjects of Tripoli of Barbary (1797), The administration of John Adams had explicitly stated:

As the Government of the United States of America is not in any sense founded on the Christian religion; it has in itself no character of enmity against the laws, religion, or tranquility, of Musselmen [sic].[63]

Somebody should tell that to Ann Coulter who suggested, "We should invade their countries, kill their leaders and convert them to Christianity."

That was not what the founding fathers intended. Thomas Jefferson illustrated this in his *Autobiography* where he discussed the passage of Virginia's Act for Religious Freedom:

Where the preamble declares, that coercion is a departure from the plan of the holy author of our religion, an amendment was proposed by inserting "Jesus Christ," so that it would read "A departure from the plan of Jesus Christ, the holy author of our religion;" the insertion was rejected by the great majority, in proof that they meant to comprehend, within the mantle of its protection, the Jew and the Gentile, the Christian and Mohammedan, the Hindoo [sic] and Infidel of every denomination.[64]

Unlike Ann Coulter, the founders were often polite when emphasizing the necessity of a secular government. In his "Memorial and Remonstrance," James Madison asked, "Who does not see that the same authority which can establish Christianity in exclusion of all other religions may establish, with the same ease, any particular sect of Christians in exclusion to all other sects?"[65]

Who indeed? Well, most conservatives have not gotten the memo.

But, our founders were not *always* so polite. Far from being Bible-believing Christians, many of them were organized-religion-loathing Deists. They damned the both the Bible and established churches in no uncertain terms. For example, Thomas Jefferson pulled no punches when he wrote:

Millions of innocent men, women and children, since the introduction of Christianity, have been burnt, tortured, fined and imprisoned. What has been the effect of this coercion? To make one half the world fools and the other half hypocrites; to support roguery and error all over the earth.[66]

Thomas Paine, the author of the patriotic pamphlet "Common Sense," was just as gentle in his book, *The Age of Reason:*

Whenever we read the obscene stories, the voluptuous debaucheries, the cruel and tortuous executions, the unrelenting vindictiveness, with which more than half the Bible is filled it would be more consistent to call it the word of a demon than the word of a god. It is a history of wickedness that has served to corrupt and brutalize mankind; and, for my part, I sincerely detest it as I detest everything that is cruel.[67]

Angry stuff. And there is *plenty* more where that came from.

Now, I am not saying that you have to be a Deist or an Atheist to be a good American. But it helps. As long as you are not trying to write your religious beliefs into laws that the rest of us must follow, you are honoring the founders' original intent. Your soul is your sole business, not your government's. "Live and let live" is the essence of the separation of church and state – and freedom itself, but I will tackle that more in the next chapter. Thomas Jefferson once put this issue rather memorably:

The legitimate powers of government extend to such acts only as are injurious to others. But it does me no injury for my neighbor to say there are twenty gods, or no God. It neither picks my pocket nor breaks my leg.[68]

Why can't conservatives grasp this simple concept?

Why must they, say, outlaw the sale of alcohol on Sundays (or throughout the year in some counties)? It is a rather odd way to honor someone who supposedly turned water into wine. But it is even odder that they can legally enforce their paradoxical theology on the rest of us. Obviously, this is the very same denominational favoritism that James Madison warned us about. Although they are not explicitly enacted to conform to the doctrine of any specific church, such obviously religiously-motivated laws violate the rights of those who do not share that particular faith. After all, what if you do not think drinking is a sin? Not all Christians do. Islam does, but Judaism does not. And why was Sunday chosen over, say, Thursday? Obviously, one denomination has written their theology into law for others to follow and that is unquestionably unconstitutional.

And why must conservatives push constitutional amendments against gay marriage? If some denominations, such as Episcopalians, Methodists, or Lutherans, decide to honor homosexual unions, how can the state deny their legitimacy without holding one faith's theology above another's? The only legitimate interest the state has in marriage is in enforcing contracts and the rights and obligations that come with them. People should be able to will their property or grant power of attorney to whoever they choose. What is it to you if the two parties are gay? It neither picks your pocket nor breaks your leg. In fact, it takes a rather acrobatic imagination to argue otherwise.

It seems pretty simple, doesn't it? This book is entitled *Conservatism is Un-American and Other Self-Evident Truths* for a reason. Much of its content *is* pretty self-evident. But some of it is also obscure.

For example, while it is no newsflash that conservatives have misrepresented the religiosity of our founding fathers, it is not widely known that they have also distorted the founders economic notions. The portrait we always get of America's architects is one of *laissez faire* zealots who felt government should never intervene in the marketplace – as if Mr. Alexander Hamilton spoke for all of them. Many conservatives are convinced that tax revolt was the sum total of the American Revolution. They insist that our founding fathers would want us to resist any redistributive legislation and give the "free market" a free hand.

Think again. The papers of Benjamin Franklin, Thomas Jefferson, and Thomas Paine paint an entirely different picture. Far from being laissez faire zealots, a lot of them sound like total socialists today. These men hated aristocracy and wanted to prevent the rich from becoming another one. They warned us of great wealth's threat to democracy.

For example, just days before signing the Declaration of Independence – that he had also helped craft – Franklin wrote: "An enormous proportion of property vested in a few individuals is dangerous to the rights, and destructive of the common happiness of mankind; and therefore every free state hath a right by its laws to discourage the possession of such property."[69]

Take a moment to recover. Did you read that correctly? Better read it again to make sure. Diagram the sentence, if you have to.

The quote comes from Dr. Franklin's first draft of Pennsylvania's Declaration of Rights. And while the Pennsylvania Assembly rejected this rather radical item, it is still interesting to see what he meant by societal happiness. After all, it was Franklin who suggested substituting the H-word into John Locke's "Life, Liberty and the Pursuit of Property." If you ever wondered what the "pursuit of happiness" meant, now you know.

Also notice that Dr. Franklin claimed that great wealth threatened humanity's *rights* as well as happiness. Clearly, he did not think that greed and freedom worked together naturally as Ayn Rand's acolytes claim.

And Thomas Jefferson shared Benjamin Franklin's skepticism of selfishness. In his *Notes on the State of Virginia*, Jefferson worried, "They will forget themselves, but in the sole faculty of making money, and will never think of uniting to effect a due respect for their rights." Obviously, they did not think the profit motive was a natural bulwark of human liberty. Instead, they saw it as a dangerous distraction.

Incidentally, that Jefferson quote comes from his chapter on religious freedom, in which he stresses the need for instituting secular safeguards. The founders often viewed great wealth and organized religion with similar suspicion. Therefore, today's conservatives either do not get – or deliberately misrepresent – many of the founders' economic beliefs just as they garble the founders' religious ones. Small surprise there.

Case in point, Thomas Jefferson is often called "The Father of Small Government" and he is frequently invoked by those opposed to regulating big business. But to him, "big government" meant large armies and broad police powers. Of course, conservatives adore those things, so it is a bit bizarre to hear those pro-business, tough-on-crime foreign policy hawks tout the man who once blasted banks as "more dangerous that standing armies."[70] Apparently, militaristic capitalists have misunderstood Thomas Jefferson. And yet, it is hard to see how they possibly could since Jefferson *repeatedly* claimed that government had not just a right but *an obligation* to protect the public from the selfish rich.

In fact, Jefferson put his beliefs into practice with his embargo of both Britain and France. He thought that avoiding getting embroiled in the Napoleonic Wars was more important than the profits of wealthy shipping interests and acted accordingly. Agreeing with a correspondent, he replied:

In your letter to Fisk, you have fairly stated the alternatives between which we are to choose: 1. licentious commerce and gambling speculations for a few, with eternal war for the many; or 2. restricted commerce, peace, and steady occupations for all.[71]

Whoa! That's hardly a summation of sacred conservative principles. In fact, it is a sacred conservative article of faith that government must never interfere with business and many hoodwinked liberals unquestioningly accept that precept as the American Way.

Thomas Jefferson would beg to differ. That slam on banks was not a one-time, off-the-cuff remark. On the contrary, look up "banks" in the index of any collection of his writings, and you will find more of the same. In his day, Jefferson saw an unregulated banking industry run amuck. Countless revolutionary veterans lost their farms and homes to foreclosures that had sparked Shays' Rebellion and many other uprisings.

Now, compare this to recent history. It is said that Rick Santelli's 2010 televised rant from the CME trading floor in Chicago launched the Tea Party. He mocked foreclosure victims as "losers" and added, "If you read our founding fathers, people like Benjamin Franklin and Jefferson – what we're doing now in this country is making them roll over in their graves!"

But if Rick Santelli had *actually* read them, he would realize that they are spinning in the *opposite* direction. Thomas Jefferson sought to rescue the so-called "losers" from greedy speculators like Rick Santelli.

As the rich got richer and the poor got poorer, many thought that another aristocracy was taking root. Jefferson felt legislators should put a stop to it (i.e. intervene in the market), but he feared they lacked the resolve to do so. Of the "bank mania," Jefferson wrote:

It is raising up a moneyed aristocracy in our country which has already set the government at defiance, and although forced at length to yield a little on this first essay of their strength, their principles are unyielded and unyielding. These have taken deep root in the hearts of that class from which our legislatures are drawn, and the sop to Cerberus from fable has become history.[72]

That is angry stuff. And, once again, there is *plenty* more where that came from. Take this similar gem from Jefferson:

I hope we shall take warning from the example and crush in it's [sic] birth the aristocracy of our monied [sic] corporations which dare already to challenge our government to a trial of strength and bid defiance to the laws of our country.[73]

Thus, in the struggle between corporations and government, the "Father of Small Government" passionately sided with government. There is no ignoring or finessing this fact.

And Thomas Jefferson was not alone in his apprehensions. In an 1813 letter to Jefferson, John Adams had attacked "aristocratical banks" with a classical allusion of his own:

[Gaius] Verres plundered temples, and robbed a few rich men, but he never made such ravages among private property in general, nor swindled so much out of the pockets of the poor, and middle class of people, as these banks have done.

The situation sounds pretty familiar. He could be writing about 2007. Naming names, John Adams added:

Our Winthrops, Winslows, Bradfords, Saltonstalls, Quinceys, Chandlers, Leonards, Hutchinsons, Olivers, Sewards, etc., are precisely in the situation of your Randolphs, Carters, and Burwells and Harrisons.[74]

Anti-Semites should probably take note of all those W.A.S.P. names. If any ethnicity is inherently predatory (and none is), then it is certainly not the one that they suspect. Consider this a teachable moment.

This emerging elite was the threat to the rights and "common happiness of mankind" that Benjamin Franklin had identified. The linkage between political and economic equality was self-evident then and suspicion of the rich was widespread. In his 1778 "Queries and Remarks Respecting Alterations in the Constitution on Pennsylvania," Franklin blasted the "disposition among some of our people to commence an aristocracy, by giving the rich a predominancy *[sic]* in government."[75] Well, today, we have informally accomplished exactly that.

But Franklin hoped it could be avoided and he had struck a more optimistic tone elsewhere. In another pamphlet, entitled "Information to Those Who Would Remove to America," he bragged about our nation's then narrow wealth-gap. There, he told potential immigrants that America suffered "few people so miserable as the poor of Europe" and "very few that in Europe would be called rich." In sum, "It is rather a general happy mediocrity that prevails."[76]

There is that H-word again. And once again it is associated with economic equality. Of course, the situation has since reversed and America now suffers the widest wealth-gap in the industrialized world.

The word "mediocrity" frequently appears in the founders' comments on property. As I mentioned in the introduction, James Madison, the "Father of the Constitution," said society's laws should "without violating the rights of property, reduce extreme wealth towards a state of mediocrity, and raise extreme indigence towards a state of comfort."[77]

Of course, conservatives think that is totally impossible because they think redistributing wealth in *any* way violates property rights. That depends on your theory of property rights. Evidently, theirs runs against original intent. Perhaps this was the egalitarian ethos that Professor Robert Bork found so "profoundly unfortunate."

Obviously a lot of the founders were not averse to leveling the playing field. Although in his youth Franklin criticized England's Poor Laws for encouraging laziness, in later life he showed himself amenable to building a ceiling, if not a floor. However, Thomas Jefferson and Thomas Paine were quite decided on the desirability of leveling-up as well as down. Shocked by the poverty that he saw in pre-Revolutionary France, Jefferson wrote, "I am conscious that an equal division of property is impracticable, but the consequences of this enormous inequality producing so much misery to the bulk of mankind, legislators cannot invent too many devices for subdividing property." He then made some suggestions. One was, "to exempt all from taxation below a certain point, and to tax the higher portions of property in geometrical progression as they rise."[78] Today, this idea is called progressive taxation, but conservatives call it "punishing success."

Thomas Paine had also advocated a progressive taxation system to foster economic equality and prevent another aristocracy from taking root. In fact, in *The Rights of Man,* Paine suggested that the highest inheritance tax bracket should be *one hundred percent.* Can you imagine the reaction of those who squall about the "death tax" today?

Paine had also outlined a Social Security plan for the aged in a pamphlet entitled *Agrarian Justice.* It is nice to have one (thanks to FDR almost a century and a half later) – at least until the right privatizes it out of existence, as they repeatedly keep trying.

These are hardly the most radical things these founders had ever said about wealth and property – or any other topic. And yet they seem so shocking today because we have gotten a false portrait of America's past. It seems many of our founding fathers were, frankly, secular intellectuals intent on social engineering. In other words, they were the very liberal "egg heads" that conservatives now love to hate.

Thomas Jefferson was clearly the Enlightenment equivalent of a "limousine liberal." Describing his many interests while living in France, Jefferson wrote, "Architecture, painting, sculpture, antiquities, agriculture, the condition of the labouring poor fill all my moments."[79] Of course, there is the matter of *his own* laborers, but I will tackle that in my next book.

Likewise, Benjamin Franklin was hardly the sort of individual who would be very welcome at a Heritage Foundation prayer breakfast or on a Cato Institute Caribbean cruise.[80] For starters, he penned an essay on Native Americans that would be at home in any diversity reader today. Entitled "Remarks on the Savages of North America," Franklin tackled the S-word in his first two lines:

Savages we call them, because their manners differ from ours, which we think the perfection of civility; they think the same of theirs. Perhaps, if we could examine the manners of different nations with impartiality, we should find no people so rude, as to be without any rules of politeness; nor any so polite, as not to have some remains of rudeness.[81]

From there, Dr. Franklin skewered his fellow Europeans with one satirical anecdote after another. White behavior was his target. And, much like Mark Twain, he seemed to take great delight in mocking Christian missionaries. No doubt if he wrote it today many conservatives would accuse him of hating white Christians. Recommended reading.

But that is just the tip of the iceberg. Franklin also wrote a story that defended unwed mothers and a ditty ridiculing people who did not drink.[82] He also wrote another article entitled "Advice on Choosing a Mistress," also known as "Old Mistresses Apologue." The Religious Right would not like him one bit. Also, in his youth, he was producing parody news centuries before *The Onion* or "The Daily Show." The targets were the same types of people who always get lampooned – pompous hypocrites in authority.

And perhaps even worse, the venerable sage of Philadelphia was – like the two Toms – *très* fond of the French. All three men lived in France for many years. There, they conversed and corresponded with other political *philosophes* (that is French for "policy wonk") and shared their irreligious socialist notions. None of this is news to historians.

For example, in a footnote to his collection of Thomas Paine's writings, historian Phillip S. Foner wrote, "It is significant to note that Paine supported the communistic aspects of Babeuf's theories, and that, although he decried the violent aspects of the Babeuf insurrection, he considered it as correctly aimed at the removal of social inequalities in property."[83]

It is funny how we can recognize that people spoke of equality in economic terms when discussing of the *French* Revolution; but when we speak of the *American* Revolution, that facet vanishes – as if America were somehow an exception to the spirit and ideas of the Enlightenment. Perhaps that is where the error of American Exceptionalism starts.

To American conservatives, the American Revolution is not a revolution insomuch as some odd restoration of tradition and the *status quo*. In his letter to Abraham Lincoln, Karl Marx had remarked how absurd the South's reactionary "revolution" was.[84] The American right's idea of the American Revolution is just as stupid because it comes from the same impulses.

As Professor Bork had begrudgingly admitted, Thomas Jefferson was a man of the Enlightenment. Well, Benjamin Franklin and Thomas Paine were no less so. These three men all championed science over superstition and placed personal freedom over tradition. They strove to build a better world after theorizing what it would look like. That is, after all, what revolutionaries *do* – they consciously try to reorganize society. If you are in any way uncomfortable with that, you live in the wrong country.

Conservatives are profoundly out of step with those founders. It seems completely inconceivable that conservatives could admire these men or the liberal nation they had tried to create. So it should come as no surprise that their definition of patriotism is the opposite of most founders' as well. And yet, it still surprises us because most people have no idea what Enlightenment Era patriotism was.

So, what was patriotism originally? Simply put, patriotism is not nationalism. Nationalism is Pat Buchanan's love of place. It is loyalty anchored in the soil or in some ethnicity. By contrast, patriotism was loyalty to liberty and equality – and solidarity with ordinary people everywhere.

Yes, the word patriotism comes from the Greek *patras* which means "of the father" so many assume patriotism just means love of the fatherland and call it a day. But the ancient Greeks and Romans wrote a lot about what civic virtues maintained political liberty and promoted the common good.[85] And that is what Enlightenment political theorists meant by patriotism – the duties and attitudes that democratic republics require to function.

This is significant since absolute monarchs only require loyalty and obedience: Simple subjects do not participate in government, so they do not need civic virtues to guide their political behavior as full citizens do. So from the get-go, we see that patriotism is not mindless us-against-them tribalism.

This explains the patriot's love of "process" that Pat Buchanan scorns. Process is important to actual patriots because it is how liberty and equality are both achieved and preserved.

Our founders were obviously very focused on process, so conservative contempt is quite damning. Pat Buchanan's "patriotism" produces subjects, not citizens.[86] Conservatives fetishize the Constitution as an object – as they do the flag. Their veneration is purely superficial so their patriotism is forever suspect. Deep feeling is a poor substitute for actual understanding; therefore, their patriotism is unreliable – to put it politely. Indeed, forget comprehension, their attitudes are actually antithetical to patriotism.

Of course, a feeling of brotherhood was part of these civic virtues. In part, this was to minimize factional infighting, which Athens and Rome both suffered from immensely. But it was also to encourage everyone to think collectively. And expanding the ideal of brotherhood to include all humanity was an Enlightenment addition.

One obvious bond between liberty, equality, and democracy is empathy. It buttresses interest in the common good and makes us more likely to defend each others' rights. Yet both Ayn Rand and Glenn Beck have equated empathy with tyranny. Whether it is conscious or not, that callousness inevitably – and invariably – sabotages free society.

I will explore this more in the next-to-last chapter; but simply put, patriotism is essentially empathy. Conservative hostility to liberty, equality, and democracy already prevents them from being patriots. Their execration of empathy only exacerbates their alienation. It is the last nail in the coffin of their claim to be patriots.

Maybe you need a little more history to see this.

Do you remember reading that Patriots fought against Tories in the American Revolution? Well, "Tory" is another word for "conservative." In fact, members of the Conservative Party in Great Britain are still called Tories today. By contrast, Patriots were the radical wing of the Whig party.

If you are still a little confused, consider this little bit of British political trivia. In 1742, a few decades before the American Revolution, a faction of young Whig reformers called the Patriot Boys accused their party leadership of acting like Tories. You know how some centrist business-friendly Democrats often act like Republicans? It was basically the same dynamic. Just as the late, great Senator Paul Wellstone (D-MN) championed "the Democratic wing of the Democratic Party," the Patriot Boys thought their party's principles had been betrayed. They moved against their own party's Prime Minister, one Sir Robert Walpole, a staunch supporter of the rigid status quo. They forced Walpole's resignation with a vote of no confidence, and thereafter, the Patriot label stuck.

It was only logical for the restless colonists to later adopt that label. When those in power lose sight of the greater good, those on the outskirts who lack access suffer first. And the American colonists were certainly on the outskirts – geographically, perceptually, and politically.

Our political labels of right and left also originate from the 1700s. When France's legislature was in session, those aligned with the king sat to his right, whereas those opposed to him sat to his left. When revolution came, the patriots logically came from those on the left.

What else would you expect?

The revolutionaries' idea of patriotism makes perfect sense once put into context. Obviously, patriotism does not mean loyalty to the government or the *status quo* since the patriots in both the American and French revolutions were those in *rebellion* against the established order.

Accordingly, Revolutionary Era patriotism was not characterized by hostility toward other countries. The two revolutions were, by definition, *internal* conflicts rather than *external* ones. Patriots' enemies were not ethnic "Others" but domestic political opponents.

In fact, many patriots were enthusiastic about "exporting revolution," to use the Cold War era term. For example, Thomas Jefferson celebrated the French Revolution and Thomas Paine temporarily participated in France's new revolutionary government. To use another Cold War turn of phrase, patriots had hoped for a crown-toppling domino effect throughout Europe, but that would not happen until World War I.

I am not saying that some nascent nationalism did not exist yet, but it was not yet the force it later became during the Napoleonic Era. Indeed, the term "nationalism" did not enter widespread usage in the English language until the 1830s – over a half century after the American Revolution.[87]

Let me set the stage. Back then, many Europeans lived in minor princedoms that had not yet been gathered into nation-states. For example, there was no Germany yet – only Prussia, Bavaria, etc. Ditto for Italy which was then Lombardy, Sicily, etc. Maps had many more borders back then.

For many, loyalties were local rather than national. This was even true for countries that had already become nation-states such as England and France. Local loyalties run deep and are very durable. As George Orwell had observed in the 1930s – a century after "nationalism" became a familiar term – "English regional snobberies are nationalism in miniature."[88]

At first, this seems difficult to imagine. But we are talking about a period where few outside of port towns ventured more than a hundred miles from where they were born or had ever seen a map or a globe. For those, the horizons of their perceptions were quite literal. Even if they thought in terms of nationalities, local issues impacted their daily lives more directly.[89] And that meant issues of wealth and class that were directly felt and lived. These topics combined "bread and butter issues" with daily indignities.

As J.C.D. Clark argued in *The Language of Liberty 1660-1832: Political Discourse and Social Dynamics in the Anglo-American World* (Cambridge Press, 1994), the only loyalty that really transcended locality was religion.

During the early 1700s, opposition to Catholicism still remained a far more potent political motivator than any collective sense of Englishness. I am not calling this a good thing, just stressing that nationalism was still weak then.

Indeed, Clark's thesis was that the emergence of America as a secular state hastened the development of national identity to create a broader loyalty as the strength of religious identity waned and needed replacement.[90]

I do not want to oversimplify because nationalism got mixed together with patriotism from the beginning. In Europe, local nobles often married foreign nobles to acquire more land and kings frequently inherited territories outside of their realms. Since aristocrats naturally opposed both democracy and national unification, they were often the common enemy of both patriots and nationalists alike. Thus, it was already easy to conflate "the people" with "the nation" back then.

Indeed ironically, nationalism's early touchy-feely stages were almost *internationalist* in nature and it hijacked patriotism's humanist rhetoric.

For example, as late as 1846, Frenchman Jules Michelet wrote that nationalism would somehow inevitably bring about world harmony(!) In his book, *The People*, he used a musical metaphor on appreciating differences:

The more man advances, the more he enters into the spirit of his country, and the better he contributes to the harmony of the globe; he learns to know his native country, both in its positive and in its relative value, as a note in the grand concert; by it, he participates therein; and in it, he loves the world. One's native country forms the necessary initiation to the country of all mankind.[91]

Trippy.

Likewise, still later in 1858, Italian Giuseppe Mazzini had believed that realizing a group's dreams of statehood advanced humanity as a whole. In his essay, "The Duties of Man," he explicitly put humanity above both nation and family by writing, "You are men before you are citizens or fathers."

After that pithy dictum, he goes into a lengthy one-sentence lecture about how we must defend the oppressed everywhere. For Mazzini, humanity was a religion – with strict religious obligations:

If you do not embrace the whole human family in your love, if you do not confess your faith in its unity – consequent on the unity of God – and in the brotherhood of the Peoples who are appointed to reduce that unity to fact – if wherever one of your fellow-men groans, wherever the dignity of human nature is violated by falsehood or tyranny, you are not prompt, being able, to succor that wretched one, or do not feel yourself called, being able, to fight for the purpose of relieving the deceived or oppressed – you disobey your law of life, or do not comprehend the religion which will bless the future.[92]

Mazzini practiced what he preached. While in exile for trying to unify Italy, he participated in many South American revolutions against Spain. Although he was no socialist, he was a kind of 19th century Che Guevara in that he fought to liberate those who were not his own countrymen.

In that same spirit, many Americans participated in the wave of revolutions that rocked Europe in 1848. And during the U.S. Civil War, many Europeans and Canadians joined the Union Army to help destroy slavery. Similarly, people from all over the world went to Spain to join the International Brigades and fight fascism in the 1930s. It is the same impulse to act "whenever one of your fellow-men groans."

This drive to free all humanity from tyranny is part of patriotism. Yes, tribal rivalries are old. But internationalist fervor is far older than most people realize. It has a proud history going back to the Enlightenment. Capital-H Humanity began to rival religion during the Renaissance. It peaked during the Enlightenment when the American and French revolutions occurred. Then, religion resurged – alongside then emerging nationalism. But Enlightenment ideals remained potent enough that it was still necessary to at least *pay lip service* to them, hence the internationalism woven into nationalist propaganda. Yeah, history is a gumbo.[93]

Now, plug all this into American history.

Many Americans initially thought of themselves as Pennsylvanians, New Yorkers, Virginians, etc. Indeed, some felt that way up until the U.S. Civil War – and some well after. Before the American Revolution, the colonists saw themselves as Englishmen; but this was evidently far less important to them than enjoying "The Rights of Englishmen." This explains why their allegiance to Whig political principles had eclipsed their allegiance to the British Empire. Process was more important than place. Nationality was secondary, if people in that locality thought about it at all.

To some, this seems like a more primitive mindset; but if you prioritized liberty, equality, and democracy is was actually more advanced.

True, the unifying effect of the Revolution and the rise of nationalism in the early 1800s had largely changed this so that most Americans began to think of themselves as Americans. But going into the conflict, patriotism was primarily a political ethos rather than any expression of national identity – thus the explicitly political labels of Patriot vs. Tory.

I have just one last caveat: Patriots can, of course, forget their principles and slip into jingoistic nationalism. The War of Jenkin's Ear between Britain and Spain serves as a dramatic example, especially since the Whigs had clamored for it themselves – it was their war. In *The Patriot Opposition to Walpole: Politics, Poetry and National Myth 1725-1742* (Oxford Press, 1994),

Christine Gerrard soberly shows such morphing among British patriots while critiquing J.C.D. Clark:

> *If the patriotism Bolingbroke derived from the civic republican legacy was originally 'a doctrine of universal libertarian benevolence ... universalist rather than specific to the English',* [here she quotes Clark, not Bolingbroke] *it soon lost its more generous internationalist spirit. In 1727 Bolingbroke had claimed that the Craftsman's brand of patriotism was 'actuated by the noble Principles of universal and unconfin'd [sic] Benevolence', conducive to 'the Peace and Prosperity of Mankind'.* [Here, of course, she quotes Bolingbroke]. *By 1730 Bolingbroke himself had become, if not xenophobic, then certainly nationalistic. His opening letter in the Craftsman's 'Remarks on the History of England' describes 'a revival of the true old English spirit, which prevailed in the days of our forefathers, and which must always be national, since it has no direction but to the national interest'. The Bolingbroke of the 'Remarks' is first and foremost a 'Brit'. 'I feel a secret pride in thinking that I was born a Briton'.*[94]

I think it is pretty interesting that he once considered it "a secret."

This goes back and forth. Across the pond, some colonists got swept up in this enthusiasm as well. But they felt quite differently by the Revolutionary Era when they were openly courting support from the mother country's traditional enemies, France and Spain. This was not simply necessity, although it was certainly that too. Both during and after the Revolution, many Americans actively worked to de-Anglicize their culture by adopting French and Indian customs – quite eye-opening so shortly after the French and Indian War.[95]

While this was certainly a conscious effort to reinvent themselves and create a separate national identity, it was also part of an international ideology of liberty. Indeed, it shows how America's identity is tightly interwoven into this internationalism. Again, it is a gumbo.

Decades later (once it became politically safe to do so), wealthy elites would emphasize their Englishness. They did this to distinguish themselves from increasing German and Irish immigrants – but also to demonstrate their growingly overt appetite for hierarchy as well as their distaste for "excessive" liberty. It was a subtle cultural repudiation of the Revolution.

But before then, the benevolent humanist internationalism of Franklin, Voltaire, and Paine prevailed. Patriots were then citizens of the world who opposed oppression everywhere. In short, original patriotism was a product of the Enlightenment and thus mostly focused on universal human rights. It was the later Romantic Era that twisted The Rights of Man into "My country, right or wrong." Thomas Paine summed up his form of patriotism when he wrote, "[M]y country is the world, and my religion to do good."[96]

Paine's idealistic humanism might seem *naïve*, but that was the spirit of the age in spades. That was the Enlightenment all over.

Ignorance of patriotism's Revolutionary Era definition has caused considerable confusion. When Samuel Johnson said, "Patriotism is the last refuge of the scoundrel," he was not bashing nationalists. Rather, he was attacking radical Whigs. Dr. Johnson's conservative politics are not in doubt: He once declared, "I am a friend to subordination, as most conducive to the happiness of society."[97] Johnson thought people were happiest when they knew their place. Thus, Dr. Johnson and Dr. Franklin wrote very different prescriptions for societal happiness.

And, as a sidebar, subordination is, of course, opposed to both liberty and equality, and thus another example of their inherent interdependence.

Samuel Johnson was a monarchist and a Tory who believed that obedience and tradition held society together. Thus, he thought that Whig demands for liberty and equality would only cause chaos. Of course, conservative icon Robert Bork claimed they have, in fact, done exactly that.

I admit I write a lot about Robert Bork because he was a treasure trove of profoundly unpatriotic thought. But he also is a really interesting comparison/contrast with the Tea Party. They say they want "liberty" while he candidly claimed that we have too much. But they all claimed to champion our founders' original intent while promoting the opposite. The Tea Party is simply Originalism applied to economics – hence the tricorn hats they sport at protests. Indeed, Originalism is their entire motif. And Robert Bork's supposed martyrdom at the hands of the "liberal elite" fits the Tea Party's victim script perfectly. It is symmetry in symbolism. Accordingly, 2012 GOP nominee Mitt Romney had hired Robert Bork to shore up his conservative credentials and help him play a young Ronald Reagan. (I suppose the pompadour was not enough.) It was to harness the grievance politics of the privileged. Ayn Rand may supply the right's economic policies, but Robert Bork sums up their social goals.

It may seem hard to swallow that some (no, not all) founders favored fostering economic equality. It may seem improbable that their patriotism embraced all humanity. But it is not any odder than acknowledging that they were largely organized religion-scorning Deists.

No, quoting the founders' scathing criticism of religion will not win over many fundamentalists. But there is everyone else – including the curious and undecided. And having a vast catalog of quotes at our fingertips certainly helps defend the Separation of Church and State.

Well, likewise, I got a metric fuck-tonne of Enlightenment quotes equating great concentrations of wealth with aristocracy and rampant corruption. And I also got a lot of Enlightenment quotes putting the whole human family above any ethnicity or nationality. What have you got?

What? A record of loathsome disappointment and hypocrisy committed by those very same founders? Okay. No argument there.

But ideas come from places: Genealogy is a thing. I hate my parents, but I do not deny their paternity. I admit that awkward and annoying fact.

We stand on the shoulders of assholes – assholes who frequently, if not invariably, insist that their terrible behavior was somehow necessary when we would actually stand far taller if they were better people.

However, that does not mean we need to reinvent the wheel either. Take the good ideas, drop the bad ones, junk the hero worship, admit to all of this candidly, and go forth and move the world forward. Get impatient and make your mortality a timetable for change.

But I must warn you that in the process you will discover the simple fact that secularism, socialism, and internationalism are as American apple pie. Like "Star Trek," they are simultaneously American and international.[98]

I am not arguing for American Exceptionalism: Other countries have made huge contributions too and many of America's contributions were actually *Native American* in origin. More on this later.

I am also not trying to rehabilitate the word "patriotism" insomuch as show how morphing the word has grossly distorted our understanding of the past. To leftists, patriotism is the polite and sanitized word for nationalism. To liberals, nationalism is the extreme and mean version of patriotism. And to conservatives, nationalism is a slur on patriotism – hence Donald Trump urging people to reclaim the n-word.[99]

They are all wrong because their definitions are essentially the same and only differ about desirability. The error is yet another example of how everyone stupidly lets conservatives frame the debate and define terms. The biggest difference, in this instance, is that all the conservatives who did this are now long dead.

We can debate whether it is worth the effort to rehabilitate the word patriotism for political purposes. But for historical purposes, people should understand that the patriot cause in 1776 was definitively against the conservative temperament entirely. That is the take-away here.

You can argue that this knowledge denies conservatives a potent political weapon. But you can *also* argue that patriotism too easily corrupts itself into nationalism – hence how quickly so many "liberals" thoughtlessly become hawks. Like the seductive One Ring in the *Lord of the Rings*, the question becomes whether to use patriotism or to destroy it.

In the original edition, I argued that Enlightenment era patriotism is what patriotism "must become again." In retrospect, I can see how that might be confusing. I may have even been carried away by my enthusiasm for my (to me) discovery. ... Okay, probably. In any case, let me correct that here. In terms of comprehending our country's history, understanding the Enlightenment version is essential. Beyond that, I am wary.

But our history is undeniably intertwined with these ideas. Secularism, socialism, and internationalism logically follow liberty, equality, and democracy. Yes, it is absurd for conservatives to assault modernity when our young country has turbo charged it worldwide; but these ideas are also part of that modernity. You may as well deny oxygen's role in making water.

We must finally confront the obvious. Most conservatives are temperamentally incapable of the form of patriotism our founders felt. They have twisted the revolutionaries' definition of patriotism into its polar opposite – a Tory loyalty to authority. Today, their "patriotism" is like macho homophobes listening to Queen, which is to say they do not get it. Like college sports fans who hate people with education, they forget or ignore the institution's original mission.

The right's historic hostility to liberty, equality, and democracy cannot be reconciled with our country's revolutionary ethos. And the fact that these three ideals cover so much ground explains why conservatives are chronically wrong on most important topics. And this includes economic ones, because many founders recognized that money is power.

I wrote this chapter as rough synopsis of the book. If you have any problems with what you have read, the rest of the book provides additional evidence. But, agree or disagree, you should know where I am going by now.

Although unusual, I think my thesis is a pretty easy to prove. Recall Robert Bork's words: "Liberalism does not vary; it is always the twin thrusts of liberty and equality, and they never change." So, it should not be too controversial to suggest that conservatism has always sought the opposite. If liberalism and conservatism are inherently in constant conflict, the latter's hostility to liberty and equality is a given. Indeed, it is *definitional*.

Therefore, it becomes a perpetual identity crisis to be an American conservative because that status is a paradox – if not an oxymoron. American conservatism is an absurdity and it always was and will be.

Of course, the term "Tory" should have told you that already.

2: The Skinny on Liberty
The Easiest Ideal to Explain

Conservatives curiously insist they love liberty. They often say they only want government off our backs. It is a strange claim for those so tight with the Religious Right. Indeed, their recurrent crusades against sex, drugs, and rock make their libertarian rhetoric seem insincere.

Of course, they carve out exceptions for themselves and things they like. No doubt very many gun owners have been scoffing at my skepticism since they started reading. Surely liberals are not permissive on gun rights. And corporate apologists also sing a song of freedom – of sorts.

Gun owners sort of have a point, but greed's cheerleaders do not.

After all, when writing the Declaration of Independence, Thomas Jefferson did not borrow John Locke's original language fully intact. He took Benjamin Franklin's suggestion and dropped "the pursuit of property" in favor of "the pursuit happiness." Conservatives typically dismiss this as trivial poetic embellishment, but the two founders' other writings tell a different story and what I have quoted so far is just the tip of the iceberg.

The right is flatly wrong on riches, but guns are a *little* different.

Guns are odd because liberals defend individual liberty in all other instances. But for some reason, guns turn liberals into conservatives and *vice versa*. Here liberals attack the symptom rather than the disease and that sort of shallow analysis is more consistent with conservative thought.

Research routinely confirms that the primary predictor of gun violence is poverty and vast economic inequality.[100] And have not liberals traditionally cited poverty as the primary underlying cause of crime?

Well, they used to. Unfortunately, poverty has fallen out of fashion as an explanation in recent years. So on this issue "liberals" ignore both science and the poor. Instead, they look for cultural causes like violent music and video games. How conservative: The only thing missing is a little religion.

This ideological contradiction has become politically costly. Guns and abortion are two issues that have alienated many poor and middle class voters who know that conservative's economic policies have robbed them. Of course, we must never abandon a woman's right to choose, but a change on the gun issue is both necessary and inevitable. Let us get rid of this political albatross as soon as possible. Doing so would surely shave away enough votes to recreate the strong, long-term political dominance the Democratic Party enjoyed in the heyday of the New Deal and the Great Society.

Fortunately, change is already afoot. John Kerry is both a gun owner and a hunter. Howard Dean was endorsed by the NRA while he was governor of Vermont, and he later advocated reaching out to gun owners.

Moreover, Michael Moore's movie *Bowling for Columbine* did not present the thesis everyone expected. Instead of calling for a ban on guns, Moore's unexpected *exposé* linked our country's culture of fear to the effects of our shredded safety net.

And sex advice columnist Dan Savage is yet another figure who is willing to talk turkey on firearms. In *Skipping Towards Gomorrah*, he suggested that First and Second Amendment advocates could end the Culture Wars by simply signing off on broad interpretations of both amendments.[101]

I agree and certainly many independents would agree as well. And there is your bulletproof Democratic majority. Plus, it would be ideologically tidy, which would make *me* happy.

Now, I support modest gun control laws, so I should probably clarify what I mean by "a broad interpretation." I am talking about recognizing that owning guns is a personal right. Like it or not, those who say the Second Amendment only applies to state militias have a strong argument. But gun owners have a strong *counter argument*, if they want it.

They can say that the founders were broadly protective of individual liberty and that the militia clause was not the *only* reason for the Second Amendment – it was simply given as an *example*. But to do that, they must also acknowledge this broad emphasis in regard to the First Amendment. And the Ninth too, but I will get to that in a moment.

I am not just talking about the political compromise that Dan Savage suggested, although that is important too. Logically, there is no other argument left for gun rights advocates. Thus, gun owners must also defend pot, porn, abortion, LBGT rights, and all those other things that cultural conservatives have always opposed. Otherwise, the Second Amendment only applies to militias and there is no personal right to own guns. So choose.

Yes, this is a libertarian argument; but I am definitely not a libertarian. In this book, I have two whole chapters devoted to mocking libertarianism as an absurd fraud if you have any doubts.

The fact is that Democrats have been reluctant to pursue gun control for quite some time. Despite numerous mass shootings, President Obama resisted calls for gun control right up until Sandy Hook Elementary. After the previous Aurora, Colorado shootings, Obama said we only needed to enforce the laws we already have on the books.[102] Recall, this was also after his friend Rep. Gabrielle Giffords (D-AZ) was shot in Tucson, Arizona.

Obama postponed taking a stand for as long as possible. Clearly, he wanted to focus on other things, but repeated tragedies had forced his hand.

And how did Obama respond? By proposing a bill to close the gun show loophole on background checks and restore the assault weapons ban. It was defeated despite solid public approval. The assault weapons ban was the most controversial component. It only enjoyed 56% approval in the polls. But closing the gun show loophole on background checks had an astounding 92% approval – and 91% in homes with guns.[103] Think about that.

There are many very popular common sense gun control proposals on the table. Indeed, the National Rifle Association's membership is a great deal more reasonable than its fanatical leadership. The rank and file support a number of safety regulations that their lobby has always fought against and will not even deign to entertain today.[104]

But once these tweaks are in place, we can go no further. Since the Supreme Court struck down municipal hand gun bans in *McDonald v. Chicago*, it is clear that no outright ban on all guns will ever hold in the courts, even if it had broad, national public support, which it does not.

Ultimately, fighting poverty and economic inequality remain the most effective means of reducing firearm fatalities. Access to social services should surpass access to firearms. After the Sandy Hook massacre, a friend of mine asked her gun-owning friends, "If mental health is the 'real issue,' are you now ready to talk about single payer?"

It was a very powerful and on-point challenge to conservative thought. But I knew at least four gun owners who had already been advocating single payer for years. This is where the Democrats should focus.

I have a whole other chapter devoted to the right's gross distortion of the founders' economic thought, and I will also revisit the issue of gun rights later on. But while we can argue over who best defends this or that particular liberty, there remains the salient and inescapable fact that only conservatives have fashioned an ideology hostile to freedom *as a whole*. As Dan Savage pointed out during the last Bush administration:

So while gun owners are always saying that owning guns is about defending freedom, the only freedom gun owners seem interested in defending with their guns is the freedom to defend their freedom to own guns. For a freedom fan such as myself, this seems a little limited. All that firepower – 200 million guns – dedicated to defending just one freedom? Charlton Heston, the actor and president of the NRA, says he "cannot stand by and watch the Constitution of the United States come under attack," and yet I don't recall seeing Charlton Heston on television complaining about John Ashcroft's recent assaults on, say, attorney-client privilege.[105]

Savage characterizes this as short-sightedness and points out that some conservatives are finally coming around. For some conservatives, it may well be a lack of forethought. But for others, it is obviously not because conservatism has always been hostile to liberty itself, as both an attitude and an ideology. And what is freedom itself?

Freedom, as everyone actually already knows, is the right to do as you please provided you do not harm anybody else in the process.

Pretty self-evident, isn't it?

And I can make it even simpler: "No harm, no foul. Play ball!"

Of course, conservatives cannot accept this commonsensical definition. For them, freedom is something so subtle and arcane that it requires philosopher-priests to interpret it for us. The obvious definition of words are ignored or turned into their polar opposites.

This is because three propositions sum up conservative thought: First, that liberty does not *really* mean liberty. "It doesn't mean you can do as you like." Second, that equality does not really mean equality. "Not for *those* people." And third, that democracy does not really mean democracy. "We are a *republic*, not a democracy." These shabby half-assed rationalizations are all interrelated. But I will elaborate on this later.

It was not always quite like this. Indeed, for the late Barry Goldwater, the no harm/no foul definition of liberty supposedly defined conservatism itself, if you can imagine that:

I am a conservative Republican, but I believe in democracy and the separation of church and state. The conservative movement is founded on the simple tenet that people have the right to live life as they please as long as they don't hurt anyone else in the process.[106]

Imagine a "conservative Republican" affirming democracy, secularism, and a broad definition of liberty to boot! Accordingly, Goldwater had to defend himself against charges that he had gone liberal.

But if Goldwater's definition of conservatism sounds liberal, it should also sound familiar since he was simply paraphrasing Thomas Jefferson. As I quoted before, "Rightful liberty is unobstructed action, according to our will, within limits drawn around us by the equal rights of others."[107]

Elsewhere, Jefferson said legislation should banish "all arbitrary and unnecessary restraint on individual action," and "leave us free to do whatever does not violate the equal rights of another."[108]

In other words, freedom is whatever does not pick your pocket or break your leg. Again: No harm, no foul. Play ball!

This simple, self-evident definition is acknowledged by nearly everyone – except, of course, those with a political motive to deny it.

In fact, it was so obvious to our founding fathers that the Constitution was originally proposed without a bill of rights. Remember reading about that? A suspicious public demanded to see one in writing and they refused to ratify the Constitution without one. But by doing so they certainly were not calling for their rights to be limited to a list of less than ten.

On the contrary, the Ninth Amendment explicitly admits that the Bill of Rights is not a complete list by plainly stating:

The enumeration in the Constitution of certain rights, shall not be construed to deny or disparage others retained by the people.

But conservatives deny and disparage these rights all the time. It is what they do. It is what makes them conservatives. They always say that they are against "finding new rights in the Constitution," apparently unaware that those rights are nothing new. They are already built-in.

Interestingly, many of the revolutionaries were against ratifying the Bill of Rights precisely because they feared it would be used it to limit liberty *in that exact fashion*. For example, on October 28, 1787, Justice James Iredell argued at the North Carolina ratification convention:

[I]t would not only be useless, but dangerous, to enumerate a number of rights which are not intended to be given up; because it would be implying, in the strongest manner, that every right not included in the exception might be impaired by government without usurpation; and **it would be impossible to enumerate every one***. Let anyone make what collection or enumeration of rights he pleases, I will immediately mention twenty or thirty more rights not contained in it.* (emphasis original)[109]

In 1789, Representative Theodore Sedgwick made a similar objection on the floor of Congress. He quipped:

[T]hey might have gone into very lengthy enumeration of rights; they might have declared that a man should have a right to wear his hat if he pleased; that he might get up when he pleased, and go to bed when he thought proper.[110]

This fear nearly sank the Bill of Rights, but James Madison argued that the problem could be corrected.

This is one of the most plausible arguments I have ever heard urged against the admission of a bill of rights into this system; but, I conceive, that it may be guarded against. I have attempted it, as gentlemen may see by turning to the last clause of the fourth resolution.[111]

That clause ultimately became the Ninth Amendment. If there is any question of original intent here is the lengthier original:

The exceptions here or elsewhere in the constitution, made in favor of particular rights, shall not be so construed as to diminish the just importance of other rights retained by the people, or as to enlarge the powers delegated by the constitution; but either as actual limitations of such powers, or as **inserted merely for greater caution**. (emphasis added in this instance).[112]

The Ninth Amendment was included to assure people that the Bill of Rights could not be used to limit liberties. And yet this is precisely how conservatives use it today. How often have they used the phrase, "Our founding fathers never intended to permit ..." or "There's nothing in the Constitution which gives you the right to ..." or some other variant against anything that offends them?

Conservatives misconstrue the Constitution to deny and disparage our rights all the time. Again, it's what they do. It is who they are.

Perhaps the Ninth Amendment should be called the Nth Amendment, because it implicitly affirms that our liberties are infinite in number.

And, yes, these are *personal* rights as opposed to states' rights, as some characters like Robert Bork have desperately suggested. They include, among literally countless other things, our right to wear a hat if we please.

Or to party. You gotta fight for your right to party.

But you only have that right provided you do not infringe on other people's right to enjoy some peace and quiet. Obviously, those un-enumerated rights go both ways. Our rights are infinite in *number* but not *breadth*. My rights end where yours begin and *vice versa*.

Conscious consideration for others is built-in. Liberty does not begin or end with anyone's dickish id. It is a constant balancing act of give and take, an ongoing dialogue between people requiring reciprocal tolerance. We all give each other a little license so that we can enjoy the same latitude ourselves later on. In other words, live and let live.

For example, my neighbors are partying a little loud tonight, but it is Saturday night so I put up with it. On a weeknight, it is different.

This is not to say that things are entirely gray. If my neighbors are trying to police my morality – especially by trying to control behavior that does not actually impact them – it is definitely *they* who are crossing a line. There is no reciprocal give and take in that particular instance.

Like and dislike should not figure into it. Forbearance and approval are very different things: Requiring another's approval is tyrannical.

Side bar: If this all sounds a tad abstract and/or academic, do not fret. I will talk about pirates and clitoral orgasms very shortly.

Under this understanding, gun ownership enjoys another layer of protection from the Ninth Amendment. Like our other enumerated rights, the Second Amendment was, "inserted merely for greater caution." In other words, the Constitution's authors were in effect *repeating themselves* by singling out certain rights for special emphasis.

Of course, the same goes for the First Amendment and all the other rights that were specifically spelled out. It turns out that Dan Savage's proposal for ending the Culture Wars was what the prevailing bulk of our founders had originally intended all along.

Naturally, conservatives want the Ninth Amendment to go away and accordingly they try to appoint Supreme Court Justices who they know will ignore it. Judge Robert Bork was the perfect candidate for this.

Remember him? I mentioned him in chapter one. He was the fellow who said the founding fathers put too much faith in the individual and should have remembered Original Sin. He thought we should interpret the Constitution according to the "original intent" of the founders.

His 1987 confirmation fight put Originalism on the map. Before then, most people had not heard of it. Because he did not get a seat on the bench he became a political martyr in conservative lore. To "do a Bork" became a verb. This made the confirmation of subsequent Originalists much easier – hence, Justices Antonio Scalia and Clarence Thomas. Even in defeat, he had an immense impact. And when people think of Originalism, they think of Robert Bork. At his confirmation hearings, Bork compared the Ninth to a meaningless ink blot:

I do not think you can use the Ninth Amendment unless you know something of what it means. For example, if you had an amendment that says "Congress shall make no" and then there is an ink blot and you cannot read the rest of it and that is the only copy you have, I do not think the court can make up what might be under the ink blot if you cannot read it.[113]

Call it "the dog-ate-my-homework" school of constitutional scholarship. The obvious problem with Professor Bork's shoddy analogy is that abundant documentation makes the founders' intent perfectly clear. We have transcripts of the debates and, as the above quotes show, there is no ambiguity to clarify. Yet, during his hearings, Bork repeatedly claimed he had no idea what the Ninth Amendment meant and that nobody else did either:

I know of only one historical piece. There may be more. You know, this is not a subject I have researched at great length, but most people say they do not know what it means.[114]

In other words, *Please confirm me, even though I have not done my homework*. A moment later Bork added:

Senator, if anybody shows me historical evidence about what they meant, I would be delighted to do it. I just do not know.

Wait. Are we to believe that this professor of constitutional law had never read any of these documents? Had he not studied the discussions around the

Bill of Rights' creation and ratification? For such an outspoken advocate of looking for "original intent," he sure had a lot of trouble finding it.

Intriguingly, Justice James Iredell had precisely predicted Robert Bork's weasel-like approach to jurisprudence way back in 1787:

No man, let his ingenuity be what it will, could enumerate all the individual rights not relinquished by this Constitution. Suppose, therefore, an enumeration of a great many, but an omission of some, and that, long after all traces of our present disputes were at end, any of the omitted rights should be invaded, and the invasion be complained of; what would be the plausible answer of the government to such a complaint? Would they not naturally say, "We live at a great distance from the time when this Constitution was established. We can judge of it much better by the ideas of it entertained at the time, than by any ideas of our own. The bill of rights, passed at that time, showed that the people did not think every power retained which was not given, else this bill of rights was not only useless, but absurd. But we are not at liberty to charge an absurdity upon our ancestors, who have given such strong proofs of their good sense, as well as their attachment to liberty. So long as the rights enumerated in the bill of rights remain unviolated, you have no reason to complain."[115]

BUSTED!

Fortunately, not all traces of their disputes have disappeared. On the contrary, they were extensively documented and remain as evidence of actual original intent. But that did not prevent Robert Bork from pretending that they had mysteriously disappeared.

Was he playing dumb under oath?

Had he read Justice James Iredell's dire prediction and decided to implement it in the hopes that nobody else had ever seen it? Because Iredell had predicted Bork's exact argument.

His testimony unsettlingly suggests that he wanted to muddy our understanding of the past – perhaps because he feared its implications.

In his second book, *Slouching Towards Gomorrah*, Bork seemed more forthright about his apprehensions. Here, he admits to his profound discomfort with our founding ideals. Yes, he mentions comfort:

For all the decade's lurid brutality and revolutionary upheaval, the Sixties were not a complete break with the spirit of the American past. Rather, those years saw an explosive expansion of certain American (and Western) ideals and a corresponding severe diminution of others. That deserves to be stressed because if modern developments are in the American grain, if they grow from our roots, as there is reason to believe they do, they will be much harder to reverse than it is comfortable to think.[116]

Bingo. To his credit, Robert Bork at least admitted to the American character of thinking he dislikes. That shows a far greater historical understanding than most conservative pundits possess.

Of course, Professor Bork's point was that the founding fathers goofed by giving people too much credit. Elsewhere in his book, he wrote, "The signers of the Declaration took the moral order they had inherited for granted. It never occurred to them that the document's rhetorical flourishes might be dangerous if that moral order weakened."[117]

How could the founders have overlooked this possibility? Bork offered this strange explanation:

We can now see the tendency of the Enlightenment, the Declaration of Independence, and On Liberty. Each insisted on the expanding liberty of the individual and each assumed that order was not a serious problem and could be left, pretty much, to take care of itself. And, for a time, order did seem to take care of itself. But that was because the institutions – family, church, school, neighborhood, inherited morality – remained strong.[118]

This is not simply one conservative's opinion. As political clout, book sales and media attention attest, Robert Bork spoke for many on the right. He was a significant figure, and it is safe to say that his *New York Times* bestselling books compose a fair portrait of conservative thought – the fears and attitudes, if not the specific rationalizations.

It is also the most laughable hogwash imaginable.

Nobody even remotely familiar with the Revolutionary Era would characterize its traditional institutions as even secure, let alone "strong." The decades before, during, and after the struggle for independence were rocked with so much social upheaval that they make the Sixties look placid by comparison. Moralists considered "wickedness" hopelessly widespread. Church attendance was scant and "bastardy" rampant. Mob mayhem was commonplace. It was a period of unprecedented public drunkenness and property destruction. Sexuality was expressed so frankly that bawdy limericks spiced up general interest newspapers and dead folks' tombstones. Insolence was ubiquitous and class antagonism had reached a fever pitch. The old social order was halfway out the door long before "the shot heard round the world" spelled the end of English rule. In fact, colonial mobs had been regularly clashing in the streets with royal authorities since the early 1740s. By the 1770s, it had become business as usual.

I am going to belabor the point because it is important, but also because it is absolutely hilarious.

If contemporary accounts can be trusted, the generation that won our liberty was a surly bunch. They were bastards from the start – both literally and figuratively. Their generation was the legacy of rising illegitimacy, falling rum prices, and parental neglect.[119] In their book *Generations: the History of America's Future 1584 to 2069*, William Straus and Neil Howe give us an interesting glimpse of their upbringing:

Colonial newspapers noted the rising number of children abandoned as "bastards," turned over to wet nurses, fed liquor to shut them up, or just left free to run around on their own. ... Jonathan Edwards warned that children "out of Christ" are "young vipers, and are infinitely more hateful than vipers." His Bostonian peer Andrew Eliot condemned them as an "evil and adulterous generation."[120]

Those were our founding fathers, folks – the troops, anyway.

According to Straus and Howe, this "evil and adulterous" bunch, "consumed more alcohol per capita than any colonial generation." And they were not quiet drunks either. "Between 1760 and 1775, they led more violent mobs than the cumulative total for all prior generations."[121]

That was no small feat, considering that their parents were not exactly slouches in this department either. In *A People's History of the American Revolution*, Ray Raphael gives us a vivid picture of colonial draft resistance in the 1740s. It apparently consisted entirely of rioting and it is not hard to see why. The Royal Navy used to abduct men and boys from the wharves and taverns of port towns in order to man its ships. This unpopular practice was called "impressment." Crowds often fought back and the resulting ruckus could involve *thousands* – especially in the famously insubordinate port of Boston town:

In 1741 a crowd beat up the sheriff and stoned a justice of the peace who supported impressments. In 1742 a crowd attacked the commanding officer of the Astrea and destroyed a barge belonging to the Royal Navy. In 1745 protestors beat up the commander of the HMS Shirley and battered a deputy sheriff unconscious; later that year they rioted again when a press gang killed two seamen.

Already versed in the art of protesting, several thousand rioters against the Knowles impressments once again challenged authority. They placed a deputy sheriff in the stocks, seized officers of the Lark as hostages, broke the windows of the Council chamber, and confronted the royal governor with "very indecent, rude expressions." Governor Shirley, understandably frightened, abandoned his mansion and retreated to an island in the harbor.[122]

The crowd was just getting warmed up. They then dragged a barge they thought belonged to the Royal Navy through the city streets to the vacant Governor's mansion and then to the Commons where they torched it.

Governor Shirley did what any governor would have done in this situation: He called out the militia. But only the officers showed up. It turned out that the rank and file had joined the protestors.

Commodore Knowles then threatened to bombard Boston from his ships, but it was an unlikely threat because the mob owned little property to lose. The crowd controlled Boston for three days until the Commodore finally relented and released most of those he had seized.

It sort of makes burning draft cards look pretty tame by comparison, doesn't it? And yet, protesting an authority-approved form of the draft was exactly what these colonials were engaged in – in 1741, 1742 and twice in 1745. These were not rare or exceptional events. The era was already, as Robert Bork had described the 1960s, a time of "lurid brutality and revolutionary upheaval."

Indeed, as historical records show, colonial America sometimes resembled a pirate movie. This was only appropriate since American merchants often funded or supplied Caribbean pirates. In the 1710s, the infamous buccaneer Blackbeard split his plunder with North Carolina's Governor, Charles Eden. And in the run up to the Revolution, colonial smugglers, trying to get around the mother country's trade laws, had to either out-run or out-gun British Naval frigates.

So yes, it was a pretty lawless century from the start.

Revolution is not a Norman Rockwell painting. But violent uprisings and mob actions marked this *entire* era – before, during, and after the Revolution. Who does not already know about the Boston Tea Party or the frequently deadly practice of tar and feathering? Remember reading about Shay's Rebellion? How about the Whiskey Rebellion?

This was not exactly a tranquil period in our nation's history. And for each well-known uprising, there is a less familiar one. In 1786, an armed mob of revolutionary veterans besieged the New Hampshire state legislature for three days demanding, among other things, the equal distribution of property. In a letter to Thomas Jefferson, John Adams catalogs a number of post-revolutionary mass actions both famous and obscure:

You never felt the terrorism of Shay's Rebellion in Massachusetts. I believe you never felt the terrorism of Gallatin's insurrection in Pennsylvania. You certainly never realized the terrorism of Tries's most outrageous riot and rescue, as I call it. Treason-rebellion – as the world, and great judges, and two juries pronounce it. You certainly never felt the terrorism excited by Genet in 1793, when ten thousand people in the streets of Philadelphia, day after day, threatened to drag Washington out of his house, and effect a revolution in government, or compel it to declare war in favor of the French Revolution, and against England. The coolest and firmest minds, even among the Quakers of Philadelphia, have given their opinions to me, that nothing but the yellow fever, which removed Dr. Hutchinson and Jonathan Dickenson Sargent from this world, could have saved the United States from a total revolution of government. I have no doubt you were fast asleep in philosophical tranquility when ten thousand people, and perhaps many more, were parading the streets of Philadelphia, on the evening of my Fast Day. When even Governor Mifflin himself, thought it his duty to order a patrol of horse and foot, to preserve the peace; when Market Street was as full as men could stand by one another, and even before my door; when some of my domestics, in frenzy, determined to sacrifice their lives in my defence [sic]; when all were ready to make a desperate sally among the multitude, and others were with difficulty and danger dragged back by others; when I myself judged it prudent and necessary to order chests of arms from the War Office, to be brought through by lanes and back doors; determined to defend my house at the expense of my life, and the lives of the few, very few, domestics and friends within it. What think you of terrorism, Mr. Jefferson?[123]

Gee, it kind of sounds like the Sixties or the Seventies, except there was small chance of dragging either Lyndon Johnson or Richard Nixon into the street. I guess order did not "take care of itself" back then as Robert Bork claimed. He expected us to swallow an awful lot. Nobody could plausibly argue that, "The signers of the Declaration *took the moral order they had inherited for granted.*" (emphasis added) Nor could anyone credibly claim that, "*It never occurred to them* that the document's rhetorical flourishes might be dangerous if that moral order weakened." As contemporary accounts attest, there was not any moral order to inherit. They were acutely aware of all the social and economic upheaval around them. After all, they grew up with it.

Perhaps Thomas Jefferson was fast asleep in philosophical tranquility, but certainly no one else was. Most of the founding fathers – and even Jefferson himself[124] – had acknowledged that freedom was messy stuff and fraught with serious risks (but preferable to the authoritarian alternative). In fact, they all wrote about it at great length. It is almost impossible to read their letters, essays, pamphlets, and personal journals without repeatedly reading their concerns.

So, I find it rather fascinating that the founders lived through such tumultuous times and still chose freedom. By sharp contrast, conservatives are ever ready to extinguish it, even in the most tranquil periods. They are not "fair weather patriots," but all-weather Tories.

By claiming the founders' words had unintended consequences, Robert Bork thought he could continue to ignore their plainly stated aims. Bork said the founders forgot about social order so all that lyrical stuff about liberty can safely be ignored. It is just window dressing that is there to be pretty. But in the wake of the revolution, the founders argued over what liberty really meant and what society required in order to function. Whatever side they took, there is no honestly arguing that they forgot to consider these things. Like his sorry inkblot analogy Robert Bork's ideas can only convince in total isolation from other information.

This is significant since Robert Bork's notions of how freedom works were far more sophisticated than most conservatives'. Like most conservatives, Bork felt we have too much freedom and that life was better in some halcyon day and age in which we enjoyed less liberty. But *unlike* most other conservatives, he at least admitted that our uppityness is ultimately the legacy of our revolutionary heritage. Whereas most other conservatives envision our founding fathers as stern, vigilant guardians of moral order, Robert Bork thought they totally dropped the ball because they forgot to bother with it entirely.

But these are trivial differences. Conservatives all oppose freedom and equate modernity with decay and ruin. For some reason, they all suppose the revolutionaries would share their opposition to "sexual anarchy." Corner them long enough and they may eventually admit to your right to wear a hat – after all, that's not a social issue they feel strongly about. "But surely," they'll likely say, "the founders would frown on today's promiscuity."

Nope. Indeed, this is where things really get hilarious.

Reading about eighteenth-century attitudes toward youth, sexuality, and freedom from a modern-day perspective is fascinating. During the past three decades, the media had assaulted us with one false crisis after another. Most of them were manufactured to justify sanctimonious crack downs on teenagers. Throughout the 1990s, pundits and politicians across the political spectrum decried a generation of decadent, violent "super predators" driven to bloodlust and every form of excess by lurid videogames and explicit rap music. The right, as always, called for broader police powers and a return to "family values" while "liberals" were either too timid to oppose them or joined in the moralistic chorus against such "chaos."

In reality, violent crime by youth was at a *fifty-year low*. Violent crime by *Baby Boomers* was rising. In fact, they were the *only* age group for which violent crime was rising; but, as researcher Mike Males observed, a campaign to crack down on this constituency was highly unlikely.[125]

The same could be said for virtually any teen "epidemic" you could mention – drug use, "binge drinking," unwanted pregnancies, you name it. Scolds claimed all were rising when they were actually falling.

As historian Stephanie Coontz noted in her 1992 book, *The Way We Never Were: American Families and the Nostalgia Trap*, the rate of teenagers bearing children was then *half* of what it was in 1957.[126] All of these figures were down and falling – and had not actually been high among youth since the Baby Boomers were young. Funny that.

In other words, the kids are all right; but mom and pop are nuts. But never mind. The conservative urge to control others was aroused and their appetite to mete out discipline for their own satisfaction would not be deterred by mere facts. It never is. The result was an ageist and racist hysteria that rewrote laws and destroyed lives – and continues to do so today.

By stark contrast, our founding fathers benefited from more sensible parentage. As Richard Godbeer shows in *Sexual Revolution in Early America*, there was an explosion in sexual activity in the 1700s and society largely reacted with acceptance. Church control over people's choices was waning and, in an era without access to contraceptives, sexual attitudes had measurable results. According to marriage and birth records, more and more colonials could answer the question "Have you ever been experienced?" with a yes. "In New Haven County, Connecticut, 19 percent of women who married during the 1690s were pregnant, up from a mere 2 percent in the 1670s. By the Revolutionary Era, between 30 and 40 percent of brides in some New England towns were already expecting."[127] In Puritan New England!

Can you imagine the effect such numbers would have today? Yet, despite these staggering statistics, there was no draconian crack down. In the face of an *actual* rise in teen pregnancy rates, rather than an *imaginary* one, colonial parents amazingly reacted practically rather than puritanically by embracing the folkway known as "bundling."

What is bundling? It was a colonial code word for premarital sex. A young woman's suitors were allowed to sleep over with the full knowledge and consent of her family. This practice enabled parents to monitor who their daughter was sleeping with, and thus know who was responsible for any resulting pregnancy. This American tradition astounded foreign observers from all over. As Godbeer writes:

Visitors were amazed by the openness with which young men and women spent the night together. "I have entered several bedchambers," wrote Alexandre Berthier, "where I have found bundling couples, who are not disturbed and continue to give each other all the honest tokens of their love." Johann Schoepf, who toured the region in 1783-84, assured his reader that "the young woman's good name [was] no ways impaired" by such nocturnal intimacies. Visits took place neither "by stealth" nor only after the young couple was "actually betrothed": "on the contrary, the parents are advised, and these meetings happen when the pair is enamored and merely wish to know each other better." Schoepf was not the only traveler to report that young people spent the night together after brief acquaintance. Luigi Castiglioni, who traveled through the United States in 1785-87, found himself in company with a fellow who had just spent the night with a young woman "after having courted her not more than six hours." He also claimed that overnight visits cast "no shadow upon the character of the girl."[128]

Sounds like something out of the 1965 Bob Hope comedy *I'll Take Sweden* – except that sexual attitudes were reversed. Hence, the U.S. and Europe have since switched both social mores and internal wealth gaps. Things change. Not only did Benjamin Franklin's "happy mediocrity" in economic income evaporate, a culture hostile to sexuality took over socially. The good Doctor would have lamented both developments.

This bed-hopping society was the "moral order" Robert Bork said our founding fathers "took for granted." In fact, while courting his future wife, Abigail Smith, John Adams wrote an essay recommending bundling.[129] Simply put, our nation was founded by sexual humanists.

Not that there was no controversy whatsoever. Some ministers sternly inveighed against the practice of bundling; but in an era of scant church membership, they could reach few from the pulpit. So they turned to putting their arguments in verse and got them published in newspapers and almanacs. Naturally, bundling's advocates replied in kind:

Some mothers too will plead their cause,
And give their daughters great applause,
And tell them, 'tis no sin or shame,
For we, your mothers, did the same;
We hope the custom ne'ere will alter,
But wish its enemies a halter.[130]

As many historians have noted, colonial society was pretty sexually open. As Stephanie Coontz wrote:

Eighteenth-century spelling and grammar books routinely used fornication *as an example of a four-syllable word, and preachers detailed sexual offenses in astonishingly explicit terms. Sexual conversations between men and women, even in front of children, were remarkably frank.*[131]

And after quoting a bawdy poem in his book, *White Over Black: American Attitudes Toward the Negro 1550 – 1812*, historian Winthrop Jordan observed:

If these contributions to the South Carolina Gazette were a trifle raw by the standards of a modern family newspaper, they reflected more than eighteenth-century literary frankness about sex. Newspapers elsewhere on the continent did not publish similar discussions on interracial sex, though everywhere (including Boston) they published some none-too-delicate pieces concerning sexual matters.[132]

Some of these historical ditties show unexpected sexual independence on the part of women. They could articulate great agency and desire – as well as a headstrong will to flaunt traditional society's weakened conventions:

I'll never marry, no indeed,
For marriage causes trouble:
And after all the priest has said,
'Tis merely hubble bubble
The rakes will still be counted rakes,
Not Hymen's chains can bind 'em,
And so preventing all mistakes,
I'll kiss whene'er I find them.[133]

Society's openness and women's independence and pleasure historically go hand-in-hand. For example, ignorance of the clitoris often results when sexual information is policed. But absent such censorship, the incentive to learn things gets a lot more done.

Let's discuss the clitoris for a bit.

Unlike their unfortunate Victorian descendants, the revolutionaries knew about the clitoris, thanks to a free press. For those who did not learn firsthand, love and marriage manuals came to the rescue.

Of course, both eras had their marriage manuals; but, as you can imagine, they differed from each other. The Victorian versions instructed men to conserve their sperm and women to tolerate sex. By contrast, the earlier Enlightenment manuals were … well, more *enlightened*.

Instead, their aim was to help couples "render their intercourse prolific" and they accomplished this in part by acknowledging women's anatomical needs. In *The Physician and Sexuality in Victorian America*, John and Robin Haller give us an interesting glimpse into these pre-Victorian manuals:

Another popular manual encouraged sexual pleasure by demanding that both sexes meet "with equal vigor" in the conjugal act. The woman's interest in sex as well as her ability to conceive depended entirely upon pleasurable reciprocity. The clitoris, which achieved an erection similar to the male penis ("yard" or "codpiece") as a result of stimulation, "both stir up lust and gives delight in copulation, for without this, the fair sex neither desire mutual embrace, nor have pleasure in them, nor conceive by them." Noted medical scientist John Hunter (1728 – 93) had identified the clitoris as the reciprocal organ of the male penis: "There is one part in common to both the male and female organs of generation, in all the animals that have the sexes distinct; in the one it is called the penis; in the other the clitoris. Its special use, in both, is to continue by sensibility, the action excited in coition till the paroxysm alters sensation."[134]

These people were serious about the pursuit of happiness.

Granted, the notion that conception depended on the woman's orgasm is not medically accurate. The species would be extinct if that were true.[135] Still, it was more reliable than the later Victorian notion that women who enjoyed sex were probably sterile. Obviously, pleasurable sex results in more frequent sex, which in turn makes pregnancy more likely – as all those eighteenth-century birth records proved. Hence, their results had at least supported their assumptions.

By contrast, Victorian birth rates fell thanks to moralistic junk science. A fear of freedom gripped America and Europe after the Enlightenment and Victorian values instilled a militant ignorance in the medical profession, so doctors actually endorsed this nonsense. Fortunately for American industrialists, there was still a steady flow of immigrants to toil in their dangerous factories.

It is comforting to think that it cannot happen again, but we saw it resume during George W. Bush's term in office. His Surgeon General, Richard H. Carmona, complained that he had encountered constant political interference. Religion was given a veto over science. As the *Washington Post* reported in 2007, shortly after he resigned:

Carmona, a Bush nominee who served from 2002 to 2006, told the House Committee on Oversight and Government Reform that political appointees in the administration routinely scrubbed his speeches for politically sensitive content and blocked him from speaking out on public health matters such as stem cell research, abstinence-only sex education and the emergency contraceptive Plan B. "Anything that doesn't fit into the political appointees' ideological, theological or political agenda is often ignored, marginalized or simply buried," he said.[136]

Consider those aforementioned abstinence-only sex education programs. The Bush Administration had funneled millions of tax dollars into over one hundred of them. The House Committee on Oversight and Government Reform looked into some of them and discovered several false claims. As the United Press reported:

The investigators found that one program teaches, contrary to accepted medical belief, that HIV is spread via sweat and tears. Other programs teach that condoms fail to stop the transmission of HIV 31 percent of the time during heterosexual sex and that the 'popular claim' that condoms prevent the spread of STDs is not supported by data. Federal research shows the failure rate for condoms is 3 percent when used properly.[137]

Then Senate Majority Leader – and licensed physician, mind you – Bill Frist rushed to Bush's defense claiming that he did not know if sweat or tears could carry HIV.[138] This was a little like Robert Bork claiming that he did not know what the Ninth Amendment meant. If he really did not know, he really should have because you want your doctor to know this stuff. Such ignorance should disqualify one from practice.

By the way, this was the same doctor who diagnosed Terri Schiavo *by videotape* and insisted that the brain dead woman was "responsive" and therefore should not be taken off life support.

Of course, conservative junk science is on the march in general. We live in an era in which every disproven theory has been fished out of the dustbin of history. Creationism is taught alongside Evolution in some states. The eugenicist's pseudoscientific notion that race determines intelligence is back in vogue, thanks to a book called *The Bell Curve*. And pre-Keynesian economics – which was totally debunked by the Great Depression – enjoys political respectability in both major political parties today. And the Tea Party wants to repeal child labor laws and the direct election of U.S. Senators. Perhaps the Flat Earth Society will eventually get equal time in geography classrooms. In a great many ways, America's scientific literacy and attitudes toward liberty and equality are almost where they were before 1920.

Of course, George Will had admitted that the conservative's goal was to return to 1900. Things have been deteriorating almost across the board. Yes, we elected an African American president, but schools are re-segregating and they have brought back the chain-gangs. As Thomas Frank wrote in *What's the Matter with Kansas?* (2004) "With a little more effort, the backlash may well repeal the entire twentieth century."[139]

Backlashes happen, and understanding that is crucial to defending our rights. For example, knowing that our founding fathers enjoyed bundling helps defend against the Victorian world that conservatives are trying to restore just as knowing what the Ninth Amendment meant helps defend liberty generally. The price of liberty is indeed eternal vigilance so taking progress for granted is accordingly not an option.

But the word "backlash" is a deceptive description because it legitimizes an accepted fiction. Both the right and the left have, seemingly by mutual consent, partitioned the timeline with liberals playing heralds of the future and conservatives playing curators of the past. Almost everyone seems to have acknowledged each other's chronological turf. But as a result, we have a false model of how progress takes place.

The problem is that conservatives are no better custodians of our heritage than they are of the environment. In *1984*, George Orwell warned, "He who controls the past, controls the future." In a seemingly unrelated statement, Ann Coulter summed up the responsibilities entailed in man's stewardship over the Earth: "God says, 'Earth is yours. Take it. Rape it. It's yours.'" Put together, these statements explain a great deal. Conservative stewardship of our national heritage is no different than their stewardship of our natural one. That is simply their conception of stewardship. And how *else* would they treat the liberal traditions that our nation was founded on?

The question answers itself.

Two side points on conservative stewardship:

First, I am no theologian. But if we are house-sitting for God, how happy is he going to be to come home and find that we have peed in the carpet and pocketed all the door knobs?

And second, while I am thinking of it, do not ever let Ann Coulter baby-sit your kids. Just saying.

This situation is rather ironic because conservatives, as a whole, are not particularly interested in history. History is the study of change over time. In other words, it is the study of how we got here from there, and why life is different now. Since conservatives are temperamentally hostile to change, they prefer to fetishize the past rather than try to understand it. As a result, they tend to become antiquarians rather than historians. They are essentially hobbyists who cannot see the forest for the logs. So they miss the big picture, which they are not really interested in anyway. They simply prefer to assume things were "better in the good old days" with "better" meaning more to their anti-egalitarian and freedom-hostile liking. This explains Robert Bork's hilarious assumption that strong traditional institutions restrained individualism during the Revolutionary Era.

But, to be fair, most liberals do not like reading history either because they hold similar assumptions. They tend to think that the past was populated almost entirely with simple-minded bigots despite the presence of countless figures they say were "ahead of their time." Hence, they assume "the exception proves the rule" and therefore ignore *entire movements* which those historic individuals often represented and have become shorthand for.

Put another way, liberals embrace a fairly linear notion of self-propelled progress in which things keep gradually getting better as time goes by. They assume social evolution and rationalize that any setbacks are a necessary part of some inevitable, organic process.

Both attitudes are extremely misleading. And no wonder! Again, they are the exact same models except with different opinions on developments. Conservatives and liberals differ only on the desirability of change, but they seem to agree on its general direction.

For Robert Bork, and conservatives as a whole, freedom has gotten too big for its britches. Bork described this as a gradual process that had only gained momentum in recent decades – the Sixties especially:

The idea of liberty has continuous change built into it, precisely because it is hostile to constraints. Men seek the removal of the constraint nearest them. But when that one falls, men are brought against the next constraint, which is now felt to be equally irksome. That is why the agenda of liberalism is in constant motion and liberals of different eras would hardly recognize each other as deserving the same label.[140]

Accordingly, most conservatives assume that the founding fathers would want us to reverse, stop, or at least slow social change as a deviation from their "original intent."

For example, in the *National Review's* 1955 mission statement, William F. Buckley Jr. wrote that it "stands athwart history shouting Stop!"[141] Buckley lamented that "literate America rejected conservatism in favor of radical social experimentation" forgetting that America is *itself* a radical social experiment and always has been.

Now, let us look at how liberals have also gotten it wrong. Thomas Jefferson significantly differed from both Bork and Buckley on the importance of making improvements:

But I know also, that laws and institutions must go hand in hand with the progress of the human mind. As that becomes more developed, more enlightened, as new discoveries are made, new truths disclosed, and manners and opinions change with the change of circumstances, institutions must advance also, and keep pace with the times. We might as well require a man to wear still the coat which fitted him when a boy, as civilized society to remain ever under the regimen of their barbarous ancestors.[142]

In other words, "original intent" says, "forget original intent."

Of course, today's barbarians beg to differ. But Originalist advertising notwithstanding, understanding original intent never was a conservative strong suit. The *whole goal* of the "original intent" judicial movement is to limit liberty and thereby violate original intent.

Their take on the Ninth Amendment proves this, but their take on other amendments support this assessment as well.

For example, the Fourteenth Amendment was explicitly written to give freed slaves the same civil rights as whites. And yet, for almost a century thereafter, the Supreme Court chose to ignore that obvious purpose.

Instead, in the interim, the court ruled in *Santa Clara County v. Southern Pacific Railroad* (1886) that the Fourteenth Amendment gave rights to *corporations* by making them "immortal persons."

This was clearly a stretch, but I doubt many conservatives will ever admit it. It was not until the 1950s that the court finally decided to apply the Fourteenth Amendment to African Americans as well and *that* was when conservatives began accusing the Supreme Court of overstepping itself!

Roll that fact around in your noggin for a moment.

This means it was not until the court finally honored original intent that it was accused of going against original intent – and we have been hearing conservatives squeal about "judicial activism" ever since. Those are the convoluted contours of conservative jurisprudence. It is neither logical nor historical. It is only authoritarian and dishonest.

Robert Bork and Thomas Jefferson disagreed on the desirability of change, but they agreed on its eventual direction. And they were both also wrong about it. There is no inherent leftward tendency in history making us increasingly free and equal, or even more enlightened. We *are* more free, equal, and enlightened; but that is something we humans decided to do and *made* happen. It did not occur in our sleep. Progress is not on autopilot.

Robert Bork warned, "Men seek the removal of the constraint nearest them," and certainly many do. But other men – i.e. those who think like Robert Bork – have a mania for reinforcing those restraints and even making new ones. Humanity has reactionary impulses as well as progressive ones, and conscious, collective efforts decide which ones prevail from one day to the next. Again, the price of liberty is eternal vigilance.

Robert Bork's tendencies lead to the very tyranny that Jefferson feared in his more sober moments. Many of the founders' letters mentioned fears of creeping tyranny and wondered how many more generations freedom would last. Indeed, two generations later, Abraham Lincoln wrote:

*Our progress in degeneracy appears to me to be pretty rapid. As a nation, we began by declaring that "all men are created equal." We now practically read it "all men are created equal, **except negroes**." When the Know-Nothings get control, it will read "all men are created equal, except negroes, **and foreigners and Catholics**." When it comes to this I should prefer emigrating to some country where they make no pretense of loving liberty - to [Tsarist] Russia, for instance, where despotism can be taken pure, and without the base alloy of hypocrisy.* (emphasis original)[143]

Conservatives seem addicted to adding new restrictions. Except perhaps for Barry Goldwater, conservatives have always strenuously objected to the self-evident truth that freedom means the liberty to do whatever does not harm another. *But surely*, they quickly interject, *that wasn't meant to include this or that particular act or group of people.*

Just as Justice James Iredell had claimed he could add twenty or thirty forgotten items to any written Bill of Rights, conservatives can and do invent countless new constraints, original intent notwithstanding.

Again, conservatives do not give a shit about original intent. It is just as empty as the Tea Party's always false talk of "liberty."

I wrote a lot about progress and original intent in this chapter about freedom because conservatives so often distort history to rob us of our rights. Robert Bork's ignoring the Ninth Amendment and its history was my central example, but twisting or ignoring history is simply what most conservatives do. The conservative version of the American Revolution has no revolutionaries. Radicals were absent and nobody was ever rude, insolent, or disobedient. In their portrayal, people spoke a great deal about freedom but refrained from personally exercising any.

In short, conservatives envision the revolutionaries using the word "freedom" as they do today – without really meaning it.

Among famous conservatives, Robert Bork came closest to saying our founding fathers were only fooling. But they all try to obfuscate freedom or make it something it is not, often its total opposite.

Take this interesting definition of liberty by Rudy Giuliani, given when he was still mayor of New York:

Freedom is not a concept in which people can do anything they want, be anything they can be. Freedom is about authority. Freedom is about the willingness of every single human being to cede to lawful authority a great deal of discretion about what you do.[144]

And Giuliani is (or was) a "liberal" Republican. Think about that.

That definition is refreshingly simple and straightforward.

It is also nutso, so you can see why most other conservatives might prefer the cover of a more complicated one. They try to make liberty mysterious, arcane, and inaccessible.

It is tempting to think that they are trying to hide something, but I am also open to the notion that freedom really is a mystery to them. Once you reject the "no harm, no foul" model, liberty pretty much *has* to be a mystery.

Perhaps conservatives see liberty and history the same way some frat boys see the functions of women's reproductive plumbing: They do not know much about it. They do not *want* to know much about it. Their discomfort leads them to make "knowing" jokes about it. And, in any case, they think these matters should be left to ideologically-tested experts, such as pro-life gynecologists, and "strict constructionist" judges. Then, they think, we should give such experts "a great deal of discretion about what you do."

I think their response is organic and honest – at least, with most of them. If you fear freedom, being an American poses a problem for you. So, proclaiming your "patriotism" while questioning your opponents' is not simply a debate tactic. It is also how you deal with this identity crisis. That nagging question of authenticity is always there and projection is the automatic reflex. If those conflicting thoughts become too uncomfortable, saying "freedom does not really mean freedom" starts to look logical to you. And when finally cornered, you can always say that nobody really knows what freedom means and seem deep and philosophical.

I have often seen this strange and anti-civic mysticism.

A few years ago, I was corresponding with a conservative who, like Robert Bork, claimed to have been a libertarian in his youth. He wrote that he appreciated the Thomas Jefferson quote on the necessity for institutional adaptation, but he added that was what constitutional amendments are for. So … I need a constitutional amendment to wear a hat?

Trying diplomacy, he said he loved freedom just as much as I did, but that freedom actually meant something *more* than being able to do whatever does not harm another. By "more" I suspect he meant "less." But rather than attacking, I asked him to explain what he meant by that.

He never got back to me.

3: Liberté, Egalité, and Rock & Roll
The Tripod in American Culture

Many conservatives say that liberty and equality are essentially at odds. They thus insist that we must resist "egalitarian schemes" if we are to remain free. Yet, as I wrote back in chapter one, Robert Bork said we now have too much liberty *and* too much equality. How did that happen? How did both grow, if they are locked in a zero-sum game?

Obviously, these two ideals are stuck in no such contest. On the contrary, as African American history starkly illustrates, liberty and equality are inherently interlinked. If society thinks you are inferior, your rights are imperiled – they will either be officially denied or informally ignored.

Supreme Court Justice Roger Taney spelled this out in his infamous 1856 Dred Scott decision. He wrote that African Americans were, "so far inferior that they had no rights which the white man was bound to respect," and thus, "the negro might justly and lawfully be reduced to slavery for his benefit."[145] Simply put, liberty and equality are two sides of the same coin: They are always won or lost together.

Of course, conservatives are not actually talking about the minority's rights but the majority's privileges. Rights and privileges are opposites because rights are universal while privileges are special. But conservatives often use these antonyms as synonyms. Hence, when minorities demand equal treatment, they are oxymoronically accused of demanding "special rights." The same sex marriage issue vividly illustrates this when its homophobic opponents say that gays want "a special right to marry." Oh, you mean like straights have?

Privileges often feel like rights to those who enjoy them. People in general are apt to take their habits as rights – and social customs even more so. And they are not wrong so long as they do not harm anyone else in the process. Remember, your rights are infinite in number, but not breadth.

Of course, Jim Crow Laws never met that criterion. Hence, the privileges Southern whites lost were not rights at all. There is no right to victimize others, even if you are in the habit of doing so. An oppressor's habits are not "rights."

Habits feel natural and we associate nature with our rights. And we Americans are all the more apt to express our desires in terms of rights. But habits are actually artificial. They need to be instilled. Customs are society's habits – and often its worst ones. As Mark Twain once wrote, "Customs do not concern themselves with right or wrong or reason."[146] But a free society must concern itself with those things in order to remain free. That is one reason why freedom and custom are so often at odds.

One reason that privileges feel like rights is that they often are *monopolized* rights, like the right to vote was – or the right to marry was for that matter. The privileged often confuse their exclusivity with their liberty. This may explain why some think allowing gay marriage will somehow destroy straight marriage. They think that recognizing others' rights will somehow ultimately ruin or diminish their own. Freedom is not a finite resource, but zero-sum assumptions still creep into some people's thinking.

Not harming others is explicitly built into the liberty's definition, but equality is implicitly built into it too. As Thomas Jefferson said, we must be "free to do whatever does not violate the *equal rights of another*."[147] (emphasis added) Equality is central to the distinction between rights and privileges.

This makes sense. For, if a right is truly universal, it is obviously enjoyed equally by everyone. Billy Bragg's version of "The Internationale" makes this perfectly clear. "Freedom is merely privilege extended, unless enjoyed by one and all." In other words, it is not real freedom.

Of course, counterfeit freedom is as insecure as it is illusory. Equality is not only essential to *defining* real freedom, it is essential to *defending* it as well. As Thomas Paine explained, "He that would make his own liberty secure must guard even his enemy from oppression: for if he violates this duty, he establishes a precedent that will reach unto himself."[148] Likewise, President Franklin D. Roosevelt had later declared, "We must scrupulously guard the civil rights and civil liberties of all our citizens, whatever their background. We must remember that any oppression, any injustice, any hatred, is a wedge designed to attack our civilization."[149] In other words, we all have an interest in acting like the American Civil Liberties Union (ACLU) and watching each other's backs. Neglecting this duty is self-evident self-sabotage.

When conservatives balk, some liberals make the mistake of saying, "Well, that's just how our system works." It is a stupid thing to say because it encourages conservatives to subvert our system. But it is also wrong because Thomas Paine was not talking about a unique quirk in our system. This is just how human freedom functions, period. As Reverend Martin Niemöller had famously described the developments he had experienced in Nazi Germany:

When they came for the communists, I wasn't a communist so I didn't do anything. When they came for the trade unions, I wasn't a trade unionist so I didn't do anything. When they came for the Jews, I didn't do anything because I wasn't a Jew. And when they came for me, there wasn't anyone left to do anything.

Different system, but same dynamic. Our founders understood this basic principle and designed our system accordingly. Paine was articulating a basic fact that ACLU-bashing conservatives still cannot grasp: That the unpopular must be protected and that we, the people, are the ultimate guardians of each other's rights. The courts cannot stop tyranny. They can only slow it down and buy time. The courts ultimately require others to enforce their decisions.

For example, in 1832, the Cherokee nation took the State of Georgia to the Supreme Court to prevent their forced removal. They won, but it did not matter. Then President Andrew Jackson had supposedly snorted, "The Supreme Court has spoken. Now let them enforce it." The quote was apocryphal, but the policy was actual. Thus began the tragic "Trail of Tears" which cost about 4,000 Native American lives.

Likewise, it took the Civil Rights Movement's civil disobedience and President Eisenhower's nationalizing the Arkansas National Guard to enforce the Supreme Court's decisions against segregation. Wider involvement is often required.

Of course, I am not arguing that people should not try to defend their rights in court. Rather, I am saying that relying on the courts alone is obviously not enough. There are two other branches of government to consider, along with the regular workaday world in which most things start.

The takeaway is we all have a duty to watch each other's backs. *The Three Musketeers'* motto "All for one and one for all" sums up what must be done. A labor union called the Industrial Workers of the World has a similar motto: "An Injury to One is an Injury to All." The practical application of that principle means aiding the injured and defending the still endangered – hence the necessity of anti-discrimination efforts. The Musketeers' motto shows the balance between the individual and the group – they are mutually supportive rather than mutually exclusive.

And duty has its dividends. Freedom is infectious and you cannot stop its spread without some kind of quarantine or apartheid, which in turn reduces everyone's freedom. These are not just pretty words, but a hard-nosed, nuts-and-bolts explanation of how freedom works.

In the Old South, both white and black behavior was strictly policed. Obviously, black behavior was policed more violently, but there was also a price to pay for being a "nigger lover." Whites watched each other for signs of straying and the penalty could be social, economic, or physical if you did not get the previous hints. Of course, blacks did not get any hints.

Smashing the Klan's power reversed this, leaving *everyone* freer. Thus, the whites who helped blacks ultimately helped themselves as well. Civil rights activist Anne Braden, one of the few whites singled out for praise in Martin

Luther King's historic "Letter from Birmingham Jail," had made this important point repeatedly.

Let's turn from Thomas Paine to James Madison for a moment. In Federalist #10, Madison argued that multiple political factions and interests often cancel each other out, thereby preventing any one of them from becoming too dominant. He then argued that a bigger country would be freer because it would have more groups. Simply put, diversity preserves liberty.

Diversity is a nexus of liberty and equality: It defends liberty but requires equality because if minorities are denied a voice, *de facto* homogeneity results regardless how diverse society really is. This permits a plurality to act as the majority. Reverse this and bullying becomes a lot harder to pull off. This is American history in a nutshell. Today, we are more free and equal than ever before and our current diversity both foments and bolsters this. As James Madison explained in the pamphlet:

The smaller the society, the fewer probably will be the distinct parties and interests composing it; the fewer the distinct parties and interests, the more frequently will a majority be found of the same party; and the smaller the number of individuals composing a majority, and the smaller the compass within which they are placed, the more easily will they concert and execute their plans of oppression. Extend the sphere, and you take in a greater variety of parties and interests; you make it less probable that a majority of the whole will have a common motive to invade the rights of other citizens; or if such a common motive exists, it will be more difficult for all who feel it to discover their own strength, and to act in unison with each other.[150]

Although James Madison was primarily thinking in terms of different groups' or factions' interests, diversity defends individual liberty as well. Taking things from the macro level to the micro level, larger groups tend to be more tolerant because the larger the group, the less homogeneous it is. If a group starts to weed out those who are different, it begins to shrink. Conversely, if it welcomes those who are different, it can grow. Tolerance promotes growth. And while the Republican Party's "big tent" rhetoric sounds insincere, it at least acknowledges this obvious dynamic.

Big cities illustrate this too since attempts to restrict individual liberty generally fail there. Take alcohol, for example. There are dry counties in sparsely populated rural areas but not in densely populated urban ones. And naturally Prohibition did not last nationally because the country is made up of diverse interests.

Likewise, small town gays often move to big cities not simply to improve their dating prospects but because big cities are more tolerant. Straights who seek more sexual freedom often do the same. Granted, the Internet has made isolation more tolerable, but only by linking people to a larger, more diverse – if virtual – environment. This way, people can at least get their porn, if not their Beer of the Month Club deliveries.[151] The latter will have to wait for either Wonka-Vision or a Supreme Court decision finally acknowledging that freedom means freedom, nosey neighbors or no. Of course, conservatives would call this tyranny.

Paine and Madison's methods for defending freedom are complimentary. Different minorities have often won their rights by finding allies among the majority and/or allying with other minorities. The historic coalition between blacks and Jews was immensely successful in combating racism and different religious minorities have frequently joined forces to defend the separation of church and state. These are classic examples of Madison's factions and when justice-minded members of the majority join in, Paine's method comes into play more visibly.

But success is not guaranteed. It is still a matter of getting enough numbers together and minorities can still be played off against one another. But, whichever way the wind blows, the physics remains the same, illustrating liberty and equality's unquestionable interdependence.

Our founders understood this. It was a fundamental assumption of Enlightenment political thought. Without equality, liberty has the life span of a fruit fly. Obviously, the "law of the jungle" eventually leads to the rule of the strong and thus tyranny. As John Trenchard and Thomas Gordon wrote in *Cato's Letters* (1720-1723), "Liberty can never subsist without equality."[152] They said this in the same sentence that they suggested capping wealth. Again, someone should really tell the Cato Institute:

Liberty can never subsist without Equality, nor Equality be long preserved without an Agrarian Law, or something like it; for when Men's Riches become immeasurably or surprisingly great, a People, who regard their own Security, ought to make a strict Enquiry how they came by them, and oblige them to take down their own Size, for fear of terrifying the Community, or mastering it. In every Country, and under every Government, particular Men may be too rich.[153]

Certainly liberty and equality *can* clash. After all, *liberty and liberty* can clash. Everyone's rights must be balanced with everyone else's. But you would not argue that we must give up our freedoms in order to preserve them. So why would you accept a comparable false tradeoff between liberty and equality? Of course, conservatives often do both. They have this "We had to destroy the village in order to save it" mindset, which explains their Cold War Era habit of installing despots to "defend democracy." Later, we were told that we must give up some of our freedoms to win the War on Terror, which we were told was about defending freedom and would last forever. Go figure.

Conservatives are fond of posing false tradeoffs because they are effective rhetorical weapons. Pitting "jobs vs. the environment" is another favorite of theirs. One problem with pitting the economy against the ecology is it has been repeatedly proven that states with stricter environmental regulations have stronger economies and this also holds true on the level of nation states.[154] If you need a nursery rhyme analogy to simplify things, do not kill the goose that lays the golden eggs.

The logic is obvious. And yet, conservatives still think liberty and equality are fundamentally at odds. They think three issues illustrate their case – hate crimes laws, gay rights ordinances, and affirmative action.

The cases for hate crimes legislation and gay rights ordinances are quite simple and can be taken together. Minorities might need more protection if they face greater threats, but their rights remain the same as everyone else's. For example, if bigots are targeting gays for assaults, then we need extra penalties until gays are just as safe as everyone else. But society's extra effort does not make gays super citizens with "special rights." Making no extra effort would be ignoring the problem.

It is like with voting rights. The federal government steps in where local authorities violate them, but everyone still gets only one vote each. That is not playing favorites. It is meeting the problem and defending the endangered. Such efforts are mostly on behalf of blacks, but in the highly unlikely event that some locality was trying to keep whites from voting, the federal government would step in to protect their voting rights as well. But once again, at the end of the day, everyone gets only one vote each.

Likewise, anti-discrimination legislation is not written to privilege a particular group. Such laws are written to protect people from being targeted "on the basis of their race, religion, sex, or sexual orientation." Therefore, if someone wants to bring a "reverse discrimination" suit, they can. Of course, if it is a stupid suit with no basis, they will likely lose.

Affirmative action is a bit more complex because it is not one specific program. The term refers to a variety of different policies adopted by different institutions, businesses, and agencies. There are both "weak" and "strong" forms of affirmative action.

Weak forms are often uncontroversial and enjoy broad public support. One example would be actively recruiting minorities who are under-represented in a field but not considering their minority status in the actual hiring process except in the case of a tie.

One example of a more controversial strong form would be the practice of creating a pool of qualified candidates and then considering other factors when selecting from that pool. This method is considered controversial because the "best" qualified candidate may not prevail, even though every single candidate in the pool is fit for the job.

But what does "best" mean? If it is a test score, a slight one or two point difference is an insignificant predictor of comparative performance and may be within the margin of error – and there may be biases in the test. Moreover, the lower-scoring candidate may have more relevant experience. It is easy to imagine a higher-scoring candidate blaming affirmative action if he does not get the job. For him, those two test points are all that matter.

Of course, college admission boards often have little more than test scores and grades to go by. Aside from extracurricular activities, there is frequently not a lot of real world experience to consider. So some colleges have instituted a point system in which being a member of a minority group adds a few more points to your total. Media coverage has framed this practice almost exclusively in terms of race, but other factors such as veteran or handicapped status also figure in. So called "nontraditional students" – i.e. older folks returning to finish their degrees – also get points. Race and sex are only two factors among many others.

Incidentally, this point system was initiated to avoid setting quotas, which are largely illegal.

Wait. You didn't know that?

The only time quotas are ever legally imposed is in the rare instance that a federal judge finds a particular company rife with discrimination and it is a very difficult ruling to get. But businesses and institutions are not allowed to set their own quota systems, thus most have none.

Of course, that does not stop conservatives from calling all affirmative action programs "quotas."

But whatever method is used, the basic aims of affirmative action remain the same. It is unabashedly about dismantling accumulated privilege and leveling the playing field. And there is no reason to apologize for that. In the next chapter, I show that Thomas Jefferson and Thomas Paine both wrote anti-aristocratic tax proposals that essentially had the same aim, so there is no calling this un-American. Moreover, the difference between rights and privileges has been established.

Of course, privilege is often invisible to those who enjoy it.

For example, many whites think racism is dead and do not acknowledge the accumulated advantages they take for granted. Tim Wise has brilliantly written quite a bit about this. Yet this is not difficult to explain and it actually never has been.

The economic legacy of slavery was recognized during the Civil War when General Tecumseh Sherman promised each freed slave family 40 acres to compensate for centuries of unpaid labor. President Andrew Johnson revoked the order after Abraham Lincoln was assassinated, but this illustrates that the concept is neither modern nor complex. It is just common sense. A *different* President Johnson – Lyndon Baines Johnson – acknowledged this logic when he signed Executive Order 11246 which created the first affirmative action program:

Imagine a hundred yard dash in which one of the two runners has his legs shackled together. He has progressed 10 yards, while the unshackled runner has gone 50 yards. How do they rectify the situation? Do they merely remove the shackles and allow the race to proceed? Then they could say that "equal opportunity" now prevailed. But one of the runners would still be forty yards ahead of the other. Would it not be the better part of justice to allow the previously shackled runner to make-up the forty yard gap; or to start the race all over again? That would be affirmative action towards equality.[155]

This is not ancient history. As Derrick Jackson reported in the *Boston Globe*, the average white baby-Boomer can expect to inherit $65,000. The average black baby-Boomer can expect only $8,000.[156] Yes, some of institutional racism's remaining legacy is made up of intangibles such as psychological effects, but much is not and it can be measured in cold, hard cash, as Derrick Jackson had illustrated.

This is not to say that no progress has been made. The black middle class has rapidly grown since the implementation of affirmative action and the 1964 Civil Rights Act. According to a 2005 briefing before the U.S. Commission on Civil Rights, the black middle class grew only two percentage points per decade until 1960.[157] But During the 1960s, the percentage of employed blacks that were middle class surged from 13.4% to 27.9%. That number swelled another 11 points in the 1970s and had reached 51% by 2002. This foot in the door has helped immensely.

But this is not to suggest that everything is hunky dory today. The data's compiler, Dr. Bart Landry, cautions that the term "middle class" is used very broadly to include almost everyone with a white collar job and, of course, these figures do not include the unemployed.

Dr. Henry Louis Gates Jr. has also pointed out that while the black middle class has expanded, poverty among the black working class and unemployed has intensified creating two, disconnected black Americas. But you cannot claim affirmative action does not work.

Conservatives often give contradictory portraits of anti-discrimination efforts. Either they have failed to change anything or they have become obsolete – victims of their own success.

Obviously, neither of these all-or-nothing assessments square with the facts on the ground. Progress has been made, but racism remains. Barack Obama's election and the Tea Party's conspicuously vicious rallies prove both facts. And then there is Fox and CNN's ugly immigration coverage.

You cannot credibly deny progress *or* say the job is now done. Yet, I have heard both from those who say the NAACP should close up shop. It seems that conservatives curiously disagree on whether or not there is still a problem, and yet somehow they perfectly agree on how to solve it.

Conservatives will say or do almost anything to undermine affirmative action. From preposterous posturing to dumb stunts, they try it all.

In 1996, Bob Dole tried to revitalize his flaccid presidential bid with this issue. This particular political Viagra proved impotent, but the product's future spokesman made a surprising proposal. "The real focus should be on helping citizens who are economically disadvantaged, to provide assistance based on need, not skin color."[158] I doubt he was serious – indeed, the suggestion sounds socialist. Still, others have suggested readjustment and it's not a bad idea.[159] I would not endorse dropping race and sex as factors, but I would approve adding poverty. After all, racism and sexism still exist; but including poverty is only logical.

Later in 2003, College Republicans at various universities decided to protest affirmative action in admissions by holding bake sales. Cookie prices were discounted by the identity of the buyer with white men paying a dollar, white women seventy five cents, Hispanics fifty cents, and blacks paying a quarter. However, veterans, the handicapped, and non-traditional students were not given any price breaks for some reason. I guess the College Republicans felt that would not help their argument.

Veterans were a significant omission considering that the G.I. Bill was arguably the first Federal affirmative action program. Passed just after World War II, the law was not just a gesture of respect from a grateful nation but an attempt to democratize higher education by making it affordable to the working poor. It was an amazing engine of upward mobility and its positive economic ripple effects had lasted a generation. The military's longstanding money-for-college offers are the legacy of that program just as much as they are a recruitment tool.

It turns out that affirmative action is not quite the hot button issue the media would have you believe. It failed to lift Bob Dole's campaign and the College Republicans at Southern Methodist University in Dallas Texas sold only three cookies, raising $1.50.[160] It seems people just were not buying what they were selling.

As a result, conservatives have gotten even *more desperate*.

How much more? Well, Charles Krauthammer, David Horowitz, and Newt Gingrich have actually claimed that Martin Luther King would have opposed affirmative action(!) Whereas in reality, King believed "A society that has done something special against the Negro for hundreds of years must now do something special for the Negro."[161]

Indeed, Dr. King had made the G.I. Bill comparison himself and initiated "Operation Breadbasket" – the first successful national affirmative action campaign for blacks – which he boasted had achieved, "800 new and upgraded jobs [and] several covenants with major industries." Not only did King feel something more must be done, he did it himself.

Martin Luther King's "something special" comment not only debunks one of the right's favorite fantasies; it also illustrates the aforementioned principle – that society must allocate efforts and resources where threats are greatest. If we are negligent in an area, we must redouble our efforts there. Again, anything else is ignoring the problem.

I am not saying we should stop framing the issue as a debt – because it is indeed a debt. I am emphasizing that society has a duty to combat all oppressions, both old and new, because that is what government is *for*.

Moreover, it is not like mistreatment of African American communities has since ceased. Witness the poisoning of Flint, Michigan's water supply or the infamous response to New Orleans after Hurricane Katrina which was initially indifferent and then predatory. America still does special things against African Americans. Because we can.

As an aside, conservatives' three most effective rhetorical weapons are wedge issues, false trade-offs, and historical fictions. Like Jerry Falwell's and Pat Robertson's 9-11 comments, this should and should not shock us. After all, these are the folks who not only say our founding fathers were devout Christians, but that Franklin Delano Roosevelt would have approved privatizing Social Security.[162] Ronald Reagan was fond of saying that FDR would agree that welfare efforts had gone too far. This is consistent with Robert Bork's notion that liberals from one era would not recognize liberals from the next, but it is not actually consistent with history. Among the New Dealers' many aims was not only a Social Security system but a national health care system. Fifty years before Bill and Hillary attempted it, Harry Truman made a push for universal coverage. Indeed, President Barack Obama had argued that this effort went back to *Theodore* Roosevelt, so we have hardly gone "too far" since the New Deal. "Obamacare" is a welcome stop-gap, but a true national healthcare program is still needed.

Ideas are often a lot older than you think. Not only did Dr. King advocate affirmative action, so did Dr. Franklin. Dr. *Benjamin* Franklin helped found the first anti-slavery society in North America and argued that slavery left psychological, educational, and economic scars that could not be ignored and that society had a duty to put things right:

The unhappy man, who has long been treated as a brute animal, too frequently sinks beneath the common standard of the human species. The galling chains, that bind his body, do also fetter his intellectual faculties, and impair the social affections of his heart. Accustomed to move like a mere machine, by the will of a master, reflection is suspended; he has not the power of choice; and reason and conscience have but little influence over his conduct, because he is chiefly governed by the passion of fear. He is poor and friendless; perhaps worn out by extreme labour, age, and disease.[163]

Here, Benjamin Franklin is answering those who would unfairly judge blacks by the harmful effects of slavery. But he is also answering those who paternalistically imagine slavery is benign and family-like.

But Franklin believed that this degradation was only temporary and the product of the slave's environment. He believed that it could be remedied. Accordingly, he announced that one of his organization's aims was:

To instruct, to advise, to qualify those, who have been restored to freedom, for the exercise and enjoyment of civil liberty, to promote in them habits of industry, to furnish them with employments suited to their age, sex, talents and other circumstances, and to procure their children an education calculated for their situation in life; these are the great outlines of the annexed plan, which we have adopted, and which we conceive will essentially promote the public good, and the happiness of these our hitherto too much neglected fellow creatures.

While it is easy to be cynical about "education calculated for their situation in life," such organizations often provided promising freedmen with college educations and professional training. Benefits went beyond feeling good. Trumpeting success stories not only proved their anti-racist arguments, it also attracted more donors and volunteers to their cause. That is where the logic of abolitionist societies often took them.

But beyond benevolence and strategic practicalities, there remained still one more important motive to consider: Duty. Benjamin Franklin felt, "Attention to emancipated black people, it is to be hoped, will become a branch of our national policy," and "that attention is evidently a serious duty incumbent on us."

Again, the notion that you must compensate those you have wronged is not a modern one. Nor is the concept of collective responsibility anything new. Benjamin Franklin believed that white society had an obligation to blacks that went beyond only freeing them. How long must we wait for modern day conservatives to catch up with him?

Conservatives can quibble over what form compensation should take. Their awkward arguments against reparations are revealing, but I will cover that in my next book.

My point here is that nothing about the act or concept of compensation proves that liberty and equality are at odds. Conservatives can claim that the compensation in question is excessive or poorly designed and we can argue over that. (And they will lose.) But it does not logically follow that liberty and equality are locked in a zero-sum game as a result.

Conservatives do not much care for equality. And, being Americans, they reflexively express their displeasure in the language of rights. But liberty, equality, and democracy are inherently interdependent, as our history repeatedly reminds us. Benjamin Franklin's affirmative action plan was the logical product of his anti-slavery work, just as his anti-slavery work was the logical product of his fighting for freedom. He obviously did not think the best way to defend freedom was to horde it away from others.

This interdependence ripples through every aspect of America's identity. As I wrote in the introduction, it is cultural as well as procedural. It is manifest in our manners and our music, as well as our attitudes toward sex, gender, and youth – which conservatives continuously gripe about too.

Rock and roll is a perfect example. It embodies personal rebellion and thus individual liberty. But it is also the voice of two historically heavily-policed groups, African Americans and youth.

Let us cut to the chase: Blacks invented rock. Elvis's "You Ain't Nothing but a Hound Dog" ain't nothing but a white boy performing a blues song a little faster. Slow the song down and this becomes obvious to everyone.

In fact, it was a black woman, Willie Mae "Big Mama" Thornton, who first performed "Hound Dog" at its more familiar, faster speed.

Likewise, "Pelvis" Presley merely legitimized "colored" dancing with white kids who previously did not gyrate their hips in school gyms. Elvis made black culture more palatable for Caucasian audiences.

Yet despite this whitening, conservatives still went ballistic. It was as if their kids started wearing baggy pants and backwards baseball caps. Yes, jazz, rock, and hip-hop have all faced the same hostility for the same reasons. In every case, the right insisted "jungle rhythms" threatened the existence of civilization itself!

Even when such assaults were not explicitly racist, they remained ridiculously alarmist. In 1922, an author in the *Atlantic Monthly* said jazz was, "an unloosing of instincts that nature wisely has taught us to hold well in check."[164] How instinct could conflict with nature was not explained.

But conservative hostility toward rock was not just racism – they also hated it for other reasons. Moralists were horrified because it expressed sexuality and rebellion. Early rock was true to its jazz and blues roots and hid sex in innuendo and slang – or did not hide it at all. Songs such as Little Richard's "Good Golly, Miss Molly" sent white parents into shock once they figured out what "sure likes to ball" meant. Likewise, Big Mama Thornton's original version of "Hound Dog" was actually about kicking a gigolo out of her house. Although the original song was metaphorical to begin with, the Elvis version was cleaned up even more.

Of course, sanitizing rock's lyrics did not work. Teenagers could not contain their glee and parents, of course, assumed the worst.

In fact, the phrase "rock and roll" itself was Southern black slang for having sex, as was "jazz." So, of course, young disk jockeys enjoyed saying it on the air as much as possible. Mind you, old rock could also be pretty overt. Elvis Presley's "A Little Less Conversation" was an unambiguous sexual come-on even before the JXL remix.

Hiding this history has had some amusing side effects. In *Slouching Towards Gomorrah*, Robert Bork compared jazz to rock and rap to illustrate the latter two's supposed depravity. Suffice to say, he probably did not listen to the same jazz records as I do. I presume, for example, that he had not heard Mae West moaning "A Guy What Takes His Time" or Dinah Washington crooning "Long John."

Of course, the music was not always light-hearted; it could also be grim. Like rappers, bluesmen had their violently misogynistic songs as well. Murder often followed infidelity in songs such as "She's Making Whoopee in Hell Tonight," (1930). Admittedly, this was not quite family-friendly fare, but the situation depicted is no less edifying in European stage (Othello) or opera (Tosca). Yet, nobody is calling to censor those.

And then there was also violent misogyny in white folk and country music. The murder ballad is practically a genre in itself. Take such songs as the "Banks of the Ohio," a traditional song, first recorded by Bill and Charlie Monroe back in 1936. In it, the singer murders his sweetheart for refusing his marriage proposal. It was later covered by Johnny Cash and the Carter Family. Indeed, Cash had recorded more than a few murder songs, such as "Cocaine Blues" and "Delia's Gone."[165]

These songs were all part and parcel of the development of country, blues, and jazz. Obviously, without the gritty originals their sanitized offspring could never have existed. And many of the sexual elements survived the bleach and iodine.

Professor Bork was probably unfamiliar with the music I mentioned, but he did claim to enjoy Cole Porter, which I find incredibly interesting. Porter wrote "Anything Goes" in a tone of mock shock but I doubt Robert Bork knew that. Porter also wrote another song called "Let's Misbehave" which clarifies things considerably. If you are looking for clues to original intent, here you are:

We're all alone.
No chaperone
Can get our number.
The world's in slumber.
Let's misbehave!

Bork's whole point was that immoral music encourages immoral behavior, so what are we to make of this little ditty? Here is pressure to put-out four decades before the pill sparked the Sexual Revolution of the 1960s!

In the same song, Porter wrote, "If you'd be just so sweet and only meet your fate, dear/it would be the great event of nineteen twenty-eight, dear."

I think Robert Bork listened to old records the same way he read old documents – with an inventive Puritanical imagination.

Also, had Robert Bork never heard a recording of Cole Porter performing his own songs? I am straight and there is a lot that I do not notice, but Porter's voice should be a pretty big blip on anyone's gaydar.

Robert Bork seemed adamantly unaware that jazz was created in the Jazz Age, which was not known for its law and order or adherence to convention. On the contrary, the "Roaring Twenties" coined the very notion of modernity. Everything about it was a rebellion from tradition.

For one thing, a sexual revolution was in full swing. In one Art Young cartoon of the period, a languid flapper asks her horrified mother, "Mama, didn't you find it an awful bore to be a virgin?"[166]

Youth abandoned Victorian notions of propriety while women "bobbed" their hair short, dressed like men, and entered occupations formerly barred to them. Women had just gotten the vote and middle class ones had gotten used to working outside the home thanks to World War I. Of course, working class women had always worked, but "respectable" women joining their ranks had lessened the stigma associated with it.

In short, the 1920s were a lot like the 1960s in many ways. In both decades, conservative coelacanths complained that, "You cannot tell the boys from the girls." Yet, conservatives today continue to lay claim to the twenties. In his book, Bork wrote, "Rock and rap are utterly impoverished by comparison with swing or jazz or any pre-World War II music, impoverished emotionally, aesthetically, and intellectually." Or, as Reagan Administration cabinet member James Watt had said of the Beach Boys, "That kind of music always attracted the wrong element."

I know what you are thinking. "Wait a minute. That hardly seems fair. What about Republican rockers?"

Well, what *about* them? What about gay Republicans, for that matter? You would not argue their existence means their party's policies are not homophobic, would you? Indeed, the right's hatreds are linked since sexual liberty is central to both rock and roll and gay rights, so there is no weaseling out there. Social conservatives define the right's stance on social policies and if economic conservatives let them then their Faustian bargain only reveals how little they love liberty.

Certainly *some* conservatives have gone from stodgy to savvy. Today, the right's hysteria in the heyday of Rock seems like ancient history. Republicans have long since welcomed such hard rockers as Ted Nugent and Dee Snyder of "Twisted Sister" (who performed his signature "We're not Going to Take It" at Arnold Schwarzenegger rallies). Likewise, Rush Limbaugh uses hard rock riffs to punctuate his show – although the Pretenders are not pleased about his leasing their music.

But this does not mean conservatives have become any more hip, tolerant or open-minded than in days of yore. Conservative accommodation is actually just acknowledgement that Rock and Roll is old and long co-opted.

After all, it has *over a half century* under its belt and the country itself is only a little over two centuries old. Think about that. The Rolling Stones are now fossils and former counterculture anthems now promote brokerage firms. Rock and roll was tamed and bleached so long ago that the culture warriors have moved on to blaming society's problems on audibly blacker forms of music such as hip hop.

Or have they?

They have for the most part. But over four decades after the fact, countless conservatives *still* claim the "culture of the '60s" is corrupting the republic. They do this every election year and every year in between. The sinister Sixties form the springboard for Robert Bork's book *Slouching Towards Gomorrah*. And later, Pat Buchanan blamed *The Death of the West* on that decade's legacy and immigration.

Blasting the Sixties is practically mandatory for all conservative thought and commentary. Prior to 9-11, it was almost impossible to find a conservative book that did not take aim at that decade and their assaults have not yet stopped – although hopefully soon.

And just what is this malignant sixties ethos that the right regularly inveighs against? The answer is, predictably, the advancement of liberty, equality, and the diverse and constantly morphing culture they create. But there is one other thing that also ties into all the others: Youth. Conservatives hate kids and always have.

Yes, you read correctly. Conservatives hate kids. After all, these are the folks who call teenagers "super-predators" and push for draconian sentencing. This is the constituency that likes to try kids as adults and whose politicians propose executing 11-year olds.[167] Their enthusiasm for youth curfews and school uniforms is ... well, to avoid triggering Godwin's Law, let's just say it is extremely creepy.

Needless to say, this hatred is also un-American in a variety of ways. Leaving the liberty issue aside for just a moment, American culture is youth culture and this even applies to "oldies." Whether we are talking about Scott Joplin or Janis Joplin, today's "classics" were yesteryear's youth music. American youth culture is our most popular export and a major part of our national identity. Again, we have African Americans to thank for that.

Moreover, there is America's identity as a young nation, which goes back to day one. The metaphor of America's adolescent rebellion from the "mother country" is well established. In fact, the revolutionaries utilized it themselves.

But back then, America's youthfulness was not just a symbol but a demographic reality as well. Immigration and short life expectancy kept the median age so low that many who fought in the American Revolution were teenagers and some hardly more than boys – and many famous officers were only in their twenties in 1776.[168]

To be precise, the median age of the population as a whole was *sixteen*.[169] This was significant since many boys were indentured servants or apprentices who fell under extensive social control in the Colonial Era. While traveling to Philadelphia as a teen, Benjamin Franklin recalled, "I found by the Questions ask'd [*sic.*] me I was suspected to be some runaway Servant, and in danger of being taken up on that Suspicion."[170] Revolutionary rhetoric spelled the end of these two systems just as much as economic changes did.

For example, Ebenezer Fox was *only twelve years old* when he and a friend ran away to shoulder muskets against the British. As he recalled in his memoir, he and his peers had no trouble connecting the actual and the metaphorical:

Almost all the conversation that came to my ears related to the injustice of England and the tyranny of government. It is perfectly natural that the spirit of insubordination that prevailed should spread among the younger members of the community; that they, who were continually hearing complaints, should themselves become complainants. I, and other boys situated similarly to myself, thought we had wrongs to be redressed; rights to be maintained. ... We made direct application of the doctrines we daily heard, in relation to the oppression of the mother country, to our own circumstances; and thought that we were more oppressed than our fathers were. I thought that I was doing myself great injustice by remaining in bondage, when I ought to go free; and that the time was come, when I should liberate myself from the thralldom of others, and set up a government of my own.[171]

America's adolescent rebellion from the mother country was not just some political metaphor cobbled together for propaganda purposes. It was also part of a widely held Enlightenment concept of how nations age – they age very badly. Doing a little amateur anthropology, the political philosophers of the day took a long, hard look at their world. They compared Native American nations with European monarchies and concluded that civilizations degenerate as they age. Societies stratify as they calcify. They become money-grubbing, authoritarian, and corrupt. In short, they sell out. Hence, America was hailed as an opportunity to start over again.

This notion could be more sobering than stirring. Although the new nation was a chance to start off with a clean slate, it was still understood that the slate would not *stay* clean. Things would eventually deteriorate here as well. The founding fathers had frequently expressed their fears in letters to each other and the fragility of liberty was a near constant theme.

This essentially pessimistic assessment is fundamentally at odds with the gospel of progress we are often taught, but Thomas Jefferson tweaked it into a more optimistic form. Jefferson repeatedly stressed that each new generation could hit the restart button. Accordingly, Jefferson suggested a nineteen-year expiration time on all laws and public debts to keep the dead hand of the past at bay and allow national renewal. Indeed, for Jefferson, political legitimacy hinged on this time limit. "Every constitution then, and every law, naturally expires at the end of 19 years. If it be enforced longer, it is an act of force, and not of right."[172] He believed that this and other measures, such as outlawing primogeniture to break up big estates, could prevent another aristocracy from taking root and preserve a simple, Arcadian republic of yeoman farmers.

Thomas Jefferson thought this was doable, but others felt more dubious. This can be seen in a skeptical letter penned to Jefferson by John Adams, July 16th of 1814:

Nothing can be conceived more destructive to human happiness; more infallibly contrived to transform men and women into brutes, Yahoos, or demons, than a community of wives and property. Yet in what are the writings of Rousseau and Helvetius, wiser than those of Plato? The man who first fenced a tobacco yard, and said this is mine, ought to be put to death, says Rousseau. The man who first pronounced the barbarous word [God], ought to have been immediately destroyed says Diderot. In short, philosophers, ancient and modern, appear to me as mad as Hindoos, Mahometans, and Christians. No doubt they would all think me mad, and, for anything I know, this globe may be the Bedlam, Le Bicatre of the universe. After all, as long as property exists, knowledge, property and influence will accumulate in families. Your and our equal partition of intestate estates, instead of preventing, will, in time, augment the evil, if it is one.

The French revolutionists saw this, and were so far consistent. When they burned pedigrees and genealogical trees, they annihilated, as far as they could, marriages, knowing that marriage, among a thousand other things, was an infallible source of aristocracy. I repeat it, so sure as the idea and existence of property is admitted and established in society, accumulation will be made; the snow-ball will grow as it rolls.[173]

John Adams is a hoot. I never thought I would see a conservative denigrate marriage, religion, and property all in one paragraph. I guess conservatives of different eras would hardly recognize each other as deserving the same label. And then there is that recurrent *human happiness* thing – and again in conflict with property. But, I digress.

This theory of deterioration appears to have been debunked by what has actually come to pass. After all, slavery is in the grave and women's rights have hugely improved.

But it is not entirely debunked. The institution of slavery was dying during the Revolutionary Era because it was then tied to tobacco, which was becoming unprofitable. Supply had overtaken demand because Southerners planted tobacco on almost every inch of land they cleared. Revolutionary rhetoric was frequently anti-slavery – not simply figuratively, but literally. And in that atmosphere, many slaveholders began to free their own slaves and even consider outlawing slavery altogether.

Then, Eli Whitney invented the cotton gin and all bets were off. Slavery not only got a new lease on life, but became more powerful than before. Plantation owners cultivated both cotton and aristocratic airs. Thus, only two generations later, Abraham Lincoln looked back and mused, "Our progress in degeneracy appears to me to be pretty rapid." The national mood had changed as a whole. Historian Larry L. Tise called this backlash *The American Counterrevolution* in a book by that title. Women's rights, which had also been rapidly advancing during the Revolutionary Era, also suffered a staggering setback. (I cover this more in my next book.) In New Jersey, propertied women had enjoyed the vote for three decades, until 1807 when women, blacks, boys, and other "irregulars" were barred from voting. Religiosity was rising and revolutionary ideals were forgotten in a mad scramble for land and wealth, just as Thomas Jefferson had warned. In short, the selling out had already begun.

At this point, let me reiterate that I do not think there is any directional tendency in history. There is no dragging weight or elevating gas. I do not subscribe to the Christian or Marxist notions that invisible historical forces guarantee that the meek shall eventually inherit the earth. Nor do I see the regular cycles that *Generations* authors William Strauss and Neil Howe suggest. The rapidly accelerating rate of change would seem to rule out an even rhythm and their whole theory sounds like some historical horoscope.

No, there is no overall pattern or direction. There is only the struggle between left and right and the only real tendency that exists is that when one side slackens, the other side advances. *There* is where we actually have a zero-sum game operating. Otherwise, the only certainty is uncertainty. In fact, the fortunes of this conflict often reverse in different theaters, thus the absurdity of Donald Rumsfeld alluding to "Old Europe" when Europe is now far more progressive than America. I am certainly not making a case for American Exceptionalism here.

And yet, adolescent rebellion *is* central to the American identity. The two themes of youth and revolt are essential ingredients. Even Robert Bork unhappily admitted that the tumult of the Sixties was "in the American grain." In fact, Thomas Jefferson thought such tumults were necessary corrective mechanisms. Although Shay's Rebellion was not a youth movement *per se*, it *was* a ruckus and Jefferson voiced his approval. As he wrote to James Madison, "I hold it, that a little rebellion, now and then, is a good thing, and as necessary in the political world as storms in the physical."[174] To Colonel Smith he wrote, "God forbid we should ever be twenty years without such a rebellion."[175]

Combine this with his nineteen-year time limit on all laws and debts and a clear picture emerges. For Jefferson, the function of youth and revolt was to keep us honest. Recurrent renewal was a recurrent theme. Ironically, progress requires hitting the reset button.

But here again, "Old Europe" has long stolen our thunder. For example, France enjoys a host of cradle-to-grave social services thanks to their frequent strikes and protests. The spectacle of French farmers hurling their sheep at riot police or French truckers parking their rigs across intersections is just the kind of spirited insubordination Jefferson would have loudly applauded.

And although the participants in these street actions were often middle-aged working Joes, they were supported by a worldwide anti-corporate globalization movement that was, as most movements are, dominated by young people. America holds no monopoly on youth movements, but our national history makes knee-jerk contempt for them grotesquely un-American and it is obvious what most conservatives think.[176]

But youth also performs another important function. Like all other vulnerable populations, the young are yet another canary in the societal coalmine. Whether it is law enforcement or budget cuts, the treatment of youth is another crude but useful indicator of any poison in the air. Like when conservatives decide they want to lock everyone up starting with their own kids.

Jailing youth became the rage in the 1980s and Generation X became the most incarcerated generation in American history. But it is not because we were especially ill-behaved. As Mike Males related in his 1999 book, *Framing Youth: 10 Myths about the Next Generation,* it is frequently the reverse:

"*Often,*" wrote a veteran California Appeals Court judge of the avalanche of youths shoveled into institutional management, the child "*was a minor nuisance some inadequate parent was trying to fob off on the court ... He usually just did not get along with his parents and, when one met the parents, this was often completely understandable.*" The director of Montana's state juvenile prison had a remedy: "*In most cases, we should leave the kid home and send the parents to Pine Hills.*"[177]

Incarceration-mania swept the nation and the private sector was quick to cash-in. I recall the Reagan phase of the War on Drugs quite vividly. One particularly salient memory was mental hospitals brazenly advertising themselves as places to lock up inconvenient teenagers. "Is your child on drugs?" their ads ominously intoned. "Look for these warning signs." The subsequent list of symptoms described a typical teenager in any day and age: "Talks back," "Wears weird clothes," "Changes friends," "Listens to strange music," etc. For those who could afford it, offspring incarceration was just a phone call away. I have friends who had gotten the business end of this business.

This industry was obscenely profitable. As Mike Males relayed, "The *annual* growth rate in private youth correctional facilities 'has been a staggering 45 percent over the last decade,' *Youth Today* reported in May 1998."(emphasis original)[178] Supply met demand with dizzying speed, and that demand was apparently immense. This reactionary, anti-teen zeitgeist was unmistakable. When an American teenager was caned in Singapore, many suggested adopting that practice stateside. It was as if the Baby Boomers had seen Stanley Kubrick's *A Clockwork Orange* but forgotten that it was actually about *them*.

Do not let them watch *Battle Royale*.

This authoritarian mood bloomed in the Eighties and worsened throughout the Nineties. Although youth homicides were down and falling (they were at their lowest point since 1966),[179] the media portrayed a pandemic of Uzi-toting "killer kids" to justify all that prison-building. Justice Policy Institute Director Vincent Schiraldi had noted that while America's homicide rate dropped 20% between 1992 and 1996, national news coverage of murders skyrocketed an astounding 721% and focused on adolescents. As a result, most Americans thought that juveniles committed *half* of all slayings when it was actually *only* 10%.[180]

Yet while juvenile violence had fallen, middle-aged violence had actually *tripled*. As Michael Males wrote, "In 1980, the FBI reported 450,000 Americans ages 30-49 arrested for serious violent, property, or drug crimes. In 1996, 1.5 million."[181]

It is pretty difficult to exaggerate how crazy things have gotten. We now live in a nation in which a six year-old little girl gets arrested for throwing a temper tantrum. The kindergartener was actually booked for felony assault *just because she flailed her arms around*.[182] When confronted by a reporter, Avon, Florida's police chief Frank Mercurio retorted, "Do you think this is the first 6-year-old we've arrested?"

This was not a rare exception – it is a trend. Indeed, the month before in Baltimore, a seven year-old boy was arrested for *allegedly riding his dirt bike on the sidewalk*. For doing such things little kids are handcuffed and hauled off to jail?

Of course, the fact that both kids were black explains a great deal. Ageist policies are often racist ones in disguise, which is why talk of "youth at risk" is usually very heavily-perfumed racial profiling. This helps explain the media's imaginary crime wave.

Racism is definitely an immense element, but code words do not mean that there is no ageism at work. Age and race are now merging factors as America's population becomes browner with each generation. As Mike Males had noted, "In most of America's big cities, white elders govern nonwhite kids. In California, two thirds of the elders are Euro-white; three-fifths of the youths are nonwhite or Latino. As California and the cities are, so America is becoming."[183] Race and age are distinct, but linked.

Like race, youth has always been a flash point for conservative anxieties. The young asserting themselves and building their own culture is an inherent threat to authority and tradition.

But, once again, it is not just freedom that conservatives hate. Their animus is against everything American – equality, democracy, diversity, and the dynamic, ever-changing culture they create. All these things are interdependent and their ripple effects touch every facet of American life. This explains conservatives' rabid reaction to jazz, rock, and hip hop. All these fundamentally American musical forms have touched their hot buttons of race, sex, youth, and rebellion. It is almost impossible to touch one hot button and not any of the others in the process because they are so close together. For example, take Rush Limbaugh's eye-opening 2005 response to Al Gore's proposed TV channel:

When does he start up this stupid little network? August? Yip yip yip yahoo. You know what Gore said about this? "It's going to be liberal. It's going to reflect the point of view of young people." What the hell is that, Al? What the hell is the point of view of young people? Blow jobs, that's what they're doing out there. They're out there getting oral sex all day long, that's what they're talking about. That's the point of view they can't wait that your boss, Al, made sure that's become the number one sport in high school today. So, I guess you're going to have a BJ network out there, Al, is that what you're going to do? You're going to call your network the oral sex channel out there, start competing with MTV? No, it's not going to have any of this stuff out there, folks, it's going to be talking about liberalism, no, no, no, that's not what we're about. Classic. [He] cannot even admit who he is.[184]

That did not go where you expected, did it? Fellatio and Al Gore are certainly not two things that I reflexively associate together. It almost makes you wonder whether Al Gore was an issue in Rush Limbaugh's last three divorces.

But other associations seem clear enough. Just mentioning youth set Rush Limbaugh off. Liberalism and protest are both associated with youth (as both Gore and Limbaugh apparently agree) and associated with America. To say that adolescent rebellion is "in the American grain," as Robert Bork had bitterly admitted, is an understatement. American culture is youth culture and *vice versa*. Both are born of rebellion and intermixing, i.e. liberty and equality. They come from crossing traditional lines, including the Color Line. America is an ongoing amalgamation, fueled by immigration and insubordination. It is therefore inherently alarming to traditionalists and that dynamic will never vanish.

That is why conservatism's hatred of America is both cultural and procedural. Like liberty and equality, policy and culture are two sides of the same coin. In the introduction, I mentioned that the Statue of Liberty shows how policy and culture interplay. The only difference is that conservatives do not pit policy against culture in a zero-sum game. On the contrary, they recognize the connection, which is why they attempt to legislate their morality. That is why the Culture War is a political one rather than a personal matter of "Your music sucks." Conservatives want to stop abortion, restore forced prayer in school, and prevent gay marriage. And Robert Bork was writing in favor of government censorship.

The Jim Crow era's phony "separate but equal" policy also shows this dynamic. The Old South's social dividers were not just meant to humiliate blacks, but to discourage and complicate the kind of interracial friendships and solidarity that would logically threaten the system. Cultural dividers were just as important as separate water fountains. Whether most people were conscious of it or not, rock and roll and the Civil Rights Movement were natural allies – they were both part of the same change. This explains conservatives' panicked, apocalyptic response to rock. They reacted exactly as Rush Limbaugh had above.

Conservatives are not just mad about getting old – although, like xenophobia, that adds more fuel to the fire. *Everything* about our dynamic, free society reminds them that they do not belong. And conformists crave belonging above all else. For them, liberty and equality form a perfect storm of alienation that is always gaining strength. Immigration is an obvious flashpoint for their anxiety. Youth is another. But so is everything else.

Liberty, equality, and democracy are interdependent. I used our culture as a metaphor for this interplay because it is the *product* of this interplay. It is a dramatic example of it. Every country's culture is a collective expression of who they are. Ours is democratic in the broadest sense of the word. It is not just egalitarian, but diverse and participatory – consciously so.

But to conservatives, any truly democratic society is, like jazz, "an unloosing of instincts that nature wisely has taught us to hold well in check." Therefore, conservatism is the perpetual (but frequently unsuccessful) suppression of America's best instincts and our identity as well.

As Franklin D. Roosevelt explained, "We must scrupulously guard the civil rights and civil liberties of all our citizens, whatever their background. We must remember that any oppression, any injustice, any hatred, is a wedge designed to attack our civilization."[185] And conservatism's zero-sum scam is almost always part of such ugly, un-American assaults.

4: Why the Right is Wrong on Property
Economic Equality is Immensely American

The American Revolution almost collapsed on many occasions.

Over eight uncertain years of hardships, the Continental Army was frequently on the verge of disintegrating. The revolutionaries needed reminding what they were fighting for and, lacking Frank Capra's *Why We Fight* to steel them against their privations, Thomas Paine penned several pamphlets collectively entitled *The American Crisis*. The first was written on a drum skin while retreating with Washington's army. In them, Paine plainly articulated the logic behind the colonists' revolution and so sustained the newborn nation.

Conservatives have always hated him.

Why? Two reasons:

First, Thomas Paine was a Deist. A Deist is someone who believes in God but not the Bible. Indeed, Deists reject organized religion as a whole. Although most of the founding fathers were Deists, Paine castigated the Bible with such ringing clarity that few conservatives attempt to call him one of their own. (Glenn Beck and Richard Barton are hilarious outliers.) Of course, Thomas Jefferson and many other founders attacked the Bible as well, but most conservatives forget or ignore that inconvenient fact and treat Thomas Paine as the sole exception.

Second, Thomas Paine invented the modern world's first Social Security plan in a pamphlet entitled *Agrarian Justice*. It seems that the seed of "creeping socialism" was in our soil from the very start. In fact, it was actually a native plant that we introduced to Europe, much like the potato or the tomato. As John Adams once groused, "Too many Frenchmen, after the example of too many Americans, pant for equality of persons and property. The impracticality of this, God Almighty has decreed, and the advocates of liberty, who attempt it, will surely suffer for it."[186] Notice the association between liberty and equality. Apparently, spreading the wealth is what "the advocates of liberty" do.

It turns out that the two reasons are actually interrelated. Today, many conservatives misconstrue the concept of natural law to shoehorn the Bible into the Constitution. And to be fair, it is an easy mistake to make. Eighteenth Century thinkers were indeed trying to distinguish "man's law" from "God's law." But since many of them were Deists, they did not use the Bible as a guide to God's will. Instead, they looked to Native American societies to see how people lived in a free and natural state. And the nearby First Nations had an altogether different concept of property. Instead of individual ownership, they focused on use rights. They shared fields and steams like Europeans shared city streets. And their society stressed an obligation to help others in times of need. This worldview was the inspiration for Thomas Paine's pamphlet.

If this all sounds like Karl Marx, there is a reason for that. The American and French revolutionaries influenced later radical thought. They had a critical analysis of where aristocracy came from – filthy rich families. On this continent, the founders saw that dynastic dynamic manifest in the South's planters and the North's bankers.

Today, the idea that America's purpose is to facilitate the acquisition of riches is widely accepted – even by its critics. That assumption is bunk. And what men like Benjamin Franklin, Thomas Jefferson, and Thomas Paine said on the topic paints a vividly different picture.

First, these three patriots believed that the earth belonged to all people in common. Therefore, nobody really owns any portion of land. But they also thought that land redistribution would be logistically difficult. So, to compensate the landless for the loss of their natural inheritance, those founders suggested redistributive taxation instead.

As for owning other things, Franklin, Jefferson, and Paine reasoned that everyone has a natural right to enough property to secure their survival and independence. Anything above and beyond that ultimately comes from society because society is what magnifies wealth beyond our puny individual efforts. Without society, we are limited to only those crude tools that we can make with our hands. Society provides us with prior innovations to build on, sturdy infrastructure, and *other people's hands*.

In other words, long before President Barack Obama, they declared "You didn't build that" and explained exactly why.

Finally, these three men felt that concentrations of wealth threatened the common good and that government therefore has the obvious right to break them up in order to prevent creeping aristocracy. As they saw it, free society depends on everyone being vigilantly egalitarian.

I know this must be awfully hard to swallow. After all, we are not encouraged to think of our founders as secular intellectuals dabbling in social engineering. And we are sure not supposed to see the revolutionaries as *revolutionaries*. But they were.

Of course, I am not arguing that the founders all agreed. There were reactionaries as well as radicals.

For example, Alexander Hamilton and John Jay felt wealth should run the country and they had no problem saying so. In fact, if Thomas Jefferson's account is accurate, Hamilton had actually advocated corruption as a desirable mechanism toward that end. He was an admirer of the British Parliament in which votes and government posts were then openly bought and sold. It kept the rich in control because only they could afford to buy legislation. Hamilton said, "Purge that constitution of its corruption, and give to its popular branch equality of representation, and it would become an *impractical* government: as it stands at present, with all its supposed defects, it is the most perfect government that ever existed." This prompted Thomas Jefferson to claim, "Hamilton was not only a monarchist, but for a monarchy bottomed on corruption."[187] If Hamilton were alive today, he would no doubt join the GOP in opposing campaign finance reform.

Some founders took more nuanced and balanced approaches toward property. Both John Adams and James Madison strongly affirmed property rights, but they agreed with Jefferson that concentrated wealth threatened a free society. There was a spectrum of opinion on the issue and, of course, individual founders moved back and forth along it over time. Thus, you can often find conflicting quotes from the same founder.

Consider this lengthy John Adams passage in which he expounds on the divinely-ordained impracticality of economic equality. Although it is not pithy enough to fit on a bumper sticker, it is a fair encapsulation of current conservative thought on property. In fact, it is an argument that conservatives keep trying to shoehorn into the mouths of other founders, like Benjamin Franklin,[188] but it is pure John Adams:

Suppose a nation, rich and poor, high and low, ten millions in number, all assembled together; not more than one or two millions will have lands, houses, or any personal property; if we take into the account the women and children, or even if we leave them out of the question, a great majority of every nation is wholly destitute of property, except a small quantity of clothes, and a few trifles of other movables. Would Mr. Nedham be responsible that, if all were to be decided by a vote of the majority, the eight or nine millions who have no property, would not think of usurping over the rights of the one or two millions who have? Property is surely a right of mankind as really as liberty.

Perhaps, at first, prejudice, habit, shame or fear, principle or religion, would restrain the poor from attacking the rich, and the idle from usurping on the industrious; but the time would not be long before courage and enterprise would come, and pretexts be invented by degrees, to countenance the majority in dividing all the property among them, or at least, in sharing it equally with its present possessors. Debts would be abolished first; taxes laid heavy on the rich, and not at all on the others; and at last a downright equal division of everything be demanded, and voted. What would be the consequence of this?

The idle, the vicious, the intemperate, would rush into the utmost extravagance of debauchery, sell and spend all their share, and then demand a new division of those who purchased from them. The moment the idea is admitted into society, that property is not as sacred as the laws of God, and that there is not a force of law and public justice to protect it, anarchy and tyranny commence. If "Thou shalt not covet," and "Thou shalt not steal," were not commandments of Heaven, they must be made inviolable precepts in every society, before it can be civilized or made free.[189]

So, the question is settled, correct? We can now forget about this, right?

Well, not quite. The quote has its problems.

For one thing, it certainly is not a picture of the middle class American dream. In the land that John Adams describes, only twenty percent of the population owns their homes. The remaining eighty percent either rents or are live-in servants (or slaves). Adams assumes permanent scarcity. Recall his description – "a great majority of every nation is wholly destitute of property, except a small quantity of clothes, and a few trifles of other movables." Is that the America you want to live in? If that is Adams' idea of capitalism, then it clearly does not work.

But as we shall see shortly, Benjamin Franklin, Thomas Jefferson, and Thomas Paine had a more optimistic outlook and they advocated using government to create greater prosperity. And they were ultimately correct. The G.I. Bill and the Federal Housing Authority helped rapidly expand the middle class after World War II, creating the strongest economy we ever enjoyed. History has debunked Adams' assumptions. If wealth redistribution encouraged laziness, the middle class would not have expanded at all – certainly not so dramatically.

Poor people will often blow a one-time windfall like found money. But when those in need get a steady benefit, they think differently – they budget and start to plan for the future. Their worldview and habits change because their circumstances do. Opportunity does that. That is in part why direct cash assistance without strings attached is the most effective anti-poverty program and a powerful argument for the Universal Basic Income.[190]

John Adams thought wealth redistribution would create a cycle of waste; but what it actually does is break the cycle of hopelessness. Again, if Adams' assumptions were accurate, postwar America would not have become so powerful and prosperous.

But such programs had many antecedents. The Homestead Act of 1862 is the most famous example, but it was preceded by many other such programs. Government giveaways began on day one – indeed, well before American independence. They just took the form of land grants instead of financing.

And the awkwardness does not stop there. This was also the same John Adams who later said that matrimony and property turn people in to "brutes, Yahoos, or demons." Adams said a lot of other things that would get him lambasted on Fox News. He blasted "aristocratical" banks and agreed with Thomas Jefferson that Alexander Hamilton was corrupt. And he saw all too clearly the devastation wrought by unregulated markets. In the twilight of their lives, Jefferson and Adams rekindled their friendship and discovered that they agreed on a lot more than they thought – although they still disagreed on much.

Yet, for some reason, men like Hamilton are the only founders ever mentioned when the topic is property. Thus, we usually presume they spoke for the founders as a whole and aroused no controversy among their contemporaries. On the contrary, when some founders spoke of the importance of property rights, they were replying to other founders who sought to spread the wealth.

Glossing over this economic conflict is dishonest. The struggle between Jefferson and Hamilton defined early party politics and that fight was ultimately about class. Few know that many of our founders feared great wealth's threat to liberty, so those who point it out now are called communists or at least labeled "un-American." But what is un-American is a one-sided debate. This is the other side.

Of course, Thomas Jefferson's side of the debate had some skeletons in the closet – Native American skeletons as well as African ones. After all, it was Native land that was being handed out.

But there is no denying that America was always the land of hand-outs. Those hardy pioneers hardly "pulled themselves up by their boot straps." In fact, that idiom is about doing the impossible – like Dr. Seus' the Lorax flying by hoisting himself by the seat of his pants. You try it sometime.

Less than a century before General Tecumseh Sherman promised freed slaves forty acres for generations of unpaid labor, Thomas Jefferson promised every new settler in Virginia fifty acres. It was in his first draft of the state's constitution:

Every person of full age neither owning nor having owned [50] acres of land, shall be entitled to an appropriation of [50] acres or to such as shall make up what he owns or has owned [50] acres in full and absolute dominion.[191]

It expanded on a 1705 Virginia law that gave fifty acres to every freed indentured servant. That law was a bribe to discourage those servants from joining in with any more slave revolts. Previously, indentured whites and enslaved blacks joined forces and rebelled together against their masters.[192]

As with General Sherman, Thomas Jefferson was overruled. But both proposals had sought to promote small farms in opposition to vast estates and thus frustrate another resurgence of aristocracy. And both had precedents in other acts and legislation: Tory property was confiscated during the Revolution.

The topic of property is problematic for almost everybody – for most whites, at any rate. There is not a lot of proud to go around. But this is a central thread in America's narrative and therefore there is no ignoring it. Arguing over property is essentially the story of America. I do not just mean arguing over who owns what, but also over what *is* and *isn't* property and where the very concept of property comes from. For example, the slavery debate was over the distinction between people and property. But landownership and its origin is another important facet. America was the battleground – both literally and figuratively – of all these philosophical and legal debates about property. We stand on ground zero.

So, let us now look at the founders' concepts in detail. And let us start, as they did, at the beginning. As Thomas Paine put it, "It is only by tracing things to their origin that we gain rightful ideas of them, and it is by gaining such ideas that we discover the boundary that divides right from wrong, and teaches every man to know his own."[193]

In his 1690 *Second Treatise on Government*, the British political philosopher John Locke wrote, "In the beginning, all the world was America." For a century thereafter, many thinkers pointed to our apparently uncorrupted continent when trying to discern how capital-N Nature intended people to live. One famous example was Jean Jacques Rousseau's romantic notion of the "noble savage." Native societies were actually far more diverse and complex than these thinkers realized, but these idealized impressions shaped how they thought people should govern themselves. As James W. Loewen wrote in *Lies My Teacher Told Me: Everything Your American History Textbook Got Wrong*:

Although leadership was substantially hereditary in some nations, most Indian societies north of Mexico were much more democratic than Spain, France, or even England in the seventeenth and eighteenth centuries. "There is not a Man in the Ministry of the Five Nations, who has gain'd his Office. Otherwise than by Merit," waxed Lt. Gov. Cadwallader Colden of New York in 1727. "Their Authority is only the Esteem of the People, and ceases the Moment that Esteem is lost." Colden applied to the Iroquois terms redolent of "the natural rights of mankind": "Here we see the natural Origin of all Power and Authority among a free People."

Indeed, Native American ideas may be partly responsible for our democratic institutions. We have seen how Native ideas of liberty, fraternity, and equality found their way to Europe to influence social philosophers such as Thomas More, Locke, Montaigne, Montesquieu, And Rousseau. These European thinkers then influenced Americans such as Franklin, Jefferson and Madison.[194]

Economic equality was among these ideas. As Thomas Paine wrote in *Agrarian Justice,* "To understand what the state of society ought to be, it is necessary to have some idea of the natural and primitive state of man; such as it is at this day among the Indians of North America. There is not, in that state, any of those spectacles of human misery which poverty and want present to our eyes in all the towns and streets in Europe."[195]

In his "Remarks Concerning the Savages of North America," Benjamin Franklin suggested that Natives appreciated this difference. "Having few artificial wants, they have abundance of leisure for improvement by conversation. Our laborious manner of life, compared with theirs, they esteem slavish and base."[196]

While Benjamin Franklin faulted our "artificial wants," Thomas Paine blamed the haphazard advance of civilization and plain old exploitation. Paine's *Agrarian Justice* was directed at France and England where population density prevented going back to nature. But if it was no longer an option, it still remained a yardstick:

The life of an Indian is a continual holiday, compared with the poor of Europe; and, on the other hand it appears to be abject when compared to the rich. Civilization, therefore, or that which is so-called, has operated two ways: to make one part of society more affluent, and the other more wretched, than would have been the lot of either in a natural state.

It is always possible to go from the natural to the civilized state, but it is never possible to go from the civilized to the natural state. The reason is that man in a natural state, subsisting by hunting, requires ten times the quantity of land to range over to procure himself sustenance ...

The thing, therefore, now to be done is to remedy the evils and preserve the benefits that have arisen to society by passing from the natural to that which is called the civilized state.

In taking the matter upon this ground, the first principle of civilization ought to have been, and ought still to be, that the condition of every person born into the world, after a state of civilization commences, ought not to be worse than if he had been born before that period.[197]

Along the quality-of-life continuum, Caucasian Americans fell somewhere between Native Americans and Europe's inhabitants. Recall how Benjamin

Franklin contrasted our new nation's standards of living with Europe's appalling wealth and poverty:

The truth is, that, though there are in that country few people so miserable as the poor of Europe, there are also very few that in Europe would be called rich. It is rather a general happy mediocrity that prevails.[198]

Again, the situation has since reversed and America now has the wider wealth gap. But back then, "misery" and "Europe" were linked in the founders' vocabularies because the difference was far greater overseas. This was the origin of both the "radical egalitarianism" that Robert Bork scorned and the notion that America is (or at least should be) a middle class society.

Both ideals are inherently entwined in the origin of our national identity. In fact, those two threads re-entwine from time to time. In the later Victorian period of monopolies, robber barons, and sweatshops, the working poor and the middle class joined forces, resulting in the subsequent Progressive Era. This alliance resumed during The New Deal and is long overdue now. Indeed, just like the anti-aristocratic rhetoric that often accompanies it, such perennial alliances date back to our nation's origin, reoccurring whenever society's "happy mediocrity" is threatened, near extinction, or requires resurrection.

For example, there was a rapidly growing wealth gap in the American colonies shortly before the revolution. Conditions were not nearly as bad as in Europe, but the colonists saw where things were going and sought to stop it. As Ray Raphael pointed out in *A People's History of the American Revolution,* it was pretty visible in Boston. "Since the late 1600s, the richest 5 percent of the population had increased their share of the taxable assets from 30 percent to 49 percent, while the wealth owned by the poorest half of the population had decreased from 9 percent to a mere 5 percent."[199]

In his endnote Raphael added, "In Philadelphia, the changes were even more dramatic. The share of the richest 5 percent increased from 33 percent to 55 percent between 1693 and 1771, while the share of the poorest half declined from 10.1 percent to 3.3 percent."[200]

I should mention that Benjamin Franklin bragged about our "happy mediocrity" *after* the Revolution. Whether or not that was the reality, it was certainly his ideal. But this rapidly widening wealth gap unquestionably radicalized the colonists in the run-up to the Revolution. As Gary B. Nash noted in his book *The Urban Crucible: Social Change, Political Consciousness and the Origins of the American Revolution:*

By mid-century, poverty in Boston had bred contempt for the rich in a number of political writers and fed the notion that great wealth and grinding poverty were organically connected. "From your Labor and Industry," proclaimed "Phileleutheros" for the mechanics, "arises all that can be called

Riches, and by your Hands it must be defended: Gentry, Clergy, Lawyers, and military Officers, do all support their Grandeur by your Sweat, and at your Hazard."²⁰¹

Nash's endnote for that 1751 quote is also worthy of showcasing. He wrote, "The pamphlet was taken almost verbatim from Cato's Letters, no. 69, first published in book form in London in 1724."²⁰² I hunted up the original quote because I thought the folks at the libertarian Cato Institute would like to see this one too. I think they have had sufficient time to recover from the shock of that last one:

*From your Labour and Industry arises all that can be called Riches, and by your Hands it must be defended: Kings, Nobility, Gentry, Clergy, Lawyers, and military Officers, do all support their Grandeur by your Sweat and Hazard, and in tyrannical Governments upon the People's Spoils: They there riot upon the Subsistence of the poor People, whose Poverty is their Riches. In corrupt Administrations, your Superiors of all Kinds make Bargains, and pursue Ends at the public Expense, and grow rich by making the People poor.*²⁰³

Of course, modern day conservatives like Robert Bork have a decidedly different take than Cato and Phileleutheros. In *Slouching Towards Gomorrah*, Bork wrote:

*It is impossible to see any objective harm done to the less wealthy by another's greater wealth. It is not, after all, the case that the richer man's income is extracted from the poorer man. Vacationing at the shore, I see a large yacht at anchor in the harbor. Though I may wish I had one, it is quite clear that I do not lack a yacht because another man has one. The economy is not a zero-sum game. A Rockefeller's or a Bill Gate's or a Michael Jackson's wealth does not diminish my wealth or anyone else's."*²⁰⁴

It is funny how Robert Bork sees liberty and equality locked in a zero-sum game, but then denies anything like it in the economy. Even if the economy is constantly growing (and it is currently shrinking, if we use employment as a yardstick), some exploitation still takes place. Bork's book was published in 1996. By then, the corporate feeding frenzy of mergers, takeovers, and subsequent layoffs had been going on for over a decade. Jobs were being exported at a staggering rate and those that remained stateside were often stripped of benefits and/or paid reduced wages after unions were forced to make repeated concessions. And then there is automation.

But who needed any excuse for layoffs? As business journalist Doug Henwood noticed, "By 1993, it was clear that the quickest way to add 5 points to your stock price was to lay off 50,000 workers."²⁰⁵

All of this was in pursuit of profits not seen since the aforementioned Victorian Era that conservatives are now enthusiastically duplicating. But the revolutionaries fought hard to avoid that world and that can be seen in one document after another. As Gary Nash added to that above Phileleutheros quote:

> Now such notions entered the consciousness of the laboring classes in other port towns. "Some individuals," charged a New Yorker in 1765, "... by Smiles of Providence, or some other Means, are enabled to roll in their four wheel'd [sic] Carriages and can support the expense of good Houses, rich Furniture, and Luxurious Living. But is it equitable that 99, rather 999, should suffer for the Extravagance or Grandeur of one? Especially when it is considered that Men frequently owe their Wealth to the impoverishment of their Neighbors?"[206]

Apparently, the "Ninety Nine Percent" that the Occupy Wall Street Movement spoke of had a Revolutionary Era precedent. When Colin Powell called the Occupy movement "as American as apple pie," he was probably only referring to their right to protest and air their grievances. But their critique of economic inequality is far more American than most people suspect. Thus, it is not the Tea Party, but Occupy Wall Street that had truly inherited the mantle of the Boston Tea Party.

Incidentally, a 2011 study had asked Americans to guess our nation's current wealth distribution. The respondents believed that the wealthiest fifth only held 59% of the nation's wealth. The actual amount is 84%.[207] Despite their lowball estimate, most still said redistribution was necessary. Indeed, when shown pie charts, 92% of respondents preferred Sweden's more equitable wealth distribution to America's.

As the colonists looked at nearby Native Americans, they began to esteem their own "laborious manner of life" as "slavish and base." This may explain why they adopted Indian imagery when inventing a new national identity – thus, the street theater of the original Boston Tea Party.

Oddly, today's Tea Party movement does not dress as Natives at their protests. If cultural sensitivity prompted some proactive memo from FreedomWorks or the Koch Brothers, it apparently said nothing about portraying President Obama as a monkey or a witch doctor.

But our founding fathers did not stop at studying the First Nations or at drawing symbolic associations with them. They also adopted Native concepts and an important one was that the earth belonged to all people in common. They thus reasoned that land ownership was not a natural right but rather a social construct. Thomas Paine was only one among many European thinkers who seized this idea, but he expressed it best and put it in humorous terms that most Europeans could easily understand by citing the *Bible:*

> *It is deductible, as well from the nature of the thing as from all the stories transmitted to us, that the idea of landed property commenced with cultivation, and that there was no such thing, as landed property before that time. It could not exist in the first state of man, that of hunters. It did not exist in the second state, that of shepherds: neither Abraham, Isaac, Jacob, nor Job, so far as the history of the Bible may credited in probable things, were owners of land. Their property consisted, as is always enumerated, in flocks and herds, they traveled with them from place to place. The frequent contentions at that time about the use of a well in the dry country of Arabia, where those people lived, also show that there was no landed property. It was not admitted that land could be claimed as property. There could be no such thing as landed property originally. Man did not make the earth, and, though he had a natural right to occupy it, he had no right to locate as his property in perpetuity any part of it; neither did the Creator of the earth open a land-office, from whence the first title-deeds should issue.*[208] (italics original)

As if anticipating J.D. Rockefeller's boast "God gave me my money," Thomas Paine wrote, "It is wrong to say God made *rich* and *poor;* He made only *male* and *female*, and He gave them the earth for their inheritance."[209] (italics original) The founders made this point repeatedly. In a 1785 letter to James Madison, Thomas Jefferson wrote, "The earth is given as a common stock for man to labor and live on."[210] In short, they thought the land was as free as the air and that nobody really owned either.

Most Enlightenment thinkers agreed that paradise was lost with the advent of private land ownership. Even the so-called "Father of Capitalism" Adam Smith admitted, "But this original state of things, in which the laborer enjoyed the whole produce of his own labor, could not last beyond the first introduction of the appropriation of land and the accumulation of (live)stock." He added, "As soon as land becomes private property, the landlord demands a share of almost all the produce which the laborer can either raise or collect from it."[211]

That guy sounds like a commie to me.

This explains the immense impact of the Native American example. But, the concept of private landownership was then relatively recent – even in the European world. In medieval times, the nation's land technically belonged to the king. But, there were these facts on the ground called "castles," and they often made enforcement problematic for the monarch.[212] In theory, the king could always strip a lord of his land and rank and give it to another. But in reality, feudal lords were often collectively – if not individually – more powerful than the king. In England, this reality was formalized into law by the Magna Carta, which permanently limited the monarch's power.

Needless to say, this situation gave local lords a strong sense of entitlement. But the concept of outright ownership had not yet fully taken hold. Hereditary control of territory was deeply rooted in tradition and had almost all the perks of outright ownership. Thus, there was not yet any need to rethink land and property. True, lords still owed traditional obligations to those both above and below them. The peasants who worked the land had various traditional land rights such as water access, the right to graze livestock, and the right to gather firewood off the ground (i.e. "windfall") on certain days of the week. In turn, the lord got a portion of the crops in exchange for his "protection."

So long as this situation suited the lords, it was unlikely to change. But change it did. In England, this metamorphosis occurred during the Enclosure Movement. Local lords discovered that it was often more profitable to graze sheep for their wool. The lords thus declared the land to be their private property and pushed their peasants off. Now homeless, these poor people drifted into the larger towns and cities looking for work. This surplus population, in turn, fueled England's desire for overseas colonies.

For the founders, this was relatively recent history. Indeed, the process of enclosure was not complete until well after American independence. This and the Native example impacted the founders' thoughts. Every single aspect of their situation logically compelled them to critically think about where property originally came from. They had a recent model of what went wrong as well an opportunity to rewrite the rules. And they justified the rewrite by saying that land ownership was the invention of social law rather than natural law. Thus, society could rewrite the rules at any time.

It was the obvious conclusion for them to make. After all, those who accept the status quo as God's will are not apt to rebel in the first place. But, once you jettison the Divine Right of Kings, you must rethink property entirely. A secular mindset invites scrutiny of human institutions to see how they might be improved or replaced. If we made them, then we can change them.

This distinction between natural law and social law is essential. To get a clearer idea of what these men meant, it is necessary to contrast land ownership with ownership of moveable objects. Both Thomas Jefferson and Thomas Paine described how concepts of property developed alongside different stages of society. In a piece entitled "The Batture at New Orleans," Jefferson contrasts land ownership with personal effects, alluding to some of the history I have just outlined:

That the lands within the limits assumed by a nation belong to the nation as a body, has probably been the law of every people on earth at some period of their history. A right of property in movable things is admitted before the establishment of government. A separate property in lands not till after that establishment. The right to movables is acknowledged by all the hordes of Indians surrounding us. Yet by no one of them has a separate property in lands been yielded to individuals. He who plants a field keeps possession till he has gathered the produce, after which one has as good a right as another to occupy it. Government must be established and laws provided, before lands can be separately appropriated, and the owner protected in his possession. Till then the property is in the body of the nation, and they, or their chief as their trustee, must grant them to individuals, and determine the condition of the grant.[213]

The quote comes from a discussion of property and feudalism. Jefferson was referring to early kings and chieftains to argue that land is public before it becomes private. A people or tribe might control a territory collectively, but individual ownership cannot exist before formal government does. After all, you need deeds and other enforcement mechanisms. Peeing around the perimeter only works until a bigger dog comes along – or until it next rains. But until government is invented, that is the best you can do.

And, as Thomas Jefferson said, this was universal. Land stolen from the Indians was the property of the federal government before being sold or simply given away to white settlers. But land is always originally public until bequeathed by government. Before then, "movables" are the only individual property that exists.

Thomas Jefferson was not afraid to carry this concept to its logical conclusions. In an 1813 letter to Isaac McPherson, he reiterates that natural law does not protect land ownership, but then he weakens "the right to movables." Even more radically, he then denies that natural law covers intellectual property. This seems counterintuitive. After all, if we inherently own anything, it is our own ideas, right? Thomas Jefferson thought not:

It is agreed by those who have seriously considered the subject that no individual has, of a natural right, a separate property in an acre of land, for instance. By an [sic] universal law, indeed, whatever, whether fixed or movable, belongs to all men equally and in common, is the property for the moment of him who occupies it, but when he relinquishes the occupation, the property goes with it. Stable ownership is the gift of social law, and is given late in the progress of society. It would be curious then, if an idea, the fugitive fermentation of an individual brain, could, of natural right, be claimed exclusive and stable property. If nature has made any one thing less susceptible than all others to exclusive property, it is the action of the thinking power called an idea, which an individual may exclusively possess as long as he keeps it to himself; but the moment it is divulged, it forces itself into the possession of every one, and the receiver cannot dispossess himself of it. Its peculiar character, too, is that no one possesses the less, because every other possesses the whole of it. He who receives an idea from me, receives instruction himself without lessening mine; as he who lights his taper at mine, receives light without darkening me. That ideas should freely spread from one to another over the globe, for the moral and mutual instruction of man, and the improvement of his condition, seems to have been peculiarly and benevolently designed by nature, when she made them, like fire, expansible over all space, without lessening their density in any point, and like the air in which we breathe, move, and have our physical being, incapable of confinement or exclusive appropriation. Inventions then cannot, in nature, be a subject of property. Society may give an exclusive right to the profits arising from them, as an encouragement to men to pursue ideas which may produce utility, but this may or may not be done, according to the will and convenience of the society, without claim or complaint from anybody.[214]

Now, before writing him off as a kook, it is important to recognize what Jefferson is and is not saying. He is not against recognizing intellectual property. He was a prolific inventor himself and felt society should encourage innovation in every way. Accordingly, it was Jefferson who first introduced the bill that created the U.S. Patent Office. But he did not believe intellectual property was a *natural right*. Like landownership, he thought intellectual property was the gift of society and that society had the right to decide how that property could best serve the common good.[215] The logical compromise gives us the best of both worlds – society rewards the inventor with temporary ownership, but the idea eventually passes into the public domain and then belongs to everybody. Obviously, nobody holds the patent on the wheel or the chair. This also keeps the inventor's descendants from sponging off his or her ideas indefinitely.

And Jefferson was not alone. Benjamin Franklin was a famous inventor himself and he shared Thomas Jefferson's public-spirited attitude towards intellectual property. In fact, in his classic *Autobiography*, the Pennsylvanian explains why he refused to put a patent on his famous Franklin Stove:

This pamphlet had a good effect, Gov. Thomas was so pleased with the construction of this stove, as described in it that he offered to give me a patent for the sole vending of them for a term of years; but I declined it from a principle which has ever weighed with me on such occasions, viz. **That as we enjoy great advantages from the inventions of others, we should be glad of an opportunity to serve others by any invention of ours, and this we should do freely and generously.***"*(emphasis original)[216]

If your goal is to better the world, un-patented inventions unquestionably spread faster because everybody likes free stuff. Franklin chose to share his invention for free. But even back then, it was still understood that intellectual ownership was only temporary. The Governor had offered Franklin an exclusive right "for a term of years" – not forever.

Many think this attitude is ultimately unproductive. Many others disagree. In such books as *Copyrights and Copywrongs, Steal This Idea,* and *The Future of Ideas*, the respective authors argue that the technology boom is fueled by the fact that nobody owns the Internet and thus everyone does. The Internet is what they call an "innovation commons" – an unregulated public space that nobody owns or controls. It has become a popular marketplace of ideas precisely because most things are free. Those who share Benjamin Franklin's technological generosity can post their shareware where anyone can download it. Tips, shortcuts, and all sorts of improvements are rapidly disseminated, discussed, critiqued, applied and fine-tuned. The motto of this "open source" software movement is "information wants to be free." (Recall Thomas Jefferson's candle analogy.) In this intellectually selfless environment, technological breakthroughs leapfrog forward to benefit all, so obviously generosity is not such a quixotic vehicle for progress. Thus, the notion that no innovation takes place without the profit motive is patently false.

But once again, the founders were not against protecting intellectual property. On the contrary, they even put it in the Constitution in order to "promote the progress of science and useful arts." They were just saying that it is a matter of social law rather than natural law. Accordingly, society can alter it at any time, in society's best interests. We, as a society, can always debate which policies are wisest, but it is our collective decision to make.

Likewise, land ultimately belongs to everyone in common. Individual ownership of land is a legal fiction which we entertain because many people believe it is useful and benefits society most of the time. But, when it ceases to benefit the public good or conflicts with some greater public good the fiction is no longer indulged. Hence eminent domain, which says that the government may take land for the public good, provided the owner is compensated at market value. This is typically done to build bridges and highways. But the underlying idea is that the legal fiction is entertained only as long as it benefits society.

Accordingly, the founders felt they were perfectly justified in seizing Tory property both during and after the revolution. The post-Civil War proposal to break up plantations among the slaves who had worked them was likewise consistent with this thinking. The concept of landownership has never been sacrosanct in America – neither to Natives nor Anglo invaders.

After the American Revolution, many veterans sought to take things beyond confiscating enemy property. In New Hampshire, the militia had to be called out on September 20th of 1786 to disperse an angry mob of veterans who had besieged the state legislature in Exeter for three days. Among their demands were the issuance of paper money, the forgiveness of debts, tax relief, and the equal distribution of property.[217] Basically, everything John Adams had feared in that long quote toward the front of the chapter.

Why? Because the vets had come home to find their farms about to be foreclosed on by bankers who had never shouldered a musket. Naturally, they felt betrayed and linked their revolt to the revolution they had just fought. They compared bankers to Tories. Therefore, it seemed consistent to confiscate their property as well.

Conservatives will predictably attribute this incident to irrational rabble. But officers were involved in the Exeter event, which suggests a much broader swath of support. As the *Columbia Magazine* reported two weeks later:

Oct 9. Colonel Stone, Major Cochran, Capt. Cochran, Lieut. Robinson, Capt. McKean, Lieut. McClary, Capt. Dow, Lieutenant Clough, and Ensign Cotton, officers of the New Hampshire militia, are to be tried by court martial on the 21st of next month, for aiding, abetting and assisting the insurgents lately assembled at Exeter.[218]

Obviously, this incident alarmed many. In Federalist # 10, James Madison obliquely acknowledged this often forgotten conflict the following year. He wrote that friction between the haves and have-nots is "the most common and durable source of factions" in society, and recognized that the have-nots have a program to be thwarted. Accordingly, he advised the voters of (then conservative) New York that:

[A] rage for paper money, for the abolition of debts, for an equal division of property, or for any other improper or wicked project, will be less apt to pervade the whole body of the Union, than a particular member of it; in the same proportion as such a malady is more likely to taint a particular county or district, than an entire State.

I imagine the state that James Madison had in mind was New Hampshire – which is quite interesting, given the Granite State's present libertarian bent.

This is not to say that James Madison was entirely in Alexander Hamilton's camp. After all, Thomas Jefferson was his political mentor. Madison was a midpoint between Hamilton and Jefferson and obsessed with maintaining balance. He was more concerned with preventing conflicts than protecting the interests of the rich, and he clearly saw the necessity of preserving Benjamin Franklin's "happy mediocrity" in order to avoid such tumults. When discussing the emergence of political parties, he gave five guidelines for mitigating their tendency to generate unrest. Two of them advocate regulating wealth:

In every political society, parties are unavoidable. A difference of interests, real or supposed, is the most natural and fruitful source of them. The great object should be to combat the evil: 1. By establishing a political equality among all. 2. By withholding unnecessary opportunities from a few, to increase the inequality of property, by an immoderate, and especially an unmerited, accumulation of riches. 3. By the silent operation of laws, which, without violating the rights of property, reduce extreme wealth towards a state of mediocrity, and raise extreme indigence towards a state of comfort. 4. By abstaining from measures which operate differently on different interests, and particularly such as favor one interest at the expence [sic] of another. 5. By making one party a check on the other, so far as the existence of parties cannot be prevented, nor their views accommodated.[219]

No, it was not just Franklin, Jefferson, and Paine who advocated economic equality. Many other revolutionary luminaries concurred, either quietly or out loud at some point. John Adams and his cousin Samuel Adams (now of beer fame) privately agreed with the above trio on the topic of property. As Gary B. Nash described in *The Urban Crucible*:

John Adams was one of those who had read his republican theory carefully enough to understand the connection between economic inequality and political corruption. In preparing his Dissertation on the Feudal and Canon Law, one of the most powerful republican statements of the 1760s, Adams wrote that "Property monopolized or in the possession of a few is a Curse to Mankind. We should preserve not an Absolute Equality – this is unnecessary, but preserve all from extreme Poverty, and all others from extravagant Riches." But Adams, caught between Whig and Evangelical modes of thinking, thought better of the statement, engaged as he was with wealthy Whig merchants in the early stages of resistance, and deleted it from his text.[220]

Yes, that era's Evangelicals favored spreading the wealth. Something about everyone being equal in God's eyes influenced them. I will cover this more in my next book.

John's cousin Sam was in a similar predicament. As Nash added on the next page:

Samuel Adams, who had no commercial aspirations, might inveigh that "Luxury & Extravagance are in my opinion totally destructive of those Virtues which are necessary for the Preservation of the Liberty and Happiness of the People." Yet Adams, though devoid of capitalist urges, was trying to lead a radical movement from New England's largest commercial center and had to work with John Hancock, who lived high on the hill and stocked his cellar with the best Madeira wines. Hancock's purse and prestige were vital to the success of the Massachusetts patriot movement and he was not risking his life and fortune for a return to Arcadian simplicity.[221]

There is that societal happiness business again – and, again, in opposition to property. Funny thing that.

But while the Adams cousins had kept their republican ideology under their hats, other founders did not. The notion that government must actively equalize fortunes and discourage concentrations of wealth was widespread and, as Gary B. Nash had noted above, a fixture in republican political theory.

Indeed, speaking of Evangelicals like John Adams, take Noah Webster (of dictionary fame). In 1787, this devout man wrote that a rough material equality was absolutely essential to preserving our free form of government:

*An equality of property, with a necessity of alienation, constantly operating to destroy combinations of powerful families, is the very **soul of a republic** – While this continues, the people will inevitably possess both **power** and **freedom**; when this is lost, power departs, liberty expires, and a commonwealth will inevitably assume some other form. The liberty of the press, trial by jury, the Habeas Corpus writ, even the Magna Charta itself, although justly deemed the palladia of freedom, are all inferior considerations, when compared with a general distribution of real property among every class of people.* (emphasis original)[222]

Of course, modern conservatives do not share our founders' concerns. The late Robert Bork doubted that, "the workings of democracy are impeded if there is too great a disparity in the wealth of the citizens." "There are many avenues to political power and wealth is not the most significant."[223] For example, Bork himself had slept his way onto the national stage.

Okay, that was probably an improper joke. But, levity aside, who was our last non-millionaire president? How many senators and congressmen are *not* millionaires? How does Mr. Smith get to Washington today without being rich and/or catering to them?

Robert Bork did not seem to understand how our political system works. He was mired in denial about a great many things and the role of money is politics is one of them. That or he was straight-up lying. But beyond his grasp of our current political system's structural mechanics, he was utterly tone deaf to our original national ethos:

Envy certainly has shaped and continues to shape our political culture. That is probably why it is front-page news in the New York Times that the United States displays greater inequality in wealth than other industrial nations. The unstated assumption that makes this worthy of the front page is that there is something morally wrong, even shameful, in having greater wealth inequalities than other societies.[224]

Of course, Robert Bork knew he was profoundly out of step with America's central ideological thrust. He even admitted that his assault on equality "verges on heresy."[225]

Verge is not the word. For Bork, egalitarianism was an ugly, irrational impulse. While the founders I just quoted above saw it as a bulwark of social harmony and our free form of government, Bork saw it as culturally-indulged envy. But of course, this is also the same Robert Bork who claimed that the founders forgot to bother with morality or social order because things were so tranquil that they could be safely taken for granted.

This brings us back to those rebellious New Hampshire veterans who besieged the state house demanding an equal distribution of property. While their aims were consistent with the concept that land ownership is the gift of social law, I am not mentioning this to make an argument for communism. On the contrary, both Thomas Jefferson and Thomas Paine favored widespread land ownership as socially beneficial and thought it should be encouraged – provided that small family plots did not grow into vast aristocratic estates. For Jefferson, the small farmer was the bedrock of American society. Accordingly, both wrote that outright land redistribution would be logistically impractical and advocated progressive taxation instead.

Jefferson acknowledged, "I am conscious that an equal division of property is impracticable, but the consequences of this enormous inequality producing so much misery to the bulk of mankind, legislators cannot invent too many devices for subdividing property."

"Cannot invent too many." Rally your imaginations.

To this end, Jefferson suggested a two-pronged strategy of: 1) Ending primogeniture, the traditional aristocratic practice of willing all property to the eldest son, and 2) Taxing "the higher portions of property in geometrical progression as they rise."[226]

Thomas Paine did not call for the equal division of land because he thought farmers owned their labor like everyone else. He distinguished between land and the cultivation of land. Since the two things are impossible to separate, Paine suggested taxation as a means of re-achieving original equality. To fund his Social Security program, Paine proposed a land tax that he called a "ground rent" to emphasize the premise that the land actually belongs to society as a whole:

And as it is impossible to separate the improvement made by cultivation from the earth itself, upon which that improvement is made, the idea of landed property arose from that parable connection; but it is nevertheless true, that it is the value of the improvement, only, and not the earth itself, that is individual property.

Every proprietor, therefore, of cultivated lands, owes to the community a ground-rent (for I know of no better term to express the idea) for the land which he holds; and it is from this ground-rent that the fund proposed in this plan is to issue.[227]

For Thomas Paine, taxation, social responsibility, and the origin of property were all fundamentally interrelated and he emphasized this idea repeatedly in *Agrarian Justice:*

Land, as before said, is the free gift of the Creator in common to the human race. Personal property is the effect of society; and it is as impossible for an individual to acquire personal property without the aid of society, as it is for him to make land originally.

Separate an individual from society, and give him an island or a continent to possess, and he cannot acquire personal property. He cannot be rich. So inseparably are the means connected with the end, in all cases, that where the former do not exist the latter cannot be obtained. All accumulation, therefore, of personal property, beyond what a man's own hands produce, is derived to him by living in society; and he owes on every principle of justice, of gratitude, and of civilization, a part of that accumulation back again to society from whence the whole came.[228]

I know what you are thinking. "I'm not rich? Dude! *I OWN A WHOLE GODDAMNED ISLAND!*"

But you still need other people to be rich. Without them, you do not meaningfully own anything. You are just another creature on the landscape. You do not own the island any more than that tiger over there. And that tiger is now going to eat you because safety in numbers does not work as well when you are all alone.

"No problem," you may say, "I will just shoot it with my gun."

But what gun? Who made the gun? This raises the question of stuff. Somebody made all of your tools and chances are that somebody was not you. The castaway Robinson Crusoe did not own a sweet set of wheels or enjoy indoor plumbing. Other people need to make that stuff. In fact, other people need to *invent* that stuff. Thus, the creation of wealth depends on the infrastructure of society – the legacy of other people's previous physical and mental efforts.

Society creates conveniences just as government confers ownership. Without either, property is nothing more than a small collection of primitive personal effects – i.e. "movables." There is no avoiding the ultimate logical conclusion of this fact: Ironically, individual ownership requires the collective consent and cooperation of other people. You only own what society says you do. Property is a social construct.

As you might imagine, Benjamin Franklin heartily agreed with Thomas Paine that society magnified our efforts and was due something back to perpetuate the process. Indeed, in a 1783 letter to fellow founding father Robert Morris, Franklin wrote:

All the property that is necessary to a man, for the conservation of the individual and the propagation of the species, is his natural right, which none can justly deprive him of: but all property superfluous to such purposes is the property of the public, who, by their laws, have created it, and who may therefore by other laws dispose of it, whenever the welfare of the public shall demand such disposition.[229]

Benjamin Franklin echoed his conclusion on other occasions:

Private property therefore is a creature of society, and is subject to the calls of that society, whenever its necessities shall require it, even to the last farthing: its contributions therefore to the public exigencies are not to be considered as conferring a benefit on the public, entitling the contributors to the distinctions of honor and power, but as a return of an obligation previously received, or the payment of a just debt.[230]

If the strength of Benjamin Franklin's emphasis escapes you, a farthing was an old English coin worth one fourth of a penny. Franklin was emphatic about the duty of giving something back.

Conservatives went totally bonkers when both Barack Obama and Elizabeth Warren articulated the same basic principle (albeit in a far softer tone) during the 2012 election. Both campaigners had reminded business that their success was built on the infrastructure and education that society had already provided. Elizabeth Warren was fired up:

There is nobody in this country who got rich on his own. Nobody. You built a factory out there? Good for you. But I want to be clear: you moved your goods to market on the roads the rest of us paid for; you hired workers the rest of us paid to educate; you were safe in your factory because of police forces and fire forces that the rest of us paid for. You didn't have to worry that marauding bands would come and seize everything at your factory, and hire someone to protect against this, because of the work the rest of us did.

Now look, you built a factory and it turned into something terrific, or a great idea? God bless. Keep a big hunk of it. But part of the underlying social contract is you take a hunk of that and pay forward for the next kid who comes along.

President Barack Obama then reasoned, "If you were successful, somebody along the line gave you some help. There was a great teacher somewhere in your life." Then he turned to public infrastructure – including the electronic infrastructure of the Internet:

Somebody invested in roads and bridges. If you've got a business – you didn't build that. Somebody else made that happen. The Internet didn't get invented on its own. Government research created the Internet so that all the companies could make money off the Internet. The point is, is that when we succeed, we succeed because of our individual initiative, but also because we do things together.

Note that neither Warren nor Obama denied the importance of individual effort. Instead, they put it in context. Just as you need both hydrogen and oxygen to make water, prosperity comes from the combination of individual and the collective efforts. That is just common sense.

Of course, conservatives ignored that context and seized on the words "You didn't build that." They called it communism and the Republican Party promptly made "We Built It" the theme of their 2012 National Convention. Amusingly, they held it in a convention center which was mostly built with taxpayer funds.[231] And to spearhead their message, they selected a speaker who had built her government contracting business with the help of government loans.[232] Oblivious to their hypocrisy, they went ballistic. Imagine if Warren or Obama had said society was entitled to the "last farthing" as Franklin had!

Conservatives often stoke the erroneous notion that the American Revolution was fought over taxes. On the contrary, it was all about reciprocity. The revolutionaries did not say "no taxation," but rather "no taxation *without representation*." They saw it as a two-way street. They believed that the legitimacy of taxation hinged on government being an agent of the people's will. It has the right to levy taxes to do the people's work because the people had approved that work to be done through their representatives. But without representation, the legitimacy of taxation evaporates. That was the point.

No, the founders were not as anti-tax as conservatives imagine. As Thomas Paine wrote in *The Rights of Man*, "The continual whine of lamenting the burden of taxes, however successfully it may be practised *[sic]* in mixed Governments, is inconsistent with the sense and spirit of a republic."[233] The word "mixed" refers to the fact that the British Parliament was half elected (the House of Commons) and half not (the House of Lords). Of course, the American colonists had no representation in either house of Parliament. That was their point.

Benjamin Franklin frequently addressed this continual whine after American independence was won because taxation no longer lacked representation. Democracy legitimizes taxation (which is another reason why conservatives and libertarians say they oppose democracy). As the new nation was no longer an exploited colony, it should logically pull together for the common good. And Franklin was all about pulling together.

Of course, this is the same Ben Franklin who wrote, "An enormous proportion of property vested in a few individuals is dangerous to the rights, and destructive of the common happiness, of mankind."[234] As I mentioned in chapter one, those jolting words come from his first draft of Pennsylvania's Declaration of Rights. He started writing it four days before he signed the Declaration of Independence. And it was he who inserted "the pursuit of happiness" in place of John Locke's original "pursuit of property."

Conservatives and libertarians alike will likely blast Benjamin Franklin as an enemy of entrepreneurs or some kind of crank bent on "punishing success." But he was in fact one of the few truly self-made men at Pennsylvania's convention. He went from being a poor printer's apprentice to being a wealthy international celebrity. Franklin embodied the American ideal of social mobility. But conservatives see remembering your humble origins as a sort of hypocrisy. They think that once you become rich, you must adopt their collective agenda. Therefore, they think Michael Moore is a hypocrite because he has not become a Republican. To conservatives, selling out is a badge of character and maturity. But Franklin did not forget where he had come from. In fact, years after he had become a success, he annoyed his fellow Philadelphia printers by supporting their workers when they went on strike.[235] He always stuck up for the underdog and aided the rank and file whenever he could. And, as a selection from the *Pennsylvania Gazette* attests, this included the rank and file on the battlefield – who shared his suspicion of the rich:

The Committee of Correspondence of the Committee of Privates in Philadelphia, wrote a circular letter to all the battalions in the State previous to the election of the members for the late Convention. In this letter the good people of this State were advised to choose no rich men, and as few learned men as possible to represent them in the Convention. They are charged to avoid choosing all such men as are under proprietary influence, "without their knowing it," and lastly they are directed to instruct their representatives when chosen to insist upon the people choosing their militia officers, and upon our having only one Legislature.

A member of the late Convention congratulated the State upon the opening of the Convention, that a set of plain men with good understandings were assembled together to make a government. It was debated for some time in the Convention, whether the future legislatures of this State should have the power of lessening property when it became excessive in individuals. [236]

Now, the *Pennsylvania Gazette* was Benjamin Franklin's own newspaper. And, of course, the member of the convention in question was Franklin himself. (No doubt so was also the reporter on the story.) Apparently, his attempt to butter up his colleagues failed since they rejected his proposal, but it still reflected a widespread sentiment. Suspicion of the rich was a frequent feature of revolutionary rhetoric.

One reason why Franklin felt society should limit wealth was that the wealthy were constantly trying to institutionalize their influence. Two years later, Pennsylvania's rich attempted to rig the new state constitution in their favor. They suggested an amendment to create a bicameral legislature in which the upper house would explicitly represent property and the lower house would represent population. Franklin wrote a point-by-point critique of this proposal. Here is his summation, which I have quoted from before:

The combinations of civil society are not like those of a set of merchants, who club their property in different proportions for building and freighting a ship, and may therefore have some right to vote in the disposition of the voyage in a greater or less degree according to their respective contributions: but the important ends of civil society, and the personal securities of Life and Liberty, these remain the same in every member of the society; and the poorest continues to have equal claim to them with the most opulent, whatever difference time, chance, or industry may occasion in their circumstances. On these considerations, I am sorry to see the signs this paper I have been considering affords, of a disposition among some of our people to commence an aristocracy, by giving the rich a predominancy [sic] in government.[237]

Benjamin Franklin won this later fight and today Pennsylvania still has only one legislative body.

Franklin's fear was real and widespread. It was not just some rhetorical cudgel. Old ways run deep and there was the threat of societal backsliding. As I mentioned, Southern planters had already cultivated aristocratic airs and New England's elite still admired old England's hierarchy. In fact, after the revolution, some disgruntled officers even wanted to see George Washington crowned king. This is why the Constitution explicitly forbids granting titles of nobility. Great concentrations of wealth were a related concern.

All of this ties into modern discussions about the size of government. Conservatives believe that the founding fathers all wanted small government and free markets. It is an article of faith for them. But their assumption is bunk for three interrelated reasons:

First, as I have just shown in great detail, the founders strongly disagreed on free markets and had very different concepts of property rights. Thomas

Jefferson wanted to regulate business and spread the wealth whereas Alexander Hamilton thought the rich should rule.

Second, the founders also strongly disagreed about the size of government. Thomas Jefferson clashed with Alexander Hamilton over this as well. And George Washington tended to agree with Hamilton, as can be seen in a 1787 letter: "The Men who oppose a strong and energetic government are, in my opinion, narrow minded politicians, or are under the influence of local views."[238]

Ooo! Stinging dis! Flintlocks fired!

I want to be charitable, but who does not know that the Federalists and Anti-Federalists bitterly fought over this issue with Federalists wanting "strong and energetic government"? Political campaigns were incredibly ugly, with both sides slandering each other. To suggest that there was consensus where there was scalding conflict is either ignorant or dishonest – hilariously so in any case.

Third, conservatives cannot find a single founder who endorsed *both* parts of their program. Again, a quick glance at Jefferson and Hamilton explains why. Big government founders like Hamilton favored free trade. Small government founders like Jefferson, sought to regulate commerce. Those might sound like odd combos to modern readers, but those were the two political sides in those times.

This was not contradictory because Thomas Jefferson's concept of "big government" meant large armies and broad police powers – something modern conservatives support. Jefferson's claim that banks were "more dangerous than standing armies" encapsulates not only his worldview but the political battle lines of his day. But today, advocating "small government" means letting big business run amuck. Thus, conservatives' small government/free market story twists history considerably.

Of course, you could argue that this is inconvenient to liberals too, but not really. This is because liberals do not see the founders as prophets handing down unchanging, eternal laws from God. While conservatives often fetishize "original intent" and blast relativism, liberals are far more comfortable with accepting change and putting things into context.

So, what had changed? What accounts for this switch in pairing? The socio-economic landscape is what changed.

Initially, the rich wanted a strong central government to overturn states' debt amnesty laws. As I wrote before, bankers were foreclosing on former soldiers' farms, so the vets voted out judges and state legislators they thought were beholden to banks. Then, the officials whom they voted-in got busy forgiving veterans' debts. Today's conservative anti-democratic arguments date back to this period. As John Adams feared, "Debts would be abolished first; taxes laid heavy on the rich, and not at all on the others; and at last a downright equal division of everything be demanded, and voted."

Needless to say, this alarmed Alexander Hamilton's friends. So, they turned to the Feds to preserve their interpretation of property rights. After all, that is what they felt the Constitution was for. As James Madison had argued in Federalist #10, "a rage for paper money, for the abolition of debts, for an equal division of property, or for any other improper or wicked project" would be less likely to prevail on the national stage. And federal authority could then intervene to squelch it locally. So conservatives then preferred a strong central government.

But much later, corporations became behemoths. The rich subsequently discovered that localities were easier to bully and bribe than Uncle Sam. State senators are much cheaper to buy than U.S. senators, and you can pit states against each other in a race to the bottom in average wages, tax rates, and safety standards, etc. So accordingly, companies now favor "devolving" power back to the states. Makes sense now, right?

Likewise, Republicans used to be the pro-tariff party when wealthy industrialists feared foreign competition. Today, those same industrial interests are moving factories overseas and therefore favor free trade. The economic landscape has changed, but conservative support for the rich remains a constant – that has not altered one jot.

About a century after independence in the Victorian Age, families like the Vanderbilts and Rockefellers realized our founders' fears by building financial dynasties. Critics called them "robber barons" for monopolizing markets, maintaining private armies, and murdering strikers.

But today corporate apologists like Arthur C. Brooks and John Stossel are not simply sympathetic, but celebratory. Lester C. Thurow's love of aristocracy was pretty obvious in his 2000 book, *Building Wealth: The New Rules for Individuals, Companies, and Nations in a Knowledge-based Economy*. First, he rhapsodizes over robber barons:

Great wealth allows individuals to place their footprints in the sands of time. Everyone knows the billionaires of the last half of the nineteenth century – Rockefeller, Morgan, Carnegie, Mellon. Few remember the U.S. presidents of that era. Those with great wealth are the stuff of history books. They are the modern immortals.[239]

Then, the author's monarchist leanings reach full froth. "Those with great wealth are important, to be courted. They are deserving of respect and demand deference." Thus, you should kiss his lordship's ring.

And these corporate troubadours are not apologetic about their desire to subvert our form of government. Thurow openly boasted, "Political influence can be quietly bought. Campaign contributions effectively give the wealthy more than one vote."

Other authors put on a more democratic gloss. In the future, they say, the market will register the people's will better than any election and do so on a moment-by-moment basis. Thomas Friedman heralded a coming "one dollar, one vote" system, prompting Thomas Frank to point out that Friedman had actually given "the definition of plutocracy, not democracy."[240] But, as Benjamin Franklin wrote, society is not a group of investors so you cannot justify giving the rich more votes.

I have heard Thomas Paine called an "outlier" for his economic concepts. And yet, I quote a lot of other founding outliers. Benjamin Franklin and Thomas Jefferson were the other two heavy hitters. Other giants, like James Madison and the two Adams cousins also agreed – albeit privately or less frequently. Lesser known luminaries of the revolution, such as Noah Webster, also confirmed that this was a fundamental fixture of republican ideology. So, Paine was no outlier.

The religious right plays the same game with deism. They cast poor Thomas Paine in Hell and pronounce all the other founders devout, Bible-believing Christians. But Paine embodied the Enlightenment on both topics. This was where revolutionary thinking was headed until greed and religion resurged in the early 1800s.

These founding outliers often get dismissed because their ideas were not applied in their lifetimes. After all, Thomas Paine's social security proposal was postponed so long that almost nobody knows about it. Well, many founders saw slavery as a contradiction to be eliminated, but abolition got postponed too. Their failure to end slavery in their lifetimes does not make their ideas irrelevant. And if their anti-slavery writings are significant, then their economic writings should be too. They certainly should be admissible when conservatives call today's social programs un-American.

Both issues pitted revolutionary ideals against deeply entrenched economic interests, so I suppose some disappointment is to be expected. But these radical ideas on property were part and parcel of their concept of natural law. The fact that those who had no analysis beyond crying "Mine!" initially prevailed does not change this. As Thomas Jefferson wrote, "It is agreed by those who have seriously considered the subject that no individual has, of a natural right, a separate property in an acre of land." The serious thinkers agreed, but lost to greed. Thus, the revolution got sold out.

Now I am not saying that the First Continental Congress was the First International or anything like that. The founders fought over this issue –

Hamilton and Jefferson clashed. And those I quote to make my case stopped just short of land redistribution.

But they did explicitly endorse wealth redistribution by taxation. They said property was not God-given but a social construct and that society was thus entitled to part of the wealth it had created. And they repeatedly emphasized that a rough economic equality was essential to preserving a free republic. Thus, the New Deal and the Great Society were completely in keeping with the revolution's ideals. Indeed, despite being denied and delayed, their ultimate thrust was built-in to our nation's ideological foundations. They are undeniably in our national DNA. Again, we introduced these Native American ideas to Europe.

Does the fact that the founders fought amongst themselves mean that they cancel each other out? Should we thus ignore what they said as irrelevant today?

Of course not. Just as Galileo and the Church fought over whether the earth orbited the sun, our founders also fought over slavery and the property qualification for voting. But we now know who turned out to be right, initial defeats notwithstanding. I argue that these progressive founders were likewise right about property all along.

Today, the immodest and unmerited riches that James Madison spoke of are flaunted. We now have the widest wealth gap since the Great Depression and the bankers who had crashed the economy awarded themselves enormous bonuses with the bailout money. Of course, CEOs have already been rewarding themselves for poor performance for years, so I suppose that last fact should not have shocked us much.

Likewise, America's wealth gap began widening with Reaganomics. Just as its critics predicted, the rich got richer and the poor got poorer. So, the writing was dry on that wall as well. Our predicament was decades in the making, and it did not creep up on us unseen.

My point is that those warnings date back to our country's origins and before. *Cato's Letters*, penned in the early 1720s, clarify current events – but not quite like libertarians imagine. The Enlightenment did not ignore the problem of poverty or the issue of class. Serious thinkers addressed these issues and ordinary people took to the streets or picked up muskets to deal with them before, during, and after the revolution.

Granted, you do not need a pamphlet from 1765 to ask if ninety nine "should suffer for the Extravagance or Grandeur of one?" But it helps.

5: *Why I am Not a Libertarian*
(It is Because I am a Libertarian)

I am not a libertarian.

I imagine that most of you have already figured this out by now.

Still, I am pretty libertarian on many issues, such as the Drug War. And, as I said in before, liberals have been illiberal on guns. They have forgotten or ignored the fact that poverty is the ultimate cause of violent crime because greedy yuppies do not want to talk about income inequality. Not only has this ideological inconsistency been ridiculously conspicuous, it has been politically costly. Granted, Reagan Democrats left the party first, but New Democrats closed the door behind them.

Fortunately, things are starting to turn around, at least on guns. As I wrote before, Howard Dean has long worked to reverse this error. And Michael Moore's *Bowling for Columbine* surprised audiences by looking at our culture of fear and shredded safety net instead of calling for more gun control.

In fact, in 2010, the Constitutional Accountability Center sided with the National Rifle Association in *McDonald v. Chicago*, the Supreme Court decision that struck down that city's 30-year-old handgun ban. The liberal group's move surprised some, but as *Newsweek* explained:

At the heart of the left-leaning dissenters' argument is a plea for consistency. For decades, liberals have insisted that the Constitution assumes – even if it does not explicitly spell out – a right to bodily autonomy. This right, long disputed by conservatives, is a basis for arguments in favor of abortion rights and gay rights.[241]

But surprisingly, my advocacy for individual liberty is why I am not a libertarian. Libertarians' assumptions about human nature and society are absolutely ass-backwards. Accordingly, their policies are often harmful to personal freedom. Simply idolizing the individual is not necessarily the best defense for individual liberty. You must look at society scientifically and then adjust your ideology accordingly.

Yes, some "libertarians" are flat-out frauds – conservatives trying to look hip. But others are well-intentioned people who fail to see the big picture.

Guns are a good example. They show the holes in libertarian thought as well as the holes in liberal thought.

For example, in a 2002 study entitled, "What Causes Violent Crime?" researchers looked at the United Nations World Crime Surveys for the period of 1970-1994 and concluded, "The results show that increases in income inequality raise crime rates."[242] Since this study covered different societies with different histories, traditions, and gun laws, it is safe to say that this is a reliable human dynamic. Recall what many founders said about economic equality ensuring societal happiness?

Another study, "Crime: Social Disorganization and Relative Deprivation" found, "Violent crimes (homicide, assault, robbery) were consistently associated with relative deprivation (income inequality) and indicators of low social capital." (parentheses original)[243]

In fact, studies that look into the specifics often acknowledge that general concept is well-covered ground. The abstract for "Social Capital, Income Inequality, and Firearm Violent Crime" begins, "Studies have shown that poverty and income are powerful predictors of homicide and violent crime."[244]

In other words, guns don't kill people – poverty and inequality kill people. That is a great argument against gun control, if libertarians want it. But I expect most of them do not. Internet libertarians frequently present themselves as friends of science. But to tweak Stephen Colbert's famous "Truthiness" routine, reality has a well-known socialist bias, so many libertarians are loathe to look at – let alone acknowledge – the data.

This is not to say that gun control does not reduce gun violence. On the contrary, that last study I quoted also noted that "The proxy for access to firearms was highly correlated with firearm homicide."[245]

However, there is no doubt that alleviating poverty would *also* reduce violent crime and in turn reduce calls for gun control. And even if gun control is effective, it is still tackling the problem from the back end rather than the front. Ignoring the root cause only perpetuates the problem. It means you are treating the symptoms instead of the disease.

Of course, most liberals would prefer to tackle gun violence from both ends. But that approach is constitutionally problematic. As I wrote about at length in chapter two, the Ninth Amendment explicitly spells out that the Bill of Rights is not a complete list. Your rights are infinite in number, but not breadth, because freedom means you have the right to do whatever does not harm another. Thus, you have a right to wear a hat or go to bed when you like, as Rep. Theodore Sedgwick put it in 1789. This means those rights that *were* specifically spelled out were singled out for special emphasis – "inserted merely for greater caution" as James Madison said.[246] Thus, the Second Amendment enjoys an extra layer of protection from the Ninth Amendment, as all the enumerated personal rights do. The Constitutional Accountability Center's argument for bodily autonomy is just another way of saying the same thing. If you are honestly looking for original intent, then there you have it. That is what the Constitution essentially says and has always said whether you want to acknowledge it or not. Here, on this specific point, libertarians are on solid ground while liberals and conservatives alike stand on shifting sands.

But libertarians are obviously wrong to tolerate poverty. Not only is their opposition to social programs wrong in itself, it subverts the gun rights that they claim to cherish.

In fact, reducing poverty – and thereby violent crime – would pay very many libertarian dividends. Think how much easier it would be to end the Drug War as a result. Arguing that drug use is a victimless crime often falls on deaf ears thanks to gang violence. Of course, it is the fact that it is an outlawed underground economy that puts it in the hands of gangs in the first place. Likewise, Prohibition put the sale of alcohol in the hands of Al Capone with the same bloody results. Libertarians are absolutely correct when they point this out. But, it is still a hard sell to the general public because fear often clouds logic. Reduce violent crime by reducing poverty and people will be far more likely to listen to reason.

Those who truly care about individual liberty must know that they can win few victories in an atmosphere of fear and having the worst murder rates in the First World does not help. Only failed states have worse homicide rates than ours – and their miserable living conditions and economy should probably dampen libertarian ardor too.

It is high time to face the facts. By prioritizing their greed, libertarians are frustrating all their other goals.

Indeed, specific issues aside, this atmosphere of fear breeds an anti-libertarian attitude – even among libertarians themselves. Why? Because the basis of libertarian thought is supposed to be the Enlightenment belief that people are basically rational and good and therefore require very little government to peaceably get along. But, if you think most people are ignorant or predatory, your politics inevitably become authoritarian.

Conservative founder John Jay wrote, "The mass of men are neither wise nor good, and virtue, like the other resources of the country, can only be drawn to a point and exerted by strong circumstances ably managed, or a strong government ably administered."[247]

As George Orwell observed, "The mental connection between pessimism and a reactionary outlook is no doubt obvious enough."[248]

And the late humorist Andy Rooney once ironically observed that liberals think people are basically good but need help from their government while conservatives think people are basically bad but will be okay if left alone.[249] (Except for trying to legislate their morality, of course.)

Alas, very many libertarians share the later attitude. For example, Ayn Rand saw ordinary people as "parasites," "looters," and "lice."

This also explains why so many former libertarians such as Robert Bork and the fellow I mentioned at the close of chapter two ultimately turn into conservatives. It is the predictable attitudinal trajectory and this built-in authoritarian drift describes the paranoid and socially conservative Tea Party to a tee. But I will write more on that shortly.

The point is that libertarianism does not perform as advertised. In fact, it often gets the opposite results.

Take Privatization, for example. Privatization mania ran rampant in the 1990s. Both Bill Clinton and Newt Gingrich hyped the myth that the market could do the government's work more cheaply and efficiently. "I've never seen anything like this," enthused the libertarian Reason Foundation's chairman Bob Poole at the time. "It's a contest to see who can privatize better and faster."[250]

And yet, about half of government's functions were *already* privatized by that time. Medicare was often trotted out as an example of government failure: It loses billions in fraud and waste annually. But that is because it is run by a vast network of private contractors and subcontractors which dilutes accountability and frustrates oversight. It is not administered by an "incompetent bureaucracy." Quite the opposite, it is run by this curious honor system called the market. Government signs the checks and then "gets out of the way," letting the Invisible Hand of Self-interest do the rest. The worst bureaucracy would be a huge improvement by comparison.

Likewise, the Department of Energy (DOE) pays 80 to 90 percent of its budget to contractors who oversee *themselves* because the agency is *that* understaffed.[251] This creates a pathetically obvious conflict of interest which the private contractors predictably take advantage of.

Take Rockwell International's Rocky Flats plant. We *paid* them to clean up their *own* toxic waste. Roll that around in your head for a moment. Simple common sense says they should swallow the cleanup cost because they made the mess themselves. Everyone else has to clean up their own messes. Kids learn this at home, but corporations don't.

Oh, but it gets much worse. Rockwell International then graded their own performance, and we paid them a *bonus* on the basis of their surprisingly glowing self-assessment, which had redefined failure as success.[252]

This is the fox guarding the hen house.

Privatization is not even cheaper – more often it is the opposite, costing taxpayers 25 to 50 percent *more* than if the government did the work itself.[253] Why? The reason is that government does stuff at cost, whereas the contractor wants to make a big dollop of profit on top of that.

And if the contractor hires subcontractors (as they nearly always do), the cost balloons even more. The dynamic is not difficult to explain: The more middlemen you add, the more the price goes up. That is why retail is always more expensive than wholesale. Who does not already know this?

The kicker is *all* these shocking examples come from one *Washington Monthly* article that ran in *1995!* It is old news. The jury is in: Privatization is a proven disaster that only wastes taxpayers' money. But it still has advocates today. They are either ludicrously delusional or corrupt as fuck.

Do libertarians approve this grotesque squandering of tax dollars? They do if they are the specific parasites that benefit from this open invitation to government corruption. But I have to ask why do *other* libertarians support them? Methinks "libertarian" propaganda is part of it.

Amazingly, this faulty policy still enjoys lots of political support. George W. Bush tried to privatize Social Security while he was president. Despite two disastrous wars, an imploded economy (thanks to regulators not regulating), and a botched response to Hurricane Katrina, he regards not passing Social Security privatization as his greatest failure.[254]

Speaking of Katrina, the Bush administration's bogus relief effort vividly illustrates what is wrong with privatization. The government cut checks to contractors, who paid themselves handsomely, and then farmed the work out to subcontractors who did the same. Repeat. The money got passed along until it disappeared so almost none of it got where it was supposed to go. The Invisible Hand of Self Interest pocketed it and then did not lift a finger to help anyone. It was theft and neglect together in one policy. This system does not perform as advertised – but it *does* perform as *designed*.

Despite this, privatization remains a cherished goal of both libertarians and Tea Party members today because they do not seem to grasp how the world actually works. This militant ignorance is not limited to the issue of privatization. Their heroic innovation narratives are another example.

In the 1990s, libertarians insisted that government could not innovate and accordingly clamored to privatize the Internet. They succeeded politically, but the problem with their underlying argument was that Uncle Sam had actually built the Internet in the first place.

In fact, almost every technological breakthrough of the last half century was the ultimate result of the Cold War spending in general, if not the Space Race in particular. If Ayn Rand's *Atlas Shrugged* were honestly brought up-to-date, Hank Reardon's revolutionary new alloy would have been developed in partnership with a state university and with funding from NASA or the Defense Department. You know, like how the Internet got built.

Libertarian notions of how the world works are fairly fanciful. Glenn Beck told his radio listeners that Fannie Mae and Freddie Mac failed "Because it is a hybrid between government and capitalism." He ended his explanation by claiming that "Capitalism put a man on the moon." This prompted Thomas Frank to point out that, "NASA circa 1969 was far more directly run by government than were Fannie Mae and Freddie Mac circa 2007. (It was also unionized.)"[255] Thomas Frank then pointed out the obvious fact that there was no profit motive to put a man on the moon.

Okay, I must mention one more amusing thing about the 2011 *Atlas Shrugged* movie. I noticed that one character in it marvels, "250 (mph)! – That's faster than any train has gone in this country." The key phrase is "in this country." America has lagged behind Europe and Japan in bullet trains since the *mid-1960s* and other, more socialist, countries *topped 250 mph long ago*. Japan's bullet trains broke 275 mph on conventional track back in 1996 and their magnetic levitation (Maglev) trains broke 361 mph in 2003. And France's TGV holds the current world record for conventional rail by reaching 357.2 in 2007 – just shy of the Maglev's 361.[256]

What is most pathetic about this is that the film is set in 2016(!) Apparently, American capitalism cannot achieve in (then) near-future *fiction* what much smaller countries have already achieved in historical *fact*. Who knew that Ayn Rand's heroic protagonist had such mediocre ambitions?

[Sidebar Edit: I first self-published this book in 2014. It is now 2019, so the "near-future" of 2016 has since passed. Suffice to say the film has not aged well. But again, their updating of the book was already sadly outdated in-utero. If only the producers had Googled "high speed trains" in 2011.]

Granted, Japan and France's high speed rail systems were built by a public/private partnership (Glenn Beck's recipe for certain failure). But we all know that government involvement was probably hands-on rather than the management model used at Rocky Flats. After all, conservatives and libertarians alike routinely criticize both countries for having too much government involvement in business.

Of course, it is odd for libertarians to say that government does not make anything when they are constantly trying to privatize things that government had made – and would not have gotten made otherwise. It is often said that government works best when people do not notice it, but the ironic upshot of this is that good government is vulnerable because people take it for granted and are oblivious to its enormous accomplishments.

This is true at every level. I am not only talking about Social Security or the national highway system, but your local public utility too. Until privatized, they provide cheap, dependable service. The next best thing is a heavily-regulated private one. But, one way or the other, the general public must have some leverage to avoid getting hosed. If they cannot take their business elsewhere, they can at least call city hall or exercise the power of the ballot if they are still not satisfied.

Invariably, deregulation means worse service at higher prices because monopolies do not function honestly or competently unless they are forced to. The public must somehow be able to punish utilities behaving badly.

For example, before Enron took over California's power grid, customers were not subject to artificial power shortages and resulting rolling black outs and price-gouging. Without competition, the market is not actually a market, but a corporate-controlled choke point.

But utilities do not practically lend themselves to competition. How would multiple water companies work? Would they all run separate pipes into your house?

In fact, most of this infrastructure would not even exist if government had not created it in the first place. How would water or sewer pipes even get laid in the ground without government involvement? They are part of the integrated systems of street construction and flood control. That metal thing you see by the sidewalk is called a drainage grate. It is nice to have drains when it rains. Many of our ancestors did not enjoy that luxury.

And, without municipal sewer systems, how would "Joe the Plumber" even have a job as a plumber? He would be digging wells and outhouses.

Infrastructure is not a natural byproduct of the market, but we often take it for granted because the sewer department does not have memorable, gratitude-inducing slogans like "We take poop out of your house."

Libertarians miss a lot of obvious things that you do not have to be an urban planner or sociologist to spot. Many of their central assumptions about human nature and society are just fundamentally flawed and subsequently many of their policies are detrimental to individual liberty.

Indeed, they almost seem designed to be.

Most libertarians believe three big fallacies, which they share with conservatives: First, they think that more equality always means less freedom. Second, they say state government is more freedom-friendly that the federal government and thus argue we should "devolve" power back to the states. And third, they assume that government becomes more oppressive as it takes on more responsibilities and thus social programs threaten our freedom. All three of these interlocking fallacies are pretty easily disproven.

Let's start with the fallacy that liberty and equality are always at odds. This was the whole focus of chapter three, so we can knock this fallacy out with a quick review. This zero-sum game is a false trade off because we have become increasingly free and equal – much to the chagrin of traditionalists like Robert Bork. Conservatives frequently feel that their rights are somehow diminished by recognizing others' rights. But rights are, in fact, universal and dependent on people recognizing that. As Thomas Paine explained, "He that would make his own liberty secure must guard even his enemy from oppression: for if he violates this duty, he establishes a precedent that will reach unto himself."[257]

Yes, some libertarians get this. But many of them are so invested in the rugged individualist image that they take an "everyman for himself" mindset. Certainly Ayn Rand encouraged this attitude. The Industrial Workers of the World's motto, "An Injury to One is an Injury to All," is too "collectivist" for them. But that is how freedom works: You give everyone a stake in it and then emphasize that fact. Each minority that is denied their freedom is another group that has no direct interest in defending it and this is how you whittle away everyone's liberty – by whittling away the solidarity that is essential to defending it.

Now let's tackle the second fallacy which claims that the states are more freedom-friendly than the federal government. The libertarian desire to "devolve" power from Washington to the state level is well known. "Devolve" was a major buzzword in New Gingrich's lexicon and the guiding idea behind breaking up Aid to Families with Dependent Children (AFDC) into block grants to the states in the libertarian-minded 1990s. The assumption was that, even with the best intentions, the federal government could not help but bungle, crush, corrupt, and oppress everything it touched. It was too distant from the needs of the people to do anything helpful so harm was the inevitable result. Like a bull in a china shop, the best thing it could possibly do was get the hell out. This was the dominant ideology of that decade and it remains powerful today.

And this was the interpretation which presumed innocent incompetence. Other interpretations ascribed deliberate evil. Timothy McVeigh's bombing of the Alfred P. Murrah building in Oklahoma City was only one symptom of that conspiracy theory-driven decade. Some believed that the Federal Emergency Management Agency (FEMA) – which later bungled Hurricane Katrina relief – was going to round us up and put us in concentration camps under the passing shadows of black helicopters. Fringe thinking was increasingly mainstreamed. "The X-Files" was a popular Fox show. The anti-government zeitgeist was undeniable. Freedom, conventional wisdom opined, was best left with the states because "Uncle Sam" was actually George Orwell's "Big Brother."

The 1990s were a bizarre libertarian rabbit hole.

But that decade's conventional wisdom flatly contradicted all available evidence. Historically, those wishing to limit liberty have always been most successful locally. This is why religious fundamentalists have focused on taking over school boards and targeting public libraries. Prohibition did not last nationally, but dry counties still exist today. "Community standards" can still be used to ban pornography. The Internet has made such ordinances less effective, but brick and mortar business are still impacted and they need the revenue. Porn is basically what keeps our few remaining book and video stores afloat. [Again, this book was finished in 2014.] Clearly, local government has a far greater propensity to interfere with our personal freedoms. Historically, prudery succeeds locally – but it fails nationally.

By contrast, federal efforts often benefit freedom. The U.S. Supreme Court decision Roe vs. Wade legalized abortion nationwide and it was federal intervention that ended segregation and Jim Crow laws throughout the South. This is hardly ancient history. Reproductive rights are currently under constant assault at the state level. Indeed, they surged with the rise of the Tea Party in 2010. Likewise, after the Roberts Court struck down a key provision of the landmark 1964 Voting Rights Act in 2013, Republican state legislators got busy trying to make it harder for blacks to vote. From slavery to today, states rights have always been a bulwark for local bullying. The main threat to freedom from the federal government is that they will let the states have their way with us.

So, why would any self-identified libertarian want to move the fight for freedom to such scattered and unfavorable terrain? Have they never heard of divide and conquer? After all, that is what they are an accomplice to, whether they are conscious of it or not.

This tendency toward local tyranny is not a side effect of our system. It is hardwired into human nature. As I had outlined back in chapter three, small groups often become homogeneous. Conformity and groupthink are more common and social mores are much easier to enforce.

Moreover, only so many people are going to share a particular trait or attitude. Once you start to turn away those who look or think different, your group starts to shrink. The Republican Party's contradictory policy of rallying the intolerant while talking about making their party a "big tent" illustrates this dynamic. Their vicious anti-immigrant rhetoric, for example, is not helping them win the Hispanic vote.

Simply put, uniformity and popularity are obviously at opposite ends of the spectrum and you have to pick a direction. You do not draw a large crowd by being purists, ideological or otherwise. In contrast to the notion that "smaller is better," it is often less tolerant. Of course, for conservatives, that is the point

– so they try to alter the political landscape accordingly by strengthening smaller units of government. "Devolving" power to the states invariably threatens individual liberty.

But in large groups, the snowball rolls in the opposite direction: More people means more diversity, and thus more liberty – if the system is democratic. As James Madison said, "Extend the sphere, and you take in a greater variety of parties and interests; you make it less probable that a majority of the whole will have a common motive to invade the rights of other citizens."[258]

Moreover, no one faction can dominate society because other factions can band together and resist. The more minorities, the more lightly society is governed because those in power have more groups to avoid offending. If a small group can swing a close election, there is greater incentive to respect everyone's rights. Authority accordingly becomes less cocky.

But this is not simply how our system was designed – this tendency is inherent to all large, and thus diverse, democratic groups. Madison had simply recognized and utilized this natural dynamic. Diversity is a feedback mechanism against the abuse of power. Those libertarians who dismiss diversity forget their Madison – and their own interests.

Some of them get this. For example, the preamble of the 2010 Libertarian Party's platform welcomes "the diversity that freedom brings."[259] Of course, James Madison would say that this goes both ways. If only the allegedly libertarian Tea Party were so observant and tolerant.

As a sidebar, I should probably mention that James Madison was actively advocating a stronger federal government over the previous Articles of Confederation. That is why he was called a *Federalist*. It makes sense when you stop and think about it. Therefore, the libertarian Federalist Society is just as misnamed as the libertarian Cato Institute.

And then there is the libertarian Benjamin Rush Society for medical school students. It is a strange name choice since Dr. Rush felt everyone must prioritize the common good. "Every man in a republic is public property."[260] Obviously, that is not the Benjamin Rush Society's motto. But let us pause to imagine Glenn Beck's likely reaction to that quote.[261]

Maybe libertarians should stop naming their organizations after 18th century groups and persons that the have never read.

This dynamic of diversity holds true in the courts as well as the electorate. Religious minorities have often joined forces to defend the separation of church and state. Contrary to the right's tired script that most church and state cases come from atheists, historically most have actually come from religious minorities like Jews and Jehovah's Witnesses.[262] Atheists became more vocal later on and U.S. Hindus and Muslims are now asserting their rights as well. Our religious liberty is defended by some unlikely coalitions.

Politics makes strange bedfellows. Consider the liberal Constitutional Accountability Center allying with the National Rifle Association or the ACLU allying with any number of conservatives – including Lt. Col. Oliver North. Our system was designed around such temporary alliances and diversity facilitates it. A large, diverse population means you have far more potential allies when your rights are threatened by the majority. Additionally, these temporary alliances that foster civic understanding also have the potential to become more durable.

And often that "majority" is actually only a plurality and/or not truly unified behind their leaders' plans. Again, during the Civil Rights struggle, blacks and Jews joined together along with other northerners and dissenting white southerners. Individuality and diversity demote both real and perceived majorities into mere pluralities. This explains Robert Bork's bemoaning how we have become more free and equal since the 1960s – and authoritarian bigots have thus felt oppressed ever since.

Size mattered because the whole nation got involved. Otherwise, protest is isolated and easily suppressed. Blacks did not happily accept a century of Jim Crow laws. They resisted as best they could in various ways, but they often lost because they needed outside allies. Again, change came once other Americans saw the situation as a national problem rather than a local one. This was James Madison's mechanics in action: The Civil Rights Movement had extended "the sphere." Indeed, it is very difficult to read that Madison quote today and not immediately think of this history.

Individuality and diversity are natural allies. Indeed, they naturally magnify each other. The more people think for themselves, the more diversity of opinion grows. This creates new subcultures and schools of thought which then advertise their existence. And accordingly seeing other people openly living differently reminds us that we have other options besides simply perpetuating how we were raised. Therefore, personal rebellion becomes more common.

In chapter three, I looked at the right's historic hostility to rock music. Rock and roll has always fostered a spirit of individuality and rebellion. Now how many subgenres of rock are there? There is almost no counting because even the subgenres have subgenres and they often cross-pollinate with each another. There is actually a subgenre called ska-billy – a ska twist on rockabilly or *vice versa*.

Paradoxical as it sounds, borrowing and copying are a large part of finding your own individual voice and it obviously helps to have more variety to choose from. Today, we live in a rich culture of enthusiastic sampling and thanks to this exponentially growing diversity Americans are now more individualistic than ever before. In the 60s and 70s, conservatives mocked non-conformists for conforming to the counter culture. But the counter culture was far more individualistic than the establishment it was rebelling from. And today's youth culture is certainly not monolithic now. The dominoes have dramatically fanned out in all directions.

The Internet gets an awful lot of credit for doing this, but it did so precisely by connecting people to *a larger, more diverse world.* Indeed, the Internet works a lot like America. It is a vast nation of immigrants with everyone bringing different ideas, customs, and flavors to the table. But long before the Internet, this dynamic could already be seen in big cities like New York. The Internet did not launch this process any more than the Baby Boomers invented sex or Gen-Xers invented irony. It is just how human societies work.

This bit about big cities brings us to my next point about liberty and population size – anonymity. The bigger the haystack, the freer the needle. The old medieval saying "City air makes men free" had referred to escaping serfs. But it still applies today, albeit for different reasons. People are freer in big cities than in small towns. As I said in an earlier chapter, most rural gays move to big cities not only to improve their potential dating pool but because cities are more free and tolerant. In the country, it is not just harder to get what you want, but harder to stay in the closet because everyone knows everything about everyone else. The big city's relative anonymity makes private life easier to achieve and living in the closet paradoxically less necessary.

The anonymity of a large, diverse population also supplements the secret ballot. Privacy protects liberty because it is harder to intimidate the electorate. The electorate, in turn, guards its privacy. Thus, freedom snowballs. Conservative scorn for your right to privacy is most obvious on the topic of abortion, but they despise the right to privacy in its entirety. Few of them respect the constitutional protection against unreasonable search and seizure. From the second Bush's administration's wiretaps to cops searching your car for pot, conservatives are very enthusiastic snoops. (And unfortunately, too many liberals reluctantly go along for fear of being called "too liberal.") Conservatives sense that the anonymity afforded by a large, diverse population tends to foster a culture that treasures its privacy, hence, once again, the right's preference for strengthening smaller units of government. It is a totally logical goal, given their proclivity for policing morality. But for libertarians, this preference makes no sense. It is a self-sabotaging strategy.

I mentioned a few folks back in chapter one who weighed in on this issue. Remember Pat Buchanan's argument that our big cities need "quasi-dictatorial rule"?[263] Or this Ann Coulter quote: "My libertarian friends are probably getting a little upset now but I think that's because they never appreciate the benefits of local fascism."?[264]

Unfortunately, a lot of libertarians are pretty okay with it, hence their senseless defense of states rights and moralistic local ordinances. Do not like the tyranny of your neighbors? Then *move*. That is the gist of their argument for "liberty."

But you should not have to move. This is a free country and you are entitled to do whatever does not harm another. I am of the opinion that personal freedom should prevail over local prudery. You would think this position would make me a libertarian, but the Libertarian Party curiously prefers local authorities.

This is not to say that there are not a few exceptions that prove the rule. Prostitution is legal only in Nevada and medical marijuana is not yet available everywhere. It had started in California, although other states are starting to follow suit. Indeed, since I first typed that sentence, other states had legalized recreational use. Events keep demanding revisions.

But to a great extent, these exceptions still illustrate the dynamic. After all, California is a very populous state and Nevada falls in its permissive cultural orbit. The Southwest as a whole is rapidly becoming more like the Bear Flag State as more Californians move there. Indeed, Las Vegas's economy is possible precisely because Californians and their wallets can easily get to it. Actual isolation would have different results. There could be no Las Vegas in the Himalayas.

In fact, the whole west coast has significantly liberalized its cannabis laws with Washington State legalizing it entirely. Yes, some more centrally located states have joined suit, with Colorado legalizing it entirely as well – but most of the change is on the west and northeast coasts. New England, New York, and New Jersey have kept pace with the Pacific states. When conservatives routinely bewail the "lack of values" they see on the east and west coasts, they are talking about the greater freedom enjoyed where the bulk of our country's population is concentrated. There is no denying that dynamic. Indeed, it is so evident that it feels redundant to even discuss it.

Of course, I am generalizing about *democratic* societies. Population density alone is obviously not enough. Otherwise, mainland China would be the freest place on earth. But when large groups *are* democratic, the dynamic set in motion benefits liberty, privacy, individuality, and diversity. These four words that end in Y all organically reinforce each other, which seriously irks conservatives.

Again, that is just how human groups work and James Madison had designed the Constitution to utilize this. And yet, many libertarians do not grasp this. If they did, they would not endorse devolving power to the states. California is fairly freedom-friendly, but Mississippi is not. The Supreme Court decision Roe v. Wade protects the personal freedom of women in Mississippi. It is a bit like the federal minimum wage law, except it is for your bodily autonomy instead of your paycheck. It builds a floor, but not a ceiling. States can give you *additional* protections just as they can pass an even higher minimum wage law. (Few do, which should tell you something.) But they cannot strip you of your baseline federal guarantees.

Of course, those opposed to individual liberty typically call this "tyranny." They see bullying in stopping bullying. How dare the United States government defend the rights of United States citizens? Over a century later, conservatives have not yet made peace with the Fourteenth Amendment. But I will talk more about this later. The point here is many conservatives and "libertarians" want to take away those baseline federal guarantees so they can control you through local authorities.

As a belated side bar, let me clarify that I do not use prostitutes. But as libertarians have accurately pointed out, most of the dangers and abuses associated with the job come from it being an unregulated underground economy with no safety mechanisms. It is hard to call a cop when your job is illegal. Likewise, many people went blind or died from drinking homemade hooch during Prohibition. But after alcohol was re-legalized, it became safe to drink again.

Here, libertarians are quite right. But, ironically, this is a libertarian argument in favor of government regulation. In Amsterdam, Holland, legal prostitution entails a certification process that includes disease screening and regular, mandatory health checkups. Yes, legalizing things often makes them safer, but it is the resulting regulation that does that – not "the magic of the market."

Except in time of war, the states are *far* more meddlesome than the feds, and this has always been the case. For better or worse, local government is literally in your backyard because they are figuratively in your backyard. Your state capitol is a lot closer to you than Washington, D.C. Thus, it is far easier for them to keep tabs on you and their actions affect you more directly. And, this dynamic is timeless. In the middle ages, local lords oppressed their peasants far more than any distant king. That is just the inherent geographical logistics of the situation.

It is the same way with the states. New data collection technology may change this, but historically local authority has always been more intimate and intrusive. Uncle Sam generally does not care what you do in your own bedroom. The exception is when "small government"-touting conservatives get elected. However, their efforts typically fail on the national stage for the reasons we have seen.

For example, President Ronald Reagan said "[G]overnment is not the solution to our problem: Government *is* the problem." Then, he appointed Attorney General Ed Meese who, in turn, launched his infamous Commission on Pornography. Its final report was so choked with anti-sex junk science that he became a national laughing stock. The political moment was immortalized in a memorable photo of Meese holding the hefty tome while standing in front of a bare-breasted statue of Lady Justice. Years later, George W. Bush's Attorney General, John Ashcroft, sought to prevent a repeat of this embarrassment. So he ordered the art deco statue's cold, aluminum fun bags draped, creating his own ridiculous visual.

Ed Meese's censorious crusade went nowhere in Washington. But we all know that it would have done well in many states and that the Supreme Court's "community standards" doctrine would have left freedom's advocates scant hope. Yet, according to libertarian dogma, the states are *inherently* more freedom-friendly. How is this possible when history almost always shows the opposite? Their predictive model is obviously pretty shoddy if it is usually wrong. I fault their fundamental assumptions.

This got me thinking about other libertarian claims about state government, such as the one that states are more "responsive" to the people. Intrusive yes, but *responsive?* How can that possibly be when most people pay even less attention to local politics than national politics? Apart from maybe their mayor or governor, most people cannot even name their local elected officials. Such political invisibility invites a lot shady activity. That is why state and local government is so often more dysfunctional, bankrupt (both fiscally and morally), and corrupt. Indeed, historically, corrupt "bosses" have often controlled local politics in many places and this phenomenon is both rural and urban.

For example, Boss Hogg on the 1980s TV show "The Dukes of Hazard" was based on a familiar rural archetype – a carryover from the old plantation aristocracy where a single family controlled a whole county. In many Country-Western songs and legends, the hero outlaw fights the local sheriff – rarely the feds. As friends of mine who know from bitter experience have told me, "You can find all the evil in the world in a small town."

But again, this is not just some "backwater" rural phenomenon. In the big cities you have pretty infamous examples like Boss Tweed's Tammany Hall political machine in New York City or the Daley Family in Chicago.

Former Illinois Governor Rod Blagojevich got into office posing as a reformer, but he subsequently proved to be cartoonishly corrupt. He is now in a federal penitentiary for trying to sell then President-elect Barack Obama's open Senate seat. Incidentally, Blagojevich is the *fourth* Illinois governor to get sent to the federal pen.

And then there is Louisiana politics, whose galloping corruption was only very recently[265] surpassed by Kentucky's.[266]

You can certainly find plenty of corruption at the federal level, but it gets so much worse as you look down the ladder. There is a familiar figure of speech that illustrates things: "You can't fight city hall." Well, I think you can, but a federal investigation often helps.

However, while such corruption can be found in urban areas as well, the fact of the matter remains that individual liberty is still much safer there. It is far harder to legislate morality where populations are more concentrated. As I wrote before, more diversity means more liberty. More eyes with different perspectives see more things, spot more problems, and disrupt uniformity and groupthink. It may slow down government action, but I thought libertarians wanted that. Am I wrong?

Again, as James Madison said, "The smaller the society, the fewer probably will be the distinct parties and interests composing it; the fewer the distinct parties and interests, the more frequently will a majority be found of the same party." No shit.

In time, this party naturally becomes complacent and corrupt because there is no serious political competition to keep them honest or incentivise even the pretense of honesty. With no real alternatives, voters give up hope. A lot of these jokers run unopposed. It is a pretty predictable result.

Of course, corporations love local corruption. As I wrote before, they already prefer state governments because they can play one off against another. The result is a "race to the bottom" in taxes, wages, working conditions, and environmental protections. It is the exact same way they play third world countries off against each other.

But the savings do not stop there. Oh no!

As also before noted, state senators are far cheaper than U.S. senators – you get a lot more bang for your campaign contribution buck.

And again, the fact that the public pays less attention to local politics means these antics largely go under the radar. Is this what libertarians mean when they say that state government works better? For whom?

Finally, I have to ask, "If government is inherently inimical to liberty, why would any libertarian *want* it to work better?" Conservatives and libertarians keep saying that your freedom is in danger every day the legislature is in session, so would not a little built-in inefficiency encumber the big bad Leviathan and act as another safety mechanism?

Yet again, size matters. Small groups are easier to control whereas large, diverse groups are like herding cats.

Given that most states are functionally one-party systems, while Washington is always stuck in gridlock, you would think that libertarians would logically prefer the latter. The national capitol shows James Madison's mechanics in action – or rather, *inaction*. So, what is not to love if you are an honest, freedom-loving libertarian and not some corporate shill?

So much for the second fallacy that the states are more freedom-friendly than the feds! Now, let us look at that last fallacy about the growth of government and how it supposedly results in snowballing encroachment.

Libertarians have a simplistic theory that governments threaten individual liberty more as they grow and their functions multiply. The rhetoric goes that government is always groping for power and controlling more areas of our lives. They say it is in government's inherent nature.

Much like the ancient discredited notion that the sun orbits the earth, it seems to make sense until you actually look into it. But a short survey of history shows that the opposite is true.

As I wrote in chapter one, before Franklin D. Roosevelt was elected you could not buy a beer or go on strike. But once FDR got in, Prohibition was out and the Wagner Act was in. The later guaranteed workers' right to organize in all fifty states. No longer did government kick your door in to see if you had any bathtub gin or were using your First Amendment right of association to organize a union in your workplace.

And, contrary to the concept that social programs and individual liberty are mutually exclusive, we got Social Security along with our booze back.

Also recall the 1914 Ludlow Massacre in which industrial tycoon J.D. Rockefeller used the Colorado National Guard as his own private army. Striking coal miners had to dig pits under their tents to protect their families from the Guard's machine gun fire and the U.S. Army actually had to intervene and disarm the Guard. The strike was to uphold the eight hour workday. It was a law that Colorado had passed, but Rockefeller decided he could ignore it since he controlled the governor.

I am sure that some regard the federal government's intervention as "tyranny;" but such incidents illustrate the threat of local dictatorship. Since the federal government has grown in size, the corrupt banana republic antics of state governments do not become so bloody anymore.

You might scoff, "That cannot happen now!" But if not, why not? What changed and who changed it? Public opinion is often insufficient to deter corporate malfeasance, so what mechanism gives the profit motive pause?

Once government becomes small enough to fit in big business's back pocket, it becomes a corporate pocketknife. And they use it. Individual liberty then gets whittled away because both social and economic conservatives want to control the public, albeit for different reasons – capitalists want a docile workforce whereas moralists want veto power over everyone's appetites. By sharp contrast, democratic governments tend to pick on those their own size, once they get big enough. They often forget to bother individual people once they have bigger fish to fry. Our history vividly illustrates it.

And examples are hardly limited to our history.

Remember Holland, where pot and prostitution are both legal? They also enjoy cradle-to-grave social services. (And, despite the active imaginations of certain Clinton Administration Drug Czars, the Dutch also suffer far less violent crime.)[267] Holland is a positive caricature of Western Europe as a whole in that regard because Europeans enjoy more social programs, yet it is far harder to legislate morality there. This is why Europe holds such horrors for conservatives. Heaven forbid everyone should have three day weekends every week and month-long vacations every year, as they do in Germany. For conservatives, this is the very definition of laziness and slavery – which strikes me as a pretty paradoxical combination. But why do so-called libertarians agree? The world rarely works the way libertarians claim – in fact, it's often the opposite.

For example, one of the countries that both libertarians and conservatives routinely tout as "freer" than ours is Singapore. As *Asia Times* wryly noted back in 2003, "[E]ach year the Cato Institute, a US-based conservative think-tank, and 50 other libertarian organizations rate Hong Kong and Singapore the two freest economies in the world. Like Groundhog Day, this has just recurred."[268] And, sure enough, the executive summary for the 2018 index, the latest available, reads. "Hong Kong and Singapore, as usual, occupy the top two positions."[269] And, of course, the Heritage Foundation routinely agrees.[270]

Singapore? Seriously? Interesting choice.

You might recall that that was where an American teenager was brutally caned for spray painting graffiti in the 1990s. While it certainly is true that corporations can pretty much do as they please with nearly negligible regulation, individual behavior is very strictly policed. Selling cigarettes and chewing gum is strictly regulated – yes, *chewing gum*. No, this is not an urban legend.[271] The 1992 ban was tweaked in 2004 to allow "medicinal gums" to quit smoking. But to buy a pack, you must present your name and ID card number. Pharmacists who fail to card you face a possible two year jail term and a $2,940 fine.[272] Talk about a "nanny state." Also, the penalty for possessing over 500 *grams* of marijuana in Singapore is death.

In Singapore, film and television are routinely censored, home satellite TV antennae are outlawed, and certain books, magazines, and popular songs are banned.[273] Granted, for a society with an *even greater* wealth gap than the United States, they suffer surprisingly little crime. But that is one of the few perks of living in a police state.

I suppose that sounds like loaded language. Others are more delicate. The Economist Intelligence Unit, a research group tied with the libertarian-leaning *Economist* magazine, had rated Singapore as a "hybrid regime."[274] That category falls between "flawed democracies," such as Estonia and Mexico, and "authoritarian regimes," such as Cuba and China. For additional comparison, Russia is yet another "hybrid regime."

Yes, the survey ranked democracy rather than personal freedom. But the two factors frequently coincide. They ranked pot-smoking Holland as the third most democratic just after two sexually-liberated Scandinavian nations, Sweden and Iceland. Holland was followed by Norway, Denmark, and Finland. These are all famously permissive societies.

Some libertarians think they can massage away this conspicuous incongruity by clarifying that Singapore is "*economically* freer" than the United States. They have become much more careful about including this qualification in recent years. But there are two huge problems with this dubious fallback position.

First, Singapore is not actually economically freer either. Singapore and Hong Kong – the other place Cato ranks at the top – are not actually free markets because competition is nearly nonexistent.

For example, in Hong Kong, a cartel of two families controls most of the economy and they do not compete with each other. This monopoly results in Hong Kong's citizens paying the highest prices in Asia.[275] I do not think that is a model we want to copy. It certainly is not a fact that libertarians widely trumpet. And since money is power, this cartel predictably controls the government as well as the economy.

I am starting to see why both Cato and Heritage rate Hong Kong so highly.

As for Singapore, the *Asia Times* reported:

Singapore is a different case. Its shops and its groceries are a good deal freer. But Singapore was not built by competition. Its industrial base was, and to a great extent still is, run by the Singaporean government. The government either wholly or largely owns six of the island republic's top 10 listed companies. They include Singapore Telecom, Singapore Airlines, DBS Group

Holdings, ST Engineering and Chartered Semiconductor. A special case in point is Singapore Press Holdings, which owns Singapore's media – the Straits Times and the pilot fish that surround it. While the editors and reporters at the Strait Times take umbrage at being described as government poodles, in fact the papers do not print anything that the government does not want printed, a fact that the Cato Institute and its 50 libertarian colleagues apparently do not find important enough to include in the factors that make up a free economy.[276]

So, why does the Cato Institute rate these two tiny island nations as "economically freer" than America *every* year? They do so because there is almost no government regulation.

But given the incredibly incestuous nature of these two nations' business and governmental elites, any regulation would be putting on a laughably phony dog and pony show. So, adding the word "economic" to "freer" does not make the Cato Institute's perennial claim any less ridiculous. They want corporate hegemony, not individual liberty.

The second problem with their fallback position is many libertarians passionately believe that economic freedom is the foundation for all other freedoms. That is also a basic tenet of corporate globalization: Give corporations *carte blanche* and all other freedoms, both individual and civil, will organically follow.

But obviously, this is not the case in Singapore, Hong Kong, China, or anywhere else, for that matter. Contrary to their property rights propaganda, freedom is not the natural byproduct of commerce. In fact, as Benjamin R. Barber soberly noted in *Jihad vs. McWorld*, "Democracies prefer markets but markets do not prefer democracies."[277]

After decades of trade with the U.S., China's position towards its people basically remains "Shut up and make stuff." In practice, "free trade" often means slave labor. Conservatives and libertarians alike routinely dismiss the importance of democracy, but I strongly suspect that democracy would bring China more freedom than sweatshops have. But to hear free traders tell it, China is only one more sneaker factory away from freedom.

So, all three fallacies have been utterly debunked:

First, liberty and equality are not locked in some zero-sum game. They are instead inherently interdependent.

Second, the feds are far more freedom-friendly than the states. The names Jim Crow and Roe vs. Wade are stark reminders of that.

And third, government involvement in the market does not inherently threaten individual liberty either. We repealed national prohibition at the same time we voted for the New Deal. And, internationally, we can contrast permissive social democratic Holland with strict capitalist Singapore.

We literally have a world of control groups to test these libertarian theories and the results are in.

Taken together, a nagging pattern emerges. What is bothersome is not just that the world does not work the way that libertarians claim or that their policies have proven to be consistently ill-suited to promote human freedom both at home and abroad. It is that these things are obvious to anyone who bothers to think about them for more than a moment. So, how do you get a durable political movement out of that?

It is tempting to think that its leaders actually know better and are running a scam. Of course, there is no leaked smoking gun memo that I know of and most of its leaders seem to be true believers.

But it certainly is a very top-down enterprise. In fact, it is odd to call it a "movement" when it had for so long consisted of only a few Koch family-funded think tanks and very little else. As one former think tank employee Bruce Bartlett admitted, "The problem with the whole libertarian movement is that it's been all chiefs and no Indians. There haven't been any actual people, like voters, who give a crap about it. So the problem for the Kochs has been trying to create a movement."[278]

Fred Koch had founded the Cato Institute in 1974. His sons inherited control, but they also founded their own organization: FreedomWorks (yes, it is spelled without the space in between) in 2004. Through that group, they funded the Tea Party in 2009 and finally got their movement.

But it seems they created a problem to solve a problem because the Tea Party's temperament is anything but libertarian. Although organized under the banner of fiscal conservatism, they could not camouflage their social conservatism for very long.

The 2010 biennial American Values Survey conducted by the Public Religion Research Institute discovered that fifty seven percent of them identify as members of the "Christian conservative movement."[279] The study flatly said that Tea Party members were "not libertarians on social issues."

For example, "Nearly two-thirds (63%) say abortion should be illegal in all or most cases, and less than 1-in-5 (18%) support allowing gay and lesbian couples to marry." You have to wonder how they would have answered if their leaders were not actively trying to downplay social issues.

The Tea Party does not like immigrants either. In contrast to the Libertarian Party's longstanding open borders advocacy, many Tea Party candidates want to build an electric fence along the Mexico border and/or patrol it with armed, remote-controlled drones.[280] Of course, this later became President Donald Trump's signature issue.

At first blush, this sounds like the familiar story about shedding stodgy respectability to win: The father's venerable enterprise being updated and perhaps cheapened for a new generation by his sons. But it is not quite.

Granted, that is an absolutely understandable assumption. The Cato Institute and the Tea Party seem pretty dissimilar. It is as incongruous as the notion of Hunter S. Thompson joining the Harper Valley PTA.[281]

I mean, just think about it: H.L. Mencken's ideological descendants have actually embraced what he had always called the "booboisie." This was the man who once wrote, "Perhaps the most revolting character that the United States ever produced was the Christian businessman." He kind of sounds like that cranky John Adams with his talk of "brutes" and "Yahoos," except that Mencken preferred words like "poltroons" and "pecksniffs." But "Christian businessmen" define the Tea Party to a T.

Yet the Tea Party is actually a resurgent strain of libertarianism that has existed in slightly different forms for many decades. Like some defeated disease, it is making comebacks. In the introduction, I called it "warmed-over Goldwaterism," but it goes back further than that. It traces its origin back to Ayn Rand's Manhattan inner circle and the John Birch Society. It is the story of libertarianism's built-in authoritarian drift.

It is easy to think that today's libertarianism has strayed from more noble origins. And to some extent it has dramatically deteriorated. But that is also part of a larger phenomenon. As I noted in the first chapter, a 2011 quadrennial Pew Research Center study had discovered that, "The long-standing divide between economic, pro-business conservatives and social conservatives has blurred."[282] In 1984, campaign strategist Lee Atwater had warned Ronald Reagan that "Populists have always been liberal on economics" and that without the Culture War to distract them, they had "no compelling reason to vote Republican."[283] But, since then, social conservatives have been reading Ayn Rand (while ignoring her atheism, of course) and economic conservatives have found religion.

Nowhere is this blurring more visible than the Libertarian Party's morphed position on abortion. Ayn Rand was staunchly pro-choice. "Abortion is a moral right – which should be left to the sole discretion of the woman involved." She reasoned, "An embryo *has no rights*. Rights do not pertain to a *potential*, only to an *actual* being."(emphasis original)[284] Her words could not possibly speak clearer.

This issue was once so central to libertarian thought that, in the early 1980s, they printed tee-shirts with the image of a pistol, a pot leaf, and a woman symbol with the slogan "Libertarians are pro-choice on everything."

Well, they are no longer pro-choice on abortion. Today, the Libertarian Party regularly fields anti-abortion candidates for president. Indeed, they began back in 1988 with Ron Paul.

Naturally, they reconcile this with their rhetoric of liberty by saying that your freedom should be left to the states – not, as Ayn Rand put it, the "sole discretion of the woman involved." And if you do not like it, sell your house and move to another state. Seriously, that is their answer. As one anti-Ron Paul graphic I saw quipped, "Government so small it fits in your uterus."

Today, the libertarian establishment would fail its own litmus test on social issues. And, for most reasonable people, its liberal stance on those issues was the most attractive thing about it. The draw was that they out-liberal-ed liberals on issues like the Drug War.

Alas, its authoritarian drift began at the beginning because its contradictions are inherent. Anyone familiar with the history of libertarianism could have seen this coming.

Consider two events in 1958 – the founding of the John Birch Society and Murray Rothbard's breaking with Ayn Rand.

In this book's introduction, I had mentioned that John Birch Society founder Robert Welch had called President Dwight Eisenhower a "Communist dupe" in the late 1950s. Another founding member of the Society was aforementioned Koch brothers father Fred Koch. The wealthy oilman was every bit as inflammatory as Robert Welch was and their conspiracy theory peddling predated Glenn Beck's and Alex Jones' by over a half century. As an article in *The New Yorker* later explained:

In 1958, Fred Koch became one of the original members of the John Birch Society, the arch-conservative group known, in part, for a highly skeptical view of governance and for spreading fears of a Communist takeover. Members considered President Dwight D. Eisenhower to be a Communist agent. In a self-published broadside, Koch claimed that "the Communists have infiltrated both the Democrat and Republican Parties." He wrote admiringly of Benito Mussolini's suppression of Communists in Italy, and disparagingly of the American civil-rights movement. "The colored man looms large in the Communist plan to take over America," he warned. Welfare was a secret plot to attract rural blacks to cities, where they would foment "a vicious race war." In a 1963 speech that prefigures the Tea Party's talk of a secret socialist plot, Koch predicted that Communists would "infiltrate the highest offices of government in the U.S. until the President is a Communist, unknown to the rest of us."[285]

The other 1958 event was Murray Rothbard breaking with Ayn Rand because she ran her "Objectivist" inner circle like a cult. It was almost Maoist in its totalitarian orthodoxy, so she made a rather problematic prophetess for personal freedom.

Unfortunately, Murray's thinking did not evolve much as a result of the break. Much like a dry drunk, the recovering Objectivist had lost his fundamentalist religion, but not the authoritarian black-and-white thinking that is typically associated with it. So, he then founded his own, similar religion. People are, after all, creatures of habit.

Murray Rothbard's cult-like thinking can be seen in Robert Anton Wilson's book *Natural Law or "Don't Put a Rubber on your Willie."* Rothbard had argued that skeptics of his natural law theory had a "duty" to "shut up" and take his word on faith. He praised clinging to "deep beliefs." This prompted Wilson to opine that Rothbard's group was "setting up shop as priests" but "want us to consider them philosophers."[286]

It was some philosophy. Murray Rothbard argued that parents should not be legally bound to feed and clothe their own children. Yet the self-described "anarcho-capitalist" had no problem with the police torturing suspects into confessions. Oddly, that did not meet the late economist's otherwise vastly expansive definition of state tyranny.

In 1989, Murray Rothbard and one Lew Rockwell launched "paleolibertarianism" to compliment Pat Buchanan's "paleoconservatism." They were well-positioned for the *zeitgeist* of the coming 1990s. It was the decade of hate radio, the militia movement, and privatization mania in both parties. Their prospects looked quite promising.

Bill Clinton's centrist neoliberal "New Democrats" were also ascendant in that era, and both subgroups advocated pandering to "values voters." Recall Bill Clinton endorsing the V-Chip or Joe Lieberman simply being Joe Lieberman. In sum, both influential subgroups urged becoming more Republican. To qualify Bruce Bartlett's assessment, long before they spawned the Tea Party, authoritarian "libertarians" were defining debates even without a movement or significantly visible voters behind them.

For neoliberals and paleolibertarians alike, imitating Republicans included co-opting the Southern Strategy. For the former, this meant subtle triangulations like Bill Clinton's infamously cynical Sister Souljah moment.[287] For the later, it meant literature that read like Willie Horton ads.

As the libertarian magazine *Reason* noted, "prominent libertarian theorist Murray Rothbard championed an open strategy of exploiting racial and class resentment to build a coalition with populist 'paleoconservatives.'"[288] Thus, Murray Rothbard was libertarianism's Lee Atwater, just without the subtly. Rothbard did not bother to speak in code.

Reason magazine is not fond of the paleos and posits that Lew Rockwell was the probable author of then Congressman Ron Paul's racist newsletters. They also noted that Paul's congressional campaign had bought their fundraising mailing list from the now defunct anti-Semitic conspiracy newsletter *The Spotlight*.[289] Although it should also be noted that *Reason* gave Holocaust deniers a platform in the 1970s.[290]

These unsavory associations between "edgy" libertarians and racist authoritarians remain a chronic problem. They are not irrelevant artifacts of the past. At the Daily Beast, conservative writer Matt Lewis noted what he called the "libertarian to alt-right pipeline" – while minimizing the conservative pipe segments in it, of course.[291]

In short, paleolibertarians are only paleoconservatives who are okay with pot. And paleoconservatives are only conservatives who think that the GOP is "too liberal." They are still angry that the party has avoided overt anti-Semitism since William F. Buckley told them to tone it down.[292]

Thus, Glenn Beck's and Alex Jones' audiences are not much different from Pat Buchanan's. And, unsurprisingly, Rothbard had enthusiastically supported Buchanan's 1992 presidential bid, touting, "With Pat Buchanan as our leader, we shall break the clock of social democracy."[293] Rothbard had also praised Klansman David Duke.[294]

The two threads that began in 1958 cumulated in the Tea Party. But they did not mutate much over that half century and they were never actually incompatible with one another at any point in time. The John Birch Society and the Pat Buchanan crowd run in the same racist, conspiracy theory-spinning circles. They attract the same type.

However, there is also a third thread in this story. But this one enters the narrative six years later in 1964. To Fred Koch's and Murray Rothbard's ignominious contributions to authoritarian libertarianism, we must add Barry Goldwater's as well. He mainstreamed extremism and paved the way for Ronald Reagan, George W. Bush, and ultimately Donald Trump.

In 1964, President Lyndon Johnson signed the Civil Rights Act and, according to lore, turned to an aide and said, "We have lost the South for a generation." It was a particularly grim prediction in an election year.

And, sure enough, that was the year that the two major political parties started to switch regional bases. Southerners began defecting to the previously despised Republican Party which they ultimately took over.

But at the time of the vote, Republicans still had a civil rights record they could be proud of – 80% of House Republicans and 82% of Senate Republicans had voted for the bill that Johnson signed.[295] By contrast, Democratic support was weighed down by its Southern wing.

Of course, it was not the bill alone that sealed the deal, but the GOP follow-up. Pat Buchanan's infamous "Southern Strategy" is often cited with first exploiting race, but it actually began with Barry Goldwater's 1964 presidential campaign. Goldwater was one of the few Republicans who had voted against the Civil Rights Act and he capitalized on that. Former president Dwight Eisenhower thought that Goldwater was playing with fire. He said if Republicans "begin to count on the 'white backlash,' we will have a big civil war."[296] But Goldwater was undeterred.

At the Republican National Convention in San Francisco, the Goldwater camp sidelined black delegates and brutally abused those they could not keep out. As the *Washington Monthly* later recalled, Goldwater strategists had shrunk the number of black delegates to 14 of 1,308 – a ratio of 1:100. It was then the fewest ever to be certified to any Republican convention.[297]

And to add insult to injury, the caucus of Southern Republicans named its hotel headquarters "Fort Sumter." Blacks were driven out of the party that they had loyally supported since the U.S. Civil War:

At the Cow Palace, the rolling invective that startled television viewers fell personally upon this tiny remnant. The Cleveland Call and Post reported that George Fleming of New Jersey ran from the hall in tears, saying Negro delegates "had been shoved, pushed, spat on, and cursed with a liberal sprinkling of racial epithets." George Young, labor secretary of Pennsylvania, complained that Goldwater delegates harassed him to the point of setting his suit jacket on fire with a cigarette. Baseball legend Jackie Robinson summarized his "unbelievable hours" as an observer on the convention floor: "I now believe I know how it felt to be a Jew in Hitler's Germany."

This predated Trump's rise to the presidency by quiet some time.

Just as the Tea Party had driven most moderates out of the Republican Party in 2010, Barry Goldwater's followers took over in 1964. The party's establishment tried their best to resist, but they could not stop Goldwater's highly-motivated machine. The convention floor roiled with rancor against the "liberal media" and "Eastern elites." The horrified electorate took note and delivered Goldwater a crushing defeat in November.

Later, in the 1980s, conservatives accused Goldwater of turning liberal because he opposed the growing power of the religious right. He had contrasted his libertarian "Old Conservatism" with Ronald Reagan's Evangelical-linked "New Conservatism." In the 1990s, he had defended the

Clintons and endorsed gay rights, sealing conservative opinion against him until he died. But Goldwater insisted that he had not changed.

Of course, Barry Goldwater had changed at least *some* since his 1964 campaign. For one thing, he later said he regretted his vote against the 1964 Civil Rights Act. That is a pretty significant change considering it was not just one Senate vote but the heart of his presidential bid.

But even if we assume the best intentions, then his political life becomes another example of libertarian efforts backfiring and getting the opposite results. As I mentioned earlier, his failed 1964 campaign had built the modern conservative movement and thus paved the way for Reagan's 1980 win. Goldwater had tried to move his party's regional base from East to West, but it instead shifted from North to South. The Arizona Senator had created a monster that in-turn turned on him.[298] But if he had become more libertarian before he died, libertarians have become more authoritarian in the meantime.

Arguing that that the Tea Party movement is libertarian in character is absurd. Are Sarah Palin, Christine O'Donnell, Michele Bachman (R-MN), and Jim DeMint (R-SC) libertarians? Not on a single social issue. But their economic rhetoric is very libertarian and the libertarian establishment is happy to play along – the Libertarian Party's Kafkaesque metamorphosis on the issue of abortion shows that. And Cato Institute fellow Penn Jillette appears on Glenn Beck's show to make nice quite a bit.

Observers often wonder how the libertarian establishment can safely harness this paranoid, authoritarian movement. No doubt Barry Goldwater's failed efforts are at the back of their minds. And if the GOP cannot control the Tea Party, what makes libertarians think they can do any better with this reactionary constituency?

Libertarians are getting taken for a ride. "Devolving" power to the states benefits big business, but it puts individual liberty at greater risk. And those who truly love freedom should never accept such a tradeoff.

Again, their ideology seems deliberately written to frustrate freedom in every imaginable fashion.

Consider their self-sabotaging hostility toward the Fourteenth Amendment. States rights fetishists despise this amendment because it gave freed slaves their civil rights and clarified that the states cannot deny Americans their rights. Thus, states rights fetishists consider it a tyrannical vehicle for federal interference. But without it state legislatures could ignore the U.S. Constitution at will by simply insisting that its protections only curb *federal* abuses of power – not abuses committed by the *states* or local government of *any* sort.

Needless to say, this would strip an important layer of protection off of individual liberty. Of course, the Tea Party is totally okay with that. They think that liberty is like lingerie – less is more.

But do you remember *McDonald v Chicago*, the Supreme Court decision that I began this chapter with? It was the one in which the court struck down Chicago's thirty-year ban on handguns. It was a great victory for the Second Amendment. But without the Fourteenth Amendment the Second would be irrelevant – it would not apply because *the city's* ban was not federal law.

Gun rights advocates should learn on which side their constitutional bread is buttered. Or would they prefer the Supreme Court to take the same "community standards" approach employed against pornography?

Somehow, I doubt it.

Yet Senator Rand Paul(R) and the Tea Party seek to repeal the Fourteenth Amendment because they fear that "anchor babies" might be giving undocumented immigrants citizenship. Of course, they also have other reasons, but this is the one they give.

I do not imagine they will triumph, but it is a window into how they think. If not covert bigots, they are at least the stupidest of purists who not only ignore history but also the likely legal ripple effects of their proposals. Sincere libertarians who truly want to liberate individuals in the real world should seriously rethink their irrational infatuation with states rights.

But that is just one area in which libertarian policy is counterproductive. In 1886, the Supreme Court had twisted the Fourteen Amendment to make corporations "immortal" persons, while totally ignoring why it was originally written. Many of my objections to libertarianism would evaporate if libertarians simply agreed that the egregious legal fiction of corporate personhood should be overturned. This would be consistent for them. After all, libertarians supposedly oppose collectives, and what is a corporation but a collective posing as an individual person? But instead they celebrate what they should condemn, and their choice is telling.

Admittedly, there was that brief and surreal moment when Ron Paul and Ralph Nader stood together in front of the cameras to condemn "corporatism." It coincided with that brief flirtation between the Tea Party and the Occupy Wall Street movements that lasted an instant most tried to forget about the morning after. But no other significant libertarians that I know of have followed suit. And that is because the Tea Party's absurd anti-corporate talk is just as empty as their loudly-trumpeted love of liberty.

Even more of my objections would vanish if libertarians read some James Madison on a plane to Amsterdam, Holland. Once there, they could sit back in a café, legally smoke a joint in public, and see how much freedom so-called "nanny states" actually have – a lot more than America has.

At some point, you have to decide what kind of libertarian you are. Do you want America to be more like Amsterdam or more like Singapore?

Point of interest: The Cato Institute has chosen Singapore for you. They hear freedom ring in the words, "Spit out that gum and put your hands on the hood." Most conservatives do.

6: Three Different Libertarians
Contrast & Compare

I met my first real life, self-identified libertarian in the late 1980s while cutting across campus early one sunny Sunday morning. Naturally, campus was pretty much empty.

She was a late middle-aged woman with a small child harnessed on a leash and playing in the dirt. (There is a metaphor there, if you want it.) She was passing out pamphlets and photocopied newspaper articles about police brutality. Her favorite phrase was "Military police state." I listened sympathetically and then finally asked if she favored the civilian review board that local civil rights activists were advocating.

"Oh, NO!" she exclaimed. "We don't want more government!"

As a result, I could not really fathom what she was actually advocating other than becoming a libertarian. Nor could I grasp how she thought things were supposed to work. She did not suggest eliminating the police department, but she did not want any civilian check on it either. Did she think that joining the party would magically make any abuse of power impossible? It was as if she imagined that you could reform a "military police state" by reducing government to nothing but the military and the police.

The checks and balances we had learned about in middle school civics classes seemed totally outside her mental framework of things. She had this fantasy that imperfect human institutions would work honestly and honorably if we only removed their safety mechanisms. Do not get me wrong: I think our society's safety measures are woefully weak and need strengthening – but she thought they needed eliminating.

This is not how the founders thought about things. On the contrary, they were acutely aware of humanity's capacity to crash systems, so they installed political seat belts and air bags. But the thought of such Nader-like bureaucratic oversight totally horrified her.

I am not saying that all libertarians are like this. On the contrary, I wrote this chapter to show their diversity. I recognize that the staff of *Reason* magazine is quite different from the paleolibertarian ranks of the Tea Party. But there are some broad commonalities, so I have written this chapter to compare and contrast. Different people identify as libertarians for different reasons. Many are single-issue voters who are primarily focused on, say, guns or pot. Libertarian leaders are trying to unite them, but this is proving difficult. As Penn Jillette said on one of his appearances on Glenn Beck's show:

[I]f you can convince the gun nuts that the potheads are okay and the potheads that the gun nuts are okay – everybody is a libertarian. I think just push for freedom right across the board.

But it is not as simple as that. You also have to persuade both groups that it is okay to let corporations poison their air, land, and drinking water. If that gun owner is also a farmer whose animals are dying from nearby hydraulic fracking, it could be a pretty tough sell.

Even among libertarian leaders, you have an interesting spectrum of perspectives. I will look at three significantly different libertarians: Ayn Rand, Penn Jillette, and Senator Rand Paul (R-KY). My goal is to show how their contradictory ideology often sabotages their stated aims. These three people exemplify stark ideological shifts in the libertarian movement over the years. Taken chronologically, they show what has changed. But they also show what has *not* changed. They illustrate how, consciously or not, libertarianism has always fostered freedom-hostile policies.

Naturally, I have to start with Ayn Rand, both chronologically and ideologically since she inspired the later two. "Ayn Rand" was the pen name of Russian *émigré* Alisa Zinovyevna Rosenbaum. When the Russian Revolution erupted, her parents sent her to the United States for safety. Eventually, she founded her libertarian philosophy of "Objectivism."

Rand infused capitalism with romantic, revolutionary fervor. She stole communist rhetoric and turned it upside down: In her inverted worldview, wealthy industrialists were "producers" and their workers were the "parasites."

Of course, communists did not originate the rhetoric that she stole. From Cato and Adam Smith forward, economic thinkers stressed that labor rather than capital was what created wealth. But I digress.

Today, Ayn Rand's reverse dichotomy is very compelling to the Tea Party. They have strip-mined our history for working class symbols to glorify The Man. Glenn Beck frequently turns New Deal iconography on its ear, as if Aaron Copland's "Fanfare for the Common Man" were written to celebrate robber barons like George Pullman or Henry Clay Frick.

But Ayn Rand's producer/parasite dichotomy could be awkward as well as absurd. Amusingly, it was revealed that she applied for Social Security and Medicaid in 1974.[299] Her Objectivist acolytes interestingly insist that this was not hypocrisy because she had paid into the system.

Oh? So payment negates hypocrisy? By that logic, I guess the Reverend Ted Haggard is off the hook for that whole six-year gay gigolo thing.

Of course, Ayn Rand's fans say that she was *forced* to pay taxes, but that argument changes nothing: Our taxes also subsidize the cattle and dairy industries, but that does not mean that a vegan can honestly chow down on a cheeseburger, does it? Not if it is made with real meat and real dairy. Payment – whether it is full or partial, voluntary or compulsory – is totally irrelevant. What matters is you are enjoying something you think nobody should ever do or have access to. That is the very *definition* of hypocrisy.

Oh, you do not think partial payment should count?

Okay, here is another metaphor for you:

Say a prohibitionist books an ocean cruise and the travel agent did not tell him that a free bar is built into the ticket price. Perhaps this was a recent change. In any case, the prohibitionist did not agree to it. Then he learns that all the *other* passengers bought the same travel package and they are getting hammered. To his horror, he realizes that he is subsidizing their drinking because *everyone* is subsiding *everyone else's* drinking!

This business practice attracts passengers and improves the cruise line's price point for booze because it is more efficient to buy in bulk. (Every business major knows that.) Thus, the liquor is already paid for in full, albeit at a great rate. Pooling resources often lowers costs.

Does this mean that the prohibitionist can therefore toss back some shots because he has already paid for them? Not without being a huge hypocrite.

The payment defense is also awfully shoddy in other ways.

Ayn Rand applied for Medicaid only eleven years after it was created and she had very expensive lung cancer. Thus, to say that she took out more than she put in would be a gargantuan understatement.

I actually have no problem with this. Nobody else in her generation had paid much into the then new system either, and the program was meant to help the elderly immediately. No humane human can begrudge that!

But accordingly, Ayn Rand's fans cannot honestly argue that she was only taking back what was hers. Other people had subsidized her care to make up the difference. There is no denying that.

Indeed, others would have been subsidizing her care even if she had been paying into the system her whole working life because employers are compelled to contribute too. Plus, the currently young and healthy subsidize the currently old and sick. This spreads the burden thin, making it relatively painless.

This is a significant sticking point. Libertarians often argue that entitlement programs like Social Security and Medicaid are "theft." They insist that investing in this theft does not legitimize it. It is still "robbing Peter to pay Paul" (except that we will all be Paul someday, Peter included). Thus, their "she paid in" defense is a ridiculously conspicuous reversal. If it is "theft," then she is guilty of "theft" herself. But if paying-in makes it okay, then nobody else is "stealing" either because they are also paying-in.

But either way, Ayn Rand was definitely a hypocrite for holding others to a different yardstick. Whether it is theft or not, she is still a hypocrite for calling others "thieves" because she did the very same thing.

Objectivists have to choose between their idol and their ideology. Thus, they must jettison their theft rhetoric in order to defend her. And by refusing to choose, they cast dark clouds of doubt over both.

But more important than Ayn Rand's obvious hypocrisy is the fact that she *needed* such programs. Without them, this wealthy, world-famous novelist could not pay her medical bills.

Now, for a moment, forget everything this "moral philosopher" said about government programs. Ignore her rhetoric of "theft" and "parasites" and pretend she was a different celebrity, perhaps an apolitical one.

Having done that, ponder this question: If she could not afford medical treatment, how could most people? She knew *lots* of rich people – and flattered them generally, if not specifically. Most other people are not so well-connected. They do not have that obvious advantage.

And if Ayn Rand was too proud or ashamed to ask her friends for help, she was not too proud or ashamed to ask Uncle Sam. And if these things are valid excuses for her, are not discretion and patient confidentiality valid for everyone else as well? Is that not another advantage to the program?

Such programs are unquestionably necessary. And if they were good for Ayn Rand, they are good for everybody else too. Beyond hypocrisy, her philosophy simply does not work. The fact that it did not even work for *her,* in her privileged position, should only show how totally broken it is. And that important fact should eclipse any trivial individual embarrassment.

Speaking of "paying Paul," let us briefly skip ahead for a moment. About half of Senator Rand Paul's (R-KY) medical practice income came from Medicaid payments, a program that he blasts as "intergenerational welfare."[300] I suppose it is, but that is not a bad thing.

Pointing out his hypocrisy is amusing, but it is also distracting. What is more important is that Paul is in a position to see the great good that this program does – after all, half of his patients could not afford his care without it.

Moreover, money that does not get spent does not circulate and his wallet directly feels how much Medicaid stimulates the economy. It is, after all, stimulating *his* economy. Yeah, that is a slam on his hypocrisy, but it is also saying that he should definitely know better.

Finally, a healthy workforce buoys the economy as well. Humanitarian considerations aside, it is like investing in infrastructure like schools, roads, and bridges. Frequent sickness is a drag on any economy apart from being a drag on society's aggregate health and happiness. Again, happiness featured frequently in the founders' writings. Maybe we should consider it too.

That last item might not be as visible to Paul – I do not know how many employees his private practice has. But if the obvious reasons escape him, then the subtle ones require highlighting. He is not a "Big Picture" guy.

More important than Rand Paul's personal hypocrisy is the fact that his ideology makes him militantly ignore the evidence of his own experience. After all, Dr. Paul is the Paul that Peter is being "robbed" to pay.

Upton Sinclair once said, "It is difficult to get a man to understand something, when his salary depends upon his not understanding it." But Senator Rand Paul has the opposite problem. His salary should make things a great deal easier to understand and yet he still does not get it. Either he is deeply indoctrinated or playing a longer con.

These are not *ad hominem* attacks. I am not attacking the messenger *instead* of their message in order to *distract* from it: I am attacking *both*, not substituting an insult for a solid argument. Good arguments and good insults are not mutually exclusive and there is no evasive substitution here.

But famous figures make memorable examples. And if their contradictory ideology is impossible to apply consistently, it is going to cause fervent adherents some awkward moments in the spotlight.

My point in this chapter is to show that libertarianism has some serious product defects and should be recalled. To further the analogy, if a celebrity dies driving an unsafe vehicle, his or her celebrity may save other lives by publicizing the dangerous product's defect. Hopefully, adopting an idiotic ideology is only embarrassing instead of fatal – and does not harm others.

To resume with Ayn Rand and Social Security, she opposes such programs on the grounds of defending individual liberty. But they actually *increase* individual liberty. The ideal of a leisurely retirement as the norm is a socialist notion that you can trace back to Thomas Paine's pamphlet "Agrarian Justice." Part of all our modern assumptions and aspirations about retirement is financial independence and having not just the money but *the time* to finally do what you always wanted to do.

Before Social Security and other such programs, most old people had to move back in with their grown children. That was the previous social norm. The majority of senior citizens were poor, even if they had previously been middle class. But government involvement has largely changed that. As Stephanie Coontz wrote in *The Way We Never Were: American Families and the Nostalgia Trap*, the 1970s' programs for seniors "were so effective that they wiped out the historical tendency for elders to be the poorest section of the population."³⁰¹ Yet conservatives and libertarians consistently seek to demolish that proud accomplishment. Why do they hate freedom?

In short, a libertarian existence could not possibly flourish under a libertarian system. Not for most anyway, and we must judge systems by their typical results. Obviously, family obligations would crowd out any individual life, unless you took Ayn Rand's advice and forsook them entirely.

Yes, I said "forsook." Ayn Rand was not a real big fan of family life. She called it "the glorification of mediocrity."³⁰² She sneered, "*Home life*. The stupid idealization of it, that tries to make it the highest ideal and aim for everybody. The dull, petty, purposeless existence that it is. The ridiculous smallness of it."³⁰³

Hey, I am not a family guy myself, but I am not a jerk about it either.³⁰⁴ As a feminist, I understand how being restricted to the home can be stifling, but I do not say family life is "pointless" either – and, conservative talk show propaganda notwithstanding, most feminists do not either. Feminism's point is that women should have a *choice* and one of those choices is "all of the above." This is only possible if her spouse pulls his or her own weight and helps out. But for Ayn Rand, the whole point is that nobody should ever help anyone else. Simply put, there is no "Ayn" in "team."

Ayn Rand's ideology ignores the fact that spreading mutual support networks beyond the family makes everyone freer. Paradoxically, by recognizing our obligations to *even more people*, we actually *lighten* our more immediate obligations to others because the efficiency frees us all up more. I appreciate that if you already feel burdened you are going to be wary of greater responsibility, but the dynamic has been repeatedly proven.

For example, Social Security has lightened the burden of having elderly parents: It is a wise investment in which everyone comes out ahead, both now and later. Likewise, countries with true universal healthcare spend less money on healthcare and their people live longer, healthier lives.³⁰⁵ Those are both win-wins for everyone that can only be denied by lying by omission.

Still skeptical? Then let us look at the other end of the spectrum.

In Third World countries, having lots of children is their form of Social Security. They do not have high birth rates because they are "obsessed with sex" as some people think – the economic logic of their situation dictates it: Lots of children can share the burden of supporting you in your old age. But some of these children will fail while others succeed, so that is another reason to have lots of them – it increases your odds of getting a winner.

Consider the facts on the ground, step by step, and the range of subtle ways in which government neglect impacts these odds. If government does not ensure safe drinking water, infant mortality rates are going to be high. So, right off the bat, you as an individual are incentivized to keep pumping out kids because you know that many of them will not survive childhood.

That is the grim economic logic of their circumstances. Children are an investment in a cynical sense. This is not to suggest that those in this situation do not love their children, but it is an economic strategy just as much as traditional arranged marriage was an economic transaction.

And all this was also the case in European cultures up until relatively recently. Consider the musical *Fiddler on the Roof* and the fact that people can live to be 100. The life depicted in it was only about 100 years ago. And, oh hey, that was also about the time that Ayn Rand was alive.

Compared to the vast breadth of human history, this shift in marital expectations happened only yesterday. The United States of America is only a little over 200 years old. That is a little more than two centenarians living back to back. Our notion that this is a long time strikes the rest of the world as almost adorable. In the greater scope of things, it is the blink of an eye.

Prosperous modern countries operate differently primarily because government reverses this spiral. I mentioned clean drinking water, but building schools is another important function. If you educate children, they are more likely to become successful. This allows the modern model of investing more time in your children instead of the more traditional scattershot approach. Instead of several unskilled children working miserable, menial jobs, you aim for a prosperous professional.[306]

Do not get a swelled head from the words "prosperous countries" if you happen to live in one and are in an advantaged class. My best guess says you did not consider any of these mechanics until I mentioned them, let alone did you agitate to actualize them. No, you inherited them. You cannot claim credit for an accident of birth, so you should not be smug about it.

This use of education is the logical extension of mammalian survival strategy. Unlike spiders or fish that need to lay *thousands of eggs* in order for some to survive, mammals nurture a smaller number of offspring until they reach maturity. It is an immensely successful strategy that, for humans, already incorporates teaching skills – whether it is how to build a fire or which plants are poisonous. Building public schools capitalizes on this: It plays to our strengths as a species. It spreads knowledge along with the tax burden of paying for it. And that ultimately enabled the exponential growth of technology that we now enjoy today.

It is absolutely astounding how many libertarians in the tech field are ignorant of the history of technology. The cult of the genius blinds them to the role of democratizing information. Teach a kid math and he or she may or may not solve a complex problem that has been frustrating people for a very long time. But teach a *million* kids math and you increase the chances that one of them is going to figure it out. Yes, give the kid some credit. But also credit the system that increased the odds by spreading the skill set; because without it, society rarely finds that diamond in the rough – and other societies find theirs sooner, giving them a relative advantage.

But this is not just about locating geniuses: The public schools are not just scouting operations. Everyone benefits from universal education, not just directly but indirectly. It is a force multiplier for society's wealth and comfort and every iota of our infrastructure requires it from our water supply to our power grid. It is not enough to have few genius engineers – you also need lots of ordinary plumbers, electricians, and machinists. Without them, the genius is near useless because there are countless production bottle necks in the application of the genius' ideas. It limits the reach and ripple effects.

This is not touchy-feely talk. It is the hard nuts-and-bolts fact of the matter: It is steely-eyed realism. As Stephen Jay Gould wrote, "I am, somehow, less interested in the weight and convolutions of Einstein's brain than in the near certainty that people of equal talent have lived and died in cotton fields and sweatshops." There is great humanity and fairness in those words, but they are also unsentimental cold, hard facts that the smug and dumb studiously ignore.

I believe that things like housing, healthcare, and education are basic fundamental human rights regardless of anyone's talent, flint, or hard work. Remember Benjamin Franklin's words from chapter four:

[B]*ut the important ends of civil society, and the personal securities of Life and Liberty, these remain the same in every member of the society; and the poorest continues to have equal claim to them with the most opulent, whatever difference time, chance, or industry may occasion in their circumstances.*[307]

Here "industry" means an individual's work ethic.

But even if you do not agree with Franklin and me, you should at least agree that it is stupid not to invest in the "important ends of civil society," i.e. things like housing, healthcare, education, etc. Indeed, it is suicidally stupid for any society to neglect such social infrastructure.

And you must admit that a society that regards them as basic fundamental rights is less apt to neglect them. Such civic attitudes are safeguards: They help us remember to do basic fucking maintenance and eschew hubris. Voters are less likely to forget them if they are framed that way.

Our own history illustrates all of this.

For example, the high tech world we enjoy today is not just the ultimate result of Cold War era research and development (R&D) spending. The G.I. Bill had democratized higher education by allowing working class veterans afford college. By stark contrast, our current student loan system basically punishes people for going to college, and that eventually hurts society as a whole. Already, employers are complaining that there are not enough qualified applicants for the high tech jobs that they are offering.

Of course, a large part of that problem is also that they *do not want* to pay qualified people what they are *actually worth* and the job market is not responding as advertised.[308] But the bottom line is that it is stupid to for any country punish getting an education. In short, the Information Age would be impossible without the liberal welfare state's infrastructure. Yet a great many opinion-smiths on the Internet bite the hand that feeds them. It is the most moronic national self-sabotage imaginable.

Having Social Security pays similar invisible dividends to education: You lighten the burden by spreading it. And in doing so, you free people up to explore ideas – not just the retired, but their adult children too. Everyone enjoys greater independence as a result of this efficiency. But that independence is threatened when people do not realize where it comes from.

Ayn Rand was childless. I do not know if she expected to eventually retire on her book sales or always work. Either way, cancer happened – as it often does. Health costs mount as you age and she did not have any children to help shoulder the burden as traditional societies typically prescribe.

I actually share Ayn Rand's childless lifestyle. It is one of the wonders of the modern world. But unlike Ayn Rand, I recognize and acknowledge the historically unique social constructs that make it possible. I am grateful for the things that she took for granted and that she sought to dismantle – even as she hypocritically took advantage of them.

Indeed, there is a vast cognitive disconnect between her rugged pioneer/cowboy ideal and the urban world she lived in. Galt's Gulch was an incongruously cosmopolitan version of the Unabomber's cabin. There are no markets in the desert – no consumers or engines of prosperity to harness. Both Benjamin Franklin and Thomas Paine had emphasized this when they explained that society creates wealth by magnifying our individual efforts.

Those who are against society investing in public schools are often those who are against society investing in a comfortable and independent retirement. But, if you truly treasure your independence, you might want to rethink euthanizing Social Security. It will benefit you when your parents are old because eit will lessen or eliminate the burden on you and, perennially manufactured myths of the program's imminent bankruptcy aside, it will benefit you when you become old too.[309] It is the most obvious win-win for you at both of these stages of your life. Or would you rather they were harder?

Intelligent self-interest points towards "socialism." And if you think that is somehow un-American, you can take it up with Thomas Paine.

Recent revelations have been awfully awkward for Ayn Rand's fans. And the one that she applied for Social Security and Medicare is actually not the worst of them.

Ever hear of William Edward Hickman? At age nineteen, he was already a career criminal as forger and multiple murderer. So, he was both "force and fraud" wrapped in the same package. Today's Tom Sawyer is a mean, mean guy – except this was in 1928.

One day, Hickman kidnapped, murdered, and mutilated an eleven-year-old girl. The crime made national headlines. He sent cruel, taunting notes to her father, who agreed to pay the ransom. Despite this, Hickman strangled the girl, drained her blood in a hotel bathtub, and cut off her arms and legs. He bound her torso up to suggest that she still had her limbs intact and sewed her eyes open to trick her father into thinking she was still alive. En route to the trade off point, Hickman littered Los Angeles with her limbs. That remorseless monster was shortly caught, tried, and executed.

So, what does this have to do with Ayn Rand?

Well, she idolized him.

In her journals, Ayn Rand sounds like a giddy school girl when listing William Hickman's qualities. She thrilled to "The fact that he looks like 'a bad boy with a very winning grin,' that he makes you like him the whole time you're in his presence."[310] I suppose she also drew hearts around his name in her notebook, adorned by rainbows and Objectivist unicorns.

This would be an *ad hominem* attack if Ayn Rand was merely smitten by him, but she based the hero of her first, unfinished novel, *The Little Street*, on him. William Edward Hickman was her philosophical ideal. For Rand, the real crime in society's eyes was not his murder and dismemberment of an innocent child but his daring to be an individual and a "real man." In her journals, she wrote, "It is repulsive to see all those beings with worse sins and crimes in their own lives, virtuously condemning a criminal, proud and secure in their number, yelling furiously in defense of society."[311]

Wait. *Worse?* It is hard to imagine anyone doing much worse without an army at his or her disposal. She writes on the next page, "It is the mob's murderous desire to revenge its hurt vanity against a man who dared be alone." No, I think it was his chopping up the little girl. You can be alone without doing anything like that.

Ayn Rand thought this guy had the right idea. "Hickman said: 'I'm like the state: what is good for me is right.' That is this boy's psychology. (The best and strongest expression of a real man's psychology I have heard.)"[312]

In this harsh light, the libertarian to alt-right connection does not seem like a great betrayal of libertarian ideals – more like the realization of them.

Obviously, her appreciation was not ironic. In the previous paragraph, she writes that, "He is born with a wonderful, free, light consciousness – [resulting from] the absolute lack of social instinct or herd feeling. He does not understand, *because he has no organ for understanding*, the necessity, meaning, or importance of other people." (italics original)

In sum, "In this respect, he has the true, innate psychology of a Superman. He can never realize and feel 'other people'."[313] In other words, he was either a sociopath or psychopath. Psychologists differ on whether there is any difference and some use the terms interchangeably.[314] But neither sociopaths nor psychopaths are known for recognizing other's rights.

On the same page, Rand qualified her admiration for Hickman and making him the model for her novel's hero:

The model for the boy is Hickman. Very far from him, of course. The outside of Hickman, but not the inside. Much deeper and much more. A Hickman with a purpose. And without the degeneracy. It is more exact to say that the model is not Hickman, but what Hickman suggests to me.

Oh well, never mind then. Forget I said anything.

Except then you have to ask, "What does a sadistic killer suggest to anyone, besides a sadistic killer?" And Ayn Rand's inside/outside distinction is a senseless oxymoron – his "deeper" "outside"? How does that work exactly? The inside decides what the outside does and she clearly adored both.

On the same page, she wrote that her novel's hero "shows how impossible it is for a genuinely beautiful soul to succeed at present; for in all modern life, one has to be a hypocrite, to bend and tolerate. This boy wanted to command and smash away things and people he didn't approve of." On the previous page, she wrote, "He is born with the spirit of Argon and the nature of a medieval feudal lord." Thus, he is not the sort of fellow many of our founding fathers would have approved of. Even John Adams blasted "aristocratical [*sic*.] banks."

Moreover, this was not quite the Ayn Rand that we associate with railways, skyscrapers, technology, and achievement, but the one with a grudge against modernity. She saw voluntary cooperation as an abomination: You do not ask – you *command!* She saw no dignity in the daily habits of being free and equal. She saw no nobility in accommodating other people. The normal give-and-take niceties of ordinary people living in a free society apparently utterly disgusted her. It is impossible to overstate her contempt.

Ayn Rand's novel, *The Little Street*, was meant to be "The tragedy of a man with the consciousness of a god, among a bunch of snickering, giggling, dirty-story-telling, good timing, jolly, regular fellows."[315] In other words, he is every other bitter comic book super villain you can think of.[316]

And he is definitely what rightists claim to hate – an "elitist."

Apologists attribute her enthusiasm to her youth and claim that she later grew out of it. They say she was still under the sway of Nietzsche's writings at the time. But she had not changed much by the time she wrote *The Fountainhead*. In her notes for it she wrote, "One puts oneself above all and crushes everything in one's way to get the best for oneself. Fine!"[317]

Of her hero, she wrote, "He has learned long ago, with his first consciousness, two things which dominate his entire attitude toward life: his own superiority and the utter worthlessness of the world."[318]

Okay, that actually sounds like only one thing.

Psychologists estimate that one in 25 people are sociopaths.[319] This is not to say they are all killers – very few are. However, when someone is *both* a sociopath *and* a killer, it is a very dangerous combination. That is why they grab headlines and our imaginations (and Ayn Rand's).

This sobering statistic may also suggest why her books are so popular. Supposedly, they are second only to the Bible in popularity.[320] And strangely there is plenty of overlap in their two readerships, if the Tea Party is any indication.

This affinity for sociopaths and psychopaths also appears in libertarians' intense identification with corporations, which the courts consider to be legal persons. Of course, corporations cannot feel guilt or empathy because they are not real people.

But quite surprisingly, corporations also have *all the other traits* associated with sociopaths: They are manipulative, superficial, self-aggrandizing, risk-seeking, reckless with others' safety, primarily focused on short term gains (i.e. quarterly profits) and completely incapable of forming long term relationships or accepting responsibility for their actions.

The documentary *The Corporation*, based on the book of the same name, explored this idea in detail. One of their interviewees was Dr. Robert Hare, an FBI profiler who had also designed the checklist that criminologists use to identify psychopaths. Going down the checklist on camera, Dr. Hare concluded that a corporation was a "prototypical psychopath."

In the 1990s, the business press was awfully fond of humanizing corporations by saying that they were people too. These cheerleaders carried things further by saying the reverse – that people were corporations. In 1999, a Merrill Lynch ad had actually asked, "Corporations like to refer to themselves as 'families.' Shouldn't it be the other way around?"[321] Cartoonist Ruben Bolling had done an excellent job of depicting how such a dysfunctional family would likely function on one Tom the Dancing Bug strip.[322]

Blurring the distinction between corporations and human beings paints a pretty picture until you look at how such legal persons typically behave. The psychopath analogy is not over the top. If a corporation is a person, it is a fair question to ask what kind of a person we are talking about. If not a casual killer, it is at least the type of asshole who reads a lot of Ayn Rand.

Ayn Rand's crush on William Edward Hickman was deeply grounded in her fiercely anti-egalitarian worldview and utter lack of compassion. The two complementary views were always central to her philosophy. Just look at her aristocratic contempt for common people in her description of the Hickman trial's jury:

Average, every day, rather stupid looking citizens. Shabbily dressed, dried, worn looking little men. Fat, overdressed, very average, "dignified" housewives. How can they decide the fate of that boy? Or anyone's fate? If a man has to be judged, why can't he be judged by his superiors, who alone would have the right to do it? Why does he have to be judged by "equals" (and what "equals"!)?[323]

As a friend pointed out, that actually *is* an *ad hominem* attack.

Now, I should mention that I *like* a lot of libertarians. Some do indeed love individual liberty and many are science-friendly, snarky atheists like me. How can I not identify to some extent? (Note: I originally wrote this before the New Atheist movement became an alt-right snake pit.)

In fact, many of my favorite entertainers are libertarians.

For example, there is Berke Breathed, the creator of *Bloom County, Outland,* and *Opus*. When an Onion AV Club interviewer described his strips as liberal he replied, "If you'll read the subtext for many of those old strips, you'll find the heart of an old-fashioned Libertarian."[324] Yes, it came as a shock, but who does not love *Bloom County*?

And I am actually old enough to remember when Dennis Miller was funny – although that may be my fuzzy memory betraying me. Is he still even a libertarian anymore? I recall his defenses of the Clintons in the 1990s were often problematic, but he went almost full-Fox News after 9/11.

And then there is the comedy magic duo of Penn and Teller.

I have often found such entertainers immensely entertaining – and not in an ironic fashion. As George Orwell said of Rudyard Kipling and Salvador Dali, you can enjoy their works while knowing what is wrong with them.

Although Orwell might have been more tolerant than I am. It is relative. We all have occasional disagreements, but degree and frequency can be deal-breakers. The difference between mistakes and deliberate deeds also factors in. People have reservoirs of goodwill which can get depleted.

Penn and Teller are an excellent example. I love a lot of their work. Their scathing *exposés* of spiritual hucksters on their show, "Bullshit," were alternately hilarious and poignant. This comparison will surely annoy them, but I thought those segments were much like Michael Moore's work. They had done a segment defending undocumented immigrants that was truly beautiful. It is must see TV – as was their piece debunking fundamentalists on abstinence-only sex education.

On such issues, Penn and Teller are fighting "the good fight" and doing it much more effectively than most. Anyone who calls former Surgeon General Jocelyn Elders one of their heroes wins some bonus points with me. The Clintons' firing her for saying masturbation is okay was typical of their craven caving on everything from Don't Ask, Don't Tell to the Defense of Marriage Act.

But "Bullshit" was sometimes, well, *bullshit*. Penn and Teller sapped their credibility with dubious segments on other things.

For example, they had called the danger of secondhand smoke a hoax claiming the only evidence is a single "discredited" study, which was never actually discredited. Just because a judge did not like it, does not mean the scientific community dismisses it – and Penn and Teller must know that. That is not how science works. Penn and Teller have since semi-recanted by saying that better evidence now exists.

They similarly dismissed mad cow disease, even hinting that the animal rights group PETA might be behind hyping it. This disease had killed over 150 people in the United Kingdom. Fortunately, immunologists had quickly traced the cause and the government outlawed feeding cow brains to other cows. This stopped the spread of an incurable disease that is 100% fatal in all who contract it. Government intervention plainly saved the day and it is insane to try and paint that as a sinister thing.

Now, to be fair, Penn and Teller were making a point about not living in fear rather than talking about the so-called "magic of the market." And yet, I cannot help wondering how worse things might have worked out if the cattle industry was left to regulate itself – as libertarians advocate.

I knew Penn and Teller were libertarians, but I was surprised to find out just how much. Penn Jillette has appeared on Glenn Beck's shows so often that I have actually caught myself saying "Penn Beck."

This was part of the larger libertarian/Tea Party love fest going on, and both men praise Ayn Rand.

In one show, Beck was broadcasting from the Alamo. At the time, Jillette's only objection was when Beck said it was the most appropriate place for a tea party. Jillette thought the people of Boston, the location of the original Boston

Tea Party, had cause to dispute that. But I wondered what the Alamo had to do with the Tea Party at all unless its agenda includes shooting Mexicans and/or defending slavery. (It does.)

The point is that Penn Jillette is cozying up to the same freedom-hostile, theocratic survivalist types that he had routinely ridiculed on his show "Bullshit," and this really surprised and disappointed me. Later, Penn Jillette expressed discomfort with the event's jingoistic patriotism. (He is a pacifist.) But how do you *not* know that this is what Glenn Beck is all about?

Similarly, Penn Jillette is cool with Rush Limbaugh since Limbaugh has always been nice to *him*. Never mind Limbaugh's long-established record of blatant racism. Cue the They Might be Giants song "Your Racist Friend."

Penn Jillette is a pretty doctrinaire libertarian, which means he frequently – if unintentionally – illustrates how libertarian goals and dogma are at cross purposes. He wants to privatize roads and schools. The later idea is a plank in the Libertarian Party platform: "Education, like any other service, is best provided by the free market."

Two sentences later, one of those frequent cross-purpose quandaries appears in that platform: "Recognizing that the education of children is inextricably linked to moral values, we would return authority to parents to determine the education of their children, without interference from government."

Moral values? Is that the Focus on the Family plank in the platform? That is an overt overture to those voters who want to take Darwin out of the classroom and put God in. Failing that, such voters want to insulate their children from exposure to competing ideas – especially secular ones. How exactly does this plank encourage libertarian attitudes?

Glenn Beck and Penn Jillette also have strange ideas about charity. On his show, Glenn Beck said he does not feel very charitable around tax time. Penn Jillette agreed that compulsory giving "Takes all the joy out of it."

Okay, two things:

First, problems exist to get fixed or treated, not to make us *feel good*. Problems are not a source of joy or satisfaction or the difficulty setting on a video game.[325] This is the mentality of people who think every motive is ultimately selfish because they cannot imagine things being any other way. To them, charity is either performative or hedonism.

It is a narrow understanding of human behavior based on limited experience. We typically think of charitable giving being the very rich giving to the very poor. But a huge hunk of it is actually lateral and invisible – the working poor giving to other members of the working poor. In other words, helping out friends, relatives, and neighbors who are often in the same socioeconomic strata. You do it out of duty, decency, and the knowledge that you might find yourself in similar dire straights someday.

You probably had plans for that money and do not relish parting with it. It does not feel great. You do not feel puffed up. Yes, you are appreciated and respected for your sacrifice; but disappointment is bundled-in with it, so it's not exactly a net gain. It's a mixed bag. You are not some "big wheel" showing off. You are just a normal decent person of modest means doing what you can.

Second, private charity is rarely adequate even in the best economy. But in a crash, it dries up just when it is needed most because everybody is obviously tightening their own belts and prioritizing their own families first. Hence the 2010 headline "Top 400 Charities See Billions Less in Donations, Biggest Percentage Drop Ever Recorded."[326]

Who cannot grasp this obvious dynamic? Local and private relief dried out in the *first year* of the Great Depression, which lasted a *decade*. This is actually why people demanded that government get involved in the *first place*. Uncle Sam can do the job. By contrast, private charity is ridiculously inadequate in a real crisis. It simply isn't a serious alternative.

There's a famous quote about bankers that applies here: "A banker is a fellow who lends you his umbrella when the sun is shining, but wants it back the minute it begins to rain." It has alternately been attributed to Mark Twain or Robert Frost, but anonymous versions have been found earlier – one of which, says "fair weather friend" rather than banker. But the dynamic aptly describes how charity fails when the economy sours. There might be an initial outpouring of support, but it does not last. This does not mean that average people are stingy hypocrites but that they literally do not have anything they can spare. Meanwhile, the wealthy typically sit on their money.

In short, conservatives and libertarians together constitute the "charity begins at home" crowd, and that callous saying vividly illustrates why charity disappears when times get rough and it is most needed – just like that umbrella.

The Libertarian Party platform parallels Glen Beck and Penn Jillette's attitude toward helping the poor as well: "The proper and most effective source of help for the poor is the voluntary efforts of private groups and individuals. We believe members of society will become more charitable and civil society will be strengthened as government reduces its activity in this realm."

Sigh. Okay, two *more* things:

First, do you really want to hand religion another recruitment tool?

Some might be immune to this lure, but desperate people are, by definition, desperate. How does that affect the electorate? How secure is the separation of church and state then? You might want to think about likely ripple effects and why today is more secular than yesteryear.

Of course, that depends on which "yesteryear" we are talking about. The "Greatest Generation," which fought World War II, was quite secular. They put their trust in science and government. But their children, the Baby Boomers, are the opposite. They gullibly turned to religion and business – usually in predatory combination. And their paradoxically materialistic spirituality showed us just how callous navel-gazing could be. One Matt Groening "Life in Hell" cartoon summed things up with a list of callous New Age bromides to deflect appeals by homeless beggars. "Follow your bliss, pal."

But, before the Baby Boomers, the historical trend has been toward secularization and that has coincided with the growth of democracy and social programs. And conservatives have noticed this. At the 2010 Values Voters Conference, Jim DeMint (R-SC) warned his audience, "It's no coincidence that socialist Europe is post-Christian because the bigger the government gets the smaller God gets and *vice-versa*."

Hey, that sounds like win-win to me. Obviously, relying on private charity would likely augment religion's influence on society. Glenn Beck would probably not have a problem with that, but Penn Jillette really should if he is going to remain an active advocate for atheism.

My second objection takes the form of an obvious question: Why are these two Ayn Rand fans trying to tell us how to foster charity? Ayn Rand *hated* charity. She actually thought altruism was "evil" and thus celebrated selfishness. She said help should only go to "equals" rather than unworthy inferiors, who would only resent it and bite the hands that feed them. She even admitted, "[H]ere is the paradox about 'helping another': *one can only help those who don't actually need it.*" (italics original)[327]

Why help at all, then? Oh, wait. I suppose that was her point.

She also wrote:

Charity to an inferior does not include the charity of not considering him an inferior. (This is so by definition.) This is what is demanded by the collectivists now. If the inferior is to be helped on the ground that he is weak and you are strong – let him remember and acknowledge his position (and this is the premise of any voluntary charity).[328]

Nice. Is this petty power trip the "joy" that libertarians get from giving?

Note how the two quotes inform each other. Naturally, the recipients are likely to resent your rubbing their noses in it – and they may actually talk back to you. I suspect such an incident might have inspired that last Rand quote. Maybe this was what made the aristocratic *émigré* sour on *noblesse oblige*.

Her reaction seems to have resulted from a lack of self-awareness. And that is sort of ironic for someone so obsessed with the capital-S Self. Perhaps some outside input might have helped Ayn Rand to become more *objective*. Criticism can be a great opportunity for self-improvement, if you have the intellect and initiative to act on it. But if you are too prickly and defensive to listen, the opportunity is lost. Thus, you need to be objective in order to become more objective. Apparently, Ayn Rand lacked practice.

Ayn Rand's "Objectivist" label is itself contradictory. Both logic and compassion require looking beyond our subjective perspectives and selfish interests. In fact, combining logic and compassion was what the Enlightenment was all about. It advocated taking in the big picture to improve the common good. In short, you cannot be selfish and objective at the same time because of bias. The word "objective" sounds trustworthy, so Ayn Rand used it. Likewise, some religious cults incorporate the word "science" into their names. But a self-interested, narrow mindset is not objective any more than a religion is scientific.

I will develop this point about the Enlightenment more over subsequent chapters. My point here is that libertarians are neither the most constant advocates of charity nor the most objective authorities on it. So, they are the last people we should consult if we truly want to encourage people to be more charitable.

But none of this brittle pettiness sounds like Penn Jillette. When I watch his "Penn Says" clips, he seems so reasonable and laid back. Yes, his height and bellowing stage persona are intimidating. But what you see in these videos is Penn unplugged – the gentle giant. And this mellow, soft-spoken Penn seems incongruous with the rigid, hyper elitist negativity of Ayn Rand. I cannot imagine that they would have gotten along in real life. Can you see it?

This is obviously the opposite of an *ad hominem* attack because I think Penn and Teller are otherwise awesome. I am an atheist who grew up in Kentucky in the 1980s. (Now the Bluegrass State is home of the Creation Museum, where you can see exhibits of Adam and Eve frolicking with dinosaurs.) Guys like them – and the Amazing Randi, Robert Anton Wilson, etc. – formed a lifeline for people like me. They give hope and support to teenage atheists the same way that Dan Savage does for teenage gays. So, if you sense that there is something personal here, you are correct. I am not saying, "These guys are idiots, so ignore their ideas." I am saying, "These guys are brilliant! So why are they siding with those who so obviously oppose individual liberty? Don't they know better?"

In fact, I think both Penn and Teller can probably see a lot of what I am talking about. For openers, they grasp that libertarianism is supposed to be based on the optimistic Enlightenment assumption that people are basically rational and good and thus need little government to get along. Bogeymen are always handy for expanding police powers which is why stoking fear of other people is conservatives' stock and trade.

Granted, the duo goes overboard when they try to soothe our fears of corporations and their poisonous products – some "Bullshit" segments sound like the dying physicist in *Repo Man*.[329] But at least they are somewhat consistent in their optimism. Their greatest lapse in this area would be allying with apocalyptic, theocratic reactionaries like Glenn Beck.

Again, this is shocking because Penn and Teller should know better. I do not just mean that they are smart guys – many of their previous statements show that they are well positioned to appreciate the various dynamics that I am highlighting. In *How to Play in Traffic*, Penn and Teller rant against senseless local stripper ordinances:

The Supreme Court said that pasties and a G-string (I'm glad that they have to humiliate themselves by using those silly words) don't infringe that much on the First Amendment (it makes my blood boil that it's okay to take our rights away a little bit). (emphasis original)[330]

(They use parentheses a lot.)

I agree completely. But I also wonder what they are complaining about. After all, the Supreme Court is only allowing local authorities to legislate morality – they are not imposing morality from the bench *themselves*. They are only doing nothing to stop local tyranny. And that, according to libertarian dogma, is how things *should* be. Any federal interference in local mores would be considered "tyranny." *Do you have prudish, nosey neighbors trying to control your sexuality? Sucks to be you. You should move to Vegas.* But that sounds like a retreat from liberty to me.

Here is another example. When promoting his latest book, *Every Day is an Atheist Holiday!* Jillette appeared on Glenn Beck's show, "The Blaze." Jillette argued that that a religious pharmacist "absolutely" had the right to deny a woman the abortion pill because the pharmacist's individual conscience is sacred.

But what about the woman's? Beck did not ask that question, but they both probably would have said that she can go to another pharmacy. But what if there are not any more in the area? Then it sucks to be her.

But individual conscience is actually not all *that* sacred to Penn Jillette. He added that the pharmacist's employer was free to fire him and that would be fine just so long as the government did not get involved. The employer has an individual conscience too and apparently that trumps the pharmacist's. Money trumps many things.

It all seems pretty reasonable until you stop and think about it. Then you realize that there is a hierarchy with women at the bottom and bosses at the top. To tweak George Orwell, some consciences are more equal than others.

If you have a problem with birth control, then do not use any. But do not interfere with other people's access to it either.

Likewise, if you think drinking is a sin, do not work in a liquor store or a bar. Or, if you do, just do your job anyway.

You do not have to be a genius to realize that allowing pharmacists to deny birth control is only going to prompt theocratic prudes to become pharmacists. Why not allow Christian Science pharmacists to deny *all* prescriptions the same way they try to deny their children medical attention? Granted, they would be unlikely to find jobs, so you could say that the market would prevent that. But the principle still remains the same: The law should not allow others' religious convictions to restrict your bodily autonomy. It is an abuse of your position to use your job to force your personal mores or desires on others.

And this principle is not a minor abstract thing. Slightly over half the human population is female, yet some "libertarians" prefer to indulge the authoritarian urges of a few prudes.

Likewise, bosses cannot demand sex from employees to grant raises or promotions. That is illegal – and should be. The predatory employer's rationale is "If you do not like it, you can work someplace else."

Notice any pattern yet? Libertarian "liberty" frequently boils down to "Might makes right." Again, we must judge philosophies by typical results.

In practice, Penn Jillette's philosophy is less pro-freedom than anti-government. He would never tolerate a cop forcing pulled over motorists to pray – but only because a cop is an agent of government. If your private sector employer found religion and forced you to practice it too, that would probably be okay with Penn because you could presumably find another job. In his worldview, there is no coercion until government gets involved.

Obviously, this poses a problem when government is trying to protect our freedoms. One of the most fundamental functions of government is protecting us from *each other*. That is why we have laws against murder, rape, etc. And this includes civil law as well as criminal law: If someone breaks a contract with you, you take them to court. Playing referee between people is government's proper role and it always has been.

Take gay marriage, for example. On Glenn Beck's show, Penn Jillette asked when government got involved in love and marriage as if this were some unprecedented new intrusion. Um, try the Code of Hammurabi.

Marriage was a monetary transaction for millenniums before love got involved. And property remains a large part of marriage and family today, thus disputes over divorce, custody, or inheritance. As long as people own homes, have children, and have disputes, government has a role to referee. And I do not see that changing anytime soon short of society abolishing property, which I don't think either Beck or Jillette support.

The notion that government should not get involved is absurd. Without a referee, "Might makes right" would decide every dispute. Libertarians ignore non-governmental bullying and insist government must never intervene to stop it. During the show, Jillette emphasized, "We do not want to be a country of bullies," But his philosophy is a bonanza for bullies and he should be smart enough to see that.

The whole show was a train wreck of phony history and shameless pandering. Penn Jillette "absolutely" agreed with Glenn Beck that our country was founded on "Christian principles." Gee, I do not recall reading that in the Treaty of Tripoli. It actually says the opposite.

Jillette then credited the birth of individualism to Martin Luther nailing his challenge to the Papacy on the Wittenberg Church door. Never mind the Renaissance's revival of ancient, pagan Greco-Roman thought. Remember? That is where the words "democracy" and "republic" come from. Also, forget Socrates taking a suicidal stand for freedom of conscience. And I suppose all those marble penises and boobies that Michelangelo chiseled all over Italy somehow sprang from the new Protestant take on Jesus' teachings.

Of course, things got most absurd when they discussed the founders. Penn Jillette said, "If I'm given a choice between a socialist and a Christian, I think it was Thomas Jefferson that said I won't hesitate to go with the later. I'll go with a Christian in a second over a socialist."[331]

Obviously, Jefferson never said that. For one thing, the word "socialist" did not even exist yet. That is why I call some of our founders *proto*-socialists – because their ideas later inspired socialism. For another thing, Jillette's sentiment is contrary to Jefferson's *whole world view*.

It is a lot like David Barton claiming that Thomas Paine said we should teach Creationism in public schools! Paine died the same year that Darwin was born, so I suppose Barton thinks the founder blasted the infant's ideas from his death bed. Moreover, Creationism is a twentieth century attempt to claim the chapter of Genesis is science, a relatively new move for people of faith. And never mind Paine's famous hatred of the Bible.

Penn Jillette's claim was just as absurd because Thomas Jefferson loathed organized religion and he advocated greater economic equality. Therefore, it was both *chronologically impossible* and *totally out of character* for Jefferson to say what Jillette claimed.

Unfortunately, Penn Jillette has a frustratingly Obama-like habit of giving away the farm to find common ground. When Glenn Beck said that the founding fathers were "devoutly Christian," Penn Jillette did not challenge him. But they *did* disagree on *one* point, prompting Beck to hilariously phone David Barton for a fact-check during a commercial break(!) Otherwise, they were in complete agreement throughout the show. Jillette's game plan was largely "Do not contradict the host." Thus, he buttressed – instead of debunked – their poisonous theocratic assumptions about American history. I would call it a missed opportunity, but that seems dishonestly generous.

As an atheist, I found Penn Jillette's charm offensive to be pretty offensive. It was as infuriating as watching President Obama agree to make cuts in Social Security, only not as important. And both moves were overtures to the same fundamentalist anti-government demographic.

This brings us back to the paleolibertarians of the Tea Party. There certainly is some friction between them and the libertarian establishment. But as Penn Jillette's frequent visits with Glenn Beck prove, they can be overlooked.

Take the issue of immigration. The Tea Party wants an electrified border fence whereas the Libertarian Party has always advocated open borders – as the aforementioned "Bullshit" segment on the fence illustrates. Again, it is must-see TV and absolutely amazing. *Reason* magazine's flow cart of the numerous hurdles and insane wait times immigrants face to become citizens is similarly brilliant and not to be missed.[332]

Sidebar edit: Almost a decade after I wrote this book, Penn Jillette stopped calling himself a libertarian. He saw how the anti-mask movement endangered others during the Covid pandemic and made him begin to reconsider things. To that he added, "Many times when I identified as Libertarian, people said to me, 'It's just rich white guys that don't want to be told what to do,' and I had a zillion answers to that — and now that seems 100 percent accurate."[333]

Jillette was always an outlier. His optimism about others made him a poor fit for a political movement that opposed community. And that paradox makes him a great comparison-contrast with most other libertarians who jettison their principles and eventually become authoritarians.

Of course, there are libertarians who were always authoritarians but totally oblivious to the contradictions. They were raised with those contradictions and stuck with them into adulthood, so there was no trajectory towards conservatism because they were already there. Take Senator Rand Paul (R-KY).

Rand Paul is the son of paleolibertarian Congressman Ron Paul (R-TX), who had run for president as the Libertarian Party's candidate in 1988. In 2008, Ron Paul sought the Republican Party's nomination. He was the lone voice against the Iraq War in the GOP primary. Accordingly, the Fox News Network dutifully sandbagged his candidacy, which infuriated Paulites. Ron Paul was as unwelcome among the Republican establishment as Ralph Nader was among the Democratic one. Father and son are close. Rand followed his father into medicine and later into politics. Both are anti-war – and anti-choice.

After Barack Obama won the 2008 presidential election, Fox News promptly morphed into the Tea Party channel. And in 2010, Rand Paul leapt aboard, declaring himself the Tea Party's candidate in Kentucky. He even got pro-war Sarah Palin's endorsement.

But Kentucky's Libertarian Party was troubled enough with Rand Paul's slippery principles that they briefly considered withholding their endorsement and running their own candidate. Citing Paul's support for a constitutional ban on abortion and his opposition to gay marriage, the state party's Vice Chairman Joshua Koch said Paul "had gone from being an outsider candidate to a Tea Party candidate to an establishment candidate in the past nine months. It's a complete identity crisis. I've never seen anything like it."[334] But they eventually relented.

For his part, Rand Paul distanced himself from the Libertarian Party shortly after he became the GOP's senate candidate.[335] Mind you, this did not stop him from playing Rush songs at has campaign rallies. But the band did, because he was not paying for the privilege.[336]

Both Pauls' economic philosophy is dogmatically business-friendly. The son's first national splash after winning the Kentucky Republican primary was appearing on the *Rachel Maddow Show*. Maddow had asked Paul about his past comments on the 1964 Civil Rights Act triggering 14 minutes of him squirming and insisting that he found "all racism abhorrent" and "bad business." Paul said he favored *most* of the act, but that he found the portion ending segregation in private establishments problematic because it infringed on business owners' "freedom of speech."

Speech? Hey, I interpret the First Amendment pretty broadly to include art, music, theater, film, and even stripping, but even I have difficulty seeing discrimination as a species of "speech." As with the meddling pharmacist that Jillette and Beck support, it is a matter of denying access, not personal expression.

And restaurants and bars *are* public spaces despite being privately owned. It is a gray area, just as public sidewalks are public property but must be kept free of hazards by private individuals and businesses. You cannot credibly stand on your front porch and shout, "Hey! You kids get off my sidewalk!" There are obvious areas where the public and private spheres intersect. That is just common sense.

Rand Paul's reaction was an example of how a rigid, highly theoretical ideology can make you paint yourself into some pretty uncomfortable corners. His supporters accused Rachel Maddow of entrapment and trying to paint him as a racist. Yet it seems to me that she was actually trying to politely point out a large problem area in his ideology. She was essentially saying, "Look, you must admit that government has done some good. Had your philosophy prevailed, lunch counters would still be segregated."

But she never got that far because Paul refused to answer whether he would have voted for the bill. Instead, he spent the *entire segment* awkwardly insisting that he opposed racism when she had not even accused him of any. She was trying to get him to confront the obvious real world consequences of his ideology. Shortly after the broadcast, his campaign said Paul *would* have voted for the bill despite his misgivings. Good to know.

Republicans depicted this fiasco as a "rookie mistake" made by an earnest non-politician who was naïve about dealing with the media. But what Paul is actually naïve about is how things work and how change takes place.

This can also be seen in Rand Paul's reaction to British Petroleum (BP)'s Deepwater Horizon oil rig explosion and spill in the Gulf of Mexico. Sarah "Drill, Baby, Drill" Palin rather surprisingly accused President Obama of dithering during the crisis. But candidate Rand Paul was more ideologically consistent and accused Obama of being too heavy-handed. "What I don't like from the president's administration is this sort of, 'I'll put my boot heel on the throat of BP.' I think that sounds really un-American in his criticism of business."[337] Apparently, he thinks there is nothing more American than letting a foreign corporation despoil our environment. Paul practices a strange species of patriotism.

But Rand Paul did not stop there. After comparing the BP spill to the Dotiki coal mine collapse in Kentucky, the ophthalmologist opined, "I think it's part of this sort of blame-game society in the sense that it's always got to be somebody's fault instead of the fact that maybe sometimes accidents happen." Paul's callous comment was inept, but not inapt. In fact, it was an unintentionally excellent comparison because both had resulted from management cutting corners on safety to save money. Yes, sometimes accidents happen. But they happen more often when safety is ignored.

This is a chronic problem in the coal fields. It is great television when men are buried alive miles under a mountain. There are candlelight prayer vigils as people feverishly try to dig the trapped miners out before their air runs out. It is compelling claustrophobic horror. Maybe that is why mine safety is routinely ignored despite one predictable – and preventable – tragedy happening after another. But more likely, it was because the Bush administration appointed regulators who were ideologically opposed to doing their jobs. After all, actually enforcing safety regulations would be putting the boot heel of government on business' throat. Accordingly, Paul wants to repeal federal mine safety laws entirely.

Incidentally, presidents Clinton and Bush appointing anti-regulation regulators also played an enormous role in the 2007 economic meltdown.[338]

James Madison took a dim view of strong local control because he was sensitive to the possibility of local tyranny. The Pauls show how this can go down to the family level. In an interview with *The New York Times*, Rand Paul was asked, "As a libertarian, did your father grant you great liberty to do what you wanted in your childhood?" Rand Paul's answer was pretty interesting. "The kind of funny thing is that there's a difference between the government and a family. A family can be a complete dictatorship."[339]

That *is* a funny kind of thing. A subsequent profile in the same publication clarified this somewhat by emphasizing that the Paul family had few rules, no chores, and lightly-enforced curfews. However, Rand's father echoed the notion that it is okay for authority to tighten with smaller groups. "Ron Paul said he was not philosophically opposed to centralized authority, as long as it existed close to home, or within it."[340]

That makes a lot of sense until you stop and think about it. The Paul home does not sound abusive, but what about families which are? Should society not be allowed to intervene? Conservatives are fond of arguing that the family is the foundation of society as a whole and thus must trump society for society's own good.

But I argue the opposite: Civilization and freedom begin when authority and group loyalties are more diffused creating an interwoven web of checks and balances that allows individualism to emerge and flourish. By contrast, concentrating all power in the family ultimately leads to hierarchical tribalism. Simply put, liberty begins when society says, "You cannot rape your children or sell them into slavery," and has the power to back it up.

Of course, those with a more "Biblical" mindset tend to differ. They take the notion that "a man's home is his castle" rather literally and do not take kindly to nosy social workers. Hence, say, the Branch Davidians, which anti-government firebrands often lionize.

Thus, the conditions that breed, benefit and defend individual liberty are obviously the opposite of what the two Pauls presume. More family and local control hurts personal freedom. Of course, conservatives already know this fact and agitate accordingly. By contrast, most libertarians either do not get this frequently played-out dynamic or just play dumb about it. But either way, liberty predictably suffers as a result.

A steam or gasoline engine that is missing important components will either not work or will explode when started. But the libertarian Federalist Society wants Federalism without the federal government. It wants hands-off decentralization without the checks and balances. This is libertarians' theoretical engine of liberty. Yet in practice, their plan for divvying up authority only creates a lot of local dictators and family tyrants.

The Pauls are apparently okay with that. This shows their poor grasp of the dynamics. After all, the Paul family's permissive childrearing practices were not prevented nor even discouraged by the federal government. But it is difficult to imagine it defining a tribal clan system where family is the last word. Such societies are hardly individualistic. And, as I wrote before, we must judge systems by their typical results. Our society has become increasingly individualistic as local authority erodes and that is obviously what angers conservatives. So, what about it angers "libertarians"?

Libertarians do not get Federalism. Our founders had studied different societies and tried to incorporate every structural defense for freedom they could find. They saw that the decentralization of power helped – including the decentralization of wealth. But they also saw that large groups governed more lightly than small ones thanks to their diversity, and so they tried to integrate the two. They also recognized the value of checks and balances where different units of government cancel each other out.

This principle works on both the national and individual levels. Abusive parents or partners can be dealt with by local authorities. And yet people still enjoy a lot of privacy since intrusive local authorities that infringe on individual liberty – for example, by passing anti-sodomy laws or trying to outlaw abortion – can be stopped by the federal government. Thus, individualism flourishes by pitting federal and state government against each other. This is how America is *supposed* to work. Federalism is a mechanism of opposing mechanisms that operates both horizontally and vertically.

Of course, abusers will cry "government tyranny" when they cannot bully others. That "whatever does not harm another" part of freedom does not fully click with them. Again, protecting ourselves from one another is one reason why people form governments in the first place. Assault is assault whether it happens on the street or in the home, but the Paul family's rhetoric plays to an audience that thinks assault is okay inside the family. Again, libertarianism is a bonanza for bullies.

As I wrote in the last chapter, there *are* instances where local government is friendlier to individual liberty, such as marijuana. Such issues are rare, but they do happen. But the ultimate goal of these mechanisms is to defend freedom. Unfortunately, devices do not always work the way they were designed. Sometimes unintended consequences result or they are hijacked for oppressive purposes. That is why when states and the federal government clash we should ask, on a case-by-case basis, "Which side benefits freedom?" That should be the tie-breaker.

But the worst thing you can do is unthinkingly default power to the entity that is least likely to defend individual liberty and that has historically been the states. That is how you wind up with a rigid, awkward ideology that tries to justify dry counties and does not desegregate lunch counters.

I have tracked libertarianism's devolution across three different individuals. Ayn Rand's hypocrisy showed that her ideology failed *even her*. Penn Jillette downplayed libertarian principles to convert authoritarian theocrats. And Senator Rand Paul is the type of politician that results from dropping those principles outright.

Today's libertarians are essentially conservatives. They are perhaps less happy with the military-industrial complex and more pro-pot, but otherwise they are regular Reagan Republicans.

And Ayn Rand was no fan of Ronald Reagan. In her last public speech, she blasted, "the appalling disgrace of his administration is his connection with the so-called Moral Majority" who were trying to "take us back to the Middle Ages, via the unconstitutional union of religion and politics."[341]

She then added, "A man who claims to defend rights and objects to the right to have abortion, who wants to dictate to a woman in the most intimate, crucial, and tragic issue of that kind, and he wants to forbid it – that's not [a] defender of rights."[342]

Her dictum was crystal clear. And it applies no less to Ron or Rand Paul and company than it did to "The Gipper."

But you really have to wonder why Ayn Rand was shocked by Ronald Reagan. Did she really think individual liberty would thrive in the selfish society she advocated? Thomas Paine said that we must defend even our enemy's rights in order to preserve our own. But Ayn Rand's ideal individual does not even acknowledge the value of other people. So how likely is liberty to last if that all-against-all attitude is celebrated? Clearly, selfishness is as unlikely to foster liberty as it is to foster charity.

The Tea Party is the most political power that the libertarian movement has ever tasted, but it cost them most of their principles. Admittedly, other stripes of libertarians remain, but their numbers are still insignificant. Before the Tea

Party, libertarianism had no foot soldiers. Its political clout was largely limited to think tanks. Now, there are finally foot soldiers, but the problem is they are not really libertarians.

It is a lot like when there were more Goths than Romans in the Roman army. The new recruits are not quite assimilated. Yet today, it is anti-immigrant bigots who are ironically the newcomers who do not fit-in.

This paradoxical problem goes far beyond the libertarian movement. Immigrants assimilate to America far faster than most conservatives who were born here. What are we going to do with this strange population which is hostile to out way of life? They have troubled us for generations.

I am only half joking. When push comes to shove, conservatives know they do not belong in a free society. This simultaneously explains their efforts to make America more to their authoritarian liking and their prickly response to every issue that touches on what America is supposed to stand for – i.e. most all of the important ones.

So small wonder they hate immigrants! Each immigrant reminds them that their claim to America is vastly inferior by comparison. We have all these conservatives who claim that ancestors arrived on the May Flower, and yet their every political impulse is fundamentally un-American.

And here we finally reach the Big Reveal that you should have already guessed by now since I have telegraphed it so frequently.

More important than libertarians themselves is the libertarian rhetoric that conservatives often co-opt: It allows them to shed their authoritarian associations. The whole Tea Party movement is only libertarian camouflage for conservatives. The right has always dishonestly fought against freedom in freedom's name; but George W. Bush's War on Terror disastrously flushed any subtlety down the toilet, so conservatives subsequently went into damage control mode and began gas-lighting voters by pretending to be libertarians. That is conservatism during the Obama era in a nutshell.

But they always have done so to some extent. And that is why I wrote two chapters on libertarianism in this book on conservatism: If I dynamite libertarian claims to liberty, conservative ones slump into dust with them.

I have illustrated libertarianism's built-in authoritarian drift. To switch metaphors, it almost seems like planned obsolescence – as if libertarianism is built to be a rickety bridge to conservatism that collapses behind you as soon as you get across, thereby stranding you there.

But today, conservatives seem to be rebuilding the bridge in the opposite direction to permit a retreat to still more dishonest libertarian posturing. So I wrote one more chapter to blow up that bridge and cut off their escape. If I did not, they would only reuse that bridge to return. I just got so bored and annoyed with their eternal evasive antics. Surely you do too.

Murray Rothbard's support for Pat Buchanan shows where libertarian "reason" eventually leads. Robert Bork shows it. The Libertarian Party's anti-abortion candidates also show it. Libertarianism is only a slippery slope to conservatism, as anyone who bothers to look at it knows.

In short, conservatives' libertarian rhetoric is a total joke. Not only is their sincerity suspect, they stole a faulty product. And that was probably done knowingly since libertarian principles have a notoriously short shelf life. Once again, Cato soberly warned that "liberty can never subsist without equality," so libertarian-style liberty is *bound* to fail, if not *built* to.

But that is okay because it does not actually have to work. Indeed, it is better that it does *not* work.

Conservatives just want the box that it comes in.

7: Participatory Democracy
The Third Leg of the Tripod

Most schoolbook donnybrooks are fought over evolution. But Texas did things a little different in 2010.

No, the traditional assault on the separation of church and state was not forgotten. The new curriculum required textbooks to reference the "laws of nature and nature's God" when discussing political concepts. But, the Texas State Board of Education also voted to diminish America's significance in world history and to distort students' understanding of our form of government – indeed, to ban the very mention of its name.

The original curriculum had asked students to "explain the impact of the Enlightenment ideas of John Locke, Thomas Hobbes, Voltaire, Charles de Montesquieu, Jean Jacques Rousseau, and Thomas Jefferson on political revolutions from 1750 to the present."[343] But the new guidelines erased the words "Enlightenment" and "revolutions." Moreover, they also dropped Thomas Jefferson in favor of Thomas Aquinas, John Calvin, and Sir William Blackstone. The *only* American political philosopher on the previous list was dumped to make room for two foreign theologians and a hardcore monarchist.

I am not kidding. In his famous *Commentaries on the Laws of England*, Sir William Blackstone wrote, "The king is not only incapable of doing wrong, but even of thinking wrong; in him there is no folly or weakness."[344] So, the king is infallible, like the Pope? I am not sure how that qualifies Sir Blackstone as a revolutionary thinker. Oh, but wait, I forgot – the Lone Star State had dropped the word "revolution" too. Perhaps Texas will next replace their state song with "God Save the King."

Texas has not gone quite that far. But the board also voted to strike the word *democracy* from any reference to America's form of government. Henceforth, Texas textbooks would call America a "constitutional republic."

But just what is a constitutional republic? Conservatives are rarely clear on that, so I do not think they know themselves. Some of them talk as if republics and democracies are opposites. This merits investigation since knowing our form of government is sort of important. So, we should probably look at what our founders thought a republic was before exploring conservatives' historic hostility to democracy. Original intent is relevant.

Let us start with the founder that Texas dumped. As I wrote in chapter one, Thomas Jefferson and many of his contemporaries used the terms *democracy* and *republic* interchangeably. Other founders agreed that the two forms of government overlapped, yet they argued over which one was the original form. But since Jefferson mixed the two, I will use him as my starting point to show how separate definitions emerged.

Thomas Jefferson's definition of an original, pure republic was the direct democracy practiced in small town hall meetings where there were no elected officials and ordinary citizens directly voted on all proposals. We can see this in an 1816 letter to John Taylor:

Indeed, it must be acknowledged, that the term republic is of very vague application in every language. Witness the self-styled republics of Holland, Switzerland, Genoa, Venice, Poland. Were I to assign to this term a precise and definite idea, I would say, purely and simply, it means a government by its citizens in mass, acting directly and personally, according to rules established by the majority; and that every other government is more or less republican, in proportion as it has in its composition more or less of this ingredient of the direct action of the citizens. Such a government is evidently restrained to very narrow limits of space and population. I doubt if it would be practicable beyond the extent of a New England township.[345]

Later in the letter, Jefferson elaborates, explaining that republican-ness is relative: "The purest republican feature in the government of our own state is the House of Representatives. The Senate is equally so the first year, less the second, and so on. The executive still less, because not chosen by the people directly. The judiciary, seriously anti-republican, because for life."

Thomas Jefferson also addressed these ideas in an 1816 letter to Isaac Tiffany. Mr. Tiffany had asked Jefferson for his reply to ancient critics of democracy like Aristotle. Again, Jefferson says a democracy is a pure republic:

They had just ideas of the value of personal liberty, but none at all of the structure of government best calculated to preserve it. They knew no medium between democracy (the only pure republic, but impractical beyond the limits of a town) and an abandonment of themselves to an aristocracy, or tyranny independent of the people. It seems not to have occurred that where the citizens cannot meet to transact their business in person, they alone have the right to choose the agents who shall transact it; and in that way a republican, or popular government, of the second grade of purity, may be exercised over any extent of country. The full experiment of a government democratical, [sic] but representative, was and is still reserved for us. (parenthetical aside original)[346]

Jefferson added, "The introduction of this new principle of representative democracy has rendered useless almost everything written before on the structure of government." In other words, Jefferson said that Aristotle was irrelevant to America.

Thomas Paine largely agreed with Thomas Jefferson. He had also pointed out that other governments called themselves republics. He wrote, "Various forms of government have affected to style themselves as a republic. Poland calls itself a republic, which is a hereditary aristocracy, with what is called an elective monarchy. Holland calls itself a republic which is chiefly aristocratical, with a hereditary stadtholdership."[347] Paine did not sound terribly impressed with their republican credentials.

Likewise, Thomas Paine agreed with Thomas Jefferson that representation allowed republics to govern a far larger area democratically. He wrote, "Simple democracy was society governing itself without the aid of secondary means. By ingrafting *[sic]* representation upon democracy, we arrive at a system of government capable of embracing and confederating all the various interests and every extent of territory and population."[348]

He then adds, "It is on this system that American government is founded. It is representation ingrafted upon democracy."

However, Thomas Paine's vocabulary was somewhat more modern than Thomas Jefferson's. Jefferson called *all* democracies republics and *vice versa*, since he used the terms interchangeably. Accordingly, he called direct democracy a "pure republic." But Paine only called *representative democracies* republics. And accordingly, he called direct democracy "simple democracy" to reflect that republics were more developed.

Their terminology differed slightly, but their essential concepts remained much the same. For both, town hall meetings were the pure, original form of popular government and adding a system of representation allowed democracy to govern more territory. As Paine wrote, "What Athens was in miniature, America will be in magnitude."[349]

James Madison mostly agreed with the two Toms. He contrasted "a pure Democracy, by which I mean, a Society, consisting of a small number of citizens, who assemble and administer the Government in person" (i.e. a local, direct democracy) with "a Republic, by which I mean a Government in which a scheme of representation takes place." What Paine called "simple democracy," Madison called "pure democracy." Therefore, he also saw a republic as a modified form of democracy.

Notice that James Madison had further sharpened the distinction. What he called a pure democracy his mentor, Thomas Jefferson, had called a pure republic. That is a big shift in terminology, whereas Thomas Paine's distinction was more subtle. And yet, this is still hair-splitting because their working ideas remained basically the same.

However, James Madison had emphasized a different difference than the amount of territory that a democracy could practically govern. For Madison, a republic was a more *refined* form of democracy with checks to protect the rights of minorities. Conservatives dislike these checks unless the minority at risk is the rich. This explains their frequent referendums against abortion and gay marriage. (James Madison would abhor putting anyone's rights up for a vote.) While Madison had acknowledged that size mattered; for him, minority safeguards were most important. Indeed, he saw them as related. That is why he said we should "enlarge the sphere" by adopting his new Constitution: Minority rights would be less threatened by local tyranny under a more centralized government. But at the end of the day, Madison agreed that a republic was a type of democracy – just one with safeguards.

Of course, there was not unanimous agreement because not everyone thought that a republic as a form of democracy – some thought it was the other way around. John Adams wrote, "The Federalist is a valuable work, and Mr. Madison's part in it as respectable as any other. But his distinction between a republic and a democracy cannot be justified. A democracy is as really a republic as an oak is a tree, or a temple a building."[350] So he agreed that one form of government was a subset of the other – he just disagreed on which was the broader category. He thought Madison had it backwards.

For John Adams, a republic was a government run by representatives whether they were elected or not. As long as one man did not hold all the power it was still a republic – thus Poland, then governed by a legislature of unelected aristocrats, was still a republic. Adams argued that there were democratic republics, aristocratic republics, and "mixed" republics. For example, the British Parliament has an elected House of Commons and an unelected House of Lords. Since both houses of Congress are now elected (Senators were originally appointed), America is a democratic republic.

In short, James Madison thought that a republic was a refined form of democracy, while John Adams thought a democracy was a more participatory republic. They disagreed over which form of government was a subcategory of the other, but they basically agreed where America was along the general spectrum of governments.

John Adams had also mentioned that other countries like Holland and Poland called themselves republics as well. But unlike Thomas Paine, he accepted their claims at face value. Adams called them "aristocratic republics" whereas Paine basically called them frauds.

This also put John Adams at odds with Thomas Jefferson who thought, "[W]here the citizens cannot meet to transact their business in person, *they alone* have the right to choose the agents who shall transact it." (emphasis added) Hence Jefferson considered such governments counterfeit republics as well. Without voter control, such "republics" lacked political legitimacy since legitimacy hinged on "consent of the governed."

No matter how you slice it, the founders clearly agreed that we were both a republic *and* a democracy. Again, they only differed on which one was the subcategory of the other. And, as I had mentioned in chapter one, John Marshall had defended his fellow Federalists against the charge that they were closet monarchists by declaring, "We, sir, idolize democracy."[351]

I should also note that many of democracy's fiercest critics also used the words *democracy* and *republic* interchangeably, just as Thomas Jefferson had.

At the Constitutional Convention of 1787, Elbridge Gerry said, "The evils we experience flow from the excess of democracy." He mentions a colleague whose "republican" enthusiasm had dimmed. "He had, he said, been too republican heretofore: he was still, however, republican; but had been taught by experience the danger of the leveling spirit." "Leveling" meant equalizing. Gerry was lamenting the democratic ethos of equality.

Speaking of the leveling spirit, Alexander Hamilton also shows how the words *democratic* and *republican* often got transposed. At the Philadelphia Convention, he deplored "the amazing violence & turbulence of the democratic spirit," and thus the recording secretary noted that Hamilton had "acknowledged himself not to think favorably of Republican Government."[352]

Alexander Hamilton's advocating a strong central government makes him a rather awkward founder for conservatives to invoke today. But Eldridge Gerry was no less so. In the same speech that Gerry spoke of "excess democracy," he had also lamented that, "It would seem to be a maxim of democracy to starve the public servants." Today, that is the aim of the antidemocratic – thus conservatives' constant assaults on government employees and their unions. Conservatives want to "starve the beast" and shrink government down to the size that it can be "drowned in a bathtub" as Grover Norquist once memorably put it. Public servants suffer as a result.

Conservatives can, of course, dig up plenty of quotes against pure democracy. But this tactic will not work for two obvious reasons:

First, nobody with any political clout is arguing for *pure* democracy. Certainly, liberals are not because minority rights are far too important. Too many liberal victories show the enormous importance of checks and balances. All three branches of the federal government had played important roles in the Civil Rights struggle and the Supreme Court's *Roe v. Wade* decision gave women greater reproductive autonomy just as *Obergefell v. Hodges* recognized gay marriage.

Liberals are certainly never going to jeopardize any of that.

Second, fears of "excess democracy" were greatest when modern democracy was still untried. Back then, public schools were far fewer and literacy rates were not that great. But these issues got fixed. After over two centuries, democracy has advanced and has stood the test of time. Like evolution, the American Experiment is no longer "only a theory." It is a settled question proven by an immense wealth of evidence that only the most hardcore reactionaries can ignore – which, of course, they still do.

Some conservatives enjoy pointing out that the Soviet Union had claimed to be a democracy. They forget to mention that it also called itself a republic. Yes, the Union of Soviet Socialist *Republics* (U.S.S.R.) may have been a mockery of democracy because a one-party system offers no choices, but it eventually became a republic by John Adams's very generous definition. After Joseph Stalin died, the Politburo made damn sure that power could never be seized by one man ever again – ditto with the People's *Republic* of China after Mao Zedong kicked the bucket. They became "republics," but that did not make them free. Undemocratic republics cannot be free. Those who denigrate democracy on the Orwellian-named Free Republic.com should probably take note.

Of course, George Orwell disputed the idea that the U.S.S.R. was even socialist, let alone a republic. In his special preface for the Ukrainian edition of *Animal Farm,* he explained why:

Since 1930 I have seen little evidence that the U.S.S.R. was progressing towards anything that one could truly call Socialism. On the contrary, I was struck by clear signs of its transformation into a hierarchal society, in which the rulers have no more reason to give up their power than any other ruling class.[353]

A page later he added:

Indeed, in my opinion, nothing has contributed so much to the corruption of the original idea of Socialism as the belief that Russia is a Socialist country and that every act of its rulers must be excused, if not imitated. And so for the past ten years I have been convinced that the destruction of the Soviet myth was essential; if we wanted a revival of the Socialist movement.

It is always odd when conservatives claim George Orwell as one of their own. In fact, in his 1946 essay "Why I Write," Orwell wrote, "Every line of serious work that I have written since 1936 has been written, directly or indirectly, *against* totalitarianism and *for* democratic socialism, as I understand it."[354] (italics original)

So *Jacobin* magazine is closer to Orwell than the *National Review*. Who knew? Well, everyone who has actually read Orwell.

It is always risky to take any group or nation's labels at face value. For example, the Nazis had called themselves the "National Socialist German Workers Party" yet they sent actual socialists to the death camps (more on that next chapter). The word "republic" has similarly been abused by many countries that are not one – except by John Adams's big tent definition, and often not even then.

Another favorite argument that conservatives love to trot out is claiming that "democrat" was an insult in the founders' day. Supposedly, the Federalists and anti-Federalists blasted each other as "aristocrats" and "democrats" respectively.

Well, not entirely. After all, Thomas Jefferson had originally name his political party the "Democratic-Republicans" Would not that be like calling your party the "Scum Sucking-Republicans"? And did John Marshall mean to say, "We, sir, idolize scum-sucking"?

Somehow, I doubt it.

Of course, being called an aristocrat or monarchist *was indeed* an insult. It was aimed to those who were hostile to democracy. The Federalists were frequently called both, thus John Marshall's defensive denial.

Tory was yet another insult. Whigs and Tories were the two political parties before the Revolution. As I wrote in chapter one, Tories were conservatives who preferred hierarchy to democracy, whereas radical Whigs preferred the reverse and had dubbed themselves "Patriots" almost a century before the American colonists grew discontent. When the revolution came, these labels defined sides. In the rest of the English-speaking world, conservatives are *still* called Tories and the meaning remains unchanged. Tories are still authority-adoring traditionalists who typically sympathize with the rich. Naturally, after the American Revolution, this attitude was highly suspect and thus the stuff of insults state side.

These insults sprung from a very real fear. Each state had its wealthy, elite families and they had long become accustomed to thinking of themselves as the aristocrats of their respective colonies. Remember that John Adams had compared Massachusetts's banking families to Virginia's plantation families in a letter to Thomas Jefferson blasting "aristocratical *[sic]* banks."[355] Our founding fathers understood that wealth and power predictably try to perpetuate and consolidate themselves by utilizing every institutional tool they can co-opt, create, or recreate. And the vocabulary of aristocracy was one the founders were obviously already familiar with. Accordingly, any aristocratic airs were kept well hidden until it became safer to flaunt them. But the pursuit of such power was ever present and worrisome to the revolutionaries. It was a very frequent theme in both public discourse and private journals and correspondence.

This aristocratic mindset was most overt in the South. Before the American Revolution, New England had rooted for the Parliament in the English Civil War and town hall meetings had fostered a strong democratic ethos. By contrast, the South had rooted for the king's cavaliers and plantation life fostered a more medieval mentality. During the American Revolution, John Adams wrote of North Carolina:

The Gentry are very rich, and the common People very poor. This Inequality of Property, gives an Aristocratical [sic] Turn to all their Proceedings, and occasions a strong Aversion, in their Patricians, to Common Sense. But the Spirit of these Barons, is coming down and must submit.[356] (emphasis original)

And as Harry Caudill later wrote in *Night Comes to the Cumberlands*:

The Antebellum South was filled with romantic legends in which handsome young men left baronial halls and came to the New World to establish spacious manor houses of their own and to preserve the chivalry and gallantry of Sir Walter Scott's fantastic novels. Coats of arms were duly supplied to bolster these outlandish claims, and they hang today on thousands of walls, attesting to the hereditary splendor of imaginary ancestors.[357]

Note that the notion of inborn superiority was already a favorite theme in the South. As Abraham Lincoln acknowledged, this attitude went beyond family vanity to influence political thought. Conservatism's hostility toward democracy was always white hot:

It continues to develop that the insurrection is largely, if not exclusively, a war upon the first principle of popular government – the rights of the people. Conclusive evidence of this is found in the most grave and maturely considered public documents, as well as in the general tone of the insurgents. In those documents we find the abridgment of the existing right of suffrage and the denial to the people of all right to participate in the selection of public officers except the legislative boldly advocated, with labored arguments to prove that large control of the people in government is the source of all political evil. Monarchy itself is sometimes hinted at as a possible refuge from the power of the people.[358]

A few lines later Lincoln added, "It is the effort to place *capital* on an equal footing with, if not above, *labor*, in the structure of the government." (italics original)

This desire to abridge the existing right of suffrage has hardly vanished. U.S. Supreme Court Justice Anthony Scalia, Texas Governor Rick Perry (R), Rep. Paul Broun (R-GA), and Sen. Mike Lee (R-UT) had all voiced support for repealing the Seventeenth Amendment. That is the one that lets us directly vote for our U.S. senators instead of having our state legislatures choose them for us. In 2010, several senatorial candidates, including Joe Miller, Ken Buck, and Steve Southerland, had also signed on to the repeal movement.[359] They were in effect saying "Vote for me, because I think you should not be able to vote for me." Of course, all were conservative Republicans.

This idea is a Tea Party favorite. Ironically, these are the same people who call their opponents "elitists." Indeed, belying their populist imagery, Tea Party Nation president Judson Phillips thinks that limiting the vote to property holders "makes a lot of sense," although he avoided overtly endorsing it. On his radio broadcast, he explained:

The founding fathers originally said they put certain restrictions on who gets the right to vote. It wasn't you were just a citizen and you got to vote. Some of the restrictions, you know, you obviously would not think about today. But one of those was you had to be a property owner. And that makes a lot of sense, because if you're a property owner you actually have a vested stake in the community.[360]

Judson Phillips was fibbing a little. The founders did not put these restrictions on – they *inherited* them. And after we won our independence, there was dispute over whether these restrictions should be left in place. Like slavery, the property qualification for voting was something that the founders had fought over and that disagreement fell along regional lines as well. The North abolished both shortly after the Revolution. But, in the South, both blacks and poor whites alike had to wait until Union troops arrived nearly a century later. Judson Phillips suggests there was consensus where there was dispute.

And remember Benjamin Franklin saying the poorest continues to have equal claim to representation as the "most opulent" before bitterly blasting "a disposition among some of our people to commence an aristocracy, by giving the rich a predominancy *[sic]* in government"? This disposition still exists. And Judson Phillips would have you believe it was what all the founders wanted.

One of democracy's more genteel discontents is David Brooks, who thinks we are "neurotically democratic" and gushes that autocratic regimes like China and Singapore get things done. In other words, he is saying that Mussolini made the trains run on time.

In David Brooks' Orwellian reasoning, filibuster abuse is a symptom of too much democracy. Of course, as Matt O'Brian had pointed out on the *Washington Post's* Wonkblog, the filibuster is actually a check on democracy.[361]

If David Brooks really wants to get things done, he should want *more* democracy, not *less*.

David Brooks' column is replete with double-speak and zero-sum word games. He says we need "to become less democratic at the national level in order to become more democratic at the local level."[362] How exactly this would promote local democracy is not quite explained. Is that how things work in China? He just plays to conservative anti-Washington sentiment without giving any details on that particular point.

To break gridlock, Brooks suggests, "The quickest way around all of this is to use Simpson-Bowles-type commissions to push populist reforms." But Brooks' paradoxical idea of "populist" includes "entitlement reform." This does not sound very much in the spirit of the 1870s Populist Movement, which incidentally had first proposed the direct election of U.S. senators.

David Brooks does admit "The process of change would be unapologetically elitist." Part of it would be to "rally establishment opinion to browbeat the plans through." It sounds a lot like how Noam Chomsky describes the system works *today*. But then Brooks argues that this elitist process "would be anything but elitist" because of something bottom-up flexibility pixie dust something. Seriously, it is a train wreck of glittering generalities written to argue that things are actually their opposites. Toss in a New Deli cabbie and it becomes a Thomas Friedman column.

I know it is very tempting to write off Franklin and Lincoln's language of aristocracy and monarchy as politically motivated hyperbole. But it was part of a longstanding understanding of how the world worked. Shortly after Lincoln's death, wealthy tycoons, who had profited from the rapid industrial development of the Civil War, began to illustrate our founders' fears. These "robber barons," as critics called them, begat an era of monopolies, sweatshops, and galloping government corruption where bribery was common. Many bragged that they had governors and congressmen in their back pockets.

America had finally vanquished slavery. So, many employers, both North and South, sought to invent the next best thing. Just as the old plantation aristocracy strove to retain total control over their former slaves, these new industrialists desired the same control over their miners and factory hands. These tycoons often ran company towns in which the company was your employer, landlord, grocer, and everything else. You were paid in company script rather than real money. Accordingly, the boss totally controlled the local economy. He could squeeze you by raising prices while lowering wages. If you could not make ends meet, the company was always happy to float a loan at outrageous interest rates. So debt servitude was endured by miners as well as sharecroppers. How could you save up for your escape when the scant cash you ever saw was only phony Monopoly money? Thus, these robber barons ran their enterprises as plantations or fiefdoms – they treated their employees like slaves or serfs. Metaphor and hyperbole bordered on reality.

This ugly history is typically omitted from textbooks, and I do not expect that Texas will correct this longstanding tradition of omission anytime soon.

The self-entitled callousness of these captains of industry was absolutely astounding. Remember the Ludlow massacre? That was the strike where miners had to dig pits under their tents to protect their families from machine-gun fire. In his 1914 congressional testimony on the strike, John D. Rockefeller swore that he had to keep the union out "at any cost." Commission chairman Frank Walsh, asked him, "And you will do that if it costs all your property and kills all your employees?" Rockefeller simply replied, "It is a great principle."[363] This was precisely the type of aristocratic arrogance that Ayn Rand glorified. Rockefeller then added, "[I]t was upon a similar principle that the War of the Revolution was carried on."

Unless he meant the Confederate side of the U.S. Civil War, I am not sure which "War of the Revolution" he was referring to. But this was the same man who had dynamited a rival's oil refinery[364] and then said that "God gave me my money," so he often drew unusual conclusions.

But this new, revised version of the Divine Right of Kings was hardly unique to Rockefeller. In 1902, Philadelphia and Reading Railroad president George Baer argued, "The rights and interests of the laboring man will be protected and cared for – not by labor agitators, but by the Christian men to whom God in his infinite wisdom has given the control of the property interests of this country."[365]

In other words, God hired the fox to guard the hen house, so how dare the poultry object? Thus, injustice is justified since the status quo must be the will of God. Today, Arthur C. Brooks says that God did indeed make Rockefeller rich to reward his piety. He and Jon Stossel agree that Rockefeller's critics were only jealous of his immense success.

Mark Twain had noticed that American culture was losing its democratic ethos and anti-aristocratic character. He wrote of the "coming American monarchy."[366] "In public we scoff at titles and hereditary privilege but privately we hanker after them, and when we get a chance we buy them for cash and a daughter."[367] After lamenting our pathetic fascination with lords and ladies, he wrote, "The next step is to rail and scoff at republics and democracies."[368] Conservatives certainly took that step a long time ago. I can just imagine what Mark Twain would make of today's silly Disney Princess shit.

The founders feared that the rich would become another aristocracy and Mark Twain believed that he was witness to the dismal metamorphosis they had predicted. "Like all the other nations, we worship money and the possessors of it – they being our aristocracy, and we have to have one."[369] In *Huckleberry Finn*, Twain wrote of "The Orneriness of Kings" and in *A Connecticut Yankee in King Arthur's Court*, he totally savaged his era's romanticization of chivalry. Twain wrote, "[A] privileged class, an aristocracy, is but a band of slaveholders under another name."[370] Thus, Twain was only half joking when he famously accused Sir Walter Scott of causing the Civil War by writing *Ivanhoe*.

This Victorian celebration of medieval English things appeared in architecture as well as literature. Victorian homes were built in Richardsonian Romanesque or Neo-Gothic. In *Life on the Mississippi*, Mark Twain called the Louisiana state capitol a "sham castle" and blamed Sir Walter Scott for that as well. "The South has not yet recovered from the debilitating influence of his books."[371]

The growth in immigration and industrialization had also made northern Anglo-Americans ethnocentric, hostile to democracy and modernity, and nostalgic for ancient English things. Earlier, the revolutionaries had adopted many Native American and French symbols and customs to create a separate, new American identity distinct from "Mother England." But the Victorians later reversed this.

Their pastoral feudal fantasy was paradoxical because England was the Industrial Revolution's birthplace and it was Southern cotton that got their textile looms humming. Most plantations were factory farms and it was Eli Whitney's mechanical cotton gin made the whole system possible. And unlike traditional agriculture that grew a variety of foodstuffs for local consumption, the South focused on growing inedible cotton for export to foreign markets. Therefore, it was inherently intertwined with international industrial trade. America's Victorian elites – both North and South – were emotionally recoiling from the very modernity that made them rich. And they spent that money building nostalgic castles.

After the Civil War, northern elites gradually began to sympathize with their southern counterparts as anti-immigrant bigotry rose. They came to see each other as being on the same page. Bullies empathize with bullies and a similar attitude could be seen elsewhere. As British historian V.G. Kiernan wrote in *The Lords of Human Kind: Black Man, Yellow Man and White Man in an Age of Empire*:

Lord Salisbury, the Conservative leader, supporting coercion in Ireland, said that Irishmen were as unfit self-government as Hottentots. ... There is a story of the Austrian representative saying to the Hungarian, when the Hapsburg empire was transformed into the Dual Monarchy in 1867, "You look after your barbarians, and we'll look after ours" – meaning the Czechs, Serbs and so on.[372]

Thus, the North abandoned blacks to the so-called "Knights" of the Klu Klux Klan. As the popularity of D.W. Griffith's 1915 film *Birth of a Nation* showed, such southern "chivalry" was openly celebrated outside the South into the early twentieth century.

But this also meant that anti-aristocratic rhetoric stayed in play as progressives attacked the same cruel, superstitious, and authoritarian medieval thinking Mark Twain had attacked in *A Connecticut Yankee in King Arthur's Court*. Indeed, such political insults continued into Franklin D. Roosevelt's day. FDR frequently attacked "economic monarchists," "economic royalists," and "Tories" in his speeches. He even borrowed the phrase "New Deal" from Mark Twain's *A Connecticut Yankee.*[373]

In his 1932 Chicago Democratic convention acceptance speech, FDR took aim at his era's Tories and what would later be called "trickle-down economics" in the Reagan Era:

There are two ways of viewing the government's duty in matters affecting economic and social life. The first sees to it that a favored few are helped and hopes that some of their prosperity will leak through, sift through, to labor, to the farmer, to the small businessman. That theory belongs to the party of Toryism, and I had hoped that most of the Tories left this country in 1776.[374]

His anti-monarchist rhetoric was more explicit in his 1936 Democratic Convention speech. This was the speech in which FDR famously declared, "This generation has a rendezvous with destiny." But a portion of it was devoted to explaining how monopoly threatened democracy by using metaphors of royalty:

For out of this modern civilization economic royalists carved new dynasties. New kingdoms were built upon concentration of control over material things. Through new uses of corporations, banks and securities, new machinery of industry and agriculture, of labor and capital – all undreamed of by the Fathers – the whole structure of modern life was impressed into this royal service. There was no place among this royalty for our many thousands of small-businessmen and merchants who sought to make worthy use of the American system of initiative and profit. They were no more free than the worker or the farmer. Even honest and progressive-minded men of wealth, aware of their obligation to their generation, could never know just where they fitted in this dynastic scheme of things.[375]

Calling monopolies monarchies was consistent with the rhetoric of the revolutionaries. In both private letters and public speeches, the founders frequently voiced their fear of concentrated power in any form. Again, remember John Adams attacking "aristocratical banks."

In fact, American political cartoonists had always portrayed ambitious men and groping industries as kings or Caesars. Richard Nixon's "imperial presidency" inspired many to depict him as a king. Hugh Haynie's take was especially memorable and Edward Sorel had portrayed Nixon as Louis XVI.[376]

But outside of cartoons, this political tradition had largely dissipated by the 1950s. The 1930s and 40s was a period of transition. The new menace of fascism was invoked literally rather than figuratively, but it was aimed at the same anti-democratic forces. Often the charges of monarchism, slavery, and fascism could be found in the same documents. As George Seldes wrote in his fiery 1943 book *Facts and Fascism*:

I call these elements Fascist. You may not like names and labels but technically as well as journalistically and morally they are correct. You may substitute Tories, or Economic Royalists, or Vested Interests, or whatever you like for the flag-waving Anti-American Americans whose efforts and objectives parallel those of the Linga Industriale which brought out Mussolini in 1920, and the ThyssenKrupp-Voegele-Flick Rhineland industry and banking system which subsidized Hitler when Nazism was about to collapse. Their main object was to end the civil liberties of the nation, destroy the labor unions, end the free press, and make more money at the expense of a slave nation.[377]

George Seldes acknowledged that others had already made this connection:

"The kingdom of Henry Ford," wrote Michael Sayers, *"is a fascist state within the United States. All the characteristics of Fascism – Jew-baiting, corruption, gangsterism – exist today wherever King Henry Ford reigns over American workers. Bur Fordism and Americanism cannot long continue to exist side by side. Already in more than half a dozen states the National Labor Relations Board has found the Ford Motor Company guilty of maintaining 'a regime of terror and violence directed against its employees.'"*[378]

Likewise, the DuPonts had financed the Black Legion, a Klan-linked fascist group that had firebombed union meetings and murdered organizers. They killed at least fifty people in Detroit, MI, many of them African Americans.[379] Henry Ford's brutal campaign of intimidation included whippings. That may explain Seldes' use of the word "slave."

Once again, metaphor and hyperbole often bordered on reality. This was the era before "big labor and big government" that conservatives recall with nostalgic fondness and seek to restore despite its horrific and long-documented side effects.

Today, the rhetorical metamorphosis is complete. Almost nobody is accused of being a monarchist or an aristocrat anymore. The term "Tory" is now only used outside of the United States and it is a legitimate label rather than an accusation or insult. It just means "conservative." Nazi name-calling remains instead. And now, misinformed misuse has morphed it into something that is almost as meaningless as it is emotional, but I will cover that more in the next chapter. The point here is that the Tory mentality still persists today and it still assaults democracy.

Does it matter if we call ourselves a democracy or a republic? Isn't that just a matter of semantics? After all, if it does not alter our form of government or how it works, who cares what we call it?

What a question! Obviously denying that we are a democracy poisons our national identity and impacts us both at home and abroad.

Witness the 2000 Supreme Court decision *Bush v. Gore*. When the court ordered Florida officials to stop the recount, conservatives justified it by saying "We are not a democracy, but a republic." It was a huge paradox for states rights advocates. Running elections is left to the states, hence the bewildering variety of different systems. The federal government must not interfere unless the states are denying citizens their civil rights under the Fourteenth Amendment. But George W. Bush's lawyers improbably claimed exactly that, even though they had no legal standing to do so.[380] If Florida wants to conduct a recount, the rest of the nation can wait. But of course conservatives were not concerned with consistency. Both hostile to democracy and afraid of losing, Republican pundits invoked their nebulous notion of a republic to justify this judicial usurpation.

Talk about "activist judges."

This anti-democratic mentality also impacts our foreign policy. We had prolonged the Cold War by supporting almost every mass-murdering, torturing despot around the globe instead of aiding emerging democratic movements in the decolonizing world.

Why? Because we could not bear to see Noah Webster's "soul of a republic" spread. Instead, we made a mockery of freedom and democracy by backing the likes of Pinochet, Branco, Banzer, Doe, Zia Ul-Haq, Suharto, Stroessner, Papadopoulous, Papa and Baby Doc Duvalier, the Samozas, Videla, Cristiani, etc. Many of these dictators had direct Nazi ties. But as long as they were anti-communist, we did not care. Our foreign policy experts thought it was better to support a fascist than anyone as socialist as our European allies. Standard Oil's profit margins were more important than democracy.

Of course, such "banana republics" were not republics any more than the communist governments that put the word in *their* names. But ambiguity and ignorance about what a republic is made such relationships easier to spin. By supporting France's attempt to hold onto Vietnam as their colony, we only made ourselves the villains and therefore further popularized Ho Chi Min. Our supporting the brutal Diem dictatorship did not help any either. Any subsequent attempts to win the Vietnamese people's "hearts and minds" were foredoomed, so the promised elections were never held. So much for the "Republic" of South Vietnam. We just buttressed autocratic puppets.

This was ironic because we were once European colonies as well. Once we won our independence, our young country tried to avoid becoming any superpower's puppet. Here is Thomas Jefferson writing on the War of 1812 – a sideshow to England's ongoing war with Napoleon. Read this passage with the Cold War in mind:

We believe no more in Bonaparte's fighting merely for the liberty of the seas, than in Great Britain's fighting for the liberties of mankind. The object of both is the same, to draw to themselves the power, the wealth and the resources of other nations. We resist the enterprises of England first, because they first come vitally home to us. And our feelings repel the logic of bearing the lash of George III for fear of that of Bonaparte at some future day. When the wrongs of France shall reach us with equal effect, we shall resist them also.[381]

That quote aptly describes the attitude of many former colonies in Asia and Africa toward the U.S. and U.S.S.R. They tried to steer between the superpowers and even dared to disagree with them. That is what happens when people have a choice – they make their own choices. Remember, Pat Buchanan's strange take on the importance of democracy: "Whether a nation is democratic should be of less concern to us than how it views America. In the Cold War, autocratic Pakistan was a better friend than democratic India, which sided with Moscow in the Afghan war."[382] As I had mentioned in chapter one, democratic India was unhappy with our training and funding of Osama bin Laden. Our paternalism rarely appreciates genuine independence. India had to look to its interests, and those did not include arming hostile Jihadists.[383]

The issue of colonialism also shows conservatism's hostility to democracy. In 1957, William F. Buckley wrote a *National Review* editorial that favorably compared Jim Crow at home with colonialism abroad. It was an unsigned editorial, which meant it was the shared opinion of the whole editorial board, but the prose was unmistakably Buckley's. Note how he pitted civilization against liberty, equality, and democracy:

The central question that emerges – and it is not a parliamentary question or a question that is answered by merely consulting a catalogue of the rights of American citizens, born Equal – is whether the white community in the South is entitled to take such measures as are necessary to prevail, politically and culturally, in areas in which it does not prevail numerically?

The sobering answer is Yes – the White community is so entitled because, for the time being, it is the advanced race. It is not easy, and it is unpleasant, to adduce statistics evidencing the median cultural superiority of white over Negro: but it is a fact that obtrudes, one that cannot be hidden by ever-so-busy egalitarians and anthropologists. The question, as far as the White community is concerned, is whether the claims of civilization supersede those of universal suffrage. The British believe they do, and acted accordingly, in Kenya, where the choice was dramatically one between civilization and barbarism, and elsewhere; the South, where the conflict is by no means dramatic, as in Kenya, nevertheless perceives important qualitative differences between its culture and the Negroes', and intends to assert its own.

National Review believes that the South's premises are correct. If the majority will what is socially atavistic, then to thwart the majority may be, though undemocratic, enlightened. It is more important for any community, anywhere in the world, to affirm and live by civilized standards, than to bow to the demands of the numerical majority. Sometimes it becomes impossible to assert the will of a minority, in which case it must give way, and the society will regress; sometimes the numerical minority cannot prevail except by violence: then it must determine whether the prevalence of its will is worth the terrible price of violence.[384]

Later, Buckley publicly backed off this awkward argument. But he continued to support, employ, and promote those who still held this white supremacist worldview.

For example, Pat Buchanan was deeply influenced by *National Review* foreign policy columnist James Burnham who wrote *The Suicide of the West.*[385] The National Review later hired Pat Buchanan as well and still later endorsed him for president in 1992.

These *Review* contributors regularly portrayed places like Apartheid South Africa and the white minority regime in Rhodesia as citadels of civilization to be defended against what they saw as egalitarian barbarism.

That racist mindset still survives today in both paleoconservatism and paleolibertarianism. One of the many charges that the Tea Party leveled against President Barack Obama is that he is an "anti-colonialist." Well, so was George Washington, so what is their point?

Their point is that defying the British Crown is simply not done if your skin is yellow, black, or brown. And the fact that they think "anti-colonialist" means "un-American" telegraphs their ass-backwards mentality pretty clearly. Their "patriotism" does not rise above petty us-vs.-them ethnic tribalism and is hostile to both freedom and democracy.

Needless to say, past anti-democratic policies have had horrific consequences abroad. Had the CIA not overthrown Prime Minister Mohammad Mosaddegh in 1953, Iran would today have a half-century of democracy under its belt and be less hostile to us now. But, alas, the Iranian people believed that the oil in their ground belonged to them and not foreign corporations. So we decided that they were "not ready" for democracy and thus installed the torture-using Shah as their monarch.[386] You have to wonder what our founders would think of our overthrowing a democracy to restore a monarchy.

For better or worse, our democratic identity has often decided which wars we fought. We entered World War I to "make the world safe for democracy" and World War II to do likewise and fight fascism. Of course, conservatives are not above co-opting the cause of democracy to get us into wars. George W. Bush had used it, among other arguments, to justify invading Iraq. Pundits such as Ann Coulter accused peace protesters of hating freedom and democracy. Likewise, many conservatives became temporary feminists for our Afghan war, which had implausibly become about *burqas*. Had conservatives finally embraced *democracy* in order to defeat Saddam Hussein's dreaded *Republican* Guard?

Not quite. During the War on Terror, some Bush Administration officials actually suggested postponing the elections,[387] presumably until the threat of terrorism had passed, which, again, Vice-President Dick Cheney said would not be in our lifetime. Although, we had held elections during the U.S. Civil War, the Bush administration considered a few guys with box cutters to be a far greater existential threat.

The spectacle of conservatives suddenly supporting abroad what they had always mocked at home was something truly special. But, as I wrote before, this singularity was short-lived. Glenn Beck was a major advocate of invading Iraq. He echoed all of the Bush Administration's talking points about bringing democracy to the Arab world. But then Barack Obama was elected president and the Arab Spring began in the streets of Cairo. Young Muslims demanded democracy and ousted despots without U.S. troops.

Suddenly, Glenn Beck did not want democracy for Arabs anymore. In fact, he saw this as threat to all we hold dear and urged viewers to stockpile food and ammunition. Yes, some conservatives still adhered to the Bush League line, but Ann Coulter, Mike Huckabee, and the religious right agreed with Glenn Beck.[388] Ann Coulter won applause and hoots of approval at the Conservative Political Action Conference (CPAC) in 2011 by saying that Egypt's dictator, Hosni Mubarak, should jail more journalists.

Conservatives have always fought against democracy in ways both large and small. First, they opposed the Civil Rights movement in the 1950s and 60s. Then, they opposed lowering the voting age to eighteen. Then, they opposed "motor voter" bills in the 1970s and 80s which made it easy to register when you got or renewed your driver's license. And now that the Supreme Court has struck down a core provision of the 1964 Civil Rights Act, they are back at their old voter suppression tactics.

Those who defend such bills insist they are not racist – they say they are just trying to hurt the Democrats' chances at the polls.[389] In other words, "We're not bigots, just cheaters." But I think there is definitely some bigotry in the mix too. After all, it is easier to violate others' rights if you dislike them. Sympathy tends to interfere with victimizing others at both the planning and execution stages, while hostility obviously facilitates it.

But this also goes beyond bigotry. Conservative hostility to democracy is a historical constant. It starts with Alexander Hamilton's aristocratic attitude and goes from there. As Abraham Lincoln said of the Confederates, conservatives make "labored arguments to prove that large control of the people in government is the source of all political evil." In the 1950s, the John Birch Society put up billboards that read "This is a republic, not a democracy! Let's keep it that way." Such thinking rings in the Texas State Board of Education's striking the word democracy from its textbooks and the Tea Party's desire to repeal the direct election of U.S. Senators. And Pat Buchanan advocates putting cities under "quasi-dictatorial rule" by arguing, "If the people are corrupt, the more democracy, the worse the government." Of course, conservatives have always thought the people are too corrupt to govern themselves – it is what makes them conservatives. That is the Tory mentality.

There are a host of obvious problems with conservative hostility to democracy. At home, it means they are quick to violate voting rights. Abroad, it means they are apt to support despots. But I would add this question: What does it say about their patriotism?

8: Springtime for Goldberg
Behind the Right's Bizarre Nazi Analogies

It is probably a positive thing that most people react to Nazi analogies with instant suspicion. Such comparisons are lurid, ridiculous, and nowadays ubiquitous. Today, Nazi-analogies pepper political discourse as never before. It has become the earmark of arguments that are lazy, crazy, or both – and there are plenty of those out there.

It would be good to have a moratorium on this metaphor, but unfortunately such a pact would probably not last. The reason goes beyond the loss of civility in political discourse. Conservatives cannot stop making Nazi analogies any more than they can stop questioning their opponents' patriotism. Both are basically the same projecting. Twisting history is a defensive reflex. It is the result of their anti-democratic animus.

And World War II is not the only historical period they distort. The Enlightenment, the Civil War, and the Progressive Era especially all go through their Orwellian meat grinder.

Conservatives really began hammering liberals with Nazi analogies in the 1990s. Rush Limbaugh called feminists "feminazis" by comparing abortion to the Holocaust while forgetting or ignoring that abortion was *verboten* in the Fatherland. Likewise, the militia movement used Nazi analogies while lionizing white supremacists like Randy Weaver. The use of this tactic has only grown since then.

This is not to say liberals have never played the Nazi card. Quite to the contrary, it admittedly has been a longstanding political tradition. But something fundamental has changed. There was once a sort of understanding in the badlands of political hyperbole that conservatives were called "fascists" and liberals were called "communists." It was how each called the other extremists along the political spectrum of left and right. But now, right is left and *vice versa*. All history and ideology are turned inside out. Except that leftists do not call conservatives "communists" – at least, not seriously.[390]

How did we get here? I have a theory. After a century of conservatives red-baiting everything from the eight-hour work day to school desegregation, the communist label had lost a lot of its emotional traction. Civil disobedience behind the Iron Curtain had torn it down so Ronald Reagan's old "evil empire" rhetoric rang irrelevant in a world with only one superpower. The crumbling of the Eastern Block made communists seem pathetic rather than scary. And since conservatives mostly motivate voters through fear, this geopolitical triumph posed to be a novel problem for them. They needed a new bogeyman.

Calling liberals "Nazis" was their solution. The beginning and end of their argument seems to be that the word "Nazi" was the German acronym for the National Socialist German Workers Party. Add a rant about big government to that and you have the sum total of their point. It is a compelling argument if you know absolutely nothing about Hitler's rise to power or what he subsequently did with it.

From there, they argue that using government to do virtually anything is inherently fascist. It is ultimately an argument against modernity. This is why they claim that fascism had actually originated with the French Revolution. As we shall see, it is not just a rhetorical weapon against liberals, but a weapon against the concept of progress itself that equates social change with guillotines and gas chambers. Any modernity is automatically associated with state terror.

Traditionalists are predictably pretty addicted to this interpretation, and getting them into detox is highly unlikely. They are almost adorably proud of their "I'm rubber, you're glue" argument. They decry Nazi analogies as if they had never done any red-baiting. But now they can do both at the same time and act like they are only hitting back.

Of course, conservatives pounce on any opportunity to turn the tables, however nonsensical – thus their favorite phrase "liberals are the *real* racists." Nazi analogies are just another variant of this.

But, as I suggested before, there is more to their narrative's attraction than that. Deep down, they know that their authoritarian, anti-egalitarian mindset is utterly un-American. Naturally, this contradiction creates tension and projection is their automatic response.[391]

And, once again, this is not limited to Nazi analogies. Conservatives are chronically on the wrong side of history, so they must constantly rewrite it – thus their many strange attempts to co-opt FDR, MLK, JFK, etc. Consider Ted Nugent claiming that Rosa Parks is one of his heroes when he is not calling President Obama a "subhuman mongrel."

Conservatives are in a perpetual identity crisis. They are touchy because their sense of patriotism and belonging feel under constant assault. This is not only because of their fear of change, but also because they hate everything America is supposed to stand for and cannot admit it. Thus, anything they say on the matter is an attempt to square a circle. But their Nazi analogies will be my central focus in this chapter because they define the current political *zeitgeist* and they say a lot about how conservatives think and operate.

Let's begin with some debunking. Unfortunately, it is necessary.

The best place to start would be with the Nazi acronym. Initially, it appears to be a great inconvenience. The words "National Socialist German Workers Party" pretty much say it all, right?

Except that it does not because the Nazis were notorious liars. Adolf Hitler said that people will swallow a big lie more easily than a small one, and their party name was a whopper. I seriously doubt that they would have gotten too far in the Great Depression calling themselves the National Capitalist German Bosses party.

In fact, the far right often founds deceptively-named groups. Take, for example, Jerry Falwell's Liberty University or Phyllis Schlafly's Independent Women's Forum. This is basically the same strategy behind company unions, phony abortion clinics, and polluter-funded "Astroturf" (as opposed to grassroots) green groups. "Truth in Advertising" is not a conservative strong suit and many contemporary observers had called out Adolf Hitler's pseudo-socialism. As journalist George Seldes wrote in 1943, "He stole the word."[392]

In fact, the party's name was a mixed message which should have red-flagged the lie. Since when did nationalists and socialists get along? Socialism is internationalist, hence the "Internationale." Therefore, socialists in every country had ideologically opposed involvement in World War I. Their slogan was "A bayonet is a tool with a worker on both ends." True, many succumbed to emotional jingoism and betrayed their principles, but others worked hard to avert war. The issue had bitterly split them. For example, in Germany, Rosa Luxemburg scathingly criticized those who had voted for war in 1914.

By contrast, nationalists happily jumped in with unified, ideologically consistent agreement. Of course they would – war validates and magnifies their violent, tribal, "us vs. them" mindset, making society brutally hunt and punish any "traitor" who does not share it. Thus, it becomes a very handy excuse for attacking actual socialists, which the Nazis later did. Thus, their name combined phony socialism with actual nationalism.

Nazi rhetoric constantly changed like a chameleon. They talked an anti-capitalist line to workers, and a pro-capitalist one to their employers. In fact, all fascist parties used this technique. Italy's dictator, Benito Mussolini, wrote quite florid pro-capitalist prose, reminiscent of the self-actualization business literature that management gurus later churned out throughout the 1990s. "Private property completes the human personality: it is a right and therefore an obligation."[393] Ayn Rand could have written that line.

Of course, Adolf Hitler could also sound like Ayn Rand. In a speech to businessmen comparing democracy with communism, he argued that great differences in talent justified great differences in wealth. Hitler wanted to communicate that he was no collectivist, and only a little pinch of religion distinguished his rhetoric from Rand's:

This entire structure of culture, down to its foundations and in each of its building blocks, is nothing other than the result of creative talent, the achievement of intelligence, and [of] the industriousness of individuals. The greatest results are the great crowning achievement of individual geniuses endowed by God ...[394]

Anticipating Ayn Rand's producer/parasite rhetoric, Adolf Hitler blasted the "exploitation of creators, of geniuses, and talented men." Turning back to the topic of democracy, he decried "subjugating the genius to the majority" and fumed, "This is not the rule of the people, but in fact the rule of stupidity, of mediocrity, of half-measures, of cowardice, of weakness, and inadequacy." Naturally, Hitler did not give the same speech to factory hands or the angry unemployed.

The Nazis talked out of both sides of their mouths. This explains how they were both a political joke and attractive to desperate voters. Mixed messages capitalize on mixed feelings, which are widespread in times of crisis and uncertainty. They are political Rorschach tests in which people see what they want to see. And while such self-contradictions often turn off thinking people, those hungry to identify with something do not care. In fact, emotional voters rarely notice. They just think the speaker shares their mixed feelings. They see the speaker as "like me" and may even become protective of the speaker. As Adolf Hitler had bragged, "Confusion, indecision, fear; these are my weapons."[395]

So, the Nazis double-crossed everyone, right?

Well, not quite. They remained very friendly to big business. During the Night of Long Knives, Adolf Hitler had any Brown Shirt leaders who took his anti-capitalist rhetoric seriously slain in their beds. He did not want to see any Aryan capitalists harassed.

In fact, the Nazis and big business got along famously. They needed each other: Adolf Hitler liquidated the Reds, for which capital was grateful. And capital was essential to Hitler's long-range plans because "mom & pop shops" do not make planes and tanks. For that, you need heavy industry.

Once in power, Hitler outlawed labor unions – a longstanding wet dream of industrialists. Actions speak louder than words and Hitler's actions dramatically showed that he was no socialist.

Again, bait-and-switch was a favorite fascist tactic. Benito Mussolini had pledged to enact land reform for Italian peasants. Great aristocratic estates were supposed to be broken up into small family plots for poor farmers. He proposed this to co-opt a land reform movement that had already been active in Italy since the end of World War I. Consider this quote that he made shortly after he seized power and was still solidifying his position. Note how he still felt it necessary to pay lip service to democracy:

I love the working classes. The supremest [sic] ambition and the dearest hope of my life has been, and is still, to see them better treated and enjoying conditions of life worthy of the citizens of a great nation. ... I do not believe in class war, but in cooperation between classes. The Fascist government will devote all its efforts to the creation of an agrarian democracy based on the principle of small ownership. The great estates must be handed over to the peasant communities: the great capitalists of agriculture must submit to a process of harmonization of their rights with those of the peasants.[396]

For those who associate socialism with fascism, this quote is a smoking gun. But Benito Mussolini betrayed Italy's peasants in less than two months. He not only stopped land reform, he even *reversed* it by returning land that the peasants had already taken for themselves.

Of course, why would any dictator want to divide up property amongst the poor to create a Jeffersonian republic of small yeoman farmers? To paraphrase the "Soup Nazi" in *Seinfeld,* no forty acres and a mule for *YOU!*

Instead, Mussolini built what he called the Corporate State, in which big business and government cooperated to ensure a docile populace and workforce.

Naturally, America's captains of industry were in love. They asked, *"How can WE get some of that sweet action?"* As U.S. ambassador William E. Dodd warned upon his return from Berlin in 1937, "Fascism is on the march today in America. Millionaires are marching to the tune. It will come in this country unless a strong defense is set up by all liberal and progressive forces."[397] He then elaborated:

A clique of U.S. industrialists is hell-bent to bring a fascist state to supplant our democratic form of government, and is working closely with the fascist regime in Italy and Germany. Aboard ship a prominent executive of one of America's largest financial corporations told me point-blank that if the progressive trend of the Roosevelt administration continued, he would be ready to take definite action to bring Fascism to America. Certain American industrialists had a great deal to do with bringing fascist regimes into being in both Germany and Italy. They extended aid to help Fascism occupy the seat of power, and they are helping to keep it there."

Note the use of the word "progressive." It does not seem to mean what Glenn Beck thinks it does. Go figure.

And in a letter to senators published in the *New York Times*, Ambassador Dodd wrote:

There are individuals of great wealth who wish a dictatorship and are ready to help a Huey Long. There are politicians who think they may gain powers like those exercised in Europe. One man, I have been told by personal friends, who owns near a billion dollars, is ready to support such a program and, of course, control it.[398]

Some of these tycoons were coy about their fascist enthusiasms and some were not. For example, Henry Ford's sympathies were quite overt. And he was not the only one. General Motors' president William S. Knudsen told a *New York Times* reporter that Hitler's Germany was "the miracle of the 20th Century."[399]

This is not to say that the press sat on the sidelines and simply reported. Publishers all over America adored Adolf Hitler and loathed Franklin D. Roosevelt. We are often told FDR's fireside chats were meant to reassure a shaken nation in the depths of the Great Depression. But they were also the only way that he could make his case to the people undistorted. Most publishers were openly pro-fascist prior to Pearl Harbor. As George Seldes noted, William Randolph Hearst's newspapers "published signed propaganda articles of Goering, Goebbels and Co."[400] Hearst interpreted his status as a press baron pretty literally. He built and lived in a Bavarian-style castle in California. Therefore, cartoonists often drew him as a king. *Fortune* magazine's July 1934 issue loved Benito Mussolini so much that Seldes called it "a song of praise for Fascism."[401]

Much of the business establishment saw fascism as a solution to communism. But to those with anti-democratic, aristocratic attitudes, fascism was already attractive even without any communist threat. If you equated liberty and equality with chaos and longed for a strongman to defend tradition, your latent monarchism was already aroused. Simply put, fascism was monarchism modernized for the 20th Century – aristocracy made sleek, streamlined, and posh like an art deco Tamara de Lempicka painting. And the fact that workers were actually in revolt only added urgency, making political reaction seem hip, edgy, and relevant. To conservatives, the birth of fascism was an affirming breath of fresh air. They saw it not as a necessary evil but as a happy model to copy.

Jonah Goldberg is a big promoter of the notion that socialism is fascism. *The National Review Online* editor had written a column called "Springtime for Slanderers; Who are you calling a Nazi?" He later expanded it into a book called *Liberal Fascism: The Secret History of the American Left from Mussolini to the Politics of Meaning*. Goldberg's article pretends to be a plea against using Nazi analogies, but it is predictably littered with them. He closed his column with this curious challenge:

And one last point I feel compelled to point out. I've never met a real social-welfare state leftist who could answer the following question without having to think real hard: "Aside from the murder and genocide, what exactly don't you like about National Socialism?" And I've never met a conservative who didn't have an answer at his fingertips. So, who's really closer to being a Nazi?[402]

Well, what can I say? I am speechless.

The obvious answer is *"Everything"* but Jonah Goldberg seems unlikely to accept that. He wants specifics and that is difficult because any specific thing I could mention pales next to genocide. Things like institutional racism, press censorship, outlawing labor unions, etc. are certainly all bad, but they are not *genocide* bad. That evil eclipses everything else. Thus, people are stunned, not stumped.

What makes Jonah Goldberg's query especially absurd is the *völkisch* (folk-ish) "family values" voters who helped put the Nazis in power in the first place. The horrors of World War I had discredited the old Victorian order throughout Europe and the Jazz Age took its place. Germany's conservative institutions were particularly hard hit. They had invested all their prestige and political credibility in eventual victory. Thus, with the ignominy of defeat, the monarchy, the military, and the church lost their all their cultural authority over society. Kaiser Wilhelm cowardly skipped the country and the blue-nosed Prussian prudery that had once rivaled Great Britain's went with it. Germany finally let her hair down – and bobbed it. Berlin quickly eclipsed Paris as the id of Europe. There was greater gay and lesbian visibility and frank talk about sex as women got jobs previously reserved for men and demanded both the vote and the right to abortion. (They got the vote, but not legalized abortion.) This revolt against Victorian mores was going on throughout the Western World, but in Germany the effect was far more jarring.

Of course, conservatives regrouped. Their attitude can be summed up in the title of Robert Bork's *Slouching Towards Gomorrah*. They thought society was suffering from a deficit of discipline and equated liberty and equality with both spiritual and material ruin. They craved a return to order and a society where everyone knew their place. Thus, Hitler appealed to cultural conservatives. Like Ronald Reagan's "Morning in America," Hitler promised national renewal in a nostalgic fashion. The only overtly welcome modernity was technology, especially military technology. All other modern ideas were considered poisonous foreign imports – infections to be purged from the German bloodstream.

This can be seen in their gender politics. They considered women's true concerns to be *"Kinder, Küche, Kirche"* – children, kitchen, and church. But the three Ks had little appeal for young German women whose ambitions went beyond being *hausfraus*.

Predictably, many older, traditional women were both jealous and horrified. Much like Phyllis Schlafly's Independent Women's Forum, these church ladies formed anti-feminist women's groups in response. Like Ann Coulter, they were anti-choice in every sense of the word and thought giving women the vote was a huge mistake.[403] But once they had it, they had no problem using it to oppose more progress.

For example, Nationalist Party Reichstag delegate Clara Mende was a longtime opponent of women's suffrage, but of course that did not stop her from running for office once she could vote.[404]

As Claudia Koontz noted in *Mothers in the Fatherland*, "these women wanted 'Emancipation from Emancipation!' – a slogan later taken up by Nazi ideologue Alfred Rosenberg."[405] Adolf Hitler stated, "[T]he term 'women's emancipation' is invented by Jewish intellectuals, and its meaning was imbued with the same spirit."[406]

When these groups merged into one umbrella organization under the Nazis, their guidelines stipulated that they would eschew "the false steps of the democratic-liberal-international women's movement which ignores the source of the woman's soul that comes from *God* [italics in original] and nationality [*Volkstum*]."[407]

They were basically Sarah Palin's anti-feminist "mama grizzlies."

This anxiety can also be seen in Fritz Lang's 1927 silent science fiction film *Metropolis*. Its message was that a return to church and tradition will save society from destructive class conflict. This was symbolized by the character Maria, the hot young church lady, bringing everyone together on the forgotten medieval cathedral's steps at the film's climax. When she repeatedly preaches that the heart must mediate between the head and the hand, she means the middle class must mediate between capital and labor.

By contrast, her evil robot doppelganger dressed like a Ziegfeld Follies chorus girl and reveled in sex. The android false Maria represented the liberated, "selfish" New Woman, and her wanton thrill-seeking had almost physically destroyed Metropolis. The metaphor could not possibly have been plainer to German audiences, and Adolf Hitler loved this film's affirmation of tradition and hierarchy.[408]

Where sexuality is feared, freedom is never safe and it was not hard for German conservatives to convert prudish discomfort into political reaction. Sexual liberty was depicted as both a symptom of social decay and a foreboding metaphor for freedom itself. Pat Buchanan summed up their attitude aptly because he shares it: "Homosexuality is not a civil right. Its rise almost always is accompanied, as in the Weimar Republic, with a decay of society and a collapse of its basic cinder block, the family."[409]

Traditionalists wanted somebody to make the gays go away and Adolf Hitler delivered – albeit more literally than they might have imagined. The Nazis immediately outlawed pornography and "degenerate art." They made the punishment for abortion far more severe and birth control far harder to obtain.[410] There was a "Reich Headquarters for the Combating of Homosexuality and Abortion."[411] Never was government so much in people's bedrooms. But bedrooms are not boardrooms, so conservative enthusiasm remained undimmed.

Most people are probably not familiar with this history. If you asked them to picture women in Nazi Germany, they would likely think of a blond dominatrix wearing an SS uniform.

Perhaps this is what Rush Limbaugh wants you to imagine when he says "feminazi." He definitely wants to make feminism threatening.

Ignorance of this history is probably another reason why people draw a blank when Jonah Goldberg asks them what was wrong with the Nazis besides genocide. Well, the Nazis' sexism is certainly one answer.

At this point, you might have noticed a pattern – the familiar marriage of economic and cultural conservatives.

Now, I am not saying that being both automatically makes you a fascist. There are some other earmarks as well. Contempt for democracy would be a big one, and racism would be another huge factor.

But I *am* saying that fascists are both and that the idea that they are "actually socialists" had long been utterly debunked.

In short, all pit bulls are dogs – but not all dogs are pit bulls. But Jonah Goldberg would have you believe that a pit bull is actually a kind of cat.

George Seldes had weighed in on this issue back in 1938:

It is becoming more and more commonplace – despite the attack of purists and the students of semantics – to use the words conservatives and Fascist as synonyms. There are of course considerable differences, although every man who is a Fascist is ipso facto a conservative, and the reverse is not necessarily true. It is true, however, that the man who founded Fascism defined it as reactionary and anti-liberal.[412]

George Seldes was referring to Benito Mussolini's article "Force and Consent" in the March 1923 issue of *Gerarchia*.[413] That was his party's official publication. Its title means "hierarchy" in Italian. Of course, real socialists do not like hierarchy. As Robert Bork wrote, "Radical egalitarians necessarily hate hierarchies."[414] By contrast, many conservatives admire hierarchy and mock democracy. *Gerarchia's* subscribers would have no doubt nodded in agreement with Bork's critique of liberty and equality, not to mention Samuel Johnson's notion that subordination is "most conducive to the happiness of society."[415] Despite this, Bork's 1997 *Slouching Towards Gomorrah* is full of the same ass-backwards Nazi analogies that we hear from Glenn Beck today.

Conservatives' confusing socialism with communism is somewhat saner because communism is indeed a form of socialism, just as a Manx is a kind of cat – and just as fascism is a kind of conservatism. But, likewise, the Islamic Republic of Iran qualifies as a republic by John Adams' very broad definition, so does that mean that all republics are thus tyrannies?

Also recall George Orwell's opinion on the Soviet Union's so-called "socialism." He thought it was a fraud.[416]

Conservatives are fond of slippery slope arguments. They say social programs are the "Road to Serfdom." Except Sweden's citizens have enjoyed all sorts of generous social programs since the end of World War II, but no Soviet-style gulags have resulted. It is a free society and it has not invaded any of its neighbors in centuries. Likewise, the United Kingdom has socialized medicine and remains a free society.

As if anticipating all this nonsense, George Seldes put things in perspective in an interview a few years before his death. He mused:

I don't think there is one American in a hundred that knows anything of the difference between socialism and communism. To me, to them, sometimes they even talk about the "-isms" as if all "-isms" were alike, including even fascism. Yes, they're all bad. All "-isms" are bad. How 'bout republicanism? Heh.[417]

Of course, if I were Jonah Goldberg, I would not ask "who is closer to being a Nazi," when we can just play Six Degrees of Joseph Sobran. Goldberg edits the *National Review Online*, and Sobran had worked for the print edition for *seven years* while championing Holocaust-denying journals.[418] Eventually, Joseph Sobran's anti-Semitic activities became a big enough liability that William F. Buckley finally fired him in 1993, but the two men later reconciled before their deaths. I should also note that Ann Coulter wrote a very warm obituary for Sobran entitled "Not Your Average Joe."[419] Suddenly, Gore Vidal calling William F. Buckley a "crypto-Nazi" starts to seem slightly less hyperbolic.

Still uncertain? Then let me jog your memory.

In 1992, the *National Review* had actually endorsed Pat Buchanan for president. Recall that Buchanan had arranged Ronald Reagan's Bitburg

Cemetery visit in 1985. Reagan defended the visit by saying that the SS officers buried there "were victims just as surely as the victims in the concentration camps."[420] (Conservatives sure have a gift for spin.) While working in the Reagan White House, Buchanan had also tried to get the Justice Department's Nazi-hunting Office of Special Investigations shut down.

Pat Buchanan has a lengthy record of defending fascists, so it is not necessary to review all the details. My point here is that the *National Review* cannot claim that they did not truly know Buchanan before they endorsed him. As I mentioned in the last chapter, Pat Buchanan wrote for the *Review* and the magazine had helped shape his ideological foundations. He was deeply influenced by the *Review*'s racist foreign policy columnist James Burnham.[421] Both supported the white minority regime in Rhodesia.

William F. Buckley himself was a McCarthyite. Yes, he was erudite, but he had thuggish politics – thus, he and Buchanan were pretty similar. Buckley might have regretted defending Jim Crow in the 1950s, but that did not alter his pro-Apartheid take on South Africa in the 1980s. Sounding a lot like Buchanan, Buckley had mocked "one man, one vote" as a "fanatical abstraction" that we should not foist on South Africa.[422]

So, there is no denying that Pat Buchanan was the direct product of this publication. The *Review* knew exactly who they were endorsing.

Of course, Jonah Goldberg says that Pat Buchanan is not really a conservative because of his reversal on free trade. He writes, "Buchanan calls himself a 'paleoconservative,' but in truth he's a neo-progressive."[423] Somehow I doubt that Buchanan embraces that label.

And, speaking of Pats, the *National Review* had even excused Reverend Pat Robertson's anti-Semitic conspiracy theories and attacked his critics. When Michael Lind tried to drive Robertson out of the conservative movement, the *Review* drove Lind out instead.[424] That is taking a stand. Thus, methinks that Jonah Goldberg doth protest too much on the name calling front.

William F. Buckley is frequently credited with driving anti-Semites out of the conservative movement, but he actually harbored and defended them as long as possible. In his book, Jonah Goldberg wrote, "Liberalism, unlike conservatism, is operationally uninterested in its own intellectual history."[425] And yet he is operationally uninterested in the intellectual history of his *own magazine*. In this light, his prickliness is pretty predictable.

Indeed, the very idea that liberals and leftists cannot face their history is absolutely hilarious. We are very adept at tearing down our own idols. That comes with practice. We are quite good at acknowledging that Thomas Jefferson owned slaves or that Franklin D. Roosevelt put Japanese Americans in internment camps during World War II. In fact, I had first read that

Woodrow Wilson was a racist from a progressive historian, James W. Loewen, in his best seller *Lies My Teacher Told Me: Everything Your American History Textbook Got Wrong*. My paperback copy has a cover blurb by Howard Zinn, author of the bestselling *A People's History of the United States: 1492 – Present*. Jonah Goldberg is projecting a conservative trait because when liberals acknowledge such ugly facts, conservatives automatically accuse them of "hating America."

What I have written thus far is largely a response to Jonah Goldberg's article. His book, *Liberal Fascism: The Secret History of the American Left from Mussolini to the Politics of Meaning*, is even loopier. Like *Plan 9 from Outer Space*, it is so bad that it is good. Yes, it is nauseating and dishonest; but it is often hard not to laugh.

For example, he actually argues that the film *Dead Poets Society* is fascist. To his Orwellian thinking, insubordination is authoritarian and encouraging people to think for themselves is starting a cult. I must admit that certainly can happen. But not everyone who tries to be a catalyst for liberty is Ayn Rand.

Jonah Goldberg's credibility is already shot, so mocking his book seems gratuitous at this point. But there is more here than a car accident-like fascination with his ridiculous revisionism. His book is part of a far larger assault on the Progressive Era that has become increasingly visible in recent years. The Cato Institute had already been putting out books like Richard A. Epstein's *How Progressives Rewrote the Constitution* for years before Goldberg wrote *Liberal Fascism*. Cato fellow Jim Powell wrote a Glenn Beck-like book called *Wilson's War: How Woodrow Wilson's Great Blunder Led to Hitler, Lenin, Stalin, and World War II*. It just barely beat *Liberal Fascism* to the shelves. Goldberg's book is part of a *genre*.

As Jonah Goldberg said on Glenn Beck's show, "I'm actually not the first person to say this. I'm actually taking a lot from other historians and putting it all in one place which you can't find anywhere else."[426]

That is one way to put it. But I think Chip Berlet was being more accurate when he called Goldberg's book a compendium of John Birch Society articles published over the last fifty years.[427] Either way, these ideas are not new. But the Tea Party has breathed new life into them and Jonah Goldberg's tome is your convenient one-stop shop for such thought.

Conservatives are hostile to every Progressive Era accomplishment. Newt Gingrich considers child labor laws to be "truly stupid." U.S. Senator Mike Lee (R-UT) thinks they are unconstitutional. And Maine Governor Paul LePage (R) wants to loosen his state's so that twelve year olds can work for two dollars less than minimum wage, which he calls a "training wage." And, as I wrote before, both John Stossel and Arthur C. Brooks have defended robber barons. Ever since historians started pointing out the ugly similarities between our era and the Gilded Age, sweatshop apologists have had job security. And since the best defense is a good offense, they paint progressives as proto-fascists.

There is a tactical aspect to this approach as well: It is the path of least resistance. Those who loathe Franklin D. Roosevelt are a tiny minority. He was a very popular president and remains so today. Accordingly, conservatives have turned their guns more on the dour Woodrow Wilson because he is a much easier target. Defaming the New Deal is a pretty difficult trick, so they start with the less well-known Progressive Era instead. Obviously, this is their backdoor assault on the New Deal. But, as I shall show shortly, it is also their backdoor assault on the Enlightenment and America's core liberal principles as well.

As I wrote before, conservatives make Nazi analogies because they are projecting. But their strategists have harnessed this defensive reflex and written an alternative narrative around it. *Liberal Fascism* is part and parcel of this far larger project. So, yes, I am going to keep mocking Jonah Goldberg. But his name is no more or less a punch line than, say, Glenn Beck's or that of any Fox News host making the same insane claims. Goldberg is simply serviceable shorthand for the conservative movement as a whole at this moment.

Let us start with Jonah Goldberg's strongest argument. He correctly mentions that some of the Progressive Era's birth control advocates had briefly flirted with the eugenics movement which had advocated the forced sterilization of "undesirable" parts of the population, meaning poor minorities. (This is a favorite argument among opponents of birth control and abortion and therefore nothing new.) The eugenics movement had attracted people from across the political spectrum including, of course, conservatives. In fact, both groups had ideologically mixed memberships. As historian Jill Lepore noted of Margaret Sanger:

She really did court eugenicists; at one point, the American Birth Control League discussed a merger with the American Eugenics Society. But Sanger was a socialist, which often put her at odds with the eugenicists and with her own organization as well. A survey conducted of nearly a thousand members of the American Birth Control League in 1927 found its membership to be more Republican than the rest of the country.[428]

It was a case of odd political bedfellows that predictably did not work out. Eugenicists opposed voluntary birth control because they thought the state must decide who should reproduce. Sterilizing the "unfit" was only half of their plan: The other half was making sure the "fit" had children – whether they wanted to or not. Therefore, eugenics movement leader Paul Poponoe wrote that "birth control is the reverse of eugenics."[429]

Jonah Goldberg at least admits that liberals do not advocate eugenics today. But he fails to mention eugenics' endurance in some conservative circles. Take, Doctor Roger Pearson, for example. When he first visited the U.S. in 1958, he was the London-based organizer for the Northern League, a white supremacist group that included former SS officials.[430] He then founded, edited, and/or wrote for many racist publications, such as *Northern World* and *Western Destiny*. In his 1966 book, *Eugenics and Race*, he bluntly wrote, "If a nation with a more advanced, more specialized, or in any way superior set of genes mingles with, instead of exterminating, an inferior tribe, then it commits racial suicide."[431]

Ugly stuff. But his activities were not limited to the fringes. For many years, he was on the editorial board of the Heritage Foundation publication *Policy Review*. And, in turn, many Heritage staffers had joined Pearson's innocuously named *Journal of Social and Economic Studies*. In 1978, *Policy Review* dropped Pearson from its masthead when the *Washington Post* exposed him. But the linkage continued. As investigative reporter Russ Bellant wrote, "Heritage's director for domestic issues, Stuart Butler, joined Pearson's *Journal*, as did right-wing sociologist Ernest van den Haag of *National Review*."[432]

Really? *The National Review*? How interesting!

Ancient history? Not quite. Roger Pearson's work was the basis for *The Bell Curve,* the 1994 book that claimed intelligence is based on race.[433] *The National Review* openly championed that racist book. Indeed, today, one of its authors, Charles Murray, remains a regular contributor to the *National Review* and *the National Review Online*. What Charles Murray says today is obviously more relevant that what Margaret Sanger had said in 1927.

Indeed, Goldberg even defends Murray in his book *Liberal Fascism*. "But whatever the merits or demerits of *The Bell Curve* may be, the simple fact is the Murray and Herrnstein were making a deeply libertarian case for state *nonintervention*."[434] In other words, racist junk science is A-Okay as long as government does not act on it.

Of course, I have grave doubts about racists resisting the temptation to use the state's power when they get it. Murray Rothbard's endorsing Pat Buchanan shows how slippery those deeply libertarian principles can be. The Tea Party loved Arizona's "papers, please" law for harassing Hispanics and I do not trust those paleo-"libertarians" on abortion or gay rights either. Their political reflexes are anything but freedom-friendly.

Also recall that, in 1986, the *National Review*'s founder, William F. Buckley, had proposed that "Everyone detected with AIDS should be tattooed in the upper forearm, to protect common-needle users, and on the buttocks, to prevent the victimization of other homosexuals."[435] That policy does not sound terribly libertarian to me.

Again, the eugenics issue is Jonah Goldberg's strongest argument. But it is still not smart for him to draw attention to it – not for him or for the conservative movement as a whole. Yes, it is particularly embarrassing for him, but the Heritage Foundation does not come off too much better. Well, Goldberg's arguments only get worse from there.

Like Glenn Beck, Jonah Goldberg preys on his audience's ignorance. He invokes obscure historical events and omits important context. Because Hollywood has largely ignored these moments, you either know about them or you do not. Most do not and Goldberg uses this as an opportunity to rewrite history.

For example, he says that progressives were responsible for loyalty oaths and the Palmer Raids without mentioning that these activities were both parts of the First Red Scare. These shameful incidents rarely make it into high school history textbooks. And where are you going to see the deportation of Emma Goldman depicted in film outside of Warren Beatty's *Reds* (1981)? Was there a recent remake? Most Americans only know about the Second Red Scare, which is more popularly known as the McCarthy Era. So for them, the First Red Scare is a blank slate which Jonah Goldberg is happy to fill.

Woodrow Wilson *was* responsible for loyalty oaths and the Palmer Raids, but that does not make them progressive actions. By that logic, liberals must oppose social programs since President Clinton signed "welfare reform." Indeed, Clinton's pro-business policies included signing NAFTA. Does that mean that labor unions, a traditional Democratic Party constituency, favored the trade pact as well? Obviously not.

Bill Clinton also signed the Defense of Marriage Act (DOMA) and "Don't Ask/Don't Tell" (DADT). So, I suppose that makes conservatives champions of gay rights. Perhaps they will claim that when they next rewrite their movement's history. Today, they compare themselves to Rosa Parks; so perhaps tomorrow they will compare themselves to Harvey Milk.

Yes, I joke. But here in the Trump era, satire frequently surpasses reality and I wrote most of this chapter long before. Such brazen lying is nothing new for them and it is best to be prepared.

Getting back to the Progressive Era, should we suppose that J. Edgar Hoover was a progressive for his role in the Palmer Raids? And did the conservatives of that era oppose any of Wilson's actions? Of course not, because they were basically conservative moves.

Likewise, Jonah Goldberg alludes to the American Legion's fascist links but not their anti-union violence. Simply put, the Legion was capitalism's storm troopers. Goldberg quotes the Legion's 1923 National Commander Alvin Owsley saying, "If ever needed, the American Legion stands ready to protect our country's institutions and ideals as the *fascisti* dealt with the destructionists who menaced Italy."[436]

Except Goldberg conveniently neglects to mention that Owsley said these "destructionists" were all leftists – "[S]oviets, anarchists, IWW, revolutionary socialists and every other 'red.'" Goldberg cites to two sources and both give the whole quote.[437] Awkward.

He then mentions in passing that these leftists were targeted by other vigilante groups with Woodrow Wilson's encouragement, but he does not acknowledge that the Legion did the same things. Their business was brutally pro-business. It was the whole point of their existence.

Jonah Goldberg has a chronic habit of chopping off the important ends of historical quotes. Frequently, the very next sentence either contradicts or undermines his point. He wrote, "What appealed to Hitler about Ford was that he 'produces for the masses. That little car of his had done more than anything else to destroy class differences.'"[438] Jonah Goldberg presents this as a socialist quote, but it is the opposite. Hitler's next sentence was "You may envy the man who owns a better machine than yours, but you do not hate him."[439] Hitler wanted to eliminate class antagonism, not class itself. By "differences" he meant conflicts, not distinctions, because other people will still have sweeter wheels.

Moreover, Hitler was making the familiar conservative argument that social change comes from markets rather than movements – products not politics. Pat Buchanan had said something similar about women's liberation: "The real liberators of American women were not the feminist noise-makers, they were the automobile, the supermarket, the shopping center, the dishwasher, the washer-dryer, the freezer."[440]

Amusingly, that Adolf Hitler quote about automobiles came from a fawning 1933 *New York Times* interview which is rich with interesting tidbits that contradict Jonah Goldberg's thesis. Hitler almost sounds like he is addressing the Chamber of Commerce. In the next paragraph, we read that Hitler warned his followers "against weakening the economic forces of the nation by hounding and bullying employers." And in the paragraph after that, the *Fuehrer* boasted, "We are cutting red tape drastically. We are plowing through the bureaucratic hierarchy that stifled us. We have to reduce the government's cost and its size." Sign that man up with FreedomWorks and the Club for Growth!

Jonah Goldberg also claims that progressives adore war because it supposedly allows them to advance their agenda. "Like [Theodore] Roosevelt, Croly and his colleagues looked forward to many more wars because war was the midwife of progress."[441] He explains, "During wartime this country has historically done whatever it takes to see things through. But in peacetime the American character is not inclined to look to the state for meaning and direction. Liberals have responded to this by constantly searching for new crises, new moral equivalencies to war."[442]

Really? Is that why we had the First Red Scare after the First World War and the Second Red Scare after the Second World War? If the Palmer Raids were "progressive" in nature, then the McCarthy Hearings must be too. Yet, I have difficulty imagining the left engineering or benefiting from either of these periods. Historically, wars make people more conservative. It is ludicrous to suggest any different, let alone the opposite.

And how many perpetual wars have conservatives started, stoked, or exploited? After the Cold War, the War on Drugs was the next excuse for expanding police powers and the surveillance state. Then there was the War on Terror, which Dick Cheney said would never end.

Incidentally, the War on Terror is conspicuously absent from the index of Jonah Goldberg's book, but the War on Poverty merits four mentions. It is an odd yardstick of liberal bellicosity.

Goldberg does mention the War on Drugs, but he lists it as a liberal enterprise.[443] Perhaps he imagines that Nancy Reagan was married to Jimmy Carter and "Just Say No" was a Seventies thing.

And to pad his strange list of liberals' war equivalents even further, Jonah Goldberg mentions the "war on cancer." That sounds like a pretty apolitical campaign to me, but Goldberg has a ready answer for that too: In the very next line, he suggests that exhorting people to "get beyond politics" is fascist.[444] Apparently, even *centrists* are Nazis, now.

Goldberg is obviously projecting. Conservatives are incentivized to promote war. Psychological research shows that reminding people of death makes them more dogmatic in their beliefs and more punitive in enforcing them.[445] People in a life-or-death mindset are impatient with details, nuance, or shades of gray. Everything is "It's either us or them," which is not terribly conducive to tolerant, liberal thought.

So no wonder conservative pundits such as Stu Bykofsky, John Gibson, and Glenn Beck say we need another 9-11 to restore our sense of purpose. They are nostalgic for the power they had after the attacks.

Of course, Goldberg sees no fascist attitudes there. But, if any "liberals" go along for fear of being labeled "too liberal," that is damning proof of liberalism's inherent fascist tendencies. By contrast, conservatives just want to give peace a chance.

I should also note that Jonah Goldberg is repurposing an old anti-Semitic trope. Where religious bigots see a Jewish conspiracy fomenting more wars (recall Mel Gibson claiming Jews are behind all the world's wars), Goldberg fabricates a near identical progressive one.

And in both cases, the conspiracy theorists are often the ones who promote war. Their enthusiasm for bombing brown people knows no bounds. The last war that conservatives opposed was coincidentally enough World War II. They have not exactly been peaceniks ever since, so this reluctant warrior shtick is pretty rich coming from the right.

Twisting history is hardly limited to Jonah Goldberg or Nazi analogies. At the 2011 Conservative Political Action Conference (CPAC), Ann Coulter said, "It's just like a liberal, they import slaves, they hold slaves, they fight for slavery, they go to war in a civil war to defend slavery. They then install legal discrimination against blacks for a hundred years." Whoa! Talk about reckless crazy talk. Obviously, she was off-message by admitting the Civil War was fought over slavery. Is she turning into a liberal?

I could point out that the two major political parties had traded regional bases since the 1964 Civil Rights Act or that the Republicans had made Barry Goldwater's race-baiting Southern Strategy a permanent fixture. But do I really need to? After all, you can hardly call yourself the "Party of Lincoln" after embracing Jefferson Davis. Yet, this remains a stock argument among conservatives who say blacks should still vote Republican. Of course, Ann Coulter did not say "Democrat" – she said "liberal," therefore conservative Democrats are presumably free from stain.

Jonah Goldberg plays the same sleight-of-hand in his book *Liberal Fascism*. When cataloging skeletons that he sees in liberalism's closet, he pads that list by writing that "the Democratic Party was home to Jim Crow for a century." Yes, it was also home to Strom Thurmond until he became a Republican for some reason. Gee, I wonder why.

Both Ann Coulter and Jonah Goldberg make the same dishonest stock argument. In fact, Coulter's rant aptly parallels how and why Goldberg wrote his book: Their motives and techniques are identical. It is the exact same reflex.

Projecting ideological tendencies is often part of conservative distortions. In 2012, Rev. Pat Robertson surprisingly came out against the War on Drugs and stiff prison sentencing. His move would have been refreshing if he had not pinned both policies on liberals:

> *Every time the liberals pass a bill – I don't care what it involves – they stick criminal sanctions on it. They don't feel there is any way people are going to keep a law unless they can put them in jail. ... What we're doing is turning a bunch of liberals loose writing laws – there's this punitive spirit, they always want to punish people.*[446]

So, to review, liberals are at fault for the military industrial complex and now the prison industrial complex too. Who knew?

Likewise, Rush Limbaugh, Glenn Beck, and Ted Nugent have all called President Barack Obama a divisive racist. These three media personalities have all made many outrageously racist statements themselves, but Obama has made none. So, where do you suppose that comes from? Obviously, it is projection. But it is not a purely spontaneous reaction: It is as organized as it is organic. This is just the latest variant of their "liberals are the *real* racists" argument that has become rhetorical motor memory. In short, "I'm rubber, you're glue" has become another stock catch-all conservative argument.

A variant of this argument is hijacking liberal causes and figures.

I think this began in the 1980s when anti-abortion protestors claimed they had inherited the mantle of the 1960s Civil Rights Movement. The homophobic Westboro Baptist church makes the same claim as they wave their "GOD HATES FAGS" signs at funerals.

As I noted before, Ronald Reagan imagined that Franklin D. Roosevelt would agree that government had gotten out of control. Likewise, Robert Bork had claimed that the past's liberal icons would not recognize their movement today and conservative pundits have subsequently run with that assumption in the most shameless fashion.

For example, on the fiftieth anniversary of the John F. Kennedy assassination, some pundits took a brief break from Kennedy-bashing to claim JFK was a conservative.[447] Glenn Beck said that JFK "would be a Tea Party radical" today – and Rush Limbaugh falsely claimed, "Kennedy was not a big believer in the Civil Rights Act," which I presume is a good thing in his book. Since their audiences are primarily made of Baby Boomers, co-opting this nostalgia was probably predictable.

Claiming Kennedy was a conservative became a talking point. It was echoed by Chris Wallace and Neil Cavuto of Fox News, as well as Jeff Jacoby of the *Boston Globe*. It was just as bizarre as the claim that Martin Luther King would have opposed affirmative action, an absurd argument made by Charles Krauthammer, David Horowitz, and Newt Gingrich.

This is just what they do now.[448] Who is next? Perhaps Glenn Beck's hatred of Woodrow Wilson will inspire him to reinvent Eugene V. Debs as a libertarian. After all, if you can turn Thomas Paine into a Creationist, anything is possible.

Are their insane claims clinical or cynical? You have got to wonder if they believe their own spin.[449] Glenn Beck likes to point out that Woodrow Wilson was a huge racist. This is quite true. But, given Glenn Beck's routine use of racist dog whistles, I question the sincerity of his outrage. And Ted Nugent is not the only racist comparing himself to Rosa Parks. Seditious rancher Cliven Bundy did the same shortly after saying that blacks were better off as slaves.[450]

All these absurdities are familiar arguments, and this is why they sound so plausible to conservative audiences. These people already live in Opposite Land. They think that welfare causes poverty, affirmative action causes racism, and sex education classes cause teen pregnancy. They believe government efforts always backfire and that "liberal elites" conspire to hide the truth. So, forget the higher teen birth rates we see where "abstinence only" programs are taught. Never mind the rise of so many blacks into the middle class – to say nothing of twice electing a black president by landslide. And pay no attention to the drop in poverty after Lyndon B. Johnson's Great Society programs started or its rise after Ronald Reagan slashed their budgets. If a government program does not completely wipe out a social ill, it must therefore be the cause – you know, the same way that having fire departments causes fires.

They are trying to rewrite the Great Depression too. As Thomas Frank wrote in *Pity the Billionaire*, they are using the iconography of the New Deal *against* the New Deal. The Dust Bowl photos of poverty that Glenn Beck used on his TV show were taken by government photographers to spur Congress to action. But Beck used them to essentially say "Look how proud and flinty we were before we got soft from government handouts." The photos do show dignity. That was to counter the right's stereotype that working class people were lazy and to build up sympathy for them. That era had its own callous Rick Santellis calling those who had lost their homes and farms "losers." But unlike the stock market speculators who had crashed the economy, these people actually *made things*.

Indeed, the right had begun rewriting economic history even before the 2007 crash. You could see this in design and fashion. When people believed the market could never fall, art directors used Russian Constructivist fonts ironically. That was part of the 1990s' Soviet kitsch that went with post-Cold War triumphalism, but things did not stop there. The retro look was in. There was an occasional nod to the posh and dapper 1920s; but the thematic emphasis was on strength, so the more muscular industrial aesthetic of the 1930s was favored. You often saw Works Progress Administration-inspired designs in business newspaper and magazine layouts.

Remember, this was when suspenders and bow ties came back into style. It was as if we had reset the twentieth century and the New Deal had never happened – it was only acknowledged to mock it. We were now in an alternate universe that had skipped that particular period. In this different timeline, America had never disappointed Ayn Rand and Atlas enjoyed society's appreciation and deference.

And when the market *did* crash, smug snark morphed into spin. This iconography was no longer used ironically, but manipulatively. The rewrite continued, albeit with a tweak. Now, there was all the more reason to milk this particular imagery.

As a result of such gross distortions, Thomas Frank found some people who thought the era's anthem "Brother Can You Spare a Dime?" was actually meant as an indictment against the New Deal and Keynesian economics(!)[451] Never mind it was written by Yip Harburg, a socialist who was later blacklisted during the McCarthy era. Never mind it was written on Herbert Hoover's watch before FDR got elected. Ideology trumps chronology.

This was no isolated absurdity. As Thomas Frank has documented in many books, conservatives have been co-opting populism for at least two decades. In their strange alternative narrative, social workers are elitists and billionaires are just ordinary folk. So, after causing the worst economic crisis since the Great Depression, doubling-down on this story was only logical for them. Obviously, they must obfuscate the past if they do not want to see a repeat of the New Deal, and so they brazenly conflate opposites.

But I see a larger pattern than Thomas Frank does. I have repeatedly stressed that liberty, equality, and democracy are the three interdependent pillars of America's identity and documented conservative hostility toward each of them. After all, that is my thesis. I have also shown that America's every ethos is problematic for conservative "patriotism," hence their tendency to project and question other people's patriotism. The right's false populism compose one example of this reflex and their Nazi analogies form another.

A lot of classic Americana comes out of the Great Depression and World War II. This period both shaped and defined what is often called "The Greatest Generation." Since conservatives like to think that they own patriotism, they probably would try to co-opt this era even without any economic incentive – although, the money definitely helps too. Remember Ann Coulter rewriting the U.S. Civil War. That was another nation-defining crisis that conservatives are desperate to redefine because it is so awkward for them. The right's attempt to hijack Kennedy's legacy and the Civil Rights Movement is just more of the same. One of the arguments that Rush Limbaugh made to claim that John F. Kennedy was a conservative was that JFK was "proud to be an American" – as if liberals are not.

Of course, Limbaugh's obvious motive is that *conservatives* are not. Consciously or not, conservatives must rewrite history to hide the fact that their ideology is inherently un-American. Every historic moment that revives our country's frequently neglected commitment to liberty, equality, or democracy is going to be awkward for them. Once again, conservatives are chronically on the wrong side of history because their un-American temperament repeatedly puts them there.[452]

Conservative "patriotism" is nothing but nostalgic tribalism, unencumbered by the high-minded liberal ideals that our country was supposedly founded on. It is only a deep need to be on a team and worship old things. But there is no real reverence for what those old things are supposed to mean. Conservatism's self-appointed guardians of tradition rarely study history. Oaths and rituals substitute for scholarship, so when they try to instruct others, they are usually spectacularly wrong.

Small wonder their movement harbors so many people who are hostile to our country's ideals. You know, the same way that William F. Buckley had harbored so many Holocaust deniers.

It is tempting to think that Jonah Goldberg is just grasping at straws in an effort to turn the charge of fascism around. But it is more than that: This is a *whole worldview*. He is either a writer who is deeply alienated from America and modernity or a one who really knows his audience.

One thing in *Liberal Fascism* that I have not fully explored vividly illustrates this reactionary mindset. For Goldberg, all forms of fascism are unified by the notion that the human condition can be improved. He writes, "Most of all they share the belief – what I call the totalitarian temptation – that with the right amount of tinkering we can realize the utopian dream of 'creating a better world.'"[453]

Wait. What? Wanting to improve conditions is totalitarian? Forget Progressivism, this super-elastic definition of fascism stretches to fit around the very concept of progress *itself*.

Goldberg cannot grasp that perfection is a direction, not a destination. By striving for it, we improve things. Was the founding fathers' forming "a more perfect union" fascist? After all, they had replaced the states rights-based Articles of Confederation with a much stronger central government. I guess those first jackboots had big, shiny brass buckles on them.

Astoundingly, Goldberg also poses as a champion of the Enlightenment against Michel Foucault. Yet, Goldberg says, "The conservative or classical liberal vision understands that life is unfair, that man is flawed, and that the only perfect society, the only real utopia, waits for us in the next life."

Um, that is certainly the Tory mentality, but it hardly defines the Enlightenment or the Patriots' cause for that matter. The emphatically secular revolutionaries did not wait for the Rapture to address their grievances. They dealt with them kinetically, in the then here-and-now. That is, after all, what revolutionaries *do*.

But Goldberg's version of the Enlightenment stops just short of endorsing the Divine Right of Kings. Are you unhappy with your lot in life? Just be patient and wait. God will fix all after-the-fact.

He then develops this idea that he is fighting for the Enlightenment. He actually writes, "All major conservative schools of thought trace themselves back to the champions of the Enlightenment – John Locke, Adam Smith, Montesquieu, Burke."[454]

That is a pretty narrow pantheon of champions considering his highly elastic definition of fascism. I suppose I should credit him with omitting Cato. Although, I imagine he would get along much better with Samuel Johnson than anyone on his woefully short list.

Are not Voltaire and Rousseau also champions of the Enlightenment? And why are there no *American* thinkers on his list? Like the Texas State Board of Education, I suppose that Jonah Goldberg had found none whom he could truly admire. That does not sound too patriotic to me.

Predictably this hostility to progress is part of their hostility to progressives. It is almost a tautology. But as I wrote before, it is also a back door assault on our founding ideals and where they lead – on the inherent trajectories that revolutionary attitudes have.

Jonah Goldberg, Glenn Beck, and those other rightwing pundits and think tank writers are ultimately trying to hide the fact that the Progressive Era was a *resumption* of the Enlightenment after a period of romanticized reaction. It was a rebirth of reason and compassion after the Victorian Era's selfish feudal enthusiasm which was epitomized by the "sham castles" that Mark Twain had mocked.

Certainly, Revolutionary Era feminists like Abigail Adams, Judith Sargent-Murray, Mary Wollstonecraft, and Marie Olympe De Gouges would have applauded women finally getting the vote. This is not conjecture – they demanded it. They argued that it was an inherent part of the Enlightenment's ideology of liberty. As Abigail Adams had warned her husband John, "If particular care and attention is not paid to the Ladies we are determined to foment a Rebellion, and will not hold ourselves bound by any Laws in which we have no voice, or Representation."[455] And across the pond, Mary Wollstonecraft wrote, "The divine right of husbands, like the divine right of kings, may, it is to be hoped, in this enlightened age, be contested without danger."[456] Alas, she was wrong about that last part. The French government guillotined Marie Olympe De Gorges for writing her "Declaration of the Rights of Women." (The Progressive Era's suffragettes also faced violence in the form of beatings by police.) For some reason, these women did not make it onto Jonah Goldberg's list either.

Conservatism is un-American in part because perpetual improvement is part of our national ethos. Like William F. Buckley, conservatives stand "athwart history, yelling Stop."[457] Like Robert Bork, they have a problem with the very concept of progress. By contrast, Thomas Jefferson thought "We might as well require a man to wear still the coat which fitted him when a boy, as civilized society to remain ever under the regimen of their barbarous ancestors." That is probably why he too is absent from Jonah Goldberg's pantheon.

But do not look for Benjamin Franklin or Thomas Paine in there either since their social program proposals obviously disqualify them. And forget other spread-the-wealth advocates like Noah Webster and James Madison, for that matter. Goldberg's "Champions of the Enlightenment" would make a disappointingly short trading card set.

Even a cursory survey of the founders' efforts shows their progressive impulses. Benjamin Franklin constantly proposed new "improvements," i.e. public works projects. Thomas Jefferson was the consummate technocrat and civil engineer. When designing the new national capitol, he laid out streets and sewer lines to facilitate sanitation and fight disease – which was quite important since Washington, D.C. was built on a drained swamp. These men were hardcore city planning geeks seeped in the spirit of idealistic civil servants. They would have thrilled to the heady, energetic days of the early New Deal. You know that Benjamin Franklin and Franklin D. Roosevelt would have hit it off. They would have been like twins! Both jolly men were charming, hard-partying policy wonks who got busy fixing things the next morning. Cartoonist Kate Beaton needs to commit this awesome team-up to paper right now.

Again, many of our founders were social engineers who always sought to advance the common good. Applying the latest scientific thinking in every area of life for the benefit of all defined both the Enlightenment and the later Progressive Era. Since the right cannot patriotically assault the first era, they must therefore assault the second. Conservatism is therefore the eternal enemy of the Enlightenment, and thus, the conservative assault on progressivism is ultimately an assault on America itself. It is the logical end product of William F. Buckley's and Robert Bork's thought. This is (and, in fact, has always been) conservatism's inherent trajectory, whether articulated with dignified erudition or lurid Nazi analogies. Whatever the classiness of the conveyance, the eventual destination remains the same.

Jonah Goldberg's contribution to modern political discourse has both left its mark and met its goal. His goal was not the cessation of Nazi analogies, but to disassociate right wing politics from right wing politics and to assault the very concept of progress itself in the process. And he accomplished both by conflating political opposites.

It is the conservative version of the Horseshoe Theory horseshit spouted by many centrists today. Both framings conflate right and left in order to call progressives racist. Both flatter their believers as sensible defenders of wholesome norms against strange alien ideas and change. And finally, both twist history and co-opt heroes to serve their narrative.

For example, in his famous Letter from a Birmingham Jail, Reverend Martin Luther King expressed his profound disappointment with white moderates who he wondered might be even greater impediments to racial justice than the Klan. Today, such moderates invoke King while erasing his scathing critiques of capitalism and warm endorsements of democratic socialism. Never mind that King was assassinated while organizing a biracial Poor People's March on Washington for economic justice.[458]

Admittedly, this is not quite as bad as insisting that King would have opposed affirmative action, but it is still a gross distortion and weaponized against those who are fighting hardest for his vision. Just as conservatives say "liberals are the *real* racists," centrists say the same of those to *their* left.

Incidentally, this predates the slandering of Bernie Sanders in the 2016 election. In the late 1990s, sweatshop apologists called their critics racist. How *dare* you object to your clothes being made by children and imprisoned political dissidents! Accordingly, Thomas Friedman accused the 1999 WTO protesters in Seattle of being inspired by Pat Buchanan.

I will cover that absurdity further in my next book. My point here is Jonah Goldberg and Glenn Beck call progressives "racists" and "fascists," and their line is echoed by every other centrist twit on Twitter.

This jumbling left with right taps into some troubling historical thought. Nazi propaganda had always blurred capitalists and communists together by arguing that Jews secretly controlled both and were using them in a "two-pronged assault" on "Christian civilization." That was the view of the original Nazis as well as their ideological descendants today. If someone uses the labels "capitalist" and "communist" interchangeably, you can safely guess where they are going from there.

For example in the late 1930s, Father Coughlin, "the radio priest," claimed that *Kristallnacht* was ultimately the comeuppance to "Jewish bankers, Kuhn Loeb & Company of New York, among those who helped finance the Russian Revolution and Communism."[459]

Likewise, Pat Robertson claimed that "Wall Street bankers" had "enthusiastically financed Bolshevism in the Soviet Union since 1917."[460] Again, the *National Review* had excused this vicious lunacy.

Today, the Tea Party tries to co-opt populist rage against Wall Street and then redirect it against Washington by arguing that rich liberals are plotting to destroy capitalism. According to Glenn Beck, rich liberals have been patiently planning this since Woodrow Wilson was president a century ago. Thus, the Tea Party is presumably trying to save capitalism from sinister capitalists. They have deftly harnessed anger *against* banks to fight any regulation *of* banks.

There is no exaggerating how bizarre their narrative is. As Thomas Frank explained in *Pity the Billionaire,* "For them, Democrats are devil figures; there was no contradiction in depicting them as both pawns of the banks and also the persecutors of them. Democrats were so malignant they could play both roles simultaneously."[461] While describing a 2010 Rand Paul campaign advertisement, Frank quipped, "The viewer is expected both to hate AIG and feel compassion for it in the space of thirty seconds."

As I noted before, mixed messages prey on mixed feelings. For decades, the pro-business religion of deregulation was preached by every talking head. But then the 2007 financial crisis triggered a crisis of faith, leaving people angry and confused. Much like how traditionalist Germans felt after the Kaiser fled to Holland after World War I, their worldview was discredited and disgraced. Many had groped for any shabby rationalization to simultaneously cling to belief and be angry too.

System failure was both indisputable and searing. But cherished certainties do not retire gracefully: They dig in, lie dormant, and wait for reinforcements to arrive with fresh rationalizations to reconcile their new reality with their old ideology, sparing folks the discomfort of introspection. Bed bugs and tardigrades might envy this lazy tenacity.

Enter the Tea Party saying the financial crisis was *not* caused by *too little* regulation, but *too much* and that liberals deliberately engineer crises to make us more dependent on government – hence Glenn Beck calling billionaire investor George Soros "the puppet master" of a vast conspiracy to destroy America.

This thinking rings familiar for two obvious reasons:

First, the right has always tried to steer working class frustration away from rich conservatives and toward rich liberals. Before Soros, the Kennedy family was frequently the target of this treatment – and before them it was the Roosevelts. It is old habit. Any assault against "Hollywood liberals" is in the same vein. Indeed, the previous needle marks have since been replaced with a convenient valve to save time. To conservatives, rich liberals are class traitors so they work to make the poor feel betrayed as well.

Second, Glenn Beck's conspiracy theory sounds like a personalized version of the *Protocols of the Elders of Zion*, the anti-Semitic tract that Hitler's friend Henry Ford had promoted. But personalization does not alter Beck's script one jot – he attacks everyone to his left the same way. What is different is he is careful to say "liberals" and "progressives" instead of "Jews." Recall how Jonah Goldberg used the same substitution on the topic of foreign wars. For Beck it is finance, but it is meant to hit the same bigoted buttons. It is easy to see projection in Glenn Beck's Nazi analogies, and I suspect that his love of wearing uniforms is not entirely ironic.

In fact, Glenn Beck has promoted fascist tracts himself. On his radio show, he praised a 1936 book called *The Red Network: A "Who's Who" and Handbook of Radicalism for Patriots*. The book's author, Elizabeth Dilling, was a rabid racist. Evidence of this is in the book itself. "Neither the races nor the sexes can ever be equal. They will always be different and have distinctive functions to perform in life."[462] On the same page she had written, "God created separate races, but Communism insists upon racial inter-mixture and inter-marriage." Perhaps that is why so many Tea Party members thought that President Obama was a red diaper baby.

Elizabeth Dilling was an avid Nazi who attended rallies in both Germany and the U.S. She attacked the Allies after Hitler invaded Poland, and resisted the war effort after Pearl Harbor. Dilling later described President Dwight Eisenhower as "Ike the kike" and called President John F. Kennedy's "New Frontier" the "Jew Frontier."[463] Right wingers love rhyming names and labels. It is their primary clever talent.

And speaking of "Who's Who"-type books, Elizabeth Dilling has her own entry in the *Encyclopedia of White Power: A Sourcebook on the Radical Racist Right*. "To Dilling, Franklin Roosevelt was in all likelihood a Jew and his administration a Trojan horse for international communism."[464]

Simply change the word "Jew" to "Muslim" and that is exactly what many Tea Party members say about President Obama today. The right might like rhymes, but originality is not their strong suit. Habit will out.

And although obsessed with racial purity, Dilling liked to mix her terminology. She oxymoronically called herself a "Tory, patriot"[465] which is just as ass-backwards as calling someone else a "fascist-socialist."

Elizabeth Dilling was a fringe figure, but today the fringe increasingly defines the debate. Forget, for one moment, the fact that Glenn Beck had Fox News's highest-rated show. A 2012 poll found that 63% of Republicans *still* think that Saddam Hussein had weapons of mass destruction when we invaded Iraq in 2003![466] Evidence does not sway them.

In fact, it does the opposite and fortifies their faith in false beliefs. As I wrote in the introduction, they will respond to my founding fathers quotes the same way Creationists react to dinosaur bones. And once you think of the Creation Museum, how they arrive at their Nazi analogies becomes quite plain – they just stir everything together. Just as they drop dinosaurs into the Garden of Eden, socialists become fascists. Because why not?

And if they ignore biologists and geologists, they will ignore historians too. So I doubt they will relinquish their cherished Nazis analogies. After all, the Scopes Trail was back in 1925. Its centennial is not far off.

Adolf Hitler bragged that sewing confusion was one of his most effective weapons. Along these lines, conservatives have always conflated patriotism with nationalism and disassociated democracies from republics. Equating progressives with fascists is only their latest trick. The conservative narrative is Orwellian: bankers are Bolsheviks, doves are hawks, egalitarians are elitists, libertines are punitive, and Tories are patriots.

Of course, once you decide that the Enlightenment boils down to the medieval idea of "life sucks and then you die," none of this seems like much of a jump anymore.

Discredited beliefs may temporarily recede into the background noise, but then they resurge. Remember that Republican presidents Dwight Eisenhower and Richard Nixon had both dismissed conservative critics of the New Deal as irrelevant, isolated cranks. But when Ronald Reagan took office in 1980, the cranks came back and even took over the Democratic Party in the 1990s. We went from Richard Nixon saying "I am now a Keynesian in economics" to Bill Clinton declaring "The era of big government is over." The reactionary fringe will always be waiting in the wings to seize control once again.

But then there is everybody else. Another thing I wrote in the introduction is that politics is not the art of converting your opponent but of swaying the political middle. Fox News had had a minor, surprisingly respectful freak-out when Pope Francis called economic inequality "tyranny," so I do not suppose they will have an open mind when I point out that many of our founding fathers had already said the same thing. Naturally, Rush Limbaugh's self-identified "Ditto-heads" will probably not listen. But it gives the undecided something to think about and that is how politics actually works and always has.

However, that leaves a question. How can we talk about the right's anti-democratic animus? After all, a literal monarchist metamorphosis is no longer in the cards and overuse has rendered fascist analogies nearly meaningless. So, how can we talk about this without mentioning kings and seeming quaintly irrelevant or mentioning Nazis and seeming utterly nuts?

Unfortunately, the frank answer is we cannot. Historical honesty demands context, as does America's identity.

But we can choose our point of emphasis, so I suggest we revive the word "Tory" as a stock insult. With only one word it both acknowledges our revolutionary heritage and reminds everyone what America is supposed to stand for, or at least sparks a debate on the topic.

Of course, this course of action has two caveats.

First, I am not saying that we should never mention fascists. Obviously, Holocaust deniers who praise Franco and Pinochet qualify, so pundits like Pat Buchanan and Joseph Sobran are still fair game. If you are talking about actual fascists, it is not an analogy anymore but a simple fact. You are not only safe saying it, accuracy actually requires it.

Second, we cannot stop conservatives from using Nazi analogies, so any liberal or leftist self-restraint will likely be a one-sided endeavor. No moratorium will enforce itself any more than the market will regulate itself. The right will still exploit whatever tactic is most effective for them. They will show all the scruples of a Joe McCarthy, Roy Cohn, Lee Atwater, or Karl Rove. Conservatives have the most to gain from this moratorium, and yet we all know that they would be the least likely to honor it.

I am not just talking about the right's typical Nixonian dickishness, although that is a factor too. Nor am I only talking about the difficulty of kicking satisfying old habits which have rewarded them with repeated Pavlovian reinforcement.

No, I am arguing that their reflexive projecting is ideologically hard-wired. They are pretty sensitive about their guilty history. Indeed, their playing the Nazi card almost sounds like a "cry for help" because rational self-interest does not explain that gambit. Throwing stones from glass houses does not even begin to describe their ingrained habit.

I am not exaggerating when I say their projecting is reflexive because I do not think that they can control it anymore. Blurting out bulletins from Opposite Land is just how they deal with the world now. Their feel-good history is oddly apocalyptic. But what else can you expect from authoritarians who think that they are libertarians?

We cannot stop conservatives from making Nazi analogies, but we can force a shift of venue by refocusing on the Revolutionary Era. Franklin D. Roosevelt's talk of Toryism had reminded us who we were and the rough economic equality that so many founders thought was essential to a republic must be restored. We can accomplish this without Nazi name-calling. It is not only possible but promising. And given our history, this is the most logical course of action.

Here is an example of how we can do this. Take that famous Rev. Martin Niemöller quote which starts "When they came for the communists, I did not do anything because I was not a communist." Strangely, a lot of conservative pundits have been invoking it lately. Some shorten the quote by dropping the communist part, so I struggle mightily to imagine them sheltering suspected Reds or any other opponent of Mussolini's Corporate State. I would certainly hesitate to tell union organizers that Glenn Beck has their backs when the Gestapo or the American Legion shows up at their front door.

But, levity aside, we are still left with the question of how do we express this societal dynamic without mentioning Nazis? Well, do you remember that Thomas Paine quote on defending your enemies that I keep mentioning? "He that would make his own liberty secure must guard even his enemy from oppression: for if he violates this duty, he establishes a precedent that will reach unto himself." This principle should not be limited to "card-carrying members of the ACLU." And the fact that conservatives use that phrase derisively displays their complete contempt for free society.

Not every World War II idea or incident has a Revolutionary Era parallel. But when one exists, we should probably default to it, if it fits. And by studying our history we are better equipped to block conservative assaults on liberty, equality, and democracy.

For example, it is important to know that the founders were mostly deists when would-be theocrats try to legislate their morality. This information does not dissuade the theocrat, but it is important for everyone else to know it. And if you can point to Thomas Paine's social security proposal, those who associate social programs with jackboots have already lost because it effectively prevents playing the Nazi card.

Okay, perhaps "prevent" is not quite the right verb.

After all, conservatives will still try. Moreover, the Nazi card is very emotional and distracting – and it is always to the right's advantage to distract. But, if we stay on track, I think the Revolutionary Era argument may carry the day. And it might even wean those covert Roosevelt haters off Woodrow Wilson and back onto Thomas Paine.

Perhaps.

But I do not want to create unrealistic expectations. Even if we could curb Nazi analogies, conservatives would still have the same reflexes. When not calling abortion "worse than the Holocaust," they say abortion is "worse than slavery." That is now a talking point for them. Sarah Palin had likewise equated the national debt to slavery and then faulted African Americans for objecting to her outrageous comparison.

I am not sure how long that practice of theirs will last. Surely it creates some tension with their Neo-Confederate "states rights" wing. Perhaps they originally adopted Nazi analogies because they made a safer foreign comparison rather than an awkward domestic one. In any case, I still think that calling them Tories will raise the tone of the discussion.

Some will object to substituting one form of name-calling for another and ask how any insult can raise the tone of political discourse. But, in politics, there is no avoiding labels or hurt feelings. And, as a sometime cartoonist and fan of satire, I recognize that insults can do good.

Calling someone a Tory in America would certainly be a direct challenge to their patriotism. I am not denying that. (That is, after all, the idea.) But, it would still be a pretty tame insult – almost a gentle rebuke. It would suggest that the target is antiquated and irrelevant. Indeed, it would almost make them cuddly, like Archie Bunker. And we already know that paleoconservatives do not strenuously object to being called political fossils. That or they do not know what the word "paleo" means.

So, how strongly could they possibly object to being called Tories? They are proud, open opponents of progress and staunch defenders of tradition and hierarchy, so they would quite likely embrace the label. And they are already big fans of Margaret Thatcher, so there is also that.

More importantly, calling someone antiquated is different from calling them evil incarnate which is what the Nazi label is meant to suggest. It is much easier to picture yourself reasoning with a Tory than with a Nazi. The Tory metaphor is admittedly Anglo-centric. However, it does, paradoxically, refocus our attention what America is all about. And we all know that conservatives do not really want to have that talk.

Again, Nazi analogies distract us from discussing America's true identity, and that ultimately benefits conservatives. So instead, we should just call them Tories. After all, some of them already identify as "Tory Patriots."

And that moronic oxymoron aptly sums up all the inherent contradictions in American conservatism.

9: Liberty, Equality, & Empathy
How Compassion Holds the Tripod Together

I neglected to mention a particularly fanciful Nazi analogy in the last chapter. In 2010, Glenn Beck implied that empathy had caused the Holocaust. President Barack Obama had used the word "empathy" in a sentence and Beck felt compelled to mention that Adolf Hitler had once used the word too. Beck explained, "Empathy leads you to very bad decisions, many times."[467]

His argument seems uniquely loopy, but Glenn Beck is not empathy's only enemy. His comment stops to shock once you recall that he is a big fan of Ayn Rand. She argued that altruism is evil and equated it with tyranny. Beck's comment was not just another random manifestation of his Hitler fixation, but an expression of his fundamental moral framework – one his Rand-reading audience already shared.

This demonization of empathy is not limited to libertarians and it is sometimes literal as well. Evangelical leader Reverend Mike Bickle thinks that compassion and tolerance are the Antichrist's calling cards. "The Harlot Babylon will be a religion of affirmation, toleration, no absolutes: a counterfeit justice movement. They will feed the poor, have humanitarian projects, inspire acts of compassion for all the wrong reasons."[468]

Reverend Bickle thinks that the herald of the Antichrist is Oprah Winfrey.

No, seriously. He actually says it is Oprah. When I picture this, all I can hear is, "EVERYBODY GETS BRIMSTONE!"

Mike Bickle's assaults on empathy are pretty similar to Glenn Beck's. Both use the same "It sounds nice, but ..." structure that conservatives have always used to oppose progressive proposals. Usually, that "but" is followed by an argument that the program will not work. Liberals are accused of being well-intentioned, but wrong-headed – naïve, but not evil. The law of unintended consequences is often invoked. Usually, they just say that the program is a waste of time and money. Only the paranoid fringe suggests that altruism conceals some tyrannical conspiracy.

But today, the fringe is in the saddle of the GOP. While the red-baiting of social programs is certainly nothing new, we have not seen this degree of it since the 1950s. In any case, the basic argument is the same. Its shrillness varies over time, but it always says that the road to hell is paved with good intentions.

Conservatism's compassion-bashing is long-established. As John Kenneth Galbraith once said, "The modern conservative is engaged in one of man's oldest exercises in moral philosophy; that is, the search for a superior moral justification for selfishness." Add to that conservatives' binary, black-and-white worldview and vilifying empathy becomes predictable. If greed is good, then compassion must be bad. It is simply going on the offensive. And that is a problem because a free society must balance everyone's rights against everyone else's. Considering other people is a basic civic duty that empathy obviously encourages. Thus, celebrating selfishness ultimately sabotages free society.

For example, "Life is not fair" is the credo of cheaters and conservatives. Now, I am not claiming that everyone who says that is either one or the other – I do not think that Jimmy Carter is either. But for conservatives, that banal phrase has become a fixture and a justification for injustice and corruption. No, life is not *inherently* fair, but it is part of our country's ethos that it can be *made* fair, or at least *fairer*. As those old Superman serials remind us, "righting wrongs" is associated with the "American way." This is the goal of those who love justice, just as "Life is not fair" is the credo of those who tolerate injustice – and thus excuse and encourage it.

But, as usual, conservatives turn every virtue on its ear. Glenn Beck tells his audience that the phrase "social justice" is a red flag for tyranny – one he associates with actual red flags. Jonah Goldberg is no more nuanced in his assault on empathy. He called George W. Bush's "compassionate conservatism" "compassionate fascism" because he thinks that any use of government to improve living conditions is automatically totalitarian.[469]

Incidentally, do you know who said, "Humanitarianism is the expression of stupidity and cowardice"?[470] Kudos, if you said Adolf Hitler. I would have guessed Ayn Rand.

This also ties into Jonah Goldberg's odd notion that those who think we can build a better world are fascists. Perfect? No. But better? Always. Ever better. As I wrote before, perfection is a direction, not a destination. Perpetual improvement is part of our national ethos. Of course, that is a fundamental human quality too, but our country was the first to really encourage it because we are an invented nation. We rejected stagnant tradition and the bankrupt notion that the status quo was its own justification and the will of God. We thus rejected the Divine Right of Kings. And, of course, many of the revolutionaries had rejected organized religion by association.

In England, this Enlightenment mindset can be seen in Mary Wollstonecraft's 1792 "A Vindication of the Rights of Women." In it, she wrote, "Let not men then in the pride of power, use the same arguments that tyrannic kings and venal ministers have used, and fallaciously assert that woman ought to be subjected because she has always been so."[471] A free people realize that they have a right to rewrite the rules. Fuck old customs if they oppress anyone. Conservatives may howl, but that is what America is about.

Thomas Paine had celebrated change and humanity's agency when arguing for American independence in his pamphlet "Common Sense." He wrote, "We have it in our power to begin the world over again." That is how real revolutionaries think.

Perhaps the purest expression of this mindset was Thomas Jefferson's principle that all laws and public debts should expire after nineteen years. He wanted each generation to start off with a fresh, clean slate – free of the dead hand of the past.

His friend and rival, John Adams, had also affirmed that we always retain a right to re-order our world. And he did this while simultaneously affirming the principle of fairness. Because stratification and tradition were linked in people's experiences, their opposites – equality and change – were organically associated as well:

Government is instituted for the common good; for the protection, safety, prosperity and happiness of the people; and not for the profit, honor, or private interest of any one man, family, or class of men: Therefore the people alone have an incontestable, unalienable, and indefeasible right to institute government; and to reform, alter, or totally change the same, when their protection, safety, prosperity and happiness require it.[472]

America's true character is humanist in nature. It believes that we human beings can govern ourselves without any heavenly-appointed spokesman. It credits human ingenuity rather than divine inspiration. It says that we have not only the ability to fix the things we think are broken but the right to try. When we forget or ignore this ethos, we sabotage our country's sense of self and lose our way. Moreover, our ethos of perpetual improvement provides every generation with goals and a sense of purpose. Without it, people become as vacuous, callous, and predatory as many conservatives are today.

That last line was not just some snarky cheap shot. There will always be greed. There will always be bullies and people who exploit others, and therefore crime. To quote those old Superman serials again, it is a "never-ending battle." But that does not mean that it has to be a losing battle. Just as we can make things safer, we can make them fairer.

There is no denying that progress is both actual and measurable. We can see it in rising literacy rates and average life spans. But what happens when school budgets get cut or food safety inspections are neglected? Other countries best us in technology and we have E. coli outbreaks. We can lose ground as well as gain it. Therefore, progress is neither foredoomed nor guaranteed. We cannot safely take it for granted. Improvement of the human condition requires conscious effort. We cannot leave society on autopilot and let the "magic of the market" take care of everything. Civilization is indeed advancing, but upgrades do not mean we can neglect regular maintenance.

And, here again, humanism is a defining factor. We humans are unique in that we consciously alter our environment. The beaver dam is the result of instinct, but Hoover Dam is the result of engineering. By contrast, termites do not write environmental impact statements. They just do what they do. Likewise, human society is not a beehive because we all make decisions. Consciousness defines us, so it seems stupid not to use it more.

Democracy is the collective conscious. By debating policy, society becomes aware of its actions and their impacts. Its competing interests are like mixed feelings. Society can second-guess itself and predict (with wildly varying degrees of accuracy) a policy's likely side effects. Moreover, society can not only change its mind, it can also examine what thinking habits had led to previous mistakes (which is more self-awareness than many individual people exercise). In short, *society thinks about itself*. This means we can decide not to shit the bed we all share – a realization applicable to both the ecology and the economy.

But it also means that we can invent and build a better bed. We can conduct studies and discover that every dollar spent on food stamps generates $1.73 for the economy[473] or that every dollar invested in prison education programs reduces incarceration costs by $4.00 within the first three years after release.[474] Our modern world of sociology and city planning is the ultimate result of Enlightenment thought – and looking out for other people's welfare is part and parcel of this. Again, the Enlightenment and the Progressive Era both fused reason and compassion – they tried to utilize the latest scientific thinking for the benefit of all. Contrary to Ayn Rand's notions, truly objective thought eschews petty selfishness, considers the big picture, and looks toward the common good.

Conservatives often succeed at sabotaging progress precisely because past advances make us take it for granted. They essentially say. "We have not had a catastrophic flood in years, so let's tear down the flood wall. We don't need it anymore." Never mind that the flood wall had prevented several floods since it was built. We do not remember them because they were prevented – not that conservatives would remember them if they *had* happened. Conservative victories depend on a certain degree of civic obliviousness.

What applies to safety applies to fairness, so the conservative response is the same in both cases. It is no mystery why those who claim that racism is dead frequently say something racist in their very next breath. Not paying attention and doing nothing go hand-in-hand, and so conservatives chronically advocate ignoring the problem.

Of course, for some this is conscious and deliberate. Those who urge gutting various civil rights protections know what they are doing. But they depend on other, less alert voters to go along with their civic sabotage.

We have a civic duty to pay attention to things and empathy helps that. It makes us more alert to possible problems or ones that have not yet affected us personally. Empathy helps society's web of information flow better. No, I am not talking about the Internet, but the Internet makes a serviceable metaphor for this social dynamic. Information comes to us from all different directions, but callousness restricts this by muting certain channels.

There is a line that Howard Zinn quotes in *A People's History of the United States 1492 – Present* that illustrates this: "The cry of the poor is not always just, but if you don't listen to it, you will never know what justice is."[475] Zinn quotes it to emphasize that he is not trying to excuse or romanticize everything oppressed populations do. In fact, he prefaces the quote by writing, "I will try not to overlook the cruelties that victims inflict on one another as they are jammed together in the boxcars of the system."

Of course, Zinn is also making an ethical claim about justice that I happen to agree with; but I am primarily citing this to make a larger, related point about the flow of information – that we must listen. Empathy encourages alertness and understanding, which is why we should listen to the cry of the oppressed.

Citizens must know what justice is to function as citizens, but that knowledge alone is not enough. Citizens also need *news* of injustices. Otherwise, the best intentioned people do nothing. Principles need up-to-date information to be activated. Thus, the oppressor's oft used line: "Everything is fine. Move along. There is nothing to see here." This is why they have always seen free media as the enemy. This goes beyond their accusing the media of costing the Vietnam War. They see reporting on problems as unpatriotic. But how are any of our problems to get solved otherwise? Unwelcome news is not just news – it is the most important news there is because we cannot do our job as citizens without it. This is the necessity of listening.

Intelligent self-interest dictates paying attention as well. Even today, there are some conservatives who still claim that it is "virtually impossible" to get HIV from straight sex.[476] Thus, callousness breeds ignorance and it is often said that "karma is a bitch." But karma has nothing to do with it. The ignorant will invariably victimize themselves along with others. The most elementary civic physics predict it. It is almost a tragicomic trope.

Like diversity, empathy is another nexus point of liberty, equality, and democracy. And the trajectory of the far right's anti-empathy mentality is not in doubt. Take this revealing little nugget of wisdom from Rush Limbaugh:

[T]here is no equality. You cannot guarantee that any two people will end up the same. And you can't legislate it, and you can't make it happen. You can try, under the guise of fairness and so forth, but some people are self-starters, and some people are born lazy. Some people are born victims. Some people are just born to be slaves.[477]

Limbaugh attributes this to God: "It's just probably a matter of intelligent design." This view was also advocated by slavery defender James Henry Hammond in his 1858 "Mudsill Theory" of history. He argued that somebody has to be at the bottom of society and some people are just born to do the shit work. And since he saw that as God's plan, Hammond argued that it was both policy folly and morally wrong to oppose it. I have heard no word yet on Rush Limbaugh's position on the Divine Right of Kings.

Thus, when I say that conservatives like Glenn Beck and Rush Limbaugh assault empathy, I am not just saying they are mean-spirited bullies. (Of course, they are that too.) I am saying their basic civic spirit and understanding are stunted. Their mentality undermines America's identity and sabotages America's democratic operations.

By contrast, our founding fathers emphasized the necessity of civic spirit repeatedly. Just as Dr. Benjamin Rush said, "Every man in a republic is public property," John Adams had similarly said a republic required "a positive Passion for the public good" that should be "*Superior to all private Passions.*"[478] (emphasis original) This was no ethos of selfish individualism, nor one that was focused on the family. So, both wings of the Republican Party are fundamentally at odds with the culture of a true republic.

Of course, how could it possibly be otherwise? Democracy is inherently about public participation and our shared stake in society. In *The Rights of Man*, Thomas Paine wrote that a republic was all about the "object for which government ought to be instituted, and on which it is to be employed, *res-publica*, the public affairs, or the public good; or, literally translated, the *public thing*."[479] (italics original) So, Republicans scorn the origin of their party's name!

The founders took civic duty seriously. They would have surely recoiled at Margaret Thatcher's strange claim that "There is no such thing as society." They would have called her a Tory – which is, of course, what the late baroness was.[480]

In *The Way We Never Were: American Families and the Nostalgia Trap*, Stephanie Coontz had expounded on this early American ethos:

In the Jeffersonian tradition, public engagement was considered the primary badge of personal character; honor and virtue were political words, not sexual ones. They designated an individual's "civic altruism," especially a man's willingness to take on political responsibilities. To describe someone as a "private" person was unflattering; a preoccupation with private morality and happiness, no matter how upright, had antisocial connotations.[481]

Unfortunately, this civic altruism evaporated shortly after the U.S. Civil War as many whites succumbed to compassion fatigue. They discarded the idealism that had defeated slavery and then abandoned blacks to the Klan. Then they turned inward and focused on sexual morality and getting rich. As Coontz noted:

The Gilded Age of the mid-1870s to mid-1890s resembles the period since the mid-1970s in some intriguing ways. ... Turning away from social activism, many people focused on their personal lives and material ambitions. It would only be a partial exaggeration to argue that this era provided a foretaste of what we would later call the yuppie phenomenon, including the recent rediscovery of the joys of "cocooning."[482]

Post Civil War Evangelicals were not immune to this change in the national mood. Indeed, they mirrored it instead of resisting it. Ministers dismissed the high-minded notions of social reform they had previously helped spearhead. They no longer preached doing good but instead preached doing well. In 1870, the Reverend Russell Conwell wrote his famous "Acres of Diamonds" sermon in which he preached "[I]t is your duty to get rich." He also argued that the poor only suffered from their own sinful lack of industry.

This civic disengagement is of course poisonous to participatory democracy. Societies have responsibilities which citizens must come together to meet. But, beyond policing people's morality, many conservatives have very little interest in community. For them, community begins and ends at ethnicity or religion. For all their talk of honoring the founding fathers, conservative "values" date back to the Victorian Era and no further.

Again, things were very different in the founders' day. That was a secular time when civic holidays like Independence Day eclipsed Christmas in importance. It was before the Victorians made almost every holiday an isolated family affair. It was back when people remembered that the first Thanksgiving was a communal meal. You celebrated national holidays rowdily in the street instead of quietly around the dinner table. And what better way is there to honor our heritage, given public protest's role in our country's origin?

I watch David Simon's HBO show *Treme* and realize that New Orleans preserves something that America has largely lost – a sense of public participation and involvement. As an introvert, this is a strange thing for me to say. I like my quiet time, I do not party often, and I find obligatory jollity obnoxious. But the historical record is quite clear here and, like it or not, I must thus honestly acknowledge it. (I do party some.)

But, this is not just about partying – although holidays are, by definition, occasions to reaffirm collective identities and strengthen mutual goodwill in any community. Empathy also safeguards our very rights. Remember how liberty and equality reinforce each other: "All for one, and one for all." Give more people freedom and more people have a stake in defending it. But, ignore the rights of those you dislike and liberty's alliances fall apart. Obviously, empathy makes you more likely to do your civic duty.

The key is seeing the larger community – to "extend the sphere" as James Madison put it. Of course, he meant a strong federal government to protect minority rights. Again, the Civil Rights Movement succeeded because we no longer ignored Jim Crow laws as a "local problem" and finally made ending them a national responsibility. But empathy is part of this as well. Widening empathy means more allies, and strengthening it means we are more likely to actually act rather than simply sympathize from a distance. Empathy adds energy to our abstract, theoretical understanding of how rights work. If we feel it, we are more likely to get up out of our chairs and take a stand. But this works both ways. Without that abstract stuff, we do not realize that we have both a right and an obligation to do something about it. And so, again, we sympathize from a distance. Both components are important: We need the theory and the energy. Alone, neither does much good.

Extending empathy to all humanity is not only consistent with this logic, it was also anticipated by Enlightenment era's patriotism. As I wrote in the first chapter, Viscount Bolingbroke's definition of patriotism was "actuated by the noble Principles of universal and unconfin'd [sic] Benevolence" for "the Peace and Prosperity of Mankind." Look at the French Revolution's motto: "*Liberté, Egalité, Fraternité*" – That last word translates as "brotherhood," and there is a reason that it goes with the other two.

Also consider the Friedrich von Schiller poem "Ode to Joy" which Ludwig van Beethoven set to music in his Ninth Symphony. It was about universal brotherhood – and, apparently, drinking.

Beethoven originally considered incorporating Schiller's poem into an opera about Bacchus, the Greek god of wine. But he eventually decided to use it in a symphony instead. According to musicologist Micaela von Marcard, "[I]n the spirit of the later Enlightenment" such a musical tribute to Bacchus "would have been associated with humanitarian ideals."[483]

This can be seen in lines like "Beggars are a prince's brother" (in the original 1786 version of the poem) and "Let our book of debts be cancell'd!"[484]

It was understood that there was an organic connection between conviviality and generosity, between feasting and community. There was a spread-the-wealth ethos in this choral drinking song, and thus it was the anthem of socialists before "The Internationale" was written. Later on, Paul Robeson would sing a different version of Beethoven's "Ode to Joy" that emphasized this brotherhood even more but, alas, omitted the wine.[485]

This explains the internationalism of Benjamin Franklin, Thomas Jefferson, and Thomas Paine. As I wrote in chapter one, the American and French revolutions were *internal* conflicts rather than *external* ones. Patriots directed their hostility against the established order rather than against outsiders. Sympathy for the oppressed defined it, which is why many of the revolutionaries explicitly tied their cause to the abolition of slavery (more on that matter is in my next book). This fact also explains American enthusiasm for revolutions in Europe in the 1700s and 1800s. While conservatives are fond of saying that "charity begins at home," that era's patriots were happy to aid other people's revolutions.

This was the exact opposite of the xenophobic authoritarianism that conservatives temperamentally tend toward. Enlightenment patriotism was solidarity with ordinary people, sympathy for the "little guy." Thus, conservative callousness is not just unconscionable but un-patriotic because actual patriotism is essentially empathy.

Needless to say, I do not give conservatives high marks in doing their civic duty. Usually, they are either bullies or bystanders who reflexively sympathize with power. Whether it is rape, sexual harassment, unsafe working conditions, economic exploitation, or anything else, conservatives' automatic response is to blame the victim and/or defend the violator. And, sadly, such examples of this tendency are legion.

No doubt conservatives will howl at being called bullies. But it is hard to for them to object when they are so often bullies' apologists.

Remember when Sean Hannity and Michelle Malkin defended former Rutgers basketball coach Mike Rice who was fired for both verbally and physically abusing his players.[486] Ms. Malkin lamented that "political correctness has run amuck." Hannity speculated, "Maybe we need a little more discipline in society and maybe we don't have to be a bunch of wimps for the rest of our lives."

This certainly illuminates Hannity's dismissive defense of the Bush Administration's use of torture. (Incidentally, he still has not made good on his promise to endure water boarding.) Hannity added, "My father hit me with a belt, I turned out okay!" This made *Daily Show* host Jon Stewart exclaim, "Seriously? You're okay? Have you *seen* your show? Because it seems like the show of a guy who was hit with a belt as a child."

But then Jon Stewart missed something essential. "By the way, it's got to be so exhausting to have to categorize everything that happens through your right/left, two dimensional goggles. This isn't a liberal, left-wing media, persecuting on politically correct grounds. This was a basketball coach who acted like an asshole and got fired." I quite agree that the coach's behavior should be condemned by people across the political spectrum. In a better world, this would be a totally apolitical story. But the authoritarian personality type is not apolitical. Where Stewart saw politicizing every news item to fill air time, I see the conservative mind at work. Defending bullies is a natural reflex, given their world view. In fact, in an old *Daily Show* segment entitled "Raging Bully," anti-feminist author Christina Hoff Sommers touted the *benefits* of bullying. She said they "toughen us up." Anticipating Sean Hannity's argument, she explained, "We don't want a nation of crybabies." Life's not fair, remember?

To the authoritarian personality, bullying is just normal and healthy male behavior. Take former New Jersey Governor Chris Christie (R), who shouts at public school teachers and possibly closed a bridge to a town to punish its mayor for not endorsing his reelection.[487]

As with Mike Rice, it is the Governor's defenders on Fox News who prove my point. As Brit Hume explained, "Well, I would have to say that in this sort of feminized atmosphere, in which we exist today, guys who are masculine and muscular like that in their private conduct and kind of old-fashioned tough guys run some risks."

I am not sure how closing a public bridge is "private conduct." But, even more interestingly, Hume found a way to both praise and insult women in the same breath by implying that integrity is just some silly girly thing. Translation: "Abuse of office is just something dudes do. Don't get your panties in a wad over it."

Brit Hume seems to feel that being a bully is fine, but that it is a sad sign of the times when someone is actually *called* one. To conservatives, that guy is the *real* victim.

Of course, Chris Christie's pugnacious public persona is precisely what made him so popular among Republicans. Before the bridge scandal broke, he was the GOP's top presidential contender for 2016. Brit Hume's comment was part of a panel discussion on how Christie's personality is a double-edged sword. Christie's thuggishness resonates with conservatives.

It is silly to contradict this verdict. After all, we are talking about voters who avidly supported torturers like Tea Party darling Allen West.[488]

Likewise, American conservatives have long loved Russian strongman Vladimir Putin. This predates Donald Trump becoming president: Jon Stewart's Daily Show did a segment on this called "Big Vladdy" back in 2014. Conservatives adore the fact that the former KGB agent is a macho, homophobic hunter who upholds traditional values. To Fox News pundits, Putin is a "real leader" who "gets things done." Something about that nationalist authoritarian really speaks to them.[489]

You have got to wonder how *Liberal Fascism* author Jonah Goldberg would spin this pre-Trump conservative enthusiasm for Vladimir Putin.[490]

Let us revisit how Chris Christie illustrates conservatism's callousness.

Hurricane Sandy hit the east coast in the midst of the 2012 presidential election. President Obama temporarily suspended his campaign to prioritize federal relief efforts. That was his job. Chris Christie, in turn, did his job and cooperated with Obama. The photo ops of them inspecting the devastation together told the hopeful story of Democrats and Republicans putting aside their partisan differences in a time of crisis.

Of course, this infuriated rabid conservatives who accused Christie of helping Obama look presidential at Mitt Romney's expense. But what was Christie supposed to do? Refuse help? Hide from the cameras?

Yes.

In fact, their ideology demanded it. Election aside, they felt accepting any help was inherently a betrayal of individualist conservative principles.

And strategy and ideology were one. Voters saw events torpedo the right's anti-government rhetoric at the most inopportune moment. Americans were glad to have their Uncle Sam; and to conservatives, that was the real tragedy which should have been avoided at all costs.

But it seems that Governor Chris Christie might not have been doing his job after all. In the wake of his bridge closing scandal, yet more "muscular" regular guy shenanigans came to light compelling even Christie's advocates to voice second thoughts. As the *Star-Ledger's* editorial board wrote in 2014, qualifying their earlier endorsement:

> Yes, we knew Christie was a bully. But we didn't know his crew was crazy enough to put people's lives at risk in Fort Lee as a means to pressure the mayor. We didn't know he would use Hurricane Sandy aid as a political slush fund. And we certainly didn't know that Hoboken Mayor Dawn Zimmer was sitting on a credible charge of extortion by Lt. Gov. Kim Guadagno.[491]

As the editorial tacitly admitted, this is predictable behavior for a bully, even if they stupidly did not predict it. They thought about degree, not direction – they never dreamed that Christie would take things *that far*.

But that is what bullies *do*. And if indulged, bullies are invariably the first people to exploit any latitude they are given and push things further. They are already drunk with power, so self-restraint ain't a hallmark of their behavior. It is ridiculously *naïve* not to realize this.

And the editorial board was still half asleep after their wake up call. They ended their editorial by arguing that Governor Chris Christie was still preferable presidential timber to Senator Rand Paul. Remember when everyone thought the 2016 GOP primary would be all about those two?

Pause to consider what this says about the Republican Party. The voice of moderation already had the ring of desperate rationalization. Again, this was well before Donald Trump won the Republican nomination. Chris Christie, the acknowledged bully, still got portrayed as the party's savior against some *other* nut. And really, Christie is just Trump minus the dementia. The petty abuse of authority, the cocky corruption – it is all there.

It is almost as if conservatives do not quite grasp that being a bully makes you the bad guy. They want to be seen as the good guys, but they also like to bully and do not see any contradiction there. It bewilders them.

This is a result of their tribal us-vs.-them mindset. To them, being the good guy is a matter of birthright rather than behavior. Everything your side does is clever and justified – it is only treachery if the other side does it. You are loyal to your team and you do not snitch. You provide for your kind, but everyone else should fend for themselves.

Therefore, playing favorites is just part of the game. You reward loyalty and punish dissent. Screw the public trust – to the victor belong the spoils. Again, John Adams wrote that government is instituted for the common good and not "for the profit, honor, or private interest of any one man, family, or class of men." But, to conservatives, that is a *naïve* and unmanly way to move in the world. Might (and guile) make right.

Of course, conservatives can quickly point to many famous examples of Democratic corruption as well. That party's history is no stranger to smoke-filled rooms with cigar-chomping good old boy networks either. But those mostly come from a less liberal time, hence Brit Hume's attack on our more "feminized" culture. In fact, Republicans had once spearheaded efforts to root out corruption in government; but that was way back in the Progressive Era that conservatives now despise and criticize. Reforming government went hand-in-hand with busting monopolies, legislation against child labor, passing the eight hour work day, and giving women the vote. It was a time when

Republicans were more liberal than they are now – and when Democrats were more conservative.

The dots just connect themselves. Acceptance of corruption rises with the acceptance of privilege and advantage, whereas honest reform is always driven by those who demand fairness. The connection between conservatism and corruption is both organic and obvious because selling legislation to the highest bidder obviously benefits the rich who can most afford it. And that arrangement has been advocated by conservatives going as far back as Alexander Hamilton. It subverts the democratic process, but conservatives have never been all that fond of democracy. Authoritarians rarely are.

What is an authoritarian personality type? Chris Mooney gives us a glimpse in his 2012 book *The Republican Brain: The Science of Why They Deny Science – and Reality*: "Authoritarians are very intolerant of ambiguity, and very inclined toward group-think and distrustful of outsiders (often including racial outsiders). They extol traditional values, are very conventional, submit to established leaders, and don't seem to care much about dissent or civil liberties."[492]

And they are bullies.

Chris Mooney hastens to clarify that authoritarians are not *inherently* conservative. For example, in a Stalinist regime, like North Korea, their loyalty would be directed toward an entirely different ideology, status quo, and set of traditions. But, here in the States, authoritarians skew conservative. Mooney quotes Vanderbilt University political scientist Marc Hetherington: "The Tea Party is an overwhelmingly authoritarian group of folks." Therefore, their libertarian rhetoric is just that – rhetoric. If they lived in Russia, they would be arresting dissidents and trying to justify Vladimir Putin's "muscular," regular guy corruption – such as the vast, galloping cronyism at the Sochi 2014 Winter Olympics.

Of course, the general population does not fare too much better. As I had noted in the introduction, almost half of Americans score over .75 on a 0 to 1 scale of authoritarian attitudes. And there is your Red State/Blue State divide.

My specific point is that conservatives reflexively sympathize with power. When British Petroleum's Deepwater Horizon oil rig exploded in 2010, the fireball could be seen from thirty-five miles away. It killed eleven men and caused the worst oil spill in U.S. history. Conservatives were appalled – appalled that the company was being made to pay for the oil spill's damages to the Gulf Coast. Michelle Bachman (R-MN) called the escrow account a "redistribution-of-wealth fund." Rush Limbaugh, Stuart Varney, and Sean Hannity all called it a political "slush fund." And when BP's CEO, Tony Hayward, was called to stand before a congressional hearing, Representative

Joe Barton (R-TX) actually *apologized* to him. "I think it is a tragedy of the first proportion that a private corporation can be subjected to what I would characterize as a shakedown."[493]

Gee, I guess dying in an oil fire because your employer ignored safety is a tragedy of the second or third proportion.

This tone-deaf, unpopular position was a sympathy-defining moment if ever there was one. But it was also an ideological stand. And when Bachman and Barton backpedaled later on, Limbaugh castigated those who did not hold firm. For Limbaugh, this was a litmus test of their personal character and conservative credentials. So there should be no objection to my judging conservatism by its own yardstick.

What accounts for this selfishness and misplaced sympathy? I am not a psychologist any more than Dr. Laura Schlessinger. I cannot stress this point enough. But I have a theory about it. It is actually someone else's theory – or rather, my take on his theory.

In Jean Piaget's pioneering studies of childhood development, he had identified a stage called the Preoperational Stage (age 2 to 7). At this point, the child still cannot yet grasp others' perspectives or connections to each other. For example, Junior knows who auntie is, but he does not yet grasp that auntie and mommy are each other's sisters.

The child is the hub of an egocentric bicycle wheel, with each isolated spoke pointing toward another person or association. As Robert Frost once wrote, "an idea is a feat of association," but the child is not yet fully equipped for this feat unless the association directly affects him. Objective thought is not yet possible so magical thinking dominates instead.

Eventually, everyone figures out who their relatives are in relation to each other and starts to develop a more objective understanding of their family and the world. The bicycle wheel then becomes more of a concentric spider web or radar screen. It is still a highly egocentric perspective, but at least it now recognizes that other people have their own outside lives and separate connections with each other.

Of course, a more objective model of the outside world would be dynamic and three dimensional, like interacting complex molecules where chunks or individual atoms break off and recombine in new ways.

But few think that objectively and, egoism aside, it is just easier to simplify things. It is like putting the earth at the center of the solar system – it was wrong, but it was tidy. And it worked well for most people, most of the time, which made the notion pretty difficult to dispel.

This egocentric model is probably not conscious for most. But for many, this flat, static, map best represents how they see things – especially for those who are selfish, tribalistic, or resistant to change.

"What's in it for me and mine?" is the central question for them. If the answer to that question is "nothing directly," then the issue at hand is simply not on their spider web-like radar screen.

I am not saying that conservatives and libertarians are all still stuck at Piaget's Preoperational Stage. But simply realizing that other people have their own lives and rights is not enough. You cannot just file that abstract concept away in your head – you actually have to apply it. You actively have to keep it in mind when dealing with them or making any decisions that might possibly affect them. That is just part and parcel of being a decent person and a fully functional citizen.

For the conscientious, this is established habit. But for others, it might be an awkward, unfamiliar difficulty or a sorely resented chore, and thus sullenly performed or deftly avoided. Unused skills get rusty, and people do not like to do things they are not good at.

So I am not arguing that conservatives are hardwired toward selfishness, but habits reinforce themselves and conservatives have constructed a subculture that self-righteously tries to justify their negligence. Therefore, they cheer greed and dismiss altruism.

This may also explain the frequent stupidity of selfish people and the tendency of intelligent people to be more compassionate. Again, empathy and objectivity both require stepping outside your subjective perspective – hence the irony of Ayn Rand's acolytes calling themselves "Objectivists."

Looking at things from other people's perspectives gives you information as well as compassion. You can spot this in the dual definition of the word "thoughtful" – it means contemplative, but it also means kind.

Ditto with "considerate" – "considering" means thinking – including thinking about others.

Getting a second opinion is also a check on misperception. Therefore, egoism breeds self-sabotaging shortsightedness. There is a reason why the vain are typically vapid: They do not solicit or listen to honest feedback, so their cluelessness endures without outside input.

Psychological studies suggest that this explanation is valid. Researchers have found that reading literature makes us both nicer and smarter. And these qualities are even linked in small children. The more stories you read to them, the sharper their mental model of other people's intentions become.[494] You can spot this in the dual definition of the word "understanding" – it means both sympathy and comprehension.

It is a great deal like how Mark Twain described travel's effect in *Innocents Abroad*:

Travel is fatal to prejudice, bigotry, and narrow-mindedness, and many of our people need it sorely on these accounts. Broad, wholesome, charitable views of men and things cannot be acquired by vegetating in one little corner of the earth all one's lifetime.[495]

Of course, by this definition, we must all remain conservatives to some extent because there is so much more going on in the world than any one person can possibly process or absorb. Thus, there has to be a cutoff point at which you say that you cannot be bothered to think or care about it. You have to prioritize your concerns and obviously you are going to start with yourself and those around you. Beyond that, you will then look and see how much energy you have left to spare. It is like that line in David Simon's HBO show *The Wire*: "It's not your turn to give a damn." In the episode, it is a sarcastic quip on widespread negligence in police work, but it also describes a greater human truth.

Thus, liberalism and conservatism are relative. They are a measure of how vast or narrow the boundaries of your curiosity and concerns are. Broader often means smarter and more compassionate, while narrower promotes the opposite.

Obviously, the elasticity of these boundaries is related to how far they can stretch. Flexible people tend to be more curious and caring. But there are still only so many hours in the day and everyday cares consume a lot of those as well. People need time to think. Without it, they may become impatient and intolerant of more information. At that point, new perspectives – and the inconvenient extra facts they bring – become unwelcome complications. In short, your behavior becomes more conservative.

This may explain why some stressed working class people can be swayed by the Culture Wars to vote against their own economic interests. Intimate issues eclipse the big picture – even when the big picture directly affects you.

However, it must be stressed that working people are far less conservative than they are stereotypically portrayed and largely do *not* vote against their own economic interests.

This came as a profound shock to some when a study discovered that most Tea Party members were actually comfy suburban professionals.[496] Later, the same was found of Trump supporters.[497] Small wonder: They are the same people. In other words, they are typical Republicans.

Alas, the shocked promptly forgot these findings both times. Stereotypes are strong. They remain resilient in the face of contradictory facts.

Moreover, this chapter is about empathy and, culturally, working class people have more of that. In an article in *The Guardian*, David Graeber opined that "caring too much" was the true "curse of the working classes."[498] Why? Because middle class people prioritize personal ambition and advancement whereas working people prioritize the community. It is a longstanding survival strategy. As George Orwell wrote in *The Road to Wigan Pier*, "You cannot have an effective trade union of middle-class workers, because in times of strikes almost every middle-class wife would be egging her husband on to blackleg and get the other fellow's job."

Additionally, my previous use of the word "stupid" should probably be qualified. When you focus your attention on developing specific areas of knowledge, they become strengths while neglected areas become weaknesses. Anyone who has played tabletop role-playing games should know that. It is all about where you allocate your character points. Yes, I am a geek. But, do not ask me about quantum mechanics, nanotech, or even computers.

In modern, complex societies, our roles become highly specialized – far beyond coopers and cobblers – and of course we are all encouraged to find out what we are best suited for and "play to our strengths." Accordingly, libertarians are hardly stupid, but their intelligence is typically restricted to technology or business and therefore their sociological and citizenship skills often suffer as a result. But they are generally more pro-science and cosmopolitan than conservatives are. Thus, they are more knowledgeable because they are less xenophobic. Of course, this does not apply to the anti-immigrant paleolibertarians who animate the sign-misspelling Tea Party.

I strongly doubt that Jean Piaget's Preoperational Stage of childhood development applies to conservatives as anything more than a metaphor. Although, it is an awesome metaphor – they answer to the description in so many ways, especially magical thinking. More on that shortly.

But whatever psychology may find, we know for certain that conservative media personalities can routinely vilify empathy, celebrate selfishness, and defend bullying without alienating their audiences. Quite the opposite – statements that repel decent people resonate deeply with their followers. And it is hardly unfair to put two and two together from there.

You might ask, "What about 'compassionate conservatives'?"

Well, what about them? President George W. Bush paraded that label and he tried to privatize Social Security. Of course, conservatives have always sought to destroy Social Security one way or another since it was signed into law by FDR.

Then there is George W. Bush's mother, former First Lady Barbara Bush, who wondered "why should I waste my beautiful mind" on body bags when the invasion of Iraq was imminent. After Hurricane Katrina, she was alarmed to learn that many New Orleans evacuees were thinking of staying in Houston. "What I'm hearing, which is sort of scary, is they all want to stay in Texas. Everyone is so overwhelmed by the hospitality. And so many of the people in the arena here, you know, were underprivileged anyway, so this is working very well for them."[499] Score!

And then there is one Arthur C. Brooks who wrote a book called *Who Really Cares: The Surprising Truth about Compassionate Conservatism* which claims that religious conservatives give more to charity. Defensive conservatives are certain to invoke the American Enterprise Institute's president. And, if I had a lesser work ethic, I would just counter with Glenn Beck and Ayn Rand and call it a day.

But Brooks and Beck make such an interesting comparison/contrast on the topic of compassion. And how could I possibly ignore a book almost as evil as *The Bell Curve* or as ass-backwards as *Liberal Fascism*? His book is also a picture window into the right's magical thinking which shapes their opinion on so many other issues.

Philanthropy professionals have not been particularly kind to Arthur Brooks' book. As the peer-reviewed *Nonprofit and Voluntary Sector Quarterly* soberly noted, "Citing the discredited generosity index, Brooks asserts that residents of states whose electoral votes went to George W. Bush in 2004 are more charitable than others. Havens and Schervish (2005) show a much more mixed list of states whose residents give more than the national average."[500] Moreover, self-reported data on charitable giving is notoriously unreliable, or as one professional calls it, "mushy."[501] Survey respondents are prone to exaggeration – especially if they feel constantly guilted into giving once a week.[502]

Number-crunching is not my *forte*, but you do not have to be a social scientist to spot big problems in Arthur C. Brooks' book. To prove that liberals are stingy, he repeatedly cites this Ralph Nader statement: "A society that has more justice is a society that needs less charity."[503] Brooks takes issue with this position since he wants more charity. And if less justice does the trick, then so be it. For him, it is only the thought that counts – real world results are irrelevant. He does not care if things get better or worse or even work. Since giving is good for the soul, he seeks to promote it for its own sake – or rather for the giver's sake.

It is hard to fathom how this is compassion. Perhaps Brooks thinks that his motives cannot be selfish if they are spiritual. Yet, they are selfish by every objective measure because others must suffer to benefit his spiritual well-being. It reduces other people to vehicles – to plot devices, like minor characters in a story that live and die only so that the hero has an opportunity to be heroic. Although necessary when writing a novel or a movie, it is a monstrous approach to real life. It sees social problems as difficulty settings on a video game – except that *others* must struggle against them. His worldview does not see this world as fully real because it is so focused on the next.

Martin Luther King once wrote, "True compassion is more than flinging a coin to a beggar; it is not haphazard and superficial. It comes to see that an edifice which produces beggars needs restructuring."[504] But Brooks much prefers the haphazard and superficial because restructuring would spoil his warm fuzzies. Again, he wants more charity, so he demands less justice. He is hostile to European social programs because they are effective and thus lessen giving. Apparently, boasting about generosity is what is most important. It is not hard to spot the sin of pride in his thinking.

Arthur Brooks makes many broken arguments. As James Halteman noted in *The Christian Century*, "[I]f all the annual religious contributions in the U.S. were used to offset public expenditure for the poor, the amount would fund less than 15 percent of current aid to poor people. If all charity, religious and non-religious, were included, about 42 percent of current aid would be covered."[505] In other words, when you add-in secular donations, total private giving *almost triples*. So how are the religious more generous?

But the more important point is that this total is still *less than half* of government social spending on the poor. Brooks assumes that people will give more once government stops being involved. But that is an assumption – like the one that tax cuts do not swell the deficit because they "pay for themselves." Of course, we already know that people do not give more in hard times when it is needed most. People give less when they have less to give. We discovered that during the Great Depression and we are seeing it once again.

On the same page, James Halteman also notes, "[T]he public sector is required to deal with all cases, including the tough ones, while private groups can skim off the easy cases or at least avoid the most problematic ventures. Private groups get blamed for errors of commission in their work, but public agencies get blamed for errors both of commission and omission and thus seem less efficient." He notes, for example, that private charities got praised for pitching-in after Hurricane Katrina, but not blamed for failing to fix problems, as FEMA was. Getting "an E for Effort" is not "good enough for government work." Private charities are judged by a more charitable yardstick.

Speaking of public vs. private efficacy, many private charities are actually incredibly inefficient, wasteful, or just plain corrupt. Some are not actually charities but scams. The majority of their donations go to hiring for-profit telemarketing outfits and their founders' consulting firms.

In other words, most of their fundraising goes to fundraising with the needy often getting almost nothing.

A year-long investigation by the *Tampa Bay Times* and the Center for Investigative Reporting discovered "The 50 worst charities in America devote less than 4 percent of donations raised to direct cash aid." Six devoted zero.[506]

I suspect that most government programs are quite a bit more efficient than that. Of course, that is, provided they are not privatized, as FEMA was under George W. Bush. In that scenario, government contractors and subcontractors had basically the same inflated overhead as charity scams, so almost nothing got to the folks who needed help. The cash got passed along from one contractor to another until the last of it finally disappeared. It seems that those who advocate trickledown economics also favor filter-out relief. And with all those subcontractors, it is a multi-filtered system.

Of course, the *Tampa Bay Times* focused on the worst offenders and there are many very excellent, well-run charities out there. But waste and fraud happen because the charity industry is effectively unregulated.[507] We need more government involvement, not less. And yet, less is exactly what Arthur Brooks urges.

By way of analogy, it is nice that the guy with the SUV is generous with giving folks rides, but he sounds a lot less benevolent when he suggests getting rid of public transit. Slashing taxes so that he can buy a bigger SUV is not practical public policy. Instead, it is like the feel-good inefficiency of a charity whose budget primarily goes to for-profit call centers and lavishly catered galas.

Arthur Brooks is, at best, ridiculously unrealistic, if not surreal. He actually blasts Jimmy Carter for saying that many Americans are indifferent to suffering around the world. Brooks invokes Alexis de Tocqueville's 1835 picture of an America filled with civic groups, charities, and other voluntary organizations and then asks the reader who is right about American generosity – Carter or Tocqueville?

Several things instantly spring to mind at this point:

First, is the indelible image of Jimmy Carter swinging a hammer for Habitat for Humanity to build low income housing shortly after leaving office. (He started in 1984.) You do not talk shit about Jimmy Carter.

Second, Jimmy Carter is discussing present day international aid rather than local giving in 1835. Times have changed and people are more moved by need that they see in person. The apples-to-oranges nature of the comparison is plain.

Third is the fact that not all of the groups that Alexis de Tocqueville described were conventional charities. On the contrary, Tocqueville was emphasizing the great diversity of organizations that Americans formed – including "for entertainments." He was arguing that Americans were joiners. Today, you would not argue that a bowling league is a philanthropy group, although they might join a blood drive or pass the hat if a member needed an operation. Many early American associations focused on fostering fellowship or affirming cultural identity. Charity was often only a corollary of community – a going concern of most groups, but not the focus.

Fourth, the mutual aid these groups provided was usually between people of roughly the same economic strata. It was often about the poor pooling their resources rather than a transfer of funds from one class to another. They were motivated by the realization that they were all in the same boat. The African American social aid and pleasure clubs of New Orleans are in this grain. They are more like Social Security or paying union dues than charity – you pay into the system because you know that one day you will need it yourself.

But pooling resources is not limited to the working class. The rich and middle class practice in-group generosity too. Not all non-profit groups are philanthropic. A lot of it is like members of a club creating or upgrading facilities that only members enjoy. For Arthur Brooks, giving to a suburban high-tech mega-church is the same as giving to an inner city soup kitchen.

Indeed, he specifically says we must not judge other's priorities lest we invite criticisms of our own. Translation: church racquetball court.

In his enthusiasm, Brooks touts efforts that are essentially ordinary dues-paying. He boasts, "About 40 percent of volunteer hours go to religious causes, followed by about 30 percent for youth-related activities, such as PTA and children's sports. Poverty-related causes, health charities, and political activism causes also receive significant amounts of volunteer time."[508] Brooks adds "These statistics are impressive." Well, no, not really. Seventy percent is devoted to getting into heaven or just being an involved parent. Actual charity is a distant afterthought and bundled-in with other things.

I am not knocking after school softball. But people often join a group because there is some perceived benefit. And, on the other side, there is often the expectation that you will also contribute in some way. These are reciprocal obligations, but you all come out ahead because the group dynamic magnifies everyone's efforts.

That is just how groups work. Recall Benjamin Franklin and Thomas Paine's argument that wealth comes from society – cooperation has a multiplier effect. See also the folk saying first coined by dramatist John Heywood (1497-1580) "Many hands make light work."

But clearly that is not charity – it is self-interest. It is a civic investment from which you expect to get dividends. If your kids are not enjoying softball, you stop – unless you are getting a bigger kick out of it than your kids and living vicariously through them. But either way, you are benefitting. This is just basic dues-paying, albeit paid in time instead of money. It would be generous to say that Brooks stretches the definition of generosity.

Fifth is the fact that Brooks totally misreads Tocqueville's take on voluntarism and democracy. Tocqueville was arguing that equality and democracy foster an ethos of cooperation that stresses that all have a stake in the improvement of the community. This can be seen in every benevolent association proposal Benjamin Franklin ever wrote – and he drafted plenty, encouraging both voluntarism *and* government involvement.

Thus, democracy is not just a system of government, but *an entire way of life*. As both Thomas Jefferson and Thomas Paine wrote, a republic is a town hall meeting *writ-at-large*. But, by saying that government should get out of the way, Arthur Brooks is de-democratizing government as a vehicle for people to get things done. Brooks is turning the collective ethos that Tocqueville saw on its ear by limiting the scope of civic participation. He is thereby denying people their most powerful tool.

Of course, that is how divide-and-conquer works – you separate large groups into smaller, weaker ones. Tocqueville was talking about Americans spreading the burden and recognizing that citizens share a wider responsibility. Where Tocqueville expands civic engagement, Brooks restricts it.

There is an old saying that goes "Half-truth is whole lie." Arthur C. Brooks is correct when he says that public efforts sometimes lessen private ones. When your neighbor's house catches fire, you do not grab a bucket anymore – you call the fire department and let them handle it. But professional fire fighters are better at it because they are both trained and equipped to go into burning buildings and you are not. The result is fewer people die. But the fire department's budget still depends on the same grab-a-bucket public spirit that Brooks is trying to undermine. His target audience does not like paying their taxes, so he crafts an argument that essentially says we were better people before fire departments – so let's get rid of them. His rationalization has a counter-persuasive desperation.

I should expound more on my previous fourth point about in-group mutual aid. Arthur C. Brooks looks at giving among the poor and finds that they give a larger portion of their income than the rest of us. I can see that. Brooks also finds that the working poor give more than those on welfare, even if they have equivalent incomes. Why this discrepancy? Brooks concludes that it is because recipients become more liberal and thus stingier(!) He is particularly critical of those miserly single moms who he presumes do not teach their children that charity is a duty. On page 105, he writes, "single parenthood is a disaster for charity." Yeah, it's pretty inconvenient for the parent too.

Two likelier explanations for this giving pattern exist.

First, research shows that welfare recipients often do not have access to the same support networks as the working poor, who often help each other in ways that are rarely tabulated in cash.[509] You may give a friend free babysitting or let relatives temporarily move in with you after they have lost their home. It is not hard to imagine working class culture evolving to promote this ethos – especially when everyone is similarly leaky boats.

Second, community involvement also means knowing more people in need as well as having access to more resources. You *see* the need. It is not a distant, abstract thing that you have to imagine like, say, poverty in another country or another part of town – which, for many, may as well be another country. In addition to seeing, there is the "grapevine" – people ask after each other. "How is your mother doing? I heard about her surgery." etc.

In short, sharing burdens frees up money for dollar donations. By contrast, the isolated must pay for all the services they need and thus they have less cash-on-hand to give than better-connected people in a similar economic situation.

Indeed, if you are in the same dire straights with nothing to spare, you are going to prioritize your family first if you have no support networks to fall back on. Thus, you are likely to be more conservative, not more liberal.

That is all just basic common sense. How is Arthur Brooks so stupid?

Oh, right: Because he has never experienced anything like this.

But whether employed or on assistance, this is money that the poor can still ill-afford to part with. On page 81 of his book, Arthur Brooks admits the working poor are more likely to belong to churches that he delicately says "are especially demanding about tithing." I believe I have an example of that. The late Reverend Jerry Falwell frequently told struggling couples that they could solve all their money troubles by giving to his church. He called holding back "robbing from God":

Let me say a word to you who are struggling with debt right now. A bad attitude about money got you in debt. Whenever I am counseling a couple who's having financial difficulties, I'll say, "Give me a budget now. What's your income? How much are you spending? Where [are] you putting it?" And if I do not see tithes and offerings at the top, [I'll say] "Oh so there's your problem right there: You are robbing from God."

"Oh, we can't afford it right now, Pastor."

"No, no. You can't afford not to. If you need a miracle, you better put the miracle-working God in your budget." I've never led people into that where they didn't come back a few months later and say, "I don't know how it works, but it does. I don't know how in the world why I give more to God and [have] less to keep, I wind up with more." That's spiritual mathematics![510]

It certainly is! It is the Laffer Curve of giving – less is magically more!

You may suspect that this is an unfair comparison or somehow taken out of context. Unfortunately, it is not, and I can prove it with a little history.

As I mentioned before, Arthur C. Brooks admires the infamous oil baron John D. Rockefeller. Brooks defends Rockefeller's boast "God gave me my money" by arguing that the quote should be taken in full context. Rockefeller said, "I believe the power to make money is a gift from God. Having been endowed with the gift I possess, I believe it is my duty to make money and still more money and to use the money I make for the good of my fellow man according to the dictates of my conscience."[511]

His conscience? You may recall that this was the same man who said he would sooner kill all his employees than see them join a union, so his idea of the public good was unique. Arthur C. Brooks does not quote John D. Rockefeller's draconian congressional testimony or mention his dynamiting a rival's oil refinery. Rockefeller's frequent bribery is likewise ignored.

No, Brooks takes Rockefeller's piety at face value and claims that God rewarded Rockefeller for his generosity. Of course, controlling ninety percent of the nation's oil refineries helped to fatten Rockefeller's wallet as well, but Brooks does not mention this immense detail.[512]

Mark Twain was a contemporary of Rockefeller, and less impressed with the oil mogul's piety. Twain sardonically described Rockefeller as the "Admiral of a Sunday school" who liked to explain "how he got his dollars." For their part, Rockefeller's flock "listened in rapture and divided its worship between him and the Creator – unequally."[513]

Arthur Brooks subscribes to Reverend Jerry Falwell's "spiritual mathematics," only he calls it "Rockefeller's Hypothesis" instead. This makes the spiritual sound scientific. Brooks writes, "Rockefeller's blending theology and capitalism may sound odd to some. But for most Americans, who are comfortable with God *and* money, it represents and intriguing hypothesis: Charity and prosperity are interconnected." (emphasis original)[514] Of course, there is that inconvenient bit in Matthew 6:24 that reads "You cannot serve both God and money." But never mind that. Brooks' book is essentially Rev. Russell Conwell's 1870 "Acres of Diamonds" sermon reheated for the twenty-first century.

The concept that God rewards the righteous in this world as well as the next is the central tenet of Prosperity Theology, so this idea is nothing new in today's conservative circles. There is also a religious business book called *God Wants You to Be Rich*. Their peculiar version of Jesus is less "eye of the needle" than "eye of the tiger."

And, speaking of religious conservatives, The Rev. Pat Robertson had told his flock that they should not adopt abused children because they might be "weird." "You don't have to take on somebody else's problems."[515] Good to know.

In short, God wants you to be rich so that you can give more to the church of your choice. Of course, Arthur Brooks argues that ending redistributive taxation would help, ultimately making the poor richer. It sounds great, but I have to ask, if "Rockefeller's Hypothesis" really works, why are the working poor – who give a larger portion of their income than anyone else – still working and poor, rather than comfortably retired on their divine dividends? God's Karmic Rewards™ program is not performing as advertised. No Dickensian *deus ex machina* benefactor arrives to rescue the humble, upright protagonists from poverty in the last act.

I suspect that Arthur C. Brooks used "spiritual mathematics" throughout his book because he makes so many suspicious claims. He says that he was converted by his data, which he says he initially disbelieved. And yet, elsewhere, he has also said that admiring Charles Murray's *The Bell Curve* was what inspired him to become a social scientist in the first place.[516] It seems he cannot keep his ideological origin story straight.

Also, remember that *The Bell Curve* used massaged data to argue that intelligence is determined by race. This may explain why *Who Really Cares* has such gems as, "Public school students (myself included) were being forcibly bussed out of their neighborhoods to comply with racial mixing criteria set by bureaucrats and judges."[517] That sentence is part of his larger catalog of Carter era grievances.

Now, ignore his racist dog whistle for a minute and consider the scientific rigor of his inspiration. Saying Charles Murray got you into social statistics is like saying Bernie Madoff got you into investing. It suggests that you are as dishonest as you are callous.

Magical thinking frequently lends itself to hard-heartedness. For example, witness *The Secret*, an Oprah Winfrey-promoted book which tells its readers that people attract or repel wealth and good fortune with their attitudes. In sum, positive thoughts bring good things, whereas negative ones invite problems. It all seems merely trite until you consider its sinister implications:

Slavery, the Holocaust, AIDS, etc. all look a lot different in this sunny light.[518] What starts out as fluffy cheerleading leads invariably to victim blaming.

Conservatives' notions of where wealth and property come from also illustrate their penchant for magical thinking. They talk a lot about hard work, but are just as keen to avoid it as anyone else. Indeed, get-rich-quick schemes have added appeal for the religious ones because of their highly faith-based mindset. "Miracle methods" of making money are a frequent motif because they believe in miracles. Spiritual mathematics is hardly limited to charity. It shapes most of their notions of how wealth is generated and therefore who is truly deserving of our sympathy.

For example, the Evangelical tent revival atmosphere seen at Amway rallies is unmistakable.[519] The Jesus flows freely, identifying both the typical foot solider and the diamond-level distributor. But surprisingly, the pro-capitalist rhetoric seems stridently anti-capitalist. Testimonials of those who say the system has failed them are a basic staple. You will usually hear several stories about how working for The Man is a dead-end and a fool's game. That is why they say you should work for "yourself," except, of course, in their network enriching the person who brought you in.

Clearly, hard work alone is not cutting it if this message resonates with so many.[520] Indeed, they explicitly say so: Success is the sum of their system, hard work, *and* God's favor. Of course, they never say that your failure is a part of God's plan, because God wants everyone to be rich. But, if despite all your hard work you still do not succeed, it means you have not yet proven yourself worthy of celestial investment. Yes, they really say that to those who do not realize their material dreams.[521]

This callous hybrid of piety and greed is hardly surprising. And it is representative of a wider mentality. After all, how different is "spiritual mathematics" from putting your faith in the stock market? As Thomas Frank observed in *One Market Under God*, the business press often portrays markets as unknowable, benevolent forces that work in mysterious ways. New Economy booster Kevin Kelly's book, *Out of Control* vividly illustrates this faith-based finance. As Thomas Frank summed it up:

We were part of a "hive mind," more akin to a swarm of bees than a collection of rational, thinking persons. We were smart, but not enough to be able to order the world in any successful way. The key was to surrender control, an imperative Kelly repeats like a mantra throughout the book, to realize that the big things are simply beyond us. The way we will finally and correctly learn to understand "network economics," he writes, is through a "new spiritualism." Appliances and even clothes may learn to talk to one another, to do miraculous things, but we humans must realize our limitations and embrace the laissez-faire way as we would a religion.[522]

Again, termites do not write environmental impact statements. They just follow their appetites and consume wood. In this worldview, humans are similar consumers. We do not need to understand the big picture because we have no business trying to reorder things anyway.

Yes, the stock market was for everyone – especially those who did not understand it. As cartoonist Tom Tomorrow had pointed out, small investors are important to the stock market the same way that stranded motorists are important to horror movies.[523]

Of course, those who bought into this spiritual mindset were heartily encouraged to congratulate themselves for being in the know even though they did not actually grasp it. The attitude was both populist and elitist. *Anyone can do this! I pity the fool who doesn't!* Thus, the typical convert was both humble and smug. This was a consistent theme in the literature that Thomas Frank surveyed, which claimed that the average salt-of-the-earth investor bought generic but invested in name brands. As Frank described this mentality, "*We are never fooled; everyone else, though is a TV-watching, ad-believing dope.*" (Italics original) Thus, the "common man" did not think much of his fellow man. There is that compassionate conservatism for you. It is like a giant game of poker – if you sit down at the table and cannot figure out who the sucker is, then you are the sucker.

Ultimately, conservatives do not really believe that wealth comes from work – at least, not from the work of workers. That is something they consider Marxist, although the idea is much older. Thomas Paine had argued that workers were robbed of the true value of their labor long before then. In *Agrarian Justice*, he wrote, "[T]he accumulation of personal property is, in many instances, the effect of paying too little for the labor that produced it; the consequence of which is that the working hand perishes in old age, and the employer abounds in affluence."[524] And Abraham Lincoln essentially said the same:

And inasmuch as most good things are produced by labor, it follows that all such things of right belong to those whose labor produced them. But it has so happened, in all ages of the world, that some have labored, and others have without labor enjoyed a large portion of the fruits. This is wrong, and should not continue. To secure to each laborer the whole product of his labor, or as nearly as possible, is a worthy object of any good government.[525]

Therefore, the Industrial Workers of the World's motto, "Labor is Entitled to All it Creates," is completely in keeping with early American thought on property. Or, as the great American poet-humorist Don Marquis had put it back in the 1930s, "When a man tells you that he got rich through hard work, ask him *whose*."

Indeed, this critique even predates Thomas Paine. Similar thinking was in wide circulation during the English Civil War in the 1600s. But I will cover that in my next book. The point here is that rhetoric against stealing other people's labor is nothing new.

Interestingly, just as Jerry Falwell told his flock that they were robbing God by not tithing, Ben Franklin accused the rich of robbing society by resisting taxation. Of course, there are two salient distinctions.

First, there is the alleged thieves' ability to pay. While Dr. Franklin favored taxing the rich, Dr. Falwell squeezed the poor.

Second, apart from Margaret Thatcher, we can all agree that society exists and we expect to see our taxes at work. Yet, the operations of the Holy Ghost remain invisible to us.

But both doctors said that the entity that had originally created all wealth was entitled to partial reimbursement to keep the engine going.

Like Franklin, I have more faith in the entity that I can see. And accordingly, I have none whatsoever in Falwell's "spiritual Mathematics" or "Rockefeller's hypothesis."

Conservatives have all the cognitive tools they need to progress beyond Piaget's Preoperational Stage, but they are not accustomed to using them because conservative culture discourages that. This is the distinction between capacity and habit, ability and atrophy, *can't* and *won't*. But the results remain the same, and thus Piaget's model aptly describes why stupidity and selfishness so often coincide. To function, a republic requires public-spirited, informed voters. Yet today's conservatives consider educated people to be the enemy and tout their own blindly selfish subjectivity as "objectivity." Out of selfish stupidity, they resist paying for schools, libraries, roads, and bridges.

We literally have bridges collapsing into rivers in the news now. A U.S. Department of Transportation study discovered that eleven percent of bridges are structurally deficient.[526] But Republicans filibustered the 2011 American Jobs Act, which would have funded repairs. In the past, such a commonsensical bill would have sailed through with bipartisan support. But today, the GOP sees government as a monster and its strategy is "starve the beast." As Grover Norquist once said, "Our goal is to shrink government to the size where we can drown it in a bathtub." And if conservatives fail to appreciate such immense, visible things like bridges, no wonder they see the far subtler infrastructure of social services as wasteful boondoggles.

But how do they *not* see this? Even the subtle stuff is pretty obvious. If we were a nation of callous bastards, intelligent self-interest would still dictate that we have a safety net because other people's misfortunes tend to have negative ripple effects.

For example, welfare slows the spread of unemployment. With food stamps, the unemployed can still shop at the grocery store, so the grocery's employees are less likely to get laid off themselves. Belt tightening means less consumer spending, which results in more unemployment. Welfare mitigates this domino effect. It exists less to help the poor than to protect the economy as a whole. It is an economic shock absorber.

Nobel Prize-winning economist Paul Krugman once made a similar observation about austerity as a whole. "An economy is not like a household. A family can decide to spend less and try to earn more. But in the economy as a whole, spending and earning go together: My spending is your income; your spending is my income. If everyone tries to slash spending at the same time, incomes will fall – and unemployment will soar."[527]

So, it is not enough to be callous to be a conservative – you have to be stupid too. Conservatism is the perfect storm of astounding callousness and infuriating stupidity. The chemical reaction requires both. Alas, selfishness and stupidity are frequently twins since, if you have ice water in your veins, it tends to cause brain freeze.

Of course, as I said before, the term "stupidity" should be qualified. Conservatives might be quite bright in other areas, but their civic intelligence is shit. They may know how to run a business, but their grasp of larger economics is nonexistent. Perhaps that is why they superstitiously imagine the market as a fickle deity.

Do you think my language is perhaps over the top? Well, it is not. In fact, the situation is difficult to exaggerate. Topeka, Kansas had actually decriminalized domestic violence to save money arguing that state law still prohibited it.[528] But that excuse just does not wash because the state was rolling out its own new tax cuts, and suspects were being released without charges because no agency was accepting new cases.

This shows the folly of "devolving" power to more local levels of government. Many states now need federal help just to make their budgets. No other cities that I know of have followed Topeka's move on domestic violence, but some localities have stopped repairing roads. That is not going to attract outside business investment and spur local economic growth.

Granted, the world economic crash was, in part, at fault. But it was a three-decade-long addiction to tax cuts at every level of government that has left us vulnerable. Public resources were stretched to the limit while the economy was strong and ill-equipped to function when the economy stumbled.

Government was told to imitate business when corporations were bewitched by daft management fads.

For example, both business and government outsourced tasks they formerly performed in-house. "Doing more with less" was the mantra as assets were sold off, department budgets cut, and experienced people let go because they had earned too many raises. Self-inflicted brain drain was all the rage, so institutional memory gave way to institutional stupidity.

Budget cutters did not seem to know or care whether they were cutting off meat or fat. As long as they were cutting, they felt serious and virtuous. It was pennywise and pound foolish (or to Americanize that English idiom, pennywise and dollar moronic). Therefore, preventative maintenance, safety inspections, and every other cost that did not directly generate profit for corporations or revenue for government often got neglected.

And things worked great – right up until they did not. All of this was done under the magical fantasy that the stock market would soar forever, as if what went up could not possibly come down. It is like selling off your roof for firewood or scrap metal: The extra money is fun, until it rains.

And what caused the economic crash of 2007? Three decades of deregulation and outsourcing. In 1933, the Glass-Steagall Banking Act was passed to prevent a repeat of the shenanigans that triggered the 1929 stock market crash. But it had been repealed because banks found it inconvenient. And conservatives and "centrists," of both parties, gave tax cuts to corporations for moving their factories overseas. Obama tried to repeal these cuts, but he could not swing the votes in Congress. So, *those* laws remain on the books.

A lot can be blamed on the magical thinking that tax cuts fix everything. But, again, there is conscious sabotage afoot as well. As Thomas Frank explained in *The Wrecking Crew*, conservatives sabotage government from within and say "See? Big Government doesn't work." Sane, patriotic people might worry about how such policies would harm our country, but conservatives do not. During the invasion of Iraq, Ann Coulter accused liberal doves of "treasonous stupidity," but I think the phrase she coined best describes conservatives. Had they pulled such stunts during World War II, they would have been shot for treason. The legislative behavior described in the previous paragraph almost seems designed to destroy our country. Yes, it was probably only the product of stupidity, greed, and wishful thinking, but other policies are indeed deliberate.

For example, their scheme to hamstring the U.S. Post Office was especially inventive. The Postal Enhancement and Accountability Act of 2006 required the agency to, within ten years, prefund healthcare retirement benefits for postal workers for the next *seventy-five*. In short, to provide for retirees who were not even born yet. No other public agency or private company has to do this. This absurd burden almost ended Saturday delivery in 2011. The strategy was to simply keep tying weights to Uncle Sam's ankles until he could no longer swim. Republicans called the Post Office "bankrupt," but before prefunding began the service boasted profits in the low billions. Remember that the Post Office has not accepted any tax money since it was made a self-sufficient, semi-private institution over thirty years ago.[529] Yet, despite this privatized status, the far right is still trying to destroy Benjamin Franklin's creation.

Why? Because conservatives think sabotage is patriotic and they feel no sympathy for those who will suffer as a result. Thus, they are fond of forcing government shutdowns – not just as a hostage-taking tactic, but because they find it desirable in itself. They love to see services suspended and government employees forced to work without pay. But the damage goes beyond that. The 2013 shutdown cost the economy $24 billion in only sixteen days.[530] The five week partial shutdown in 2018, cost the economy $11 billion with a quarter of it lost permanently.[531]

Conservatives do not acknowledge how much government spending stimulates the economy. They simply take its positive ripple effects for granted. They forget that World War II pulled us out of the Great Depression. While growing up, I had noticed that they often said that "war is good for the economy" but that government spending was not. I wondered where they thought the Pentagon got its money. At least Ron Paul and son are more consistent since they want to cut the military budget too – consistent, but fiscally suicidal. But both forms of conservatism ignore how government magnifies our wealth, albeit in slightly different ways.

Conservatives' anti-civic attitude does not stop at defunding public schools or at demonizing teachers unions. It threatens every single bolt of our rusting infrastructure. Conservatism desires the literal disintegration of American civilization. I would say they are the secular equivalent of Evangelicals who want to hasten the Apocalypse, except they are not that secular. But the impulse is identical. They yearn to see the Last Days at Galt's Gulch and this selfish, pessimistic yen is the very essence of every Glenn Beck broadcast. Starkly put, we are in a fight between those who want to improve society and those who want to implode it. And those who see tyranny in empathy have plainly chosen implosion.

It may sound touchy-feely to say that compassion is society's attitudinal glue. Yet, recognizing how liberty, equality, and empathy all reinforce each other is simply steely-eyed realism. It is self-evident and conservative contempt does not change that.

Liberals often say conservative scorn for the poor is not very nice. But this goes far beyond nice. We have a civic duty which reactionaries reflexively deny and disparage. I do not go much for touchy-feely speak either. I believe all real writing is both tactile and tactless. Hey, I can be just as blunt and abrasive as, say, a Chris Christie. And if that is the only language that conservatives understand, I can do like Dr. Doolittle and "Talk to the Animals," if any conservatives are still reading. I have actually done this throughout the book to various degrees – and, yes, I am doing it now. I have also written in second person on occasion. (I have noticed that conservative political literature does that a lot.) But this is not only an effort to speak their language. This is what I really think. And yet, ironically, this bluntness itself requires some explanation.

It is a familiar truism that conservatives are motivated by anger while liberals are motivated by guilt. And, as I explore more in the next chapter, psychological studies have shown that conservatives also respond to the rhetoric of disgust. Conservatives certainly do not have a monopoly on anger or disgust. But, in the interests of diplomacy, liberals typically hide these feelings. Since conservatives seem capable of expressing little else, their example makes liberals check themselves even further. In *Poor Richard's Almanac*, Benjamin Franklin wrote, "Take this remark from Richard poor and lame, Whate'er's *[sic]* begun in anger ends in shame." Or as Yoda put it, "Anger is the way to the dark side." So liberals pull their punches. And, of course, empathy helps temper them as well.

The liberal temperament defaults to fairness and peace-keeping. All too often, this results in the mistake of soft-pedaling arguments or keeping silent. You can see this in a letter that Abraham Lincoln wrote to his slave-owning friend, Joshua Speed. Lincoln wrote it in 1855, when the prospects for abolition looked dim and it seemed that the only thing that could be done against slavery was to stop its spread westward:

> *I confess I hate to see the poor creatures hunted down, and caught, and carried back to their stripes, and unrewarded toils; but I bite my lip and keep quiet. In 1841 you and I had together a tedious low-water trip, on a Steam Boat from Louisville to St. Louis. You may remember, as I well do, that from Louisville to the mouth of the Ohio there were, on board, ten or a dozen slaves, shackled together in irons. That sight was a continual torment to me; and I see something like it every time I touch the Ohio, or any other slave-border. It is hardly fair for you to assume that I have no interest in a thing which has, and continually exercises, the power of making me miserable. You*

ought rather to appreciate how much the great body of the Northern people do crucify their feelings, in order to maintain their loyalty to the constitution and the Union.[532]

The upshot is liberals are often seen as weak. On most debate shows, the conservative jock beats up on the liberal geek. Apart from two exceptionally charismatic presidents, Democrats cannot hold the White House because all their other presidential candidates are too nice to hit back. So, they all get Willie Horton-ed or Swiftboat-ed.[533] Having fighting spirit is often seen as suspect. Just ask Howard Dean.

On the other hand, this reluctance to express anger or disgust is also a social lubricant and thus a civic virtue. That is why liberals have it. Liberal political culture promotes the habits and attitudes that participatory democracy requires and empathy is one of them. But empathy can definitely be its own worst enemy and, eventually, you are forced to ignore the rule of etiquette that says it is rude to point out rudeness.

John Adams said we must put the public good before "all private Passions." And what is patriotism but a loyalty to something beyond your front lawn? It is certainly not the Tea Party's selfish fallout shelter ethics. It is obviously the opposite. It is looking out for your neighbors across the hall and across the ocean. It rings in Schiller's "Ode to Joy" and in Aaron Copland's "Fanfare for the Common Man." It is the "civic altruism" that Stephanie Coontz found in the Jeffersonian tradition. It is the majesty of ordinary, everyday decency towards other people.

Of course, you do not have to be compassionate to be a patriot, but it helps. You can do the right thing out of duty. But empathy makes doing your duty far more likely. This explains why liberals are often excellent patriots even if they do not loudly trumpet it. All our country has to be proud of comes from acting on our liberal traditions and all we have to be ashamed of comes from neglecting them.

By sharp contrast, conservatives are frequently failures as Americans. What they consider a liberal guilt trip is simply citizenship and they resent it intensely. When they see poverty, they say, "I already gave at church" and buy Arthur C. Brooks' book. When they hear about violations of minority voting rights, they just shrug or, worse, try to justify it.

Conservatives' political reflexes are anti-civic. They typically vilify empathy, praise the bully, and blame the victim. They are at best oblivious drags on America's character and at worst they are conscious saboteurs of the common good. The latter are politely called "conservative ideologues."

This is not an unfair caricature. On the contrary, it is a photographic portrait that they are happy with and they have ordered duplicate prints. If it were otherwise, conservative media figures' insane, callous statements would alienate their audiences. Instead, their audiences applaud and enthusiastically demand more. Therefore, these political pundits constantly compete to out-do each another and come up with something worse.

But what delights conservatives disgusts true patriots.

10: The Tory's Phony Loyalty
Conservatism's Defensive Patriotism

During the 2008 presidential election, country singer John Rich caused a minor stir by claiming that the late Johnny Cash would have supported John McCain over Barack Obama. The problem was that Cash was actually a liberal Democrat.

The gaffe was made all the more embarrassing by the fact that Cash, "The Man in Black," literally wore his politics on his sleeve. In his signature song, he wrote, "I wear the black for the poor and the beaten down, living in the hopeless, hungry side of town." This does not sound like someone who would end welfare. "I wear it for the prisoner who has long paid for his crime, but is there because he's a victim of the times." Nor does it sound like he would support stiff sentencing. In fact, the song even has a slam on the Vietnam War. "Each week we lose a hundred fine young men." So, I cannot imagine that Cash would support continuing the quagmire in Iraq as McCain had.

Indeed, despite country music stations banning the Dixie Chicks for not adoring George W. Bush, a lot of country music stars and fans are Democrats and/or progressives – Willie Nelson and Kris Kristofferson, for example. And Merle Haggard is now very different from the man who wrote "Okie from Muskogee." In fact, Haggard has defended President Barack Obama. "It's really almost criminal what they do with our President. There seems to be no shame or anything. They call him all kinds of names all day long, saying he is doing certain things that he is not."[534]

The genre is far more complex than the stereotype suggests. And this is to say nothing of country music's roots in folk music, which is often quite progressive. The names Woody Guthrie and Pete Seeger should confirm that. Of course, that community can be pretty complex too, as is proved by the Johnny Cash song, "The One on the Right Is on the Left."

John Rich's mistake was human and understandable. We all do this from time to time. I must admit that I was quite surprised to learn that the late actress Dixie Carter was a Republican – a gay-friendly, libertarian Republican, but a Republican nonetheless. I made the mistake of confusing the actress with the liberal character she had played on "Designing Women." By contrast, I do not know on what basis John Rich had made his mistake because Johnny Cash usually played himself.

In a way, this little struggle over country music mirrors the far larger struggle over America's identity. Indeed, the first is part of the second. And although I know that I am making a harsh and controversial claim in this chapter, I want to be as charitable as the facts allow. Questions of belonging and authenticity are often paradoxical. They are seldom cut and dry.

Take Coca Cola, for example. The brand is firmly anchored in Americana. And yet, if you feel a nostalgic longing for "The Real Thing," as Coke had formerly touted itself, you must buy Mexican Cokes. Fans say they taste more like the original. Today, if you want that classic Americana, you must import it. This irony may seem pretty trivial, but nostalgia is a powerful factor in what most consider patriotism.

We all have different nostalgic attachments and emotional claims to America. Take mine. My parents were never U.S. citizens, but I was born here in 1967. I suppose I would be called an "anchor baby" if my parents had not returned to Europe in the late 1990s. I was nine years old during the 1976 Bicentennial Celebration of the American Revolution.

I was raised on "Schoolhouse Rock." And despite the Manifest Destiny message in "Elbow Room," these cartoons were otherwise both progressive and patriotic. Songs like "Suffering until Suffrage" and "The Great American Melting Pot" depicted struggle and synthesis. They portrayed America imperfectly evolving.

In school, my post-Watergate civics textbooks stressed that a free press was essential and singled out the 1735 John Peter Zenger liable case which established the right to print unflattering facts about public officials.[535]

These textbooks also gave space to the immigrant experience, as more Americans began to explore their roots in the 1970s.

The emphasis was on Ellis Island, but my family's odyssey was less troublesome. Being Europeans, my parents had arrived by jet and gotten green cards. Nobody misspelled their names on important documents and it certainly was nothing like the horrors seen in the film *El Norte* (1983).

Still, having immigrant parents made me different from my peers. It made me think about questions of identity and belonging. I appreciated what it felt like to be an outsider. I guess being a geek helped there as well. The Chris Claremont and John Byrne "X-Men" comics encouraged me to think critically about these issues.

The Statue of Liberty featured prominently in the patriotic imagery of my youth and I was a teen during its restoration and centennial celebration in the mid 1980s. I gave some thought to the poem inscribed on it.

Almost every youth rebels at some point, but my controlling immigrant parents gave the defiant idiom "It's is a free country" great personal resonance for me. When they eventually left, I stayed.

That background had an impact. Even as a teen, I saw through conservatives' lip service to liberty and I wondered how their urge to control others was not obvious to everyone. I watched one moral panic after another wash over the country.

In the 1980s, religious idiots claimed that playing Dungeons & Dragons led to satanic ritual murder and teen suicide.[536]

In the 1990s, authoritarians claimed that rap music was behind a teen crime wave even as youth violence was dropping dramatically.

Any trumped-up excuse to crack down on youth would do. The right's constant assaults on the already long-extinct "culture of the Sixties" showed their hostility toward personal freedom. The Culture Wars were obviously always about policing morality and a broader assault on liberty generally.

I also recognized that conservatives' favorite "patriotic" imagery was primarily air power displays or other high-tech military hardware. You were obviously supposed to associate the word "freedom" with this fetishized weaponry and ignore the right's habitual constitutional abuses from Watergate to Iran-Contra on forward.

It quickly became clear to me that the right's idea of "patriotism" was not a love of country, but an immature infatuation with something they hardly knew. True mature love acknowledges faults. But conservatives do not love America, warts and all, because they refuse to see any warts. They cannot love America because they refuse to *see* America. Not being able to stomach criticism of our country is not patriotic – it is pathetic.

There is a line in the Dead Kennedys punk rock song "The Stars and Stripes of Corruption" which illustrates this. "Tell me who's the real patriots/The Archie Bunker slobs waving flags/Or the people with the guts to work for some real change?" A serious citizen must adult-up and face the facts, however unflattering. You do not defend America's honor by denying problems but by *facing* them and *fixing* them.

Mark Twain had said something similar in *A Connecticut Yankee in King Arthur's Court*. "[T]he citizen who thinks he sees that the commonwealth's political clothes are worn out, and yet holds his peace and does not agitate for a new suit is disloyal; he is a traitor."[537] Criticism is part of citizenship. Stifling dissent is a form of sabotage. It is like disconnecting an important dashboard warning light.

For example, Frederick Douglass' famous 1852 speech "What, to a Slave, is the Fourth of July?" is a patriotic document despite its scathing condemnation of America's hypocrisy. Douglas was agitating for a new suit. And accordingly, Abraham Lincoln, in his Gettysburg Address, called for "a new birth of freedom" because the founders had failed to end slavery. Unfinished business had swelled and festered from neglect. And, as the Civil War showed, it was those who *resisted* change who were the true traitors.

Reactionaries predictably have great difficulty grasping this.

In Tennessee, the Tea Party had demanded that the school curriculum not mention that any founders owned slaves. The spokesman bemoaned that there was, "an awful lot of made-up criticism about, for instance, the founders intruding on the Indians or having slaves or being hypocrites in one way or another."[538] Oh, and they also wanted it known that "the Constitution created a Republic, not a Democracy."

And in Texas, Republicans were not satisfied with striking democracy and the Enlightenment out of textbooks. Nope. They want to eliminate critical thinking courses from the curriculum entirely.[539] They actually put it in their 2012 party platform. They are simply allergic to basic citizenship.

Conservatives often accuse liberals of being ashamed of America. Every nation has things to be ashamed of. If it does not, it has no history. But when we assess America's history, we notice that every shameful stain came from betraying our country's liberal principles. Therefore, conservatives are not really defending America's reputation – they are defending *their own*. No wonder they take it personally. Our collective guilt is much less collective than one might think. It is more conservatism's than America's.

Consider the hypocrisy that Frederick Douglass condemned. If we had not laid claim to any liberal principles in the first place, there would be no hypocrisy to criticize – immense injustice yes, but no hypocrisy. There would be no contradiction to ignore or deny.

Of course, the democratic process means America as a whole must accept its fair share of the blame – the nation cannot ignore its responsibility. But it would be dishonest to ignore the conservative temperament behind our country's most ignominious deeds.

Yes, an illiberal act might be committed by a liberal administration. For example, it was Franklin D. Roosevelt who put Japanese Americans in internment camps during WWII. But nobody outside Glenn Beck's audience and that ilk would consider the policy *itself* to be liberal in character.

On the contrary, the policy was a betrayal of everything the American Civil Liberties Union stands for. Indeed, often such travesties are committed in the fear of being perceived as "soft on" crime, communism, or terrorism. Liberals often copy conservative policy in fear of being called "too liberal."

Thus, we have bipartisan consensus *for* policies that we should have bipartisan consensus *against* – policies that are both illiberal and un-American. But I repeat myself. And, paradoxically, anyone criticizing such policies is called "anti-American" – typically by the type of conservative voter who does not want any talk about the founders owning slaves.

But the right's idea of patriotism is not simply prickly. It is also quite shallow. Conservatives are shockingly uncurious about American history and culture. Their phony patriotism is actually a defensive reflex rather than any real appreciation for our country's complex and tumultuous history and culture. Whitewashes are like that.

Let us take a look at two examples of how conservatives treat the texts and lore that they claim to honor, both sacred and secular:

I will start with Rush Limbaugh's remarkable market-based Bible study. The racist radio bloviator once claimed that Joseph told the Pharaoh to cut taxes from 90 percent to 20 percent, resulting in seven years of bounty. "You can trace individual prosperity, economic growth back to the Bible, the Old Testament. Isn't it amazing?"[540]

But the Bible tells the story somewhat differently.

In it, the Pharaoh had dreamt of seven fat years followed by seven lean ones. Joseph suggested a new tax during the years of plenty and setting aside the collected grain for the coming famine. In other words, the story is pro-taxes rather than anti-taxes and thus the *opposite* of what Limbaugh claims.

If only he read his Bible.

This is not just a flippant quip, but a window into how Rush Limbaugh thinks. I find it difficult to imagine being excited by something but not wanting to actually *see* it for myself. If I think I have found a golden quote or story, I want to see it myself – not just to verify it, but to *revel* in it.

This goes beyond basking because double-checking great bits frequently results in finding *more* of them – and even *better* ones.

But Rush Limbaugh's religious fervor is enthusiasm without interest. Thus, he does not look at what he is pointing to. It never even occurs to him that he might *want* to. And his listeners are no different.[541]

This paradox marks conservatives' patriotism as well as religiosity. Take Sarah Palin's version of Paul Revere's midnight ride:

And you know, he who warned the British that they weren't going to be taking away our arms, by ringing those bells and making sure, as he is riding his horse through town, to send those warning shots and bells, that we were going to be secure and we were going to be free.

Of course, Paul Revere actually rode to warn his *fellow colonists* that the British were coming to seize the militia's arsenal. He was certainly not telling the *British* that. He was trying to *avoid* royal patrols, not *alert* them.

Naturally, the redcoats were trying to conceal their movements too. That is why they marched at night to seize the patriots' stockpiles before morning. Everybody was trying to be stealthy that night.

Once Paul Revere warned Lexington's patriot leaders, *they* rang the church bells to wake the town while Revere rode on, again in secret, to alert the next town of Concord.

Unfortunately, a royal mounted patrol caught him before he got there, and *that* was when he told them there was a large, armed force ready for them in Lexington. It was a ruse to scare them off with big talk and buy the patriots more time to mobilize.

In short, Sarah Palin turned a covert operation into a public protest.[542]

She could have admitted that she had garbled her facts or her words. We all do this occasionally. In fact, just above, I first typed "the state militia's arsenal" even though I obviously knew that Massachusetts was still only a colony at that time. Fortunately, I caught my mistake.

By contrast, Palin stubbornly doubled-down on her version of events, compounding the problem, and drawing more attention to it. "I didn't mess up about Paul Revere," she insisted. "[P]art of his ride was to warn the British that we're already there, that hey, you're not going to succeed. You're not going to take American arms."

Yeah, the unplanned part of his ride where he got captured before he could warn Concord.

Why did she do it? A halfway savvy speaker could have used the clarification as an opportunity to talk about guns more. Acknowledge the error and move on. For example, when Michelle Bachman said that Lexington and Concord were in New Hampshire, she quickly admitted the error, turned her gaffe into a joke on Massachusetts, and most everyone forgot about it. This makes her a shrewd politician in comparison with Sarah Palin. But most conservatives would rather *feel* right that *be* right.

And why is that? It is because *becoming* right often means admitting you were wrong before. They would rather dig their heels in quicksand than cede a single inch of ground. Their goal is not to be right at the end of the day, but to avoid ever feeling any doubt or admitting error in the meantime.

Whether she was conscious of it or not, Sarah Palin was primarily defending Sarah Palin rather than gun rights. It was pure, emotional "fight or flight" – and, in her eyes, admitting a mistake is flight. And while that might be understandable in the heat of the moment, she was still stuck in that mode the next day. Reptilian brain jokes aside, I strongly suspect very many conservatives are stuck in that mode their entire lives.

Of course, liberals can be stubborn too: Nobody enjoys being proven wrong. But liberal culture does not reward such dumb stubbornness the way that conservative culture does. Liberal culture encourages curiosity and keeping an open mind and that necessarily means living with some uncertainty. Therefore, it acts as a check on human egoism.

By contrast, conservative culture throws gasoline on that fire. It fetishizes faith because it is terrified of uncertainty – feeling doubt is feeling weak, so they avoid doubt at all costs. Thus, sticking to your guns in the face of contradicting reality is something conservative culture admires – whereas changing your mind in light of new facts is seen as vacillating. A *wrong* conviction is honored as long as it is a *strong* conviction.

Of course, this is not just stubbornness. It is additionally a failure of reverence. Conservatives lack a humble "reverence for the facts." You have to value the facts over your own ego, pet theory, or worldview. And when they clash, you must yield to the facts. But very few conservatives can do that and such scientific thinking is highly suspect in conservative circles.

But, specific facts aside, I am also talking about a reverence for the subject matter itself. If you actually appreciate something, you are, well, interested in it. Passion wants information. By contrast, blind obedience obviously discourages curiosity.

For Sarah Palin, patriotism is about invoking images, symbols, and feelings. She might not be doing it cynically: She may just be duplicating what works for her as cheerleading. But strong emotions are not necessarily deep ones. They can still be quite superficial and uncurious – often stupendously so.

Conservative patriotism is often only nostalgic button-pushing with no interest in the wires behind those buttons. Thus, conservatives are not geeky enough to be true patriots. Yes, part of this is a question of intelligence. But part of this is also that passionate (and often obsessive) interest that *defines* geeks. Think of the Trekkies or Whovians who must know the minutiae of every episode of their show.

Sarah Palin has never been a geek of any description. At least, she did not bring that attention to detail to Paul Revere's ride. Nor for that matter, did Rush Limbaugh bring such loving scrutiny to the *Bible*. Neither is really geeking out about either topic.

Speaking of geeks, witness the alt-right nitwits who rant that "political correctness" is encroaching on science fiction, fantasy, and other speculative fiction which depicts different civilizations. The xenophobes are actually trying to steal the genres of xenophiles!

In their horror and sci-fi titles, EC comic books had explicitly blasted bigotry in the 1950s. So Imagine thinking that *Star Trek* is being "ruined" by diversity today! That whole mentality is ludicrously clueless. As George R.R. Martin marveled on his blog, "I mean, we're SCIENCE FICTION AND

FANTASY FANS, we love to read about aliens and vampires and elves, are we really going to freak out about Asians and Native Americans?"[543]

Likewise, superhero comic books have been switching around established characters' race or sex since the early 1960s using magic, passing the mantle, alternate universes, or other familiar narrative devices, so it is a bit late to start complaining about it now.

These are long-established tropes, yet historically illiterate reactionaries ridiculously insist that they are "real fans" and challenge the authenticity of actual enthusiasts who they do not want around. Their absurd projecting parallels conservative "patriotism."

It is immensely tempting to think that conservatives do not actually believe in anything. Perhaps their constant bluster about patriotism, faith, and values is only to hide the fact that they do not actually have any. Like people who are in love with the idea of being in love, they are in love with the idea of having deep beliefs.

I suspect that conservative patriotism is a lot like being a certain sort of sports fan. Fans who only want to have a team to root for and an opponent to root against: Fans who feel no contradiction between hating people with education and loving a college ball team.

After all, sports teams do not clash over ideological or religious issues. The New England Patriots are not fighting for democracy or trial by jury any more than the Minnesota Vikings are trying to get into Valhalla.

No, the home team only represents the home town – and often not even that. After all, players are recruited from far and wide and the franchises are owned by investors and thus as portable as any car or sneaker factory.[544]

These allegiances are quite shallow. And yet, despite this, sports fans are *passionately committed* to their teams. Conservative "patriotism" rarely rises above this superficial, tribal mindset.[545]

I am not saying that sports fans are stupid – I know some pretty brilliant ones. But they admit that sports are ultimately not that important. It is entertainment and they know that a Supreme Court decision has a lot more impact on their daily lives than the outcome of any game. But it still shows how a loyalty can be both strong and shallow.

Consider conservative Christians who do not turn the other cheek, love their enemy, or give to the poor. What do they stand for besides calling themselves Christians?

Not much. Indeed, many say that simply professing your faith is sufficient. "TESTIFY!" Forget Matthew 6:5 condemning ostentatious displays of faith:

And when thou prayest, thou shalt not be as the hypocrites are: for they love to pray standing in the synagogues and in the corners of the streets, that they may be seen of men.

Except for shaming sexuality, they are largely unconcerned with Christian behavior. What actually matters to them is belonging to Team Jesus and crushing every other team. It is just us-vs.-them.

The War on Terror has magnified this. Thus, many in the Tea Party insisted that President Obama is a secret Muslim despite his attending church, eating pork, and drinking alcohol. (Muslims cannot have "beer summits.") But, never mind. To them, he is the Other, and all the Others are the same to them – hence their bizarre but fiercely earnest belief in a Muslim/gay conspiracy to destroy America.

Likewise, the right's "patriots" scorn America's central ideals. For Robert Bork, these were "resounding generalities" – ornamental distractions that we should ignore. But after gutting America's identity what is left to feel patriotic about except a sense of place? Faith in the free market? Then move to Singapore where markets are supposedly so much freer. (And again, they actually are not.) Otherwise, you obviously have got nothing but vacuous platitudes.

For example, on the 2012 campaign trail, Republican presidential nominee Mitt Romney had uttered the most tortured tautology in modern politics. He proclaimed, "I believe in an America where millions of Americans believe in an America that's the America millions of Americans believe in. That's the America I love."[546] Okay, thanks for clarifying.

Of course, there are also committed conservative ideologues, and those on the staff of *National Review* were initially displeased that Mitt Romney was not making a more full-throated proclamation of conservative principles. But, that was before Romney tapped Ayn Rand fan Paul Ryan to be his running mate and claimed that forty seven percent of Americans only want government handouts and vote accordingly.

But what do these ideologues stand for? They always *say* that they want smaller government, but they always augment the size of government when they get in office. As I wrote before, their beliefs are less a coherent ideology than a grab bag of dislikes that include liberty, equality, and democracy (and empathy as well). Thus, if government is providing social services, they are anti-government. Otherwise, they are all for expanding police powers and legislating morality. Despite their loud libertarian rhetoric, the Tea Party is not opposed to profiling brown people or dictating women's reproductive choices.

All of these monumental contradictions become a lot less confusing when we stop thinking of conservatism as a logically cohesive ideology and recognize it as only a crude reactionary animus. So, of course, their "patriotism" is going to be either blandly vague or blatantly un-American. What else could it possibly be?

For conservatives, patriotism and religion function much the same way. For openers, they like to make a big show of both. But more importantly, Robert Bork's constitutional "Originalism" is a great deal like religious fundamentalism. Both insist on a "strict literal interpretation" of sacred texts while twisting them into pretzels. Both promote fervor over consistency and group loyalty eclipses any political principle.

Again, it is all about belonging to a team. Details are just trivial things for geeks to worry about. Don't sweat them.

For example, during the 2012 GOP presidential primaries, Mitt Romney's Tea Party-favored rivals attacked how he amassed his great wealth. Newt Gingrich and Rick Perry called Romney's years running Bain Capital "vulture capitalism." This was odd because conservatives had always called such rhetoric "punishing success." The irony was not lost on *all* conservatives. As Charles Krauthammer quipped, "Richard Trumka of the AFL-CIO nods approvingly. Michael Moore wonders aloud whether Gingrich has stolen his staff."[547] Then, Sarah Palin waded into the fray backing Gingrich and Perry. The crowning irony was that these three all objected to Romney because they doubted his conservative convictions.

Again, team sports can be both passionate and shallow. But that shallowness is consciously encouraged. Pat Buchanan calls a love of democracy "idolatry" because it replaces "a love of process for a love of country." But it is conservatives who are committing idolatry because the symbol or vessel eclipses the real thing. Without process, the country is only a vast expanse of dirt like any other landmass on this planet. Indeed, without process, the country ceases to be free. So, why do conservatives dismiss the love of process?

Likewise, the right is quick to trample the First Amendment to ban flag burning (among other things). But if sacrificing freedom for its symbol is not idolatry, then nothing is. For all their tough, concrete language, conservatives prefer vague, airy symbols over hard facts because symbols are abstract, emotional, and pliable. Facts can be manipulated, but it is far easier to manipulate feelings. And given conservatives' hostility toward real freedom, it is no wonder they exalt its symbols over its actual applications.

Of course, almost everything I have said about conservatives applies, to a lesser degree, to liberals as well. We are all human. But different groups encourage and discourage different traits. They reward or suppress different human impulses. And this, in turn, decides who they alienate or attract.

For example, we can all be selfish sometimes, but an ideology that cheers greed is naturally going to be a bigger scrooge-magnet. We can all get angry from time to time, but a movement that runs on perpetual rage is going to draw more bullies. Not all identity politics is explicit or even conscious.

In any serious discussion of American patriotism, two important topics stand out – symbols and the rhetoric of rights. We have just discussed symbols, so let's turn to how conservatives currently distort the rhetoric of rights.

We Americans have always used the rhetoric of rights to explain our behavior and justify our desires. Some claims are implausibly lofty. The personal is not always political and hyperbole is almost always just around the corner. But there is absolutely no questioning that this is a very American trait and that it is a good problem to have. After all, you *want* the public to be hyper-vigilant about their rights, even if some frivolous lawsuits burden the courts. And, contrary to tort reformers' favorite urban legends, such suits are routinely tossed out before they waste much of anyone's time.

You do not want a timid populace that permits abuse by government or each other. Free society is not free of annoyances. So, while the rhetoric of rights certainly has its unavoidable excesses, it is totally worth the headache when you consider the alternatives. What Winston Churchill said about democracy applies here: It is the worst system, except for all the others.[548]

Traditionally, conservatives have criticized this American trait. They say it leads to "inventing new rights" and a "culture of entitlement" which they say strengthens the welfare state. Every word Robert Bork ever wrote against liberty and equality was a reaction against this facet of the American character, so it is a pretty familiar critique.

But today, things have changed quite a bit. As part of their libertarian makeover, conservatives have embraced the rhetoric of rights with a vengeance and their sense of entitlement is immense. The Tea Party is essentially every type of privilege you can think of on steroids with a loopy, paranoid persecution complex to boot. Of course, this attitude is not entirely new. In Robert Bork's 1996 book, *Slouching Towards Gomorrah*, there are sixteen separate entries under the index heading "white males, heterosexual."

Conservatives consider anything they do not like to be against the constitution. For example, many on the far right nourish the fantasy that the national income tax amendment was never actually ratified. And many Tea Party people believe that the states retain the right to nullify any federal law that they dislike, despite the U.S. Civil War.

This mindset went ballistic when President Barack Obama first got elected. It prompted the *Daily Show's* Jon Stewart to suggest some perspective was in order:

I think you might be confusing tyranny with losing. And I feel for you because I've been there. A few times, in fact one of them was a bit of a nail biter.

But see, when the guy that you disagree with gets elected, he's probably going to do things you disagree with. He could cut taxes on the wealthy, remove government's oversight capability, invade a country that you thought should not be invaded. That's not tyranny. That's democracy.

See, now you're in the minority. It's supposed to taste like a shit taco.

And by the way, if I remember correctly, when disagreement was expressed about that president's actions when y'all were in power, I believe the response was, "Why do you hate America?"[549]

Conservatives often do not grasp that everyone's rights must be balanced with everyone else's, or that there is therefore no right to deny others *their* rights. They feel oppressed because they are no longer allowed to oppress. This explains the resentment exploited by the Republican Party's Southern Strategy, which Ann Coulter insists does not exist despite Lee Atwater candidly explaining it on tape:

You start out in 1954 by saying, "Nigger, nigger, nigger." By 1968, you can't say "nigger" – that hurts you, backfires. So you say stuff like, uh, forced busing, states' rights, and all that stuff, and you're getting so abstract. Now, you're talking about cutting taxes, and all these things you're talking about are totally economic things and a byproduct of them is, blacks get hurt worse than whites.[550]

But the voters who respond to that code resent having to get so abstract. Subtlety is not their thing, so they see dog whistles as oppressive political correctness. Donald Trump won the 2016 GOP nomination in large part because he dispensed with feigning plausible deniability. When Senator Rick Santorum called President Barack Obama an "anti-war government ni-" stopping short of finishing the word, I thought it would give him a huge boost. But then I realized that the party's base was disappointed by his lack of follow-through. By contrast, Donald Trump just barrels on. And when he does backpedal, it drips with such sarcasm that the faithful are not offended.

Remember the distinction between rights and privileges drawn in chapter two: Rights are universal, whereas privileges are special. So they are, by definition, opposites. But the privileged feel entitled to special treatment and regard denying that as a violation of their rights – thus their indignant declaration that "This is a Christian nation." They see tyranny in government recognizing and protecting other people's rights. They do not understand why they can be sued for sexual harassment or cannot fire an employee for being gay. To them, this is a tyrannical violation of their sacred right to do unto others whatever they like. What is the fun of being a boss if you cannot impose your sexuality on your employees and meddle in their private lives, right?

They even see acknowledging other people's identity as oppression. If you say "Happy Holidays," that is a "War on Christmas" according to Bill O'Reilly and other Fox News hosts. Of course, the phrase does not negate Christmas, it simply accommodates other holidays too. But for conservatives, accommodation is an abomination.

One of conservatives' objections to "Obamacare" is it covers birth control and they say they do not want to subsidize immorality. Hey, my tax dollars pay for *lots* of things I do not like, but my dislike does not make those things tyranny. What makes conservatives so special? As Jon Stewart reasoned, "You've confused a 'war on your religion' with not always getting what you want. It's called being part of a society. Not everything goes your way."

Of course, we all want what we want and grumble when we lose some struggle in government. But contrary to Robert Bork's writings, liberal culture is actually a check on selfish entitlement, especially where others' rights are concerned. It encourages us to see the other person's side – so much so that Robert Frost once joked "A liberal is a man too broadminded to take his own side in a quarrel."[551] This explains the bully/wimp format of debate shows like *Hannity and Colmes* and the Buchanan and Kinsley era *Crossfire*.

By sharp contrast, conservative culture does the opposite. It rabidly discourages compromise and accommodation. Barack Obama discovered that shortly after his first inauguration. We faced the greatest economic catastrophe since the Great Depression and many conservatives were conspicuously uncooperative. Remember how Rush Limbaugh set the tone? "I hope he fails." Forget the fate of the country. This says a lot about conservative "patriotism": Their eternal mantra is "Fuck the greater good."

Second edition clarification: Liberals have been tolerant to a fault. And after *decades* of giving and not getting, it is high time the left check its reflexes and take back lost ground.

There is an ***immense*** difference between balancing everyone's rights and seeking a political midpoint between left and right. I fear this immense, self-evident distinction escapes centrists – particularly when said midpoint keeps moving right thanks to compromising with those who will not compromise and when denying others' rights is the right's *organizing fucking principle*.

This is how liberties get whittled away. There can be no compromise when the other side aims to deny others' rights and/or will not compromise in turn. Period. This is simply definitional.

Missing this is inexcusably stupid. It is like the New Jersey *Star-Ledger's* missing the predictable trajectory of Chris Christie's bullying. Oh hey, the bully is a bully. Who knew it would go where it was going?

And so we have Trump now.

I thought this was all obvious from what I had written in the first edition. After all, this book is entitled *Conservatism is Un-American*; so obviously, I have no bipartisanship fetish. What I *do* have is a hot hostility towards centrist quislings who try to sabotage our democratic promise from within. Those people enable conservative purists.

Sure, I charitably threw centrists a few bones, giving them the benefit of the doubt. But I now fear those bones will only help them miss the point. And having invested almost two decades into writing this book, I am pretty damn invested in people getting the point. Agree or disagree, I will make myself understood: Self expression is the aim of every writer. And I believe that conservatism is forever antithetical to liberty, equality, and democracy.

So let us get back to that.

Much like Ayn Rand's description of William E. Hickman, conservatism does not acknowledge "the necessity, meaning, or importance of other people" except as prey or potential competitors.

For them, every public sphere is an arena with winners and losers, and they do not want to hear any whiny liberal talk about cooperation or fair play. Considering other people is a totally foreign notion to their mindset and therefore suspect. They think that self-interest is patriotic, so being civic therefore seems subversive.

Again, conservatives are not accustomed to thinking in terms of others' rights. Indeed, values rhetoric aside, they do not really think in terms of right and wrong. Instead, they *feel* in terms of like and dislike. This is the distinction between morality and ethics. Contrary to the running gag in the movie *Election* (1999), there is a big difference.

Basically, morality is disgust against things you were taught were wrong by some authority such as your clergy or your parents. It is a visceral reaction that requires no thought.

By contrast, ethics is a reasoned consideration of everyone's rights and wellbeing. In short, ethics are secular and essential to a free society while morality is linked with religion and obedience to authority.

Still skeptical? No sweat. Consider this:

Psychological studies have discovered that disgust is big in conservative thought. For example, one study concluded that conservatives could be persuaded to care more about the environment by using the language of purity and sanctity.[552] So emphasize water quality and link literal pollution to metaphorical pollution, because the metaphorical *somehow seems more real to them. It bothers them more.*

Yes, you read that right. Apparently, they find a Strangelovian appeal to Purity of Essence much more persuasive than any scientific data.

The researchers had also suggested framing environmental arguments in terms of "patriotism and reverence for a higher authority." I guess this is because making some commonsense argument against poisoning the village well is too complex for them to process or absorb.

Although I agree that the rhetoric of disgust drives conservative thought, I am slightly skeptical of this strategy. After all, if conservatives had any real reverence for "God's Country," they would already be environmentalists. Remember what Ann Coulter said about human stewardship: "God says, 'Earth is yours. Take it. Rape it. It's yours.'" So, conservative pundits have already anticipated this approach, and they can easily rationalize around it. Just as they deny both evolution and climate change, they still insist that the chemical DDT had never threatened the bald eagle.

Yes, some conservatives actually say that.[553]

While conservatives are indeed more visceral than intellectual, their flexibility must never be underestimated. Preserving their narrative trumps preserving all else, and avoiding doubt is paramount. The bald eagle is an important symbol of America, but they will throw the bird under the bus in an instant rather than admit to being wrong.

Another study found that the link between disgust and politics was clearest on "purity-related issues – specifically abortion and gay marriage."[554] When the Supreme Court struck down the Defense of Marriage Act, Senator Rand Paul (R-KY) appeared on Glenn Beck's show and asked if marrying animals would be next.[555] Never mind that animals cannot consent because they cannot talk. Even beings who can speak cannot necessarily consent due to mental capacity or an unbalanced power relationship. That is why minors cannot be held to contracts and why child brides are no longer legal currency, sacred biblical norms of behavior aside.[556]

Of course, Rand Paul was not the first to make this bestiality comparison. Before him was Bill O'Reilly, and before him was Rick Santorum. It is just a standard conservative talking point now. It says a lot about how they think. They simply throw everything they see as disgusting, threatening, or contemptible together into one conceptual slop-bucket and that is all the guilt-by-association they need to make any comparison. That is their mental filing system. Therefore, their metaphors and conspiracy theories make strange leaps. They do not like President Obama or Muslims, thus he must be one, etc.

Again, it is all about like and dislike. To many conservatives, most nouns are either positively or negatively charged with little meaning beyond that. Yes, they understand the dictionary definitions of those words, but the good or bad association is more important. They grasp that the word "racist" is a negative label, so they add it to their verbal arsenal. But there is not much thought about what racism really is or how it works behind their usage. The word is just a rhetorical hand grenade to lob back over the wall. Likewise, they realize that the word "stupid" is an insult and they routinely sling it at scientists, academics, and other accredited experts they disagree with – which is most of them.

Of course, part of this is projecting, but their binary mindset is also part of it. Everything is either good or bad, us or them, desirable or disgusting, pure or mongrel, food pellet or electric shock. All the good things are linked together and all the bad things are linked together. It is all emotion and no logic.

Conservatives' bestiality argument will remain in circulation as long as it works on their base. But why does it still work when it is so easily debunked? Every time they repeat it, someone totally torpedoes it by bringing up consent – *and yet they still keep repeating it*. One likely supplemental explanation is that conservatives do not take the concept of consent seriously. Their near constant tone-deaf comments on rape certainly prove that.[557]

But the concept of consent is *central* to *any* question of liberty from "the consent of the governed" to everything else. If you do not take this thing seriously, you do not think about rights seriously. A selfish, us-vs.-them mindset does not lend itself to objectivity or recognizing others' rights. And using the rhetoric of rights without actually respecting rights will always show.

But, again, conservatives are new at this. They are more accustomed to *attacking* the rhetoric of rights as Robert Bork had done. They are still relative novices, so perhaps they will eventually get more persuasive with practice.

I doubt that will actually happen because the only way to improve their game is to recognize other people's rights and wellbeing. But doing that would make them less conservative. It might turn them into moderate, east coast Republican RINOS or perhaps even – perish the thought – *progressive* Teddy Roosevelt-style Republicans!

It is an attitudinal Catch 22 for them. Faking always shows, so sincerity is the only way to avoid embarrassing blowback. And yet sincerity appreciating liberty requires thinking like a liberal. Yup, it sure is a toughie.

I may be wrong, but my best guess says they will eventually dodge the problem by dialing down their rhetoric of rights – probably as more of the Me Generation dies off, taking its 1960s anti-establishment attitude with it. Then Robert Bork's more traditional "law and order" approach will return. They will turn their rhetorical dial back from Liberty toward Stability and start talking about how too much freedom causes chaos. Of course, Liberty will always be on their dial because they like to think they are patriotic Americans. They will just qualify it into an empty word as they usually do.

But all this rhetorical dial-fiddling is simply that – they can adjust the treble and the bass, but they are still playing the same song. Conservatives will still have the very same unconscionable goals and incoherent arguments because they cultivate the same entitled, binary us-vs.-them mindset.

Yet, a free republic cannot function on indoctrination and disgust. A democracy requires a liberal, Enlightenment mindset in at least half the population, and without it liberty expires. We cannot be coy about this core fact any longer.

All these themes tie together, which is why conservatism is inherently hostile to our form of government. It is part and parcel of conservatives' distorted notion of patriotism that fetishizes false republics. In the Dead Kennedys song I quoted before, Jello Biafra sings, "You say you'll fight to the death to save your useless flag. If you want a banana republic that bad, why don't you go move to one?" And again, Mark Twain said something similar in *A Connecticut Yankee in King Arthur's Court*. Referring to the country's worn political clothes, he wrote, "To be loyal to rags, to shout for rags, to die for rags – that is a loyalty of unreason, it is pure animal; it belongs to monarchy, was invented by monarchy; let monarchy keep it."[558]

Yes, a monarchist mentality endures centuries after monarchy has ceased to be a political possibility here – only today we call it an authoritarian personality. It did not vanish. It reinvented itself. It has adapted, not adeptly or gracefully, but it has adapted. And its scorn for liberty, equality, and democracy remain. This mentality longs for a bygone hierarchal society when "everyone knew their place" and did not "question their betters." That "pure animal" that Mark Twain talked about is the passionate shallowness that I keep talking about – the "loyalty of unreason." Likewise, George Orwell saw in totalitarianism, "the horrors of emotional nationalism and a tendency to disbelieve in the existence of objective truth."[559] Although Orwell saw this tendency in both the extreme left and extreme right, today in America, it primarily defines the right. We see it in the "deep beliefs" that paleolibertarian Murray Rothbard had both praised and promoted.

In fact, today, some ex-libertarians in the technology field actually endorse a return to monarchy.[560] They identify as "neoreactionaries" and blast democracy as a great mistake. They attribute human progress to technology, blissfully oblivious to the fact that today's technology would be totally impossible without democracy and public education spending. As Abraham Lincoln said of the Confederates, "Monarchy itself is sometimes hinted at as a possible refuge from the power of the people." It seems the hinting continues.

Today's conscious monarchists are a politically insignificant, micro-minority, so I will not make too much of them. But their authoritarian impulses are far more widespread. The difference is that other authoritarians say things like "This is a republic, not a democracy," and those people compose a much larger minority – one big enough to take over a major political party and repeatedly hold the country hostage over the budget.

Thomas Jefferson had noticed the endurance of the Tory mentality a long time ago. In an 1802 letter to Joel Barlow, he wrote that the "division into Whig and Tory is founded in the nature of man."[561] Thus, he thought this conflict was eternal, defining past, present, and future. In 1813, Thomas Jefferson wrote to John Adams:

Men have differed in opinion and been divided into parties by these opinions from the first origin of societies, and in all governments where they have been permitted freely to think and to speak. The same political parties which now agitate the U.S. have existed through all time. Whether the power of the people or that of the [aristocracy] should prevail were questions which kept the states of Greece and Rome in eternal convulsions, as they now schismatize every people whose minds and mouths are not shut up by the gag of a despot. And in fact the terms of Whig and Tory belong to natural as well as to civil history. They denote the temper and constitution of mind of different individuals.[562]

Thomas Jefferson had made this exact same point repeatedly over the years to different people in one letter after another. In an 1817 letter to Albert Gallatin, Jefferson wrote, "[N]ature has made some men monarchists and [T]ories by their constitution, and some, of course, there always will be."[563] To the Marquis de Lafayette, he wrote 1823, "The parties of Whig and Tory are those of nature. They exist in all countries, whether called by these names or by those of Aristocrats and Democrats, *Cote Droite* and *Cote Gauche*, Ultras and Radicals, Serviles and Liberals."[564] And, in 1824, Jefferson rattled off the same list of opposing forces to Henry Lee:

Men by their constitutions are naturally divided into two parties: 1. Those who fear and distrust the people, and wish to draw all powers from them into the hands of the higher classes. 2. Those who identify themselves with the people, have confidence in them, cherish and consider them as the most honest and safe, although not the most wise depositary of the public interests. In every country these two parties exist, and in every one where they are free to think, speak, and write, they will declare themselves.

Call them, therefore, Liberals and Serviles, Jacobins and Ultras, Whigs and Tories, Republicans and Federalists, Aristocrats and Democrats, or by whatever name you please, they are the same parties still and pursue the same object. The last one of Aristocrats and Democrats is the true one expressing the essence of all.[565]

I think Thomas Jefferson's binary take is a little oversimplified, but I agree that reactionary people will always be with us and that they exist in every country.

But the ones in our country are in a uniquely awkward position. They only want to be on a team, follow a leader, and bully outsiders. But, by our country's inclusive egalitarian ethos, *they* are the outsiders and that fact drives them crazy because they cannot square that circle. Of course, they will still try – hence, their ridiculous Rosa Parks comparisons.

You may say you know conservatives who are not that crazy. Then they are not that conservative. Then they are not hardcore ideologues. It is all relative. Maybe they do not hate liberty, equality, and democracy, but just do not think about them very much. But if they fail to consider these things, then selfish appeals will prevail. As the saying goes, "If you do not stand for something, you will fall for anything." That is how the snake oil of supply side economics got sold. It is just what happens when you believe in the same America that Mitt Romney does.

I acknowledge this is a controversial take. But, that is only because we have grown so accustomed to ignoring the obvious. Thus, we must look at things with fresh eyes.

So, let us imagine a whole new nation founded on liberty, equality, and democracy. It would be *naïve* to believe that all of its inhabitants would share these ideals. Many would subtly resist from the inside. They would try to postpone, sabotage, or at least minimize its democratic promise – some of them consciously, others thoughtlessly. As Thomas Jefferson had feared, "They will forget themselves, but in the sole faculty of making money, and will never think of uniting to effect a due respect for their rights." They will put their trust in the magic of the market.

Now, in this context, consider Abraham Lincoln's Gettysburg Address in which he quasi-anonymously referred to "a new nation" founded "on this continent" that was "conceived in Liberty and dedicated to the notion that all men are created equal."

It is not a nationalist document but a patriotic one in the Enlightenment sense. As historian John T. Cumbler had pointed out to me, Lincoln did not refer to *this* nation. Instead he said, "Now we are engaged in a great civil war, testing whether *that* nation, *or any nation so conceived and so dedicated* can long endure." (emphasis added) Remember that there were then many who still insisted that our form of government could not work. But if we failed, another country could pick up where we left off. In any case, humanity must ensure that "government of the people, by the people, and for the people, shall not perish from the earth." There again is that "love of process" that Pat Buchanan hates. And that "for the people" sounds like activist government to me.

Now, picture the reactionary elements in our imaginary young country. Would they not deny they were a democracy? Would they not pit liberty against equality in a zero-sum game in order to severely restrict both? Would they not "deny or disparage" their unenumerated rights and call acknowledging them "inventing new rights"? Would they not demean the empathy that makes us more likely to defend each other's rights and wellbeing? And finally, would they not be quick to question other people's patriotism to project their profound sense of alienation in our free egalitarian society?

To ask these questions is to answer them.

Notes

[1] Paul Slansky, *The Clothes Have No Emperor: A Chronicle of the American 80s*, (New York: Fireside Press, 1989), 31.

[2] Adam Bernstein, "Conservative GOP Congressman John G. Schmitz, 70, Dies," *Washington Post*, January 12, 2001, Page B7.

[3] "Preview of Two Primaries," *Newsweek*, June 7, 1982, 32.

[4] Adam Bernstein, "Conservative GOP Congressman John G. Schmitz, 70, Dies," Adam Bernstein, *Washington Post*, January 12, 2001, Page B7.

[5] *Extra!* Dec. '87, *Best of Extra!*

[6] Many Republicans have admitted that Ronald Reagan would be too liberal for today's Tea Party-controlled GOP, including Jeb Bush and Mike Huckabee. The later said "Ronald Reagan would have a very difficult, if not impossible time being nominated in this atmosphere of the Republican Party." Rep. Duncan Hunter (R-CA) said Reagan "would never be elected today in my opinion." (Bruce Bartlett, "Why Ronald Reagan Would Not Lead Today's GOP," *Fiscal Times*, June 15, 2012.)

[7] Morris Udall, "Some Political Laughs for an Unfunny Week," *Washington Post*, October 25, 1987, C1.

[8] Andrew Sullivan, "The Mullah," New Republic Online, Thursday, March 15th, 2007.

[9] Ibid.

[10] Stephanie Coontz, *The Way We Never Were: American Families and the Nostalgia Trap* (New York: Basic Books, 1992) 98-99

[11] John Trenchard and Thomas Gordon, *Cato's Letters: Essays on Liberty, Civil and Religious* (New York: Da Capo Press, 1971), 2:16.

[12] Michael Lind, *Up From Conservatism: Why the Right is Wrong for America* (New York: Free Press Paperbacks, 1996) 3.

[13] Pam Belluck, "Libertarians see fertile soil in New Hampshire," *New York Times*, October 27, 2003, section A, p. 1. Also, libertarian billionaire Peter Theil seeks to build new sovereign nations on oil rig-like platforms in international waters. He has thus far sunk $1.25 million into this project. *Slate*'s Jacob Weisberg has called it, "the most elaborate effort ever devised by a group of computer nerds to get invited to an orgy." Jonathan Miles, "The Billionaire King of Techtopia," *Details,* September 2011.

[14] Paul Nussbaum, "Evangelicals want a biblically governed state; Pa. pilgrims join exodus to S.C.," *Philadelphia Inquirer*, July 25, 2005 sec. A, p.1.

[15] Rosa Brooks, "The 'Real' America, Really," *Los Angeles Times*, October 23, 2008.

[16] John Andreini, "Michele Bachmann: Call of the Loon," *Minneapolis Examiner*, April 29, 2009

[17] Paul Slansky, *The Clothes Have No Emperor: A Chronicle of the American '80s*, (New York: Fireside Books, 1989), 48.

[18] Chris Mooney, *The Republican Brain: The Science of Why They Deny Science –*

and Reality (Hoboken, NJ: John Wiley & Sons, Inc.), 71.

[19] "Too Many Conservative Columnists, Says Conservative," *Extra!* May/June '89, *Best of Extra!*

[20] "Jon Stewart: Pat Robertson admits GOP field is nuckin' futs!," Daily Kos, October 26, 2011, http://www.dailykos.com/story/2011/10/26/1030143/-Jon-Stewart-Pat-Robertson-admits-GOP-field-is-nuckin-futs# (accessed September 7, 2013).

[21] Laurie Goodstein, "Falwell's finger-pointing inappropriate, Bush says," *New York Times*, September 15, 2001, sec. A, p. 15.

[22] Press release, Americans United for the Separation of Church and State, June 9, 1998.

[23] Richard Zoglin, "A devilishly good deal for the Family Channel," *Time Magazine*, May 12, 1997, 65.

[24] "Suspicion Following Sun Myung Moon to Brazil," *New York Times*, November 28, 1999, sec. A, p. 3.

[25] "Behind the Times: Who Pulls the Strings at Washington's No. 2 Daily?" *Extra*, August/September, 1987

[26] "The GOP's Asian Connection: Rev. Moon," *Pittsburgh Post-Gazette*, November 23, 1997, sec. E, p. 1.

[27] "Moon Eclipses Birthday Bash For Times," *Washington Post*, May 22, 2002, sec. C, p. 1.

[28] Patrick J. Buchanan, *Death of the West* (New York: St. Martin's Press, 2002), p. 6.

[29] "McCain seeks to mend fences, Will address conservative critics today," *Boston Globe*, February 7, 2008, sec. A, p. 17.

[30] Thomas Jefferson, *Political Writings of Thomas Jefferson: Representative Selections*, ed. Edward Dumbauld, (New York: Liberal Arts Press, 1955), 55. The quote comes from a letter to Isaac Tiffany on April 4th, 1819. The Manuscript Division of the Library of Congress has a scan of it online: http://hdl.loc.gov/loc.mss/mtj.mtjbib023463

[31] Gary B. Nash, *The Unknown American Revolution: The Unruly Birth of Democracy and the Struggle to Create America* (New York: Penguin, 2005) 48, 51.

[32] Robert H. Bork, *Slouching Towards Gomorrah* (New York: Reagan Books, 1997), 5.

[33] Ibid., 57.

[34] Ibid., 66.

[35] Ibid., 63.

[36] Ibid., 57.

[37] Eric Zorn, "Coming out of the political closet with pride" *Chicago Tribune*, April 2, 1995.

[38] Robert H. Bork, *Slouching Towards Gomorrah* (New York: Reagan Books, 1997), 58. Before I forget, I would like to thank Professor Bork for providing

invaluable assistance in proving my thesis.

[39] Robert H. Bork, *Slouching Towards Gomorrah* (New York: Reagan Books, 1997), 64.

[40] Ibid., 67.

[41] Ibid., 57.

[42] Abraham Lincoln, *Complete Works of Abraham Lincoln*, ed. John G. Nicolay and John Hay, (Harrogate, TN: Lincoln Memorial University, 1894), 5:125-6.

[43] "Behind the Times: Who pulls the strings at Washington's No. 2 daily?" *Extra!*, August/September, 1987.

[44] Both still dead, incidentally.

[45] Pat Buchanan in His Own Words," FAIR press release, February 26, 1996.

[46] Patrick J. Buchanan, *A Republic, Not an Empire* (Washington, D.C.: Regnery Publishing, 1999), 14.

[47] "FAIR Report: Pat Buchanan In His Own Words" February 26, 1996.

[48] Patrick Buchanan, *Washington Times*, January 9, 1991.

[49] "The Wisdom of Ann Coulter," *Washington Monthly*, October 2001, p. 18.

[50] *Records of the Federal Convention of 1787*, ed. Max Farrand, (New Haven: Yale University Press, 1911-37), 1:135.

[51] *Debates in the Several State Conventions on the Adoption of the Federal Constitution as Recommended by the General Convention at Philadelphia in 1787 : Together with the Journal of the Federal Convention, Luther Martin's letter, Yates's minutes, Congressional opinions, Virginia and Kentucky resolutions of '98-'99, and other illustrations of the Constitution*, ed. Jonathan Elliot (Philadelphia: Lippincott, 1937), 3:222.

[52] Margaret Carlyle Duncan, "Buchanan and Duke: Playing the Same Hand," *Extra!*, March 1992.

[53] Mark Boal, "Good Samaritans?," *Village Voice*, May 27, 1997, 59.

[54] Ryan Lizza, "Leap of Faith: The Making of a Republican Front Runner," *The New Yorker*, August 15, 2011, 54.

[55] James Madison, *Letters and Other Writings of James Madison* (New York: R. Worthington, 1884), 4:492

[56] Bob Woodward, "CIA Told to Do 'Whatever Necessary' to Kill Bin Laden," *Washington Post*, October 21, 2001, sec. A, p.1.

[57] Matthew Bigg, "Election of Obama provokes rise in US hate crimes," Reuters, November 24, 2008.

[58] Air date Thursday, May 31, 2007. Plug it into any Internet search engine and you can watch the video itself and even see an official transcript on Fox News's own site, which is where I had cut and pasted this quote.

[59] David Weigel, "Fear of a Brown Planet," *Reason,* 17. The video and transcript can also be found on the Media Matters site. John Gibson insisted that he was talking about overall population decline and not attacking Hispanics. Indeed, he enclosed an

escape hatch at the end of the segment. "So far, we are doing our part here in America but Hispanics can't carry the whole load. The rest of you get busy." But the rest of the segment sends a different message. Three red flags suggest that he is actually upset about something else: First, Gibson admits that America's Caucasian population is not only holding but growing some, so what is the fuss? "Now, in this country, European ancestry people, white people, are having kids at the rate that does sustain the population. It grows a bit. That compares to Europe where the birth rate is in the negative zone." Second, he clearly portrays greater immigration as a peril of lower birth rates, so his message is ultimately anti-immigrant. "They are not having enough babies to sustain their population. Consequently, they are inviting in more and more immigrants to take care of things and those immigrants are having way more babies than the native population, hence Eurabia." Obviously, he is inviting his viewers to picture the same scenario here. Otherwise, why mention it? Except that the largest group of immigrants to the U.S. is not Arabs but Hispanics, who Gibson warns will be the majority in a short 25 years. Clearly, Gibson is making a cautionary comparison with Europe. Indeed, whether the issue is secularism, socialism or anything else, the Right's distorted picture of Europe is a favorite example. Third, Gibson implies that a lower birth rate means there will not be enough people to do the work. But America currently has a chronic unemployment problem thanks to exporting jobs and building robot assembly lines. More technology always means fewer jobs, and the march of technology is certainly not stopping or slowing, but accelerating exponentially. So, why preach that we need more people when we do not have enough jobs for the population we have? David Simon, the creator of the HBO series *The Wire*, has said that his show was not just about the Drug War but the fact that our economy does not need as many people anymore. So, what happens to all these people who live in dying cities with dying industries? I can only imagine that John Gibson thinks we need more people for cannon fodder, but war has become more automated as well. President Obama has largely turned President Bush's wars over to remote-controlled drones. Unless you want to occupy another country, you do not need boots on the ground anymore. Drones played a big role in keeping Obama's campaign promise for troop withdrawal. Thus, we must ask, "If we do not need more people for employees or troop deployments, what does John Gibson really want them for?" In his subsequent self-defense, Gibson said his critics were motivated by their hatred for Fox News. Well, Fox's coverage is rife with racism against immigrants and Hispanics, so Gibson's defense would be more credible if he contrasted himself with the other figures on his network instead of circling the wagons.

[60] "Dobbs' Dubious Disease Numbers: CNN host stands by faulty leprosy statistics," FAIR Action Alert, May 11, 2007

[61] Julie Hollar, "CNN's Immigration Problem: Is Dobbs the exception—or the rule?" *Extra!* May/June 2006

[62] David Corn, "Faith and commandments on the campaign trail," *The Nation*, September 28, 1998, 20.

⁶³ You would think that such blatantly secular language would arouse controversy, but not in 1797. It was a different time then. The treaty was passed by the Senate and signed by the President without an uproar or problem of any kind. In fact, it was the third recorded unanimous vote in the Senate's history. And, yes, treaties are indeed U.S. law. According to Article VI of the Constitution, "all Treaties made, or which shall be made, under the Authority of the United States, shall be the supreme Law of the Land." The political entity that we signed that treaty with no longer exists, so it is no longer current law; but if you are honestly looking for original intent, there it is: "the Government of the United States of America is not in any sense founded on the Christian religion." The fact that these words do not appear in the surviving Arabic version is irrelevant because we are examining American attitudes. All official U.S. versions of the treaty contain those words, including the *Senate Journal* for 1797. The treaty was then published in several newspapers such as the *Philadelphia Gazette* and *Universal Daily Advertiser* for Saturday, 17 June 1797. It would be suspect if the situation was reversed and the words were only missing from the English language version because that would mean they were being withheld from the voting public, but such is not the case.

⁶⁴ Thomas Jefferson, *Writings of Thomas Jefferson*, ed. Andrew Adgate Lipscomb and Albert Ellery Bergh (Washington DC: Thomas Jefferson Memorial Association, 1905), 1:67.

⁶⁵ James Madison, *Letters and Other Writings of James Madison*, (New York: R.Worthington Press, 1884), 1:163.

⁶⁶ Thomas Jefferson, *Writings of Thomas Jefferson*, ed. Andrew Adgate Lipscomb and Albert Ellery Bergh (Washington DC: Thomas Jefferson Memorial Association, 1905), 2:223.

⁶⁷ Thomas Paine, *The Life and Major Writings of Thomas Paine*, ed. Philip S. Foner (New York: Citadel Press, Carol Publishing Group Edition 1993), 474.

⁶⁸ Thomas Jefferson, *Writings of Thomas Jefferson*, ed. Andrew Adgate Lipscomb and Albert Ellery Bergh (Washington, DC: Thomas Jefferson Memorial Association, 1905), 2:221.

⁶⁹ Benjamin Franklin, *The Papers of Benjamin Franklin*, ed. William B. Willcox, (New Haven & London: Yale University Press, 1982), 22:533.

⁷⁰ Thomas Jefferson, *Writings of Thomas Jefferson*, ed. Andrew Adgate Lipscomb and Albert Ellery Bergh (Washington DC: Thomas Jefferson Memorial Association, 1905), 15:23. Actually it was John Taylor who first coined the phrase but Jefferson expressed his agreement in a letter to him on June 7th 1816. Jefferson's reply reads, "And I sincerely believe, with you, that banking establishments are more dangerous than standing armies; and that the principle of spending money to be paid by posterity, under the name of funding, is but swindling futurity on a large scale."

⁷¹ Ibid., 15:29. There is that concern over perpetual warfare again.

⁷² Ibid., 15:112.

⁷³ Thomas Jefferson, *Writings of Thomas Jefferson*, ed. Paul Leicester Ford (New

York: G.P. Putnam's Sons, 1899), 10:69. I was initially skeptical about this quote when I ran across it because corporations had not yet gained the great power that they wield today. Banks were the exception, so Jefferson was probably talking about banks (and he blasted banks a lot). But he usually just said "banks" rather than "corporations" so the quote seemed fairly fishy. Moreover, I had already seen several un-cited variants that frustrated my every effort to verify them. One person, thinking he or she could improve on Jefferson's prose, had apparently replaced the word "birth" with "infancy," further complicating my search. Often such tweaks made the language seem dubiously modern. Jefferson was famously fond of rambling at length and the variants I had seen were suspiciously pithy. If a quote is short and to the point, it is probably not one of Mr. Jefferson's. I had also seen numerous Frankenstein variants – quotes stitched together with parts of other quotes. Some elusive variants turn out to be legitimate because a historical figure had a favorite phrase that frequently reappears in their works. Today, we call tem "buzz words;" but before radio and television, whole paragraphs got recycled. The same speech might be given in different cities with only slight tweaks. Although a variant may be consistent with other verified quotes, consistency is insufficient by itself. Each quote must be individually verified in a published collection of historical papers and this quote finally fits the bill. For example, except for the use of the word "corporations," this quote is quite similar to the quote I used immediately previous to it: Both speak of a moneyed aristocracy trying to subvert the government. But until I found a source, I could not use this quote no matter how similar it sounded to the previous one. This is an anal-retentive business.

[74] Thomas Jefferson, *Writings of Thomas Jefferson*, ed. Andrew Adgate Lipscomb and Albert Ellery Bergh (Washington DC: Thomas Jefferson Memorial Association, 1905), 14: 9.

[75] Benjamin Franklin, *Writings of Benjamin Franklin*, ed. Albert Henry Smith (New York: MacMillan Co., 1907), 10:55.

[76] Benjamin Franklin, *Works of Benjamin Franklin; Containing Several Political and Historical Tracts Not Included in Any Former Edition., and Many Letters Official and Private, not Hitherto Published; with Notes and a Life of the Author*, ed. Jared Sparks (Boston: Tappan & Whittemore,1836), 2:468.

[77] James Madison, *Papers of James Madison*, ed. Robert A. Rutland, et al. (Charlottesville: University Press of Virginia, 1983), 14:197-198. The quote comes from a discussion the emergence of political parties. Two of his five guidelines for mitigating their dangers focus on regulating the accumulation of wealth: "In every political society, parties are unavoidable. A difference of interests, real or supposed, is the most natural and fruitful source of them. The great object should be to combat the evil: 1. By establishing a political equality among all. 2. By withholding unnecessary opportunities from a few, to increase the inequality of property, by an immoderate, and especially an unmerited, accumulation of riches. 3. By the silent operation of laws, which, without violating the rights of property, reduce extreme wealth towards a

state of mediocrity, and raise extreme indigence towards a state of comfort. 4. By abstaining from measures which operate differently on different interests, and particularly such as favor one interest at the expence *[sic]* of another. 5. By making one party a check on the other, so far as the existence of parties cannot be prevented, nor their views accommodated."

[78] Thomas Jefferson, *Writings of Thomas Jefferson*, ed. Andrew Adgate Lipscomb and Albert Ellery Bergh (Washington DC: Thomas Jefferson Memorial Association, 1905), 19:18.

[79] Thomas Jefferson, *Papers of Thomas Jefferson*, (Charlottesville: University of Virginia Library, 1950), 11:215.

[80] Incidentally, I highly recommend looking up the article "Ship of fools: Johann Hari sets sail with America's swashbuckling neocons." It is about a *National Review* cruise rather than a Cato one, but it is the same basic idea.

[81] Benjamin Franklin, *Works of Benjamin Franklin*, (New York & London: G. P. Putnam's Sons, 1904), 10:385.

[82] Benjamin Franklin, *Benjamin Franklin, Writings*, ed. J.A. Leo LeMay (New York: Library of America, 1987), 303 & 305. The poem is called "The Antediluvians Were All Very Sober" and the story is called "The Speech of Polly Baker." and they can be found on pages 303 and 305, respectively.

[83] Thomas Paine, *The Life and Major Writings of Thomas Paine: Includes Common Sense, The American Crisis, Rights of Man, The Age of Reason and Agrarian Justice*, ed. Phillip Sheldon Foner (New York: Carol Publishing Group, 1993, 1974) 607.

[84] Robin Blackburn, "Lincoln and Marx: The transatlantic convergence of two revolutionaries," *Jacobin Magazine*, 28 August 2012, https://www.jacobinmag.com/2012/08/lincoln-and-marx (accessed 04/14/2019).

[85] Andrea Baumeister, "Patriotism," *Encyclopedia Britannica* web article https://www.britannica.com/print/article/446715 (accessed 2/10/19).

[86] Interestingly, conservatives frequently claim to "love and honor" the Constitution; but their ignorance of its history strongly suggests they only fetishize it as an object – as they do the flag. What they call "love" is actually a superficial infatuation with an unknown quantity that they are not particularly curious about. I expand on this aspect later on in the book.

[87] J.C.D. Clark, *The Language of Liberty 1660-1832: Political Discourse and Social Dynamics in the Anglo-American World* (Cambridge: Cambridge University Press, 1994), 54-5.

[88] George Orwell, *The Road to Wigan Pier* (San Diego: Harvest Books, 1937), 114.

[89] Of course, maps and globes are not absolutely necessary. We Americans still routinely invade places many of us cannot find on a map. Most empires do. But back then, there was no great incentive for governments to cultivate national feeling. National armies existed, but they were supplemented by mercenaries as well. Remember, the Minutemen faced Hessians as well as Redcoats. Prior to recent privatization, most assumed this practice had gone the way of the dodo or at least

become a minor component. Alas, we live in the Haliburtion/Blackwater world now – or rather once again. But the point here is that empires do not require place nostalgia – only money. They may shamelessly utilize place nostalgia, but so many other tools exist and get used first. The Romans offered citizenship, as we do now. (Or did before Trump.) To that, we have added money for college. And of course, there has always been the "poverty draft."

[90] If so, it is awfully ironic because America was already vastly more multicultural than Europe. New York was originally New Amsterdam because it was settled by the Dutch. And the "Pennsylvania Dutch" were actually German immigrants. (Both communities published newspapers in their own languages.) The latter were already a potent voting bloc in Benjamin Franklin's early political career. Franklin actually published the first German language newspaper, but it failed as soon as German immigrants began publishing their own.

[91] Jules Michelet, *The People*. Translated by C. Cocks (London: Logman, Green Brown, and Logman's, 1846), 229.

[92] Giuseppe Mazzini, *The Duties of Man and Other Essays*, Everyman's Library (New York: E.P. Dutton, 1907), 51-58.

[93] Indeed, patriotism and nationalism remain a strangely intertwined in empathy and hostility toward others. To get Americans behind entering World War I, the myth of Belgian babies being impaled on German bayonets was shamelessly circulated. More recently, during the first Gulf War, it was the myth of Iraqi soldiers tossing premature Kwaiti babies out of incubators. Atrocity propaganda works even if foreigners are the victims. Sure, the opportunity to play hero is a part of it, but I think there is something fundamentally human about getting angry about such stories. Subtract machismo and nationalism, and consider people's typical reaction to reading a newspaper story about fatal child abuse stateside. It has already happened so there is no chance to swoop-in and stop it. And the abuser is another American. In fact, let's say it is a local story. Do you feel your blood rise anyway? Yes, as a superpower, we Americans are fed a pretty daily diet of heroic intervention stories; but I do not think we are unique, which is why our action movies are so popular around the world. This human trait to help and protect is routinely abused by the military industrial complex. It is not inherently narrow or xenophobic – although those attitudes frequently piggy back onto it.

[94] Christine Gerrard, *The Patriot Opposition to Walpole: Politics, Poetry and National Myth 1725-1742* (Oxford: Clarendon Press, 1994), 7. Christine Gerrard, *The Patriot Opposition to Walpole: Politics, Poetry and National Myth 1725-1742* (Oxford: Clarendon Press, 1994) 7. Viscount Bolingbroke started out a Tory leader before joining the Patriot Whigs. After his death, Tory writers reconverted him into a conservative, the same way American conservatives claim our founding fathers. In an article entitled "A Patriot for Whom? The Afterlives of Bolingbroke's Patriot King" (*Journal of British Studies* 36, no. 4, 397-418), David Armitage wrote of the efforts to portray him as a Tory: "Yet this is not the Bolingbroke whom the American rebels of the 1770s, the petitioners of 1775, the English radicals of the 1780s, or the supporters of Reform in the 1830s would have recognized." (418) Earlier he notes, "In a

visionary version of the King's closing speech to Parliament of 1796-97, The Speech of a Patriot King to his Parliament imagined George III as a peacemaker above party, determined to renovate the constitution, restore the nation's trade, reform Parliament and, if necessary, step down from his throne in favor of a republic, if that were the wish of the people. This phantasmal monarch proclaimed his disdain for stock-jobbing, speculation, and corruption; decried the necessity of a standing army, 'that engine of Despotism, especially in a maritime country'; and warned against continental alliances." (414) This wishful thinking made George III sound like George Washington. Bolingbroke died in 1750 – well before the crisis with the 13 colonies. His utopian work was set into the future, but he was an influence on the colonists' thought and expectations. Initially, they thought their conflict was with Parliament rather than the crown. Indeed, in the early days, Washington toasted the king and expressed his hopes that his majesty would intervene on their behalf – which was precisely the type of thing Bolingbroke said a patriot king should do.

[95] I will cover this more in my next book. But you can find details in James W. Loewen's *Lies My Teacher Told Me: Everything Your American History Textbook Got Wrong* (New York: Touchstone, 1996), 110-112. And also in Susan Branson's *These Fiery Frenchified Dames: Women and Political Culture in Early National Philadelphia* (Philadelphia: University of Pennsylvania Press, 2001).

[96] Thomas Paine, *The Life and Major Writings of Thomas Paine: Includes Common Sense, The American Crisis, Rights of Man, The Age of Reason and Agrarian Justice*, ed. Phillip Sheldon Foner (New York: Carol Publishing Group, 1993, 1974) 414.

[97] James Boswell, *The Life of Samuel Johnson*, G.B. Hill. Rev. L.F. Powell ed., (Oxford: Clarendon Press, 1887), 1:408.

[98] It is speculated that Gene Roddenberry conceived "Star Trek" after seeing the East German science fiction film *The Silent Star* (1960), about an international mission to Venus. I have seen it and am convinced. But Trek was an American production, imbued with Kennedy era optimism.

I am not negating the importance of socialist internationalism by saying so. I am only saying that there is a subtle feedback loop spanning centuries and that America is a part of it, along with other countries.

So why single out America? To stress that internationalism is inherent to America and therefore American nationalism is even more absurd than other forms of it. Apart from Native Americans, we are the descendants of slaves and immigrants. Multiculturalism is in our DNA.

[99] "You know, they have a word. It sort of became old-fashioned. It's called a nationalist. And I say, really, we're not supposed to use that word. You know what I am? I'm a nationalist, O.K.? I'm a nationalist. Nationalist! Use that word! Use that word!" Peter Baker, "'Use That Word!': Trump Embraces the 'Nationalist' Label" *New York Times*, Oct. 23, 2018, https://www.nytimes.com/2018/10/23/us/politics/nationalist-president-trump.html (accessed 04/14/2019).

[100] Mike Males, "Exposing the Myth of 'Youth Violence,'" *San Francisco Attorney*, April-May 2000.

¹⁰¹ Dan Savage, *Skipping Towards Gomorrah* (New York: Penguin Books, 2002), 246.

¹⁰² Jules Witcover, "Obama's timid talk a weak response to Aurora shooting," *Chicago Tribune*, July 25, 2012.

¹⁰³ "Over 90 percent of Americans support gun background checks: poll," Reuters, February 7, 2013.

¹⁰⁴ Mayors Against Illegal Guns Press Release, "New Poll of NRA members by Frank Luntz shows strong support for common sense gun laws, exposing significant divide between rand-and-file members and NRA leadership," July 24, 2012.

¹⁰⁵ Dan Savage, *Skipping Towards Gomorrah* (New York: Penguin Books, 2002), 249.

¹⁰⁶ Barry Goldwater, "Job Protection For Gays," *Washington Post*, July 13, 1994.

¹⁰⁷ Thomas Jefferson, *The Political Writings of Thomas Jefferson: Representative Selections*, ed. Edward Dumbauld, (New York: Liberal Arts Press, 1955), 55. The quote comes from a letter to Isaac Tiffany on April 4th, 1819. The Manuscript Division of the Library of Congress has a scan of it online: http://hdl.loc.gov/loc.mss/mtj.mtjbib023463

¹⁰⁸ *Journal of the House of Delegates of the Commonwealth of Virginia, Richmond, 1818, 11*. This public document was also reprinted in various magazines such as Page 107-108, Vol. 13 of the *Analectic Magazine*, Philadelphia, 1819 and Page 81, Vol. 15 of *Niles Weekly Register*, Baltimore, 1818-19.

¹⁰⁹ *Debates in the Several State Conventions on the Adoption of the Federal Constitution as Recommended by the General Convention at Philadelphia in 1787: Together with the Journal of the Federal Convention, Luther Martin's letter, Yates's minutes, Congressional opinions, Virginia and Kentucky resolutions of '98-'99, and other illustrations of the Constitution*, ed. Jonathan Elliot (Philadelphia: Lippincott, 1937), 4:167.

¹¹⁰ *Annals of Congress*, ed. Joseph Gales & William Seaton, (Washington: Gales and Seaton, 1834), Column 532 Vol. 1.

¹¹¹ Ibid., Column 456 Vol. 1.

¹¹² Ibid., Column 452 Vol. 1.

¹¹³ *Nomination of Robert H. Bork to be Associate Justice of the Supreme Court of the United States: Hearing Before the Senate Comm. on the Judiciary 117* (Washington, D.C.: Government Printing Office, 1989), 249.

¹¹⁴ Ibid., 248.

¹¹⁵ *Debates in the Several State Conventions on the Adoption of the Federal Constitution as Recommended by the General Convention at Philadelphia in 1787: Together with the Journal of the Federal Convention, Luther Martin's letter, Yates's minutes, Congressional opinions, Virginia and Kentucky resolutions of '98-'99, and other illustrations of the Constitution*, ed. Jonathan Elliot (Philadelphia: Lippincott, 1937), 4:149.

¹¹⁶ Robert Bork, *Slouching Towards Gomorrah: Modern Liberalism and American*

Decline (New York: Regan Books, 1996), 56

[117] Ibid., 57.

[118] Ibid., 63-64.

[119] In the first edition, I mistakenly mentioned Halloween youth mayhem, but that had not become a major problem until the 1800s.

[120] William Straus & Neil Howe, *Generations: The History of America's Future, 1584 to 2069* (New York: William Morrow & Co. 1991), 168.

[121] Ibid., 167.

[122] Ray Raphael, *A People's History of the American Revolution: How Common People Shaped the Fight for Independence* (New York: Perennial Press, 2002), 13-14.

[123] Thomas Jefferson, *Writings of Thomas Jefferson*, ed. Andrew Adgate Lipscomb and Albert Ellery Bergh (Washington DC: Thomas Jefferson Memorial Association, 1905), 13:297.

[124] In a letter to James Madison, Thomas Jefferson wrote of free government: "It has it's [*sic.*] evils too: the principal of which is the turbulence to which it is subject. But weigh this against the oppressions of monarchy, and it becomes nothing. *Malo periculosam, libertatem quam quietam servitutem*" The Latin translates as "I prefer the tumult of liberty to the quiet of servitude." https://www.monticello.org/site/jefferson/i-prefer-dangerous-freedom-over-peaceful-slavery-quotation (accessed 02/17/19).

[125] Mike Males, "Exposing the Myth of "Youth Violence," *San Francisco Attorney*, April-May 2000.

[126] Stephanie Coontz, *The Way We Never Were: American Families and the Nostalgia Trap* (New York: Basic Books, 1992), 202.

[127] Richard Godbeer, *Sexual Revolution in Early America* (Baltimore & London: John Hopkins University Press, 2002), 228.

[128] Ibid., 247.

[129] Ibid.

[130] Ibid., 254-5.

[131] Stephanie Coontz, *The Way We Never Were: American Families and the Nostalgia Trap* (New York: Basic Books, 1992), 10.

[132] Winthrop Jordan, *White Over Black: American Attitudes Toward the Negro,1550-1812* (Chapel Hill: University of North Carolina Press, 1968), 147.

[133] Richard Godbeer, *Sexual Revolution in Early America* (Baltimore & London: John Hopkins University Press, 2002), 307.

[134] John S. Haller and Robin M. Haller, *The Physician and Sexuality in Victorian America* (New York: W.W. Norton & Co. Inc., 1974), 92.

[135] I credit Catherynne M. Valente for pointing this out to me. Of course, I already knew this, but I probably would have neglected to mention it without her nudge.

[136] Christopher Lee, "Ex-Surgeon General Says White House Hushed Him," *Washington Post*, July 11, 2007, sec. A, p. 1.

[137] Christian Bourge, "Analysis: Abstaining from best policies?" UPI, December 2, 2004.

¹³⁸ Frank Rich, "A High-Tech Lynching in Prime Time," Frank Rich, *New York Times*, April 24, 2005.

¹³⁹ Thomas Frank, *What's the Matter with Kansas? How Conservatives Won the Heart of America* (New York: Henry Holt & Co., 2004), 8.

¹⁴⁰ Robert Bork, *Slouching Towards Gomorrah: Modern Liberalism and American Decline* (New York: Regan Books, 1996), 61.

¹⁴¹ William F. Buckley, "Our Mission Statement," *National Review*, November 19,1955.

¹⁴² Thomas Jefferson, *Works of Thomas Jefferson*, ed. Paul Leicester Ford (New York: Kickerbocker Press, 1904), 12:12.

¹⁴³ Abraham Lincoln, *Collected Works of Abraham Lincoln*, ed. Roy P. Basler (New Brunswick, NJ: Rutgers University Press, 1953), 2:323.

¹⁴⁴ "'Freedom Is About Authority': Excerpts From Giuliani Speech on Crime," *New York Times*, March 20, 1994, 35.

¹⁴⁵ *United States Reports*, 60:393, (60 U.S. 393 in legal notation)

¹⁴⁶ Mark Twain, *Wit and Wisdom of Mark Twain*, ed. Alex Ayers (New York: Meridian, 1989), 53.

¹⁴⁷ *Journal of the House of Delegates of the Commonwealth of Virginia* (Richmond, 1818), 11. This public document was also reprinted in various magazines such as Page 107-108, Vol. 13 of the *Analectic Magazine*, Philadelphia, 1819 and Page 81, Vol. 15 of *Niles Weekly Register*, Baltimore, 1818-19.

¹⁴⁸ Thomas Paine, *Common Sense and Other Political Writings*, ed. W.F. Adkins (New York: Liberal Arts Press, 1953), 174.

¹⁴⁹ National Park Service, Franklin Delano Roosevelt Memorial website, http://www.nps.gov/frde/photosmultimedia/quotations.htm (accessed 1/7/2014).

¹⁵⁰ Alexander Hamilton, James Madison, and John Jay, *The Federalist Papers* (New York: Oxford University Press, 2008), 54.

¹⁵¹ "Group agitating for end to Internet beer sales, cyberspace liquor merchants." *Modern Brewery Age*, January 5, 1998.

¹⁵² John Trenchard and Thomas Gordon, *Cato's Letters: or, Essays on Liberty, Civil and Religious* (New York: Da Capo Press, 1971), 2:16.

¹⁵³ Or if you prefer the original, archaic spelling: "Liberty can never fubfift without Equality, nor Equality be long preferved without an Agrarian Law, or fomething like it; fo[r] when Mens Riches are become immeafurably or furprizingly great, a People, who regard their own Security, ought to make a ftrict Enquiry how they came by them, and oblige them to take down their own Size, for fear of terrifying the Community, or maftering it. In every Country, and under every Government, particular Men may be too rich."

¹⁵⁴ An overwhelming wealth of data supports this. For a state comparison, see Stephen M. Meyer's "Environmentalism and Economic Prosperity: Testing the Environmental Impact Hypothesis" (MIT Project on Environmental Politics and Policy, October 5, 1992) and his follow up study "Environmentalism and Economic

Prosperity: An Update" (MIT, February 16, 1993). See also E.B. Goodstein's "Jobs and the Environment: The Myth of a National Trade-Off" (Washington, D.C.: Economic Policy Institute, 1994), "Green and Competitive," *Harvard Business Review*, September/October, 1995, 120-134, "Toward a New Conception of the Environment-Competitiveness Relationship," *Journal of Economic Perspectives* 9 (Fall 1995): 97-118 and "Environmental Regulation and the Competitiveness of U.S. Manufacturing: What Does the Evidence Tell Us?" *Journal of Economic Literature* 33 (March 1995): 132-163. For international comparisons, see these three reports from the Organization for Economic Cooperation & Development (OECD): "Environmental Performance in OECD Countries," "Environmental Performance Reviews: United States" and "Integrating Environment and Economy: Progress in the 1990s" All three publications— Paris: 1996.

[155] *Affirmative Action: Social Justice or Reverse Discrimination?* ed. Francis Beckwith and Todd E. Jones (Amherst: Prometheus Press, 1997), 10.

[156] *Should America Pay?* ed. Raymond A. Winbush (New York: Amistad Press, 2003), 177.

[157] "The Economic Stagnation of the Black Middle Class: A Briefing Before The United States Commission on Civil Rights Held in Washington, D.C., July 15, 2005," 23.

[158] "Doles sees failure of three decades in anti-bias fight," *New York Times*, October 29, 1996, sec. A, p. 1.

[159] President Bill Clinton had also suggested this, but I wanted to go with the Viagra joke. Richard Kahlenberg, "Class-Based Affirmative Action: A Natural for Labor," *New Labor Forum*, Spring 1998, 37.

[160] "Dallas University halts race-based bake sale," Knight-Ridder Tribune Business News, September 25, 2003, 1.

[161] Paul Rockwell, "The Right Has a Dream; Martin Luther King as an Opponent of Affirmative Action," *Extra!*, May/June, 1995.

[162] Thomas Frank, *One Market Under God*, (New York: Anchor Books, 2001), 371.

[163] Benjamin Franklin, *Writings of Benjamin Franklin*, ed. Albert Henry Smyth (New York: Macmillan Co., 1907), 10:67.

[164] Carl Engel, "Jazz: A Musical Discussion," *The Atlantic Monthly*, August, 1922, 182. The author was actually sympathetic to Jazz, but he had a gift for articulating its critics' fears: "Such excesses have not infrequently attained to tragic madness. The silly, lewd gyrations for which jazz is held responsible by some are the release of tension in a witless neurotic stratum of society. But such dances were common long before the word Jazz was coined."

[165] Thanks to Rachel Rosen for pointing these out to me.

[166] The American Social History Project, *Who Built America? Working People and the Nation's Economy, Politics, Culture and Society* (New York: Pantheon Books, 1989), 2:289.

¹⁶⁷ Vincent Schiraldi, "Media misleading on school shootings," Knight-Ridder News Service, May 28, 1998.

¹⁶⁸ Todd Andrlik, "Ages of the Revolution: How Old Were they on July 4th, 1776?" *Journal of the American Revolution*, August 8, 2013, https://allthingsliberty.com/2013/08/ages-of-revolution-how-old-1776/ (accessed 4/14/2019).

¹⁶⁹ Stephanie Coontz, *The Way We Never Were: American Families and the Nostalgia Trap* (New York: Basic Books, 1992), 189.

¹⁷⁰ Benjamin Franklin, *The Autobiography: With an introduction by Daniel Aaron*, (New York: Vintage Books/Library of America, 1990), 23.

¹⁷¹ *Narratives of the American Revolution as Told by a Young Sailor, a Home-sick Surgeon, a French Volunteer, and a German General's Wife*, ed. Hugh F. Rankin (Chicago: R.R. Donnelley & Sons, 1976), 10-11.

¹⁷² Thomas Jefferson, *Papers of Thomas Jefferson*, ed. Julian P. Boyd (Princeton: Princeton University Press, 1958) 15:396. Jefferson repeatedly emphasized that new generations should not and could not be bound by previous ones. To Major John Cartwright he wrote in 1824: "Can one generation bind another, and all others, in succession forever? I think not. The Creator has made the earth for the living, not the dead. Rights and powers can only belong to persons, not things, not to mere matter, unendowed with will. The dead are not even things. The particles of matter which composed their bodies, make part now of the bodies of other animals, vegetables or minerals, of a thousand forms. To what then are attached the rights and powers they held while in the form of men?" The year before he wrote to Thomas Earle, "a preceding generation cannot bind a succeeding one by it's laws or contracts; these deriving their obligation from the will of the existing majority, and that majority being removed by death, another comes in its place with a will equally free to make its own laws and contracts; these are axioms so self-evident that no explanation can make them plainer; for he is not to be reasoned with who says that non-existence can control existence, or that nothing can move something."

¹⁷³ Thomas Jefferson, *Writings of Thomas Jefferson*, ed. Andrew Adgate Lipscomb and Albert Ellery Bergh (Washington DC: Thomas Jefferson Memorial Association, 1905), 14:157.

¹⁷⁴ Ibid., 6:65

¹⁷⁵ Ibid., 6:372

¹⁷⁶ Incidentally, Francophobia is also un-American. As I wrote in the introduction, when conservatives suggested sending the Statue of Liberty back it wasn't just over France's opposing the Iraq War: They loath everything Lady Liberty stands for – particularly immigration. But conservatives would also prefer we forget our shared revolutionary heritage because of the ideas contained within it and France-bashing certainly serves that end.

¹⁷⁷ Mike Males, *Framing Youth: 10 Myths about the Next Generation* (Monroe, ME: Common Courage Press, 1999), 12.

¹⁷⁸ Ibid.

[179] Lori Dorfman and Vincent Schiraldi, "Off balance: News media coverage of youth crime," *San Diego Union-Tribune*, April 13, 2001, sec. B, p.9.

[180] Vincent Schiraldi, "Media misleading on school shootings," Knight-Ridder News Service, May 28, 1998.

[181] Mike Males, *Framing Youth: 10 Myths about the Next Generation* (Monroe, ME: Common Courage Press, 1999), 11.

[182] Bob Herbert, "6-Year-Olds Under Arrest," *New York Times*, April 09, 2007.

[183] Mike Males, *Framing Youth: 10 Myths about the Next Generation* (Monroe, ME: Common Courage Press, 1999), 8.

[184] He said this on his April 14th, 2005 show. The actual audio clip I heard was priceless, although I suspect it may have been sped up a notch to make him sound more like Alvin and the Chipmunks. The next day he apologized for saying "blowjob" on his "family" program. And yet he still accuses those he dislikes of giving each other "ass cancer," as he calls AIDS.

[185] National Park Service, Franklin Delano Roosevelt Memorial website, http://www.nps.gov/frde/photosmultimedia/quotations.htm (accessed 1/7/2014).

[186] John Adams, *Works of John Adams*, ed. Charles Francis Adams (Boston: Little, Brown & Co., 1850-56) 9:564.

[187] Thomas Jefferson, *Writings of Thomas Jefferson*, ed. Andrew Adgate Lipscomb and Albert Ellery Bergh (Washington DC: Thomas Jefferson Memorial Association, 1905), 1:270. Summing up, Jefferson qualified, "Hamilton was, indeed, a singular character. Of acute understanding, disinterested, honest, and honorable in all private transactions, amiable in society, and duly valuing virtue in private life, yet so bewitched and perverted by the British example, as to be under the thorough conviction that corruption was essential to the government of a nation."

[188] Strangely, Benjamin Franklin seems to be their favorite patient for this postmortem oral surgery. "When the people find that they can vote themselves money, that will herald the end of the republic." That quote (and its very many variants) are alternately attributed to Benjamin Franklin, Alexis de Tocqueville, and a Scottish jurist and historian of that time named Alexander Fraser Tytler, a.k.a. Lord Woodhouselee. But it cannot be found among their works and its earliest appearance in print is a 1951 newspaper. Since then, it has been used by personalities as different as Ronald Reagan and Penn Jillette.

[189] John Adams, *Works of John Adams*, ed. Charles Francis Adams (Boston: Little, Brown & Co., 1850-56) 6:8-9.

[190] Charles Kenny, "Give Poor People Cash: There's a simple way to reform welfare: Send money to those who need it, without conditions" *Atlantic Monthly*, 25 September 2015. https://www.theatlantic.com/international/archive/2015/09/welfare-reform-direct-cash-poor/407236/

[191] Thomas Jefferson, *Writings of Thomas Jefferson*, (New York: Library of America, 1984), 343.

[192] Howard Zinn, *A People's History of the United States: 1492 – Present* (New York: Harper Collins, 2005), 36-37.

[193] Thomas Paine, *The Life and Major Writings of Thomas Paine: includes Common Sense, The American Crisis, Rights of Man, The Age of Reason and Agrarian Justice*, ed. Phillip Sheldon Foner (New York: Carol Publishing Group, 1993), 612.

[194] James W. Loewen, *Lies My Teacher Told Me: Everything Your American History Textbook Got Wrong* (New York: Touchstone, 1996), 110-112.

[195] Thomas Paine, *The Life and Major Writings of Thomas Paine: includes Common Sense, The American Crisis, Rights of Man, The Age of Reason and Agrarian Justice*, ed. Phillip Sheldon Foner (New York: Carol Publishing Group, 1993), 610.

[196] Benjamin Franklin, *The Writings of Benjamin Franklin*, ed. Albert H. Smyth (New York: MacMillan, 1905-1907), 20:97.

[197] Thomas Paine, *The Life and Major Writings of Thomas Paine: includes Common Sense, The American Crisis, Rights of Man, The Age of Reason and Agrarian Justice*, ed. Phillip Sheldon Foner (New York: Carol Publishing Group, 1993), 610. Of course, some will say that things are now better than ever for everyone. Yet somehow I doubt that the six year old boy scrounging for edible scraps in the garbage dunes around Rio de Janeiro is really better off than the one in a rainforest village.

[198] Benjamin Franklin, *Works of Benjamin Franklin; Containing Several Political and Historical Tracts Not Included in Any Former Edition., and Many Letters Official and Private, not Hitherto Published; with Notes and a Life of the Author*, ed. Jared Sparks (Boston: Tappan & Whittemore, 1836), 2:468.

[199] Ray Raphael, *A People's History of the American Revolution: How Common People Shaped the Fight for Independence* (New York: Perennial, 2002), 16.

[200] Ibid., 405.

[201] Gary B. Nash, *The Urban Crucible: Social Change, Political Consciousness and the Origins of the American Revolution* (Cambridge, MA: Harvard University Press, 1979), 263.

[202] Ibid., 263.

[203] John Trenchard and Thomas Gordon, *Cato's Letters: Essays on Liberty, Civil and Religious*, (New York: DaCapo Press, 1971), 2:8. This is an exact facsimile of the original edition except that it was republished in two volumes instead of the original four. But, the original title pages for each volume have been retained.

[204] Robert Bork, *Slouching Towards Gomorrah: Modern Liberalism and American Decline* (New York: Regan Books, 1997), 68.

[205] Thomas Frank, *One Market Under God: Extreme Capitalism, Market Populism and the End of Economic Democracy* (New York: Anchor Books, 2001), 191.

[206] Gary B. Nash, *The Urban Crucible: Social Change, Political Consciousness and the Origins of the American Revolution* (Cambridge, MA: Harvard University Press, 1979), 263.

[207] Michael I. Norton and Dan Ariely, "Building a better America – one wealth

quintile at a time," *Perspectives on Psychological Science* 6, no. 1 (January 2011): 10.

[208] Thomas Paine, *The Life and Major Writings of Thomas Paine: includes Common Sense, The American Crisis, Rights of Man, The Age of Reason and Agrarian Justice*, ed. Phillip Sheldon Foner (New York: Carol Publishing Group, 1993), 611.

[209] Ibid., 609.

[210] Thomas Jefferson, *Writings of Thomas Jefferson*, ed. Andrew Adgate Lipscomb and Albert Ellery Bergh (Washington DC: Thomas Jefferson Memorial Association, 1905), 19:18.

[211] Adam Smith, *The Wealth of Nations* (New York: P.F. Collier and Son, 1901), 1:121.

[212] As both a fact and a symbol, castles represented decentralization. When France began centralizing, part of the process was tearing down castles and the walls around fortified towns. By contrast, Germany did not unify until 1871 and still has lots of castles left. There, local control remained dominant until Prussia absorbed all the smaller German states and baronies.

[213] Thomas Jefferson, *Writings of Thomas Jefferson*, ed. Andrew Adgate Lipscomb and Albert Ellery Bergh (Washington DC: Thomas Jefferson Memorial Association, 1905), 18:45.

[214] Ibid., 13:333.

[215] For those interested in learning more about Jefferson on this topic, I recommend Jeffrey H. Matsuura's *Jefferson vs the Patent Trolls: A Populist Vision of Intellectual Property Rights*.

[216] Benjamin Franklin, *Autobiography* (New York: Library of America, 1990), 113.

[217] *Boston Magazine*, September/October 1786, 401. Available on reel 9 of the American Periodical Series. The exact same "Account of the Insurrection in the State of New Hampshire – Written by a Gentleman who happened to be present" can also be found reprinted in *The New Haven Gazette & Connecticut Magazine* for Thursday October 5th, 1786 on reel 20.

[218] *Columbian Magazine or Monthly Miscellany*, October 1786, 96. Available on reel 9 of the American Periodical Series.

[219] James Madison, *Papers of James Madison*, ed. Robert A. Rutland, et al. (Charlottesville: University Press of Virginia, 1983), 14:197-198.

[220] Gary B. Nash, *The Urban Crucible: Social Change, Political Consciousness and the Origins of the American Revolution* (Cambridge: Harvard University Press, 1979), 349.

[221] Ibid.

[222] *The Founders' Constitution*, ed. Philip B. Kurland and Ralph Lerner (Chicago: University of Chicago Press, 1987), 1:596.

[223] Robert Bork, *Slouching Towards Gomorrah: Modern Liberalism and American*

Decline (New York: Regan Books, 1997), 71.

[224] Ibid., 69.

[225] Ibid., 66.

[226] Thomas Jefferson, *Writings of Thomas Jefferson*, ed. Andrew Adgate Lipscomb and Albert Ellery Bergh (Washington DC: Thomas Jefferson Memorial Association, 1905), 19:18.

[227] Thomas Paine, *The Life and Major Writings of Thomas Paine: includes Common Sense, The American Crisis, Rights of Man, The Age of Reason and Agrarian Justice*, ed. Phillip Sheldon Foner (New York: Carol Publishing Group, 1993), 611.

[228] Ibid., 620.

[229] Benjamin Franklin, *The Writings of Benjamin Franklin*, ed. Albert H. Smyth (New York: MacMillan, 1905-1907) 9:139. In the full quote, he repeats himself for emphasis: "All property, indeed, except the savage's temporary cabin, his bow, his match coat, and other little acquisitions, absolutely necessary for his subsistence, seems to me to be the creature of public convention. Hence the public has the right of regulating decents, *[sic]* and all other conveyances of property, and even limiting the quantity and users of it. All the property that is necessary to a man, for the conservation of the individual and the propagation of the species, is his natural right, which none can justly deprive him of: but all property superfluous to such purposes is the property of the public, who, by their laws, have created it, and who may therefore by other laws dispose of it, whenever the welfare of the public shall demand such disposition. He that does not like civil society on these terms, let him retire and live among savages. He can have no right to the benefits of society, who will not pay his club towards the support of it." Again, the references towards "savages" sound hostile today, but remember that Franklin subverted the pejorative use of the term in his "REMARKS Concerning the Savages of North America" which was clearly intended to shame his fellow Europeans. Also recall that the First Nations did not practice individual landownership, so I suspect there is a little joke here. "Going Galt" and fleeing into the wilderness to escape taxation does not secure ownership. Like that tiger, you are just another figure on the landscape. And that was Franklin's point: Property requires society.

[230] Benjamin Franklin, *Benjamin Franklin's Autobiography: An Authoritative Text, Backgrounds, Criticism*, ed. J.A. Leo LeMay and P.M. Zall (New York: W.W. Norton & Co., 1986), 222.

[231] Caitlin Ginley and Eric Hananoki, "Fox-Approved Convention Theme Contradicted by Publicly Financed Site," Media Matters, http://mediamatters.org/blog/2012/08/22/fox-approved-convention-theme-contradicted-by-p/189507 (accessed January 26, 2013).

[232] Caitlin Ginley, "How She 'Built It': Fox's RNC Theme Undercut by Key Speaker's Business Success," Media Matters, http://mediamatters.org/blog/2012/08/23/how-she-built-it-foxs-rnc-theme-undercut-

by-key/189537 (accessed January 26, 2013).

[233] Thomas Paine, *The Life and Major Writings of Thomas Paine: includes Common Sense, The American Crisis, Rights of Man, The Age of Reason and Agrarian Justice*, ed. Phillip Sheldon Foner (New York: Carol Publishing Group, 1993), 340.

[234] Benjamin Franklin, *The Papers of Benjamin Franklin*, ed. William B. Willcox (New Haven: Yale University Press, 1982), 22:533.

[235] Henry P. Rosemont, "Benjamin Franklin and the Philadelphia typographical strikers of 1786," *Labor History* 22, no. 3 (Summer 1981): 398-429.

[236] *Dunlap's Pennsylvania Packet or The General Advertiser*, November 26, 1776, 2. Available on microfilm reel 94 of the American Periodical Series.

[237] Benjamin Franklin, *The Writings of Benjamin Franklin*, ed. Albert H. Smyth (New York: MacMillan, 1905-7), 10:59. One pamphlet found among Franklin's papers was a list of principles for reforming the British system of government. It was entitled "A Declaration of those RIGHTS of the Commonalty of Great Britain, without which they cannot be FREE." (emphasis original) The third item proclaimed "for the all of one man is as dear to him as the all of another; and the poor man has an equal right, but more need, to have representatives in the legislature than the rich one." (again, italics original) Benjamin Franklin wrote on his copy "Some good Whig principles." (Ibid.,10:130) Incidentally, Franklin's first foray into public affairs was an attempt to put Philadelphia's night watch tax on a sliding scale. He thought it was unfair that "a poor Widow Housekeeper, all of whose Property to be guarded by the Watch did not perhaps exceed the Value of Fifty Pounds, paid as much as the wealthiest Merchant who had Thousands of Pounds-worth of Goods in his Stores." Accordingly, he proposed "a Tax that should be proportion'd to Property." Benjamin Franklin, *The Autobiography of Benjamin Franklin* (New York: Library of America, 1990), 101.

[238] George Washington, *The Papers of George Washington: Confederation Series*, ed. W.W. Abbot (Charlottesville: University Press of Virginia, 1983), 5:257.

[239] Lester C. Thurow, *Building Wealth: The New Rules for Individuals, Companies, and Nations in a Knowledge-based Economy* (New York: Harper Collins, 2000), 14.

[240] Thomas Frank, *One Market Under God: Extreme Capitalism, Market Populism and the End of Economic Democracy* (New York: Anchor Books, 2001), 97.

[241] Ben Adler, "Gun rally: Liberals and the NRA have found common cause in a pending Supreme Court case," *Newsweek*, March 8, 2010, 45. The article acknowledged that this particular argument for gun rights remains a minority view for the present. But in the next breath, is also acknowledged that change is already underway: "As a result, for now the liberal stand in favor of gun rights remains a novel argument in search of a judicial home. For different reasons, most scholars on the left and right want nothing to do with it. Politicians aren't rushing to embrace it. One could see how moderate Democratic members of Congress – always looking for

ways to woo back rural voters – might adopt this thinking. But they had begun to tone down their opposition to gun ownership even before this new legal argument started making the rounds in Washington."

[242] Pablo Fajnzylber, Daniel Lederman, and Norman Loayza, "What Causes Violent Crime?" *European Economic Review* 46 (2002): 1323.

[243] Ichiro Kawachia, Bruce P Kennedy, and Richard G Wilkinsonc, "Crime: Social Disorganization and Relative Deprivation," *Social Science and Medicine* 48 (1999): 719.

[244] Bruce P. Kennedy, et al., "Social Capital, Income Inequality, and Firearm Violent Crime," *Social Science and Medicine* 47 (1998): 7.

[245] Ibid., 15.

[246] Ibid,. vol. 1, col. 452.

[247] Gordon S. Wood, *The Radicalism of the American Revolution* (New York: Vintage Books, 1993), 261.

[248] George Orwell, *A Collection of Essays* (New York: Harcourt, Inc., 1948), 230.

[249] Andrew Rooney, *And More by Andy Rooney* (New York: Atheneum, 1982), 119.

[250] Joshua Wolf Shenk, "The Perils of Privatization," *Washington Monthly*, May 1, 1995.

[251] Ibid.

[252] The 1995 article notes: "At Rocky Flats, DOE officials gave Rockwell $27 million to clean up five 'ponds' of radioactive and hazardous waste that it had helped create. But Rockwell bungled the complicated procedure--supervisors caught their error, but not before the 'cleanup' was nearly complete--and the General Accounting Office now estimates that cleaning the pond will take until 2009, at a cost exceeding $170 million. The DOE's market-driven response: From 1986 to 1988, when Rockwell's performance was dismal, it received a rating of 90 out of 100--and $26.8 million in bonuses." The site has finally been declared clean after a cleanup effort that was estimated at $7.3 billion.

[253] Ibid.

[254] Becky Schlikerman, "Bush promotes book in Chicago: Former president reflects on his legacy — and pokes fun at himself," *Chicago Tribune*, October 21, 2010.

[255] Thomas Frank, *Pity the Billionaire* (London: Harvill Seckler, 2012), 69.

[256] "French Train Hits 357 MPH Breaking World Speed Record," Associated Press, April 04, 2007. I got it from the Fox News website: http://www.foxnews.com/story/2007/04/04/french-train-hits-357-mph-breaking-world-speed-record/ (accessed 4/29/2014).

[257] Thomas Paine, *Common Sense and Other Political Writings*, ed. W.F. Adkins (New York: Liberal Arts Press, 1953), 174.

[258] Alexander Hamilton, James Madison, and John Jay, *The Federalist Papers* (New York: Oxford University Press, 2008), 54.

²⁵⁹ As adopted in Convention, May 2010, St. Louis Missouri.

²⁶⁰ I owe a hat tip to Prof. Kurt X. Metzmeier for alerting me to this group's existence. Kurt speculates the Benjamin Rush Society's founders "knew he was a Revolutionary era doctor and not much else." But I think they saw "Rush" in his name and ran with that. On a local note, the Society had invited Senator Rand Paul (R-KY) to speak at the University of Louisville Medical School and, during the Q&A, one med student asked him if he had any advice for the final exams. Paul's response was unexpected. "I never, ever cheated and I don't condone cheating. But I would sometimes spread misinformation. So, and, this is a great tactic. Misinformation can be very important." Then he expounded. "We just started spreading the rumor that we knew what was on the test and it was definitely all about liver … We tried to trick all of our competing students into over-studying for the liver and not studying for the kidney and every other organ." Summing up, he said, "So, that's my advice: Misinformation works." Perhaps the Cato Institute, the Federalist Society, and the Benjamin Rush Society all knew what they were doing when they chose their names after all.

²⁶¹ The next sentence in Dr. Benjamin Rush's "Address to the American People" reads, "His time and talents – his youth – his manhood – his old age – nay more, life, all, belong to his country." I imagine Glenn Beck would consider this patriotism fascist. And, no, Dr. Rush was not urging personal sacrifice to win the war. "The American war is over: but this is far from being the case with the American revolution. On the contrary, nothing but the first act of the great drama is closed." He was also not a big fan of states rights. He was a Federalist who emphasized the importance of the national government. "The people of America have mistaken the meaning of the word sovereignty: hence each state pretends to be *sovereign*. In Europe, it is applied only to those states which posses the power of making war and peace – of forming treaties, and the like. As this power belongs only to congress, they are the only *sovereign* power in the United States. We commit a similar mistake in our ideas of the word independent. No individual state, as such, has any claim to independence. She is independent only in union with her sister states in congress." (italics original) Thus, Rush is an odd poster boy for libertarianism. Indeed, in his proposal for a public school system, he wrote, "Let our pupil be taught that he does not belong to himself, but that he is public property. Let him be taught to love his family, but let him be taught at the same time that he must forsake and even forget them when the welfare of his country requires it." You can read it in his "A Plan for the Establishment of Public Schools and the Diffusion of Knowledge in Pennsylvania; to Which Are Added, Thoughts upon the Mode of Education, Proper in a Republic."

²⁶² Tom Flynn, *The Trouble With Christmas* (Buffalo, NY: Prometheus Books, 1993), 184.

²⁶³ Patrick Buchanan, *Washington Times*, January 9, 1991.

²⁶⁴ "The Wisdom of Ann Coulter," *Washington Monthly*, October 2001, 18.

²⁶⁵ Tim Morris. "The most corrupt state? Louisiana owns it: Opinion," 25 July 2017, https://www.nola.com/opinions/2017/07/louisiana_most_corrupt_state.html (accessed May 8, 2019).

²⁶⁶ Joseph Gerth, "Kentucky politicians are rated the most corrupt, and it's not surprising," *Courier-Journal*, 26 January 2018.

²⁶⁷ "Dutch erupt at speech by American envoy: U.S. drug czar wrongly cited higher crime rate in Holland," *San Francisco Chronicle*, July 15, 1998, sec., A, p. 8.

²⁶⁸ John Berthelsen, "The 'Freest Economies in the World,'" *Asia Times Online*, July 9, 2003.

²⁶⁹ Cato Institute, Economic Freedom of the World: 2018 Annual Report https://object.cato.org/sites/cato.org/files/pubs/efw/efw2018/efw-2018-exec-summary.pdf (accessed 04/14/2019).

²⁷⁰ Heritage Foundation, 2019 Index of Economic Freedom https://www.heritage.org/index/book/chapter-3 (accessed 04/14/2019).

²⁷¹ "Singapore sticks to gum-chewing ban," *Calgary Herald*, March 5, 2010.

²⁷² Ed Wray, "Gum returns to Singapore after 12 years," Associated Press, May 26, 2004.

²⁷³ Ibid.

²⁷⁴ Economist Intelligence Unit, The Economist Intelligence Unit's Index of Democracy 2008, 5-7.

²⁷⁵ John Berthelsen, "The 'Freest Economies in the World,'" *Asia Times Online*, July 9, 2003.

²⁷⁶ Oh, SNAP! - Two servile animal epithets in one paragraph! Pilot fish eat the parasites off sharks, thus performing an important grooming function. The sharks accordingly do not eat the pilot fish. Everybody wins: The sharks get a manicure and the pilot fish get free munchies and protection from other predators. Biologists call this a "symbiotic relationship." And, well, you know what a poodle is: It's a small, toy dog. During the Iraq War, Britain's Prime Minister Tony Blair was often called "George W. Bush's poodle."

²⁷⁷ Benjamin R. Butler, *Jihad vs. McWorld* (New York: Times Books, 1995), 243.

²⁷⁸ Jane Mayer, "Covert Operations: The Billionaire Brothers Who Are Waging a War Against Obama," *New Yorker*, August 30, 2010.

²⁷⁹ Robert P. Jones, Ph.D. and Daniel Cox, "Religion and the Tea Party in the 2010 Election: An Analysis of the Third Biennial American Values Survey," Public Religion Research Institute, October 2010, 1.

²⁸⁰ The Libertarian Party's 2004 Platform advocated "the elimination of all restrictions on immigration, the abolition of the Immigration and Naturalization Service and the Border Patrol, and a declaration of full amnesty for all people who have entered the country illegally." The plank has since been scaled back, but it is still eye-opening after the 9-11 attacks.

²⁸¹ Libertarians claim Hunter S. Thompson for his love of drugs and guns, but the left can claim him as well. Arvind Dilawar, "Gonzo Socialism," 18 July 2018, https://jacobinmag.com/2018/07/hunter-thompson-gonzo-socialism-iww (accessed 04/14/2019).

²⁸² Ryan Lizza, "Leap of Faith: The Making of a Republican Front Runner," *The New Yorker*, August 15, 2011, 54.

²⁸³ Michael Lind, "The Radical Center of the Moderate Middle?" *New York Times Magazine*, December 3, 1995.

²⁸⁴ Anne C. Heller, *Ayn Rand and the World She Made* (New York: Doubleday,

2009), 320-321.

[285] Jane Mayer, "Covert Operations: The Billionaire Brothers Who Are Waging a War Against Obama," *New Yorker*, August 30, 2010.

[286] Robert Anton Wilson, *Natural Law or "Don't Put a Rubber on your Willie"* (Port Townsend, WA: Loompanics, 1987), 27.

[287] "Clinton's Willie Horton?" FAIR, 1 September 1992. https://fair.org/extra/clintons-willie-horton/ (accessed 04/14/2019).

[288] Julian Sanchez and David Weigel, "Who Wrote Ron Paul's Newsletters? Libertarian movement veterans, and a Paul campaign staffer, say it was 'paleolibertarian' strategist Lew Rockwell," Reason.com, January 16, 2008.

[289] Ibid.

[290] Mark Ames, "As Reason's editor defends its racist history, here's a copy of its holocaust denial 'special issue'," Pando, entry posted July 24, 2014, https://pando.com/2014/07/24/as-reasons-editor-defends-its-racist-history-heres-a-copy-of-its-holocaust-denial-special-issue/ (accessed 04/14/2019).

[291] Matt Lewis, "The Insidious Libertarian-to-Alt-Right Pipeline: Is it just a phase they go through—or is there something about libertarianism that attracts, well, uh, you know, racist kooks?," Daily Beast, posted on August 23, 2017, https://www.thedailybeast.com/the-insidious-libertarian-to-alt-right-pipeline (accessed 04/14/2019).

[292] Full credit for this encapsulation of paleolibertarianism goes to my friend Rachel Rosen.

[293] Lee Edwards, *The Conservative Revolution: The Movement that Remade America* (New York: Free Press, 1999), 329.

[294] Sam Tanenhaus and Jim Rutenberg, "Rand Paul's Mixed Inheritance," *New York Times*, January 25, 2014, http://www.nytimes.com/2014/01/26/us/politics/rand-pauls-mixed-inheritance.html (accessed 4/1/14).

[295] Taylor Branch, "The Year the GOP went South," *Washington Monthly*, Mar 1, 1998.

[296] Ibid.

[297] Ibid.

[298] His political protégé, Senator John McCain, defended Goldwater from other conservatives this way: "I always say that Barry Goldwater has the right to say whatever he wants to. He has made his contribution – which transformed the Republican Party from an Eastern elitist organization to the breeding ground for the election of Ronald Reagan." (Lloyd Grove, "Barry Goldwater's left turn," *Washington Post*, July 28, 1994) Senator McCain was later forced to defend himself against the charge of turning liberal. An anti-immigrant, Tea Party-affiliated challenger in the 2010 Republican primary forced McCain into intolerant mode. He accordingly promised a border fence and to filibuster any bill that let gays serve openly in the military. McCain beat his challenger by stealing his issues. Thus, political satirist Stephen Colbert sent McCain a message of "congratulations/condolences on your victory/defeat."

[299] Scott McConnell, *100 Voices: An Oral History of Ayn Rand* (New York: New

American Library, 2010), 520-521.

[300] Bruce Schreiner, "Rand Paul: Medicaid has turned into welfare," Associated Press, Oct 4, 2010.

[301] Stephanie Coontz, *The Way We Never Were: American Families and the Nostalgia Trap* (New York: Basic Books, 1992), 81.

[302] Ayn Rand, *Journals of Ayn Rand*, ed. David Harriman (New York: Dutton, 1997), 25.

[303] Ibid., 35.

[304] In the interests of full disclosure, I have a vasectomy and no dependents to raise (or to support me when I grow old). Plus, my rugged individualist parents are both rich and enjoying the largess of the French welfare state where health care is covered. Thus, I am free of financial familial obligations. But, I am realistic and realize that not everyone is similarly situated. This proves my point: Our "independence" is paradoxically underwritten by others – often through the state. My thanks to the people of France for both supporting, and putting up with, my parents. I know they can be difficult.

[305] Lisa Rapaport, "U.S. health spending twice other countries' with worse results," Reuters, 13 March 2018, https://www.reuters.com/article/us-health-spending/u-s-health-spending-twice-other-countries-with-worse-results-idUSKCN1GP2YN (accessed 04/14/19).

[306] Of course, the old dynamic is not totally unknown in affluent countries. One headline on the parody news website the Onion clarifies that: "Pretty Obvious Which Sibling Going to Have to Deal with All the Nursing Home Stuff."

[307] Benjamin Franklin, *The Writings of Benjamin Franklin*, ed. Albert H. Smyth (New York: MacMillan, 1905-7), 10:59.

[308] Barbara Kiviat, "The Big Jobs Myth: American Workers Aren't Ready for American Jobs," *Atlantic Monthly*, JUL 25, 2012, https://www.theatlantic.com/business/archive/2012/07/the-big-jobs-myth-american-workers-arent-ready-for-american-jobs/260169/ (accessed 04/14/2019).

[309] Doug Henwood, "The Myth of Social Security's Imminent Collapse," *Extra!* July/August 1995.

[310] Ayn Rand, *Journals of Ayn Rand*, ed. David Harriman (New York: Dutton, 1997), 43.

[311] Ayn Rand, *Journals of Ayn Rand*, ed. David Harriman (New York: Dutton, 1997), 36.

[312] Ibid., 27.

[313] Ibid.

[314] Generally, psychopaths are planners and also better at blending in with society. They may have stable families and be very successful in their careers. By contrast, sociopaths are impulsive, which constantly gets them into trouble. They often cannot hold a job for too long and thus lack the respectability that psychopaths find useful in getting people to trust them. Psychologists disagree on whether these are two similar conditions or just one found in both fuck-ups and those who have their shit together.

So for now, the DSM-IV (*Diagnostic and Statistical Manual of Mental Disorders* version Four) lumps them together under Anti-social Personality Disorder. If the label matters that much, Hickman was probably a sociopath since he killed the girl on an impulsive whim and sloppily left lots of clues which resulted in his quick capture. By contrast, Psychopaths are more careful and calculating. In any case, Ayn Rand's description was apt – he had "no organ for understanding, the necessity, meaning, or importance of other people." She thought this was a good thing.

[315] Ibid., 29.

[316] Many libertarians saw the Pixar/Disney film *The Incredibles* as championing their cause. Yes, the film says society promotes mediocrity. But, it also has a rather overt anti-corporate subplot and the villain is the type of self-made evil genius who Ayn Rand would probably admire. By contrast, our hero is an insurance company employee who helps his clients navigate its complex bureaucracy. Claims get paid, cutting into the company's profit margins and this infuriates his tyrannical boss. The hero says, "We are supposed to help people." His boss roars back, "We are supposed to help OUR people! Starting with our stockholders!" It seems that the profit motive does not always generate the best social outcomes. And, in contrast to this evil private sector bureaucracy, the long-suffering government agent is a benevolent character. Taken together, it is odd that they did not reflexively call the film liberal Hollywood propaganda. Also note that the film's hero must help others. Yes, he has a frustrated spirit of adventure, but he also feels compelled to help strangers in small, quiet ways even when it is inconvenient and offers no public glory. That is what makes him a hero. He also grows, eventually admitting that his family is his "greatest adventure." Recall that Ayn Rand had scorned such thinking as "dull, petty" and "purposeless." In this light, the film seems more like a gentle refutation of her philosophy. I'm sure that she would prefer watching *Silence of the Lambs*, anyway. So what made libertarians claim this film as one of their own? Well, they think that they are better than most people and latched onto the anti-mediocrity bits, which may not be as significant as they think. Comic book writers have always grappled with how superheroes deal with concealing their secret identities, and the great temptation of super kids to use their powers at school is an old plot. Thus, the only thing that libertarians have to grapple onto is a sense of superiority and it is a slippery handle at that. For them, life is "The tragedy of a man with the consciousness of a god, among … regular fellows." As a geek, I kind of get this. A lot of smart kids get picked on. But at some point you must get over yourself and decide to be Spiderman rather than Doctor Octopus. Indeed, ironically, you do not start to get really smart until you get over yourself. Otherwise, you are largely resting on your laurels. And I mentioned how hubris breeds stupidity, citing Wile E. Coyote. Libertarian intelligence is typically so narrowly focused that they frequently win at tech and business but fail at life and citizenship. Seeing *Real Genius* (1986) had saved me. Libertarianism is like Professor Jerry Hathaway: "We are different from most people, Mitch – better." This is why I try not to be an evil elitist. Also, they always have annoying, dimwitted minions and I would rather have smart, interesting friends. A Pinky and the Brain-like life does not appeal to me. Ayn

Rand had learned that the hard way. Later in life, she reflected, "[M]y fans disappointed and depressed me more than my enemies." Anne C. Heller, *Ayn Rand and the World She Made* (New York: Doubleday, 2009), 303. If she had consumed cartoons and comic books, she might have anticipated this situation.

[317] Ayn Rand, *Journals of Ayn Rand*, ed. David Harriman (New York: Dutton, 1997), 78.

[318] Ibid., 93.

[319] Martha Stout, *The Sociopath Next Door: The Ruthless Versus the Rest of Us* (New York: Random House, 2006), 6.

[320] Zogby poll: "Atlas Shrugged by Ayn Rand read by 8.1 percent," October 17, 2007.

[321] Thomas Frank, *One Market Under God: Extreme Capitalism, Market Populism, and the End of Economic Democracy* (New York: Anchor Books, 2001), 220.

[322] http://boingboing.net/2010/06/23/tom-the-dancing-bug-8.html

[323] Ayn Rand, *Journals of Ayn Rand*, ed. David Harriman (New York: Dutton, 1997), 39.

[324] Tasha Robinson, "Interview: Berkeley Breathed," Onion AV Club, posted June 25, 2003, https://www.avclub.com/berkeley-breathed-1798208298 (accessed 04/14/2019).

[325] I came up with this metaphor before I ran across John Scalzi's excellent blog post on privilege "Straight White Male: The Lowest Difficulty Setting There Is," Whatever, http://whatever.scalzi.com/2012/05/15/straight-white-male-the-lowest-difficulty-setting-there-is/ (accessed 05/04/14).

[326] Brett Zongker, "Top 400 charities see billions less in donations, biggest percentage drop ever recorded," Associated Press, October 17, 2010.

[327] Ayn Rand, *Journals of Ayn Rand*, ed. David Harriman (New York: Dutton, 1997), 270-271.

[328] Ibid., 434.

[329] "Ra-di-a-tion. Yes, indeed. You hear the most outrageous lies about it. Half-baked goggle-box do-gooders telling everybody it's bad for you. Pernicious nonsense!"

[330] Penn Jillette and Teller, *Penn and Teller's How to Play in Traffic* (New York: Boulevard Books, 1997), 173.

[331] http://youtu.be/i3LnVa7zXgc, accessed 3/26/2013.

[332] Mike Flynn, Shikha Dalmia, and Terry Colon (Illustrator), "What Part of Legal Immigration Don't You Understand?" *Reason*, October 2008, https://reason.org/wp-content/uploads/files/a87d1550853898a9b306ef458f116079.pdf (accessed 04/14/2019).

[333] Tim Grierson, "Penn Jillette Wants to Talk It All Out," Cracked, posted January 23, 2024, https://www.cracked.com/article_40871_penn-jillette-wants-to-talk-it-all-out.html (accessed 11/12/24).

[334] Roger Alford, "KY.'s Rand Paul faces possible Senate challenge from

Libertarians; shakes up campaign staff," Associated Press, May 26, 2010.

[335] Roger Alford, "Paul distances himself from Libertarian Party," Associated Press, June 8, 2010.

[336] James R. Carroll, "Rock band Rush says Rand Paul's campaign can't use its songs," *Courier Journal*, Jun 3, 2010, sec. B, p.1. Apparently, their attorney was unmoved by the "But I'm your biggest fan" excuse. (In the interests of full disclosure, I own their *Moving Pictures* CD, which I purchased legally. It was for research.) This would not be the last time that Rand Paul acted cavalier about other people's intellectual property. In 2013, it was revealed that he was a serial plagiarist. Perhaps he had misinterpreted Thomas Jefferson's thoughts on intellectual property.

[337] Michele Salcedo, "Rand Paul: Obama's criticism of BP 'un-American,'" Associated Press, May 21, 2010.

[338] "25 People to Blame for the Financial Crisis," *Time Magazine*, http://content.time.com/time/specials/packages/article/0,28804,1877351_1877350_1877322,00.html

[339] Deborah Solomon, "Tea time," *The New York Times*, April 4, 2010, sec. MM, p. 13.

[340] Mark Leibovich, "For Paul family, libertarian ethos began at home," *New York Times*, June 6, 2010, sec. N, p. 1.

[341] LibertarianismDotOrg, "Ayn Rand's Last Public Lecture: The Sanction of the Victims," YouTube video, 26:22, http://youtu.be/7XiBU8geK08 (accessed June 2, 2013).

[342] Ibid., 49:55.

[343] David Knowles, "Texas yanks Thomas Jefferson from teaching standard," AOL News, March 12, 2010.

[344] William Blackstone, *Commentaries on the Laws of England*, ed. William Carey Jones (San Francisco: Bancroft-Whitney Co., 1915), 1:247. I am grateful to Kurt X. Metzmeier for pointing this out to me.

[345] Thomas Jefferson, *Writings of Thomas Jefferson*, ed. Andrew Adgate Lipscomb and Albert Ellery Bergh (Washington DC: Thomas Jefferson Memorial Association, 1905), 16:19.

[346] Ibid., 15:65.

[347] Thomas Paine, *The Life and Major Writings of Thomas Paine: Includes Common Sense, the American Crisis, Rights of Man, the Age of Reason and Agrarian Justice*, ed. Phillip S. Foner (New York: Citadel Press, 1993), 370.

[348] Ibid., 371.

[349] Ibid., 371-372.

[350] John Adams, *Life and Works of John Adams, Second President of the United States: With a Life of the Author, Notes and Illustrations, by his Grandson Charles Francis Adams* (Boston: Little, Brown & Co., 1854), 10:378.

[351] *Debates in the Several State Conventions on the Adoption of the Federal Constitution as Recommended by the General Convention at Philadelphia in 1787* :

Together with the Journal of the Federal Convention, Luther Martin's letter, Yates's minutes, Congressional opinions, Virginia and Kentucky resolutions of '98-'99, and other illustrations of the Constitution, ed. Jonathan Elliot (Philadelphia: Lippincott, 1937), 3:222.

[352] Gordon S. Wood, *The Radicalism of the American Revolution* (New York: Vintage Books, 1993), 261.

[353] George Orwell, *Animal Farm: A Fairy Story*, illust. Ralph Steadman (London: Secker & Warburg, 1995), 178.

[354] George Orwell, *The Orwell Reader*, (New York: Harcourt-Brace, 1984), 394.

[355] Thomas Jefferson, *Writings of Thomas Jefferson*, ed. Andrew Adgate Lipscomb and Albert Ellery Bergh (Washington DC: Thomas Jefferson Memorial Association, 1905), 14:9.

[356] John Adams and Abigail Adams, *My Dearest Friend: Letters of Abigail and John Adams*, ed. Margaret A. Hogan and C. James Taylor (Cambridge: Belknap Press of Harvard University Press, 2007), 111.

[357] Harry M. Caudill, *Night Comes to the Cumberlands: A Biography of a Depressed Area* (Boston: Little Brown & Co., 1962), 7.

[358] Abraham Lincoln, *The Complete Works of Abraham Lincoln*, ed. John G. Nicolay and John Hay (Harrogate, TN: Lincoln Memorial University, 1894), 5:51.

[359] David Knowles, "8 candidates who want to amend the US Constitution," AOL News, October 7, 2010.

[360] Zaid Jilani, "Tea Party Nation President Says It 'Makes A Lot Of Sense' To Restrict Voting Only To Property Owners," Think Progress, http://thinkprogress.org/politics/2010/11/30/132532/tea-party-voting-property/# (accessed 12/26/2013).

[361] Marr O'Brian, "No, David Brooks, we don't need less democracy," Wonkblog, *Washington Post,* May 20, 2014, http://www.washingtonpost.com/blogs/wonkblog/wp/2014/05/20/no-david-brooks-we-dont-need-less-democracy/ (accessed 5/30/14).

[362] David Brooks, "The Big Debate," *New York Times*, May 19, 2004.

[363] The American Social History Project, *Who Built America? Working People & The Nation's Economy, Politics, Culture & Society* (New York: Pantheon Press, 1992), 2:197.

[364] "Greed Is Bad Reporting," *Extra!*, April 1993.

[365] Thomas Frank, One Market Under God: Extreme Capitalism, Market Populism and the End of Economic Democracy (New York: Anchor Books, 2001), 37.

[366] Mark Twain, *Mark Twain in Eruption: Hitherto Unpublished Pages about Men and Events*, ed. Bernard De Voto (New York: Harper & Brothers, 1940) 61.

[367] Ibid., 64 -65.

[368] Ibid., 66.

[369] Ibid., 65. He then shows how the media feeds this. "We like to read about rich people in the papers; the papers know it, and they do their best to keep this appetite liberally fed. They even leave out a football game or a bull fight now and then to get

room for all the particulars of how – according to the display heading – 'Rich Woman Fell Down Cellar – Not Hurt.' The falling down the cellar is of no interest to us when the woman is not rich, but no rich woman can fall down a cellar and we not yearn to know all about it and wish it was us."

[370] Mark Twain, *A Connecticut Yankee in King Arthur's Court* (New York: Bantam Classic reissue edition, 2005) 165. Twain's hostility to aristocracy can not be overstated. In the same book is his ringing defense of the French Revolution's Reign of Terror. Twain thought aristocracy was worse calling the Reign of Terror a "minor terror" by comparison. (Page 75)

[371] Mark Twain, *Life on the Mississippi* (New York: Perennial Classics edition, 1965), 229.

[372] V.G. Kiernan, *The Lords of Human Kind: Black Man, Yellow Man and White Man in an Age of Empire* (Boston: Little Brown & Co., 1969), 28.

[373] Mark Twain, *The Wit and Wisdom of Mark Twain*, ed. Alex Ayers (New York: Meridian, 1989), 163-164. After marveling that only six persons in every thousand had any say in how medieval England was run, Mark Twain's protagonist declared, "It seemed to me that what the nine hundred and ninety-four dupes needed was a new deal."

[374] Franklin D. Roosevelt, *The Roosevelt Reader*, ed. Basil Rauch (New York: Rinehart & Co., 1957), 69. He also had some words for conservatives Democrats as well. "But it is not and never will be the theory of the Democratic Party. This is no time for fear, for reaction or for timidity. And here and now I invite those nominal Republicans who find that their conscience cannot be squared with the groping and the failure of their party leaders to join hands with us; here and now, in equal measure, I warn those nominal Democrats who squint at the future with their faces turned toward the past, and who feel no responsibility to the demands of a new time, that they are out of step with their party. Yes, the people of this country want a genuine choice this year, not a choice between two names for the same reactionary doctrine. Ours must be a Party of Liberal thought, of planned action, of enlightened international outlook, and of the greatest good to the greatest number of citizens." Obviously, this was well before the Clintons betrayed the legacy of the New Deal and the Great Society. It was rather ironic that Bill Clinton dedicated the Roosevelt memorial in 1997.

[375] Ibid., 149.

[376] Hugh Haynie, *Perspective* (Louisville: Courier Journal and Louisville Times, 1974), 186. And Edward Sorel, *Unauthorized Portraits* (New York: Knopf, 1997), 129. Two pages later, Sorel depicts Richard Nixon in a big wig as "Millhouse I: Lord of San Clemente, Duke of Key Biscayne, and Captain of Watergate." On Page 151, Henry Kissinger is also depicted as Louis XVI.

[377] George Seldes, *Facts and Fascism* (New York: In Fact, 1943), 12.

[378] Ibid., 123.

[379] Charles Highman, *Trading with the Enemy: The Nazi-American Money Plot 1933-1949* (New York: Barnes & Nobel Books, 1983), 165.

³⁸⁰ Erwin Chemerinsky, "Bush v. Gore was not justiciable," *Notre Dame Law Review* 76 (2001): 1093.

³⁸¹ Thomas Jefferson, *Writings of Thomas Jefferson*, ed. Andrew Adgate Lipscomb and Albert Ellery Bergh (Washington DC: Thomas Jefferson Memorial Association, 1905), 13:147.

³⁸² Patrick J. Buchanan, *A Republic, Not an Empire* (Washington, D.C.: Regnery Publishing, 1999), 14.

³⁸³ Also, Pakistan would have been a better ally anyway since India does not border Afghanistan. It really helps arms smugglers to know something of geography. Did Pat Buchanan imagine that we could have routed shipments through India first? Because that would have been complicated by the fact that India and Pakistan do not get along and have clashed over Kashmir since partition and independence. So, again, I can see why India took a pass on arming Islamic militants.

³⁸⁴ William F. Buckley, "Why the South must prevail," *National Review*, August 24, 1957, 148-149.

³⁸⁵ John B. Judis, "White House Vigilante: Pat Buchanan takes matters into his own hands." *New Republic*, January 26, 1987, 18.

³⁸⁶ Second Edition Edit: Kudos to Senator Bernie Sanders for mentioning the coup against Mosaddegh in the 2016 Democratic primary debates! I bet this was the first time most Americans had ever heard of it.

³⁸⁷ David Johnston, "Justice Dept. says threat is not issue for election," *New York Times*, July 17, 2004. Read the article. The contradictory internal back and forth within the Bush Administration is alternately amusing and terrifying.

³⁸⁸ Michelle Goldberg, "Uprising in Egypt splits U.S. conservatives," The Daily Beast, February 1, 2011.

³⁸⁹ Steve Benen, "N.C. Republican ousted following *'Daily Show'* interview," MSNBC, http://www.msnbc.com/rachel-maddow-show/gop-official-resigns-after-racist-comments (accessed 12/26/2013).

³⁹⁰ Admittedly, it is amusing to point out Objectivism's Maoist streak. It had a cult of personality and lists of banned or approved books and music. But nobody is saying that Ayn Rand's acolytes were actually reds. Only conservatives reach that degree of total distortion. In his book, Jonah Goldberg plays an interesting game: If fascists ever used a particular technique or strategy, anyone else who uses the same is painted as a kindred spirit. This calls to mind a footnote in Richard Hofstadter's essay "The Paranoid Style in American Politics" on extremists' tendency to copy their opposites. "In his recent book, *How to Win an Election*, Stephen C. Shadegg cites a statement attributed to Mao Tse-tung: 'Give me just two or three men in a village and I will take the village.' Shadegg comments: 'In the Goldwater campaigns of 1952 and 1958 and in all other campaigns where I have served as consultant I have followed the advice of Mao Tse-tung.' 'I would suggest,' writes Senator Goldwater in *Why Not Victory?* 'that we analyze and copy the strategy of the enemy; theirs has worked and ours has not.'" Although it is fun to imagine Barry Goldwater in a frumpy uniform waving a copy of Mao's "Little Red Book," it is not a vision I think anyone should take seriously.

³⁹¹ I am certainly not the first person to notice psychological projection in politics. In "The Paranoid Style in American Politics" Richard Hofstadter wrote about it, albeit with a slightly different emphasis: "It is hard to resist the conclusion that this enemy is

on many counts the projection of the self; both the ideal and the unacceptable aspects of the self are attributed to him. The enemy may be the cosmopolitan intellectual, but the paranoid will outdo him in the apparatus of scholarship, even of pedantry. Secret organizations set up to combat secret organizations give the same flattery. The Ku Klux Klan imitated Catholicism to the point of donning priestly vestments, developing an elaborate ritual and an equally elaborate hierarchy. The John Birch Society emulates Communist cells and quasi-secret operation through 'front' groups, and preaches a ruthless prosecution of the ideological war along lines very similar to those it finds in the Communist enemy. Spokesmen of the various fundamentalist anti-Communist 'crusades' openly express their admiration for the dedication and discipline the Communist cause calls forth." Although I rely on the assumption of projection throughout the book, I am open to alternate interpretations of this behavior. It could just be that conservatives' lack of empathy and imagination simply make it difficult for them to see things from other people's perspectives or imagine anyone thinking in any other way.

[392] George Seldes, *Facts and Fascism* (New York: In Fact, 1943), 25.

[393] Benito Mussolini, *The Corporate State*, ed. Grafici A.Vallecchi, (Firenze: Viale dei Mille, 1936), 32.

[394] Adolf Hitler, *Hitler: Speeches and Proclamations 1932-1945: The Chronicle of a Dictatorship*, ed. Max Domarus, trans. Mary Fran Gilbert (Wauconda, IL: Bolchazy-Carducci Publishers, 1990), 1:92.

[395] George Seldes, *Facts and Fascism* (New York: In Fact, 1943), 210.

[396] George Seldes, *Facts and Fascism* (New York: In Fact, 1943), 42.

[397] Ibid., 122. Seldes cited a Federated Press interview published January 7th, 1938.

[398] William E. Dodd, "Letter of Ambassador Dodd to Senators," *New York Times*, May 12, 1937, p. 4.

[399] George Seldes, *Facts and Fascism* (New York: In Fact, 1943), 77. I must confess that I am amused by the New York Times's October 26, 1938 headline: "KNUSEN WARNS LABOR ON OUTPUT: Production Must Be Kept Up if Hours Are Cut, He Says on Return from Europe: TELLS OF REICH'S GAINS: Calls It's Transformation the 'Miracle of the 20th Century' – Musicians Arrive" They were on the boat as well.

[400] Ibid., 44.

[401] Ibid., 43. For some reason, that era's plutocrats loved Mussolini the most. Was it because he had invented fascism or because of the former socialist's shift from left to right? I have often heard Mussolini's early socialism invoked to bolster the claim that socialists are fascists. I suppose the thinking goes, "Once a socialist, always a socialist." But if that is how it works, then David Horowitz is still a 1960s campus radical and Ronald Reagan died a New Deal Democrat.

[402] Jonah Goldberg, "Springtime for Slanderers; Who are you calling a Nazi?" National Review Online January 5, 2001.

[403] "Coulter Culture," *The New York Observer*, October 2, 2007. The quote goes: "If we took away women's right to vote, we'd never have to worry about another Democrat president. It's kind of a pipe dream, it's a personal fantasy of mine, but I

don't think it's going to happen. And it is a good way of making the point that women are voting so stupidly, at least single women."

[404] Claudia Koonz, *Mothers in the Fatherland; Women, the Family and Nazi Politics* (New York: St. Martin's Press, 1987), 105.

[405] Ibid. To quote more fully, "Antifeminist women seized upon the rhetoric of rights, but twisted its meaning to mean the 'right' of women to remain in the domestic sphere. Many women, who had been apathetic about national issues before they could vote, used their newly won rights to mobilize against further change. Few grasped the paradox of their double mission of entering public life to defend women's private family sphere. Without either education or upbringing that might have prepared them to take advantage of their new rights, these women wanted 'Emancipation from Emancipation!' – a slogan later taken up by Nazi ideologue Alfred Rosenberg. Two-thirds of all married German women considered themselves primarily housewives. Swearing to reinforce, not threaten, male prerogatives, they set out to defend traditional morality against decadence, which they linked to large cities and poor people."

[406] Ute Frevert, *Women in German History: From Bourgeois Emancipation to Sexual Liberation* (Berg: New York, 1989), 207.

[407] Claudia Koonz, *Mothers in the Fatherland; Women, the Family and Nazi Politics* (New York: St. Martin's Press, 1987), 116.

[408] The film's story was written by Fritz Lang's wife who later became an ardent Nazi. Lang himself was not so enthusiastic and skipped the country for Hollywood shortly after Hitler came to power. His wife stayed, but he never regretted his decision. Shitty politics aside, the film is a visually magnificent, seminal science fiction masterpiece that later inspired *Star Wars*. Find the latest Criterion edition. Even the goofy-ass, quasi-colorized version with 1980s pop songs inserted is worth watching once.

[409] Jeff Cohen, "In his own words: The history book on Patrick Buchanan," FAIR, October 3, 1999.

[410] Ute Frevert, *Women in German History: From Bourgeois Emancipation to Sexual Liberation* (Berg: New York, 1989), 231

[411] Ian Kershaw, *Hitler 1889-1936: Hubris* (New York: W.W. Norton & Co., 1998), 751n.

[412] George Seldes, *Lords of the Press* (New York: Julian Messer, Inc., 1946), 195.

[413] Benito Mussolini, "Forza e Consenso," *Gerarchia*, March 1923, 801-803.

[414] Robert H. Bork, *Slouching Towards Gomorrah* (New York: Reagan Books, 1997), 201.

[415] James Boswell, *The Life of Samuel Johnson*, G.B. Hill. Rev. L.F. Powell ed., (Oxford: Clarendon Press, 1887), 1:408.

[416] Of course, conservatives do not have a monopoly on hostility to democracy. Soviet era Stalinists were just as openly contemptuous of the democratic process as any paleoconservative on Free Republic.com – just as contemptuous and just as confused, since Karl Marx had specified that economic equality required political

equality to survive. Obviously, without democracy, you cannot keep those in power from taking a bigger slice of the pie, hence George Orwell's pointing out that the Soviet leaders had become just another ruling class.

[417] *Tell the Truth and Run: George Seldes and the American Press*, dir. Rick Goldsmith, 111 min., Never Tire Productions, 1996 and 2006, DVD. Quote starts at 1:30:47. Incidentally, every American has a patriotic duty to watch this documentary.

[418] Jim Naureckas, "The Philadelphia Inquirer's new spectrum: From centrism to anti-Semitism," *Extra!*, November/December 1995.

[419] Ann Coulter, "Not your average Joe," *Human Events*, October 6, 2010.

[420] Paul Slansky, *The Clothes Have No Emperor: A Chronicle of the American 80s* (New York: Fireside Press, 1989), 128-129. Start reading on April 11, 1985. Also, note the entry for February 16, 1984 on page 85.

[421] John B. Judis, "White House Vigilante: Pat Buchanan takes matters into his own hands." *New Republic*, January 26, 1987, 18.

[422] William F. Buckley, "Meddling in South Africa," *Palm Beach Post*, August 21, 1985. Buckley pointed out that we do not practice "one man, one vote" because the Senate gives equal weight to smaller states. However, we have unquestionably been moving toward that "fanatical abstraction" as the direct election of senators illustrates. And in 1985, we were certainly closer to it than Apartheid South Africa. Buckley's argument was that we were in no position to lecture South Africa. On the contrary, we were in an excellent position considering our recent, similar experience.

[423] Jonah Goldberg, *Liberal Fascism: The Secret History of the American Left from Mussolini to the Politics of Meaning* (New York: Doubleday, 2007), 398.

[424] Michael Lind, *Up from Conservatism: Why the Right is Wrong for America*, (New York: Simon and Schuster), 1996), 109-111.

[425] Jonah Goldberg, *Liberal Fascism: The Secret History of the American Left from Mussolini to the Politics of Meaning* (New York: Doubleday, 2007), 20.

[426] "Glenn Beck talks with Jonah Goldberg, author of Liberal Fascism," http://www.glennbeck.com/content/articles/article/196/4199/, Tuesday, January 15, 2008 (accessed February 13, 2014).

[427] Chip Berlet, "The Roots of Liberal Fascism: The Book," HNN Special: A Symposium on Jonah Goldberg's *Liberal Fascism*, http://www.hnn.us/article/122245 (accessed 02/24/14).

[428] Jill Lepore, "Birthright: What's next for Planned Parenthood?" *The New Yorker*, November 14, 2011, 49.

[429] As Jill Lepore expounded on her article on NPR's Fresh Air, "She founds a journal called the Birth Control Review, and she asks [Paul] Poponoe, [the co-author of Applied Eugenics] to contribute to it. She goes to D.C. to debate Poponoe. These eugenicists that Sanger is courting are actually generally opposed to birth control because they considered it, and Poponoe writes at the time, that 'birth control is the reverse of eugenics.'" Air date November 9, 2011.

[430] Russ Bellant, *Old Nazis, the New Right, and the Republican Party: Domestic Fascist Networks and Their Effect on U.S. Cold War Politics* (Boston: South End Press, 1988), 60.

⁴³¹ Roger Pearson, *Eugenics and Race* (London: Clair Press, 1966), 26.

⁴³² Russ Bellant, *Old Nazis, the New Right, and the Republican Party: Domestic Fascist Networks and Their Effect on U.S. Cold War Politics* (Boston: South End Press, 1988), 61-63.

⁴³³ Jim Naureckas, "Racism resurgent: How media let The Bell Curve's pseudo-science define the agenda on race," *Extra!* January/February 1995.

⁴³⁴ Jonah Goldberg, *Liberal Fascism: The Secret History of the American Left from Mussolini to the Politics of Meaning* (New York: Doubleday, 2007), 245.

⁴³⁵ William F. Buckley, Jr., "Crucial Steps in Combating the Aids Epidemic; Identify All the Carriers," *New York Times*, March 18, 1986. But perhaps I see contradiction where there is consistency. After all, that was Buckley trying to be compassionate toward uninfected gays and drug addicts and Goldberg equates compassion with fascism. Maybe this is what he means when he says "We are all fascists now."

⁴³⁶ Jonah Goldberg, *Liberal Fascism: The Secret History of the American Left from Mussolini to the Politics of Meaning* (New York: Doubleday, 2007), 115.

⁴³⁷ The interview exchange goes: *"If ever needed, the American Legion stands ready to protect our country's institutions and ideals as the Fascisti dealt with the destructionists who menaced Italy."*

"By taking over the government?" he was asked.

"Exactly that," he replied. "The American Legion is fighting every element that threatens our democratic government – soviets, anarchists, IWW, revolutionary socialists and every other 'red.'... Do not forget that the Fascisti are to Italy what the American Legion is to the United States."

⁴³⁸ Jonah Goldberg, *Liberal Fascism: The Secret History of the American Left from Mussolini to the Politics of Meaning* (New York: Doubleday, 2007), 147.

⁴³⁹ Annie O'Hare McCormick, "Hitler Seeks Jobs for all Germans," *New York Times*, July 10th, 1933, 1.

⁴⁴⁰ Pat Buchanan in His Own Words," FAIR press release, February 26, 1996.

⁴⁴¹ Jonah Goldberg, *Liberal Fascism: The Secret History of the American Left from Mussolini to the Politics of Meaning* (New York: Doubleday, 2007), 99.

⁴⁴² Ibid., 160.

⁴⁴³ Ibid., 6. Amusingly, he does mention Christina Hoff Sommers's book *The War Against Boys* much later on. But at least he does not call that a "liberal equivalency of war." Doesn't he realize that entry is going to be near the War on Poverty in the index?

⁴⁴⁴ Fascists did indeed preach getting "beyond politics" and finding a "third way" between left and right. But they meant getting beyond class conflict. I have already given a few examples – from Mussolini's "harmonization" to Hitler's enthusiasm for Ford's affordable cars. This poses a problem for those who conflate fascism with communism. Obviously, the communists sought to *stoke* class conflict, not get beyond it. Of course, Goldberg ignores this and instead paints any urgent bi-partisan appeal as fascist. Absent this context, things morph into their opposites and any talk of class gets called fascist. In January of 2014, venture capitalist Tom Perkins predicted a

"Progressive Kristallnacht" in a letter to the *Wall Street Journal* that compared the Occupy Wall Street movement's criticism of the rich to the Nazis' anti-Semitism. Two months later, billionaire Home Depot co-founder Ben Langone echoed Perkins' attack on populist rhetoric, "[I]f you go back to 1933, with different words, this is what Hitler was saying in Germany. You don't survive as a society if you encourage and thrive on envy or jealousy." Actually, Langone's last line was what Hitler was saying in 1933.

[445] Abram Rosenblatt, et al., "Evidence for Terror Management Theory: I: The effects of mortality salience on reactions to those who violate or uphold cultural values," *Journal of Personality and Social Psychology* 57, no. 4 (1989): 681-690. My thanks to Jordan S. Carroll for alerting me to this study.

[446] The quote sandwiches a segment in which the CBN reporter conscientiously stressed that this issue is uniting unlikely allies on Right and Left. But Robertson ignores this, portraying being punitive as a liberal trait. Amusingly, conservatives have two central concerns in this matter: tax costs and shielding white collar crooks I guess Pat's friends are terrified of being sent to "Club Fed." This is an unexpected dividend of the era of Enron. Apparently, Wendy Kaminer was correct when she said, "If 'a conservative is a liberal once mugged,' then a liberal is a conservative once arrested." A simple keyword search will turn up the video of Robertson.

[447] Oliver Willis, "Stealing Kennedy: Conservatives Try to Hijack the JFK Legacy," Media Matters, posted November 22, 2013 10:58 AM EST, http://mediamatters.org/blog/2013/11/22/stealing-kennedy-conservatives-try-to-hijack-th/197020 (accessed November 26, 2013).

[448] At one point, Jonah Goldberg sort of claims that liberals do the same, but it does not quite work. He writes, "As for Ronald Reagan, he is enjoying what may be the most remarkable rehabilitation in modern American history – as is Barry Goldwater, who all of a sudden has become a hero to the liberal establishment. It seems that American liberals can appreciate dead conservatives when they become useful cudgels to beat up on living ones." (pg. 394) This sample of Jonah Goldberg's deceptiveness is trivial but typical. Liberals began to soften on Goldwater way back in the 1980s when, like Ayn Rand, the Arizona senator had criticized Ronald Reagan's association with the Moral Majority. This was also why liberals had liked Goldwater's political *protégé* and successor, John McCain (R-AZ). The "Maverick" was also openly contemptuous of the religious right – at least until he began running for president. Goldwater's stock with liberals grew even more in the 1990s. During Whitewater, he called a press conference to defend Bill Clinton telling his fellow Republicans to "get off his back and let him be president." (Lloyd Grove, "Barry Goldwater's Left Turn," *Washington Post*, July 28, 1994.) Goldwater also wrote an op-ed advocating allowing gays to openly serve in the military and that sealed his reputation among both liberals and conservatives. Contrary to Jonah Goldberg's ugly picture of liberals cynically using the dead, liberals befriended Barry Goldwater when conservatives shunned and punished him. "They want to change the name of the party headquarters from the Goldwater building to something else," Goldwater boasted. "They want to take my name off the airport. They want to take my name off the high school. They want to take my name off the lake up north." In fact, Barry Goldwater is

today enjoying a postmortem political rehabilitation among *conservatives* – but only because the Tea Party's phony libertarian rhetoric makes it necessary. Talk about grave robbing! And there is a big difference between heroicizing a figure and saying his ideological descendants are even more extreme. As I noted in the introduction, many prominent Republicans have said that not even Ronald Reagan could get ahead in today's GOP. If Republicans can say this, why can't liberals?

[449] While reading *Liberal Fascism*, you keep expecting Jonah Goldberg to say that he is just kidding and that his whole 400 page book is just a clever exercise written to show how all Nazi analogies are only word games and should therefore be unceremoniously ignored. It never quite happens. Instead, his book is littered with disclaimers of dubious sincerity. Again and again he basically says "I'm not saying that liberals are Nazis, but liberals are Nazis. Just nice Nazis." That is certainly his desired takeaway. Eventually, his frequent qualifiers take on an almost "I'm not a racist, but …" quality. There are two reasons for this. First is the fact that his disclaimers have zero impact on his argument. They exist only so that he can say they exist. As Michael Tomasky wrote in *The New Republic*, "As always in this book, the canard survives the complexities." Secondly, actually taking Jonah Goldberg's disclaimers at face value essentially renders his thesis meaningless. Reviewers across the political spectrum have noticed this. Tomasky asked in exasperation, "Isn't all this at once so broad and so qualified as to be meaningless?" In *The American Conservative* Austin Bramwell wrote, "Goldberg does at times display a blush of shame. He qualifies his conclusions to the point of taking them all back, insisting that he does not actually mean to say that liberals are dangerous totalitarians. He grants that some of his points are trivial and others may appear outrageous, so that nothing he says should be taken as both true and interesting at the same time. He claims that movement conservatives also suffer from the totalitarian temptation, so that we are 'all' fascists now. Why then link liberalism in particular with fascism? Here Goldberg is surprisingly candid: because, he argues, liberals do it to conservatives all the time." Tomasky suspects another motive besides revenge. "Lurking behind all these futile disclaimers may be Goldberg's well-founded fear that intelligent or knowledgeable readers might conclude that he is crazy." The two theories are not mutually exclusive. Just what Jonah Goldberg really believes is elusive, but it is clear what he wants his audience to think. The same dynamic plays out in his appearances on Glenn Beck's show. Like Penn Jillette, Goldberg pretends to gently correct the audience's misconceptions, but he is really only there to tweak and reaffirm them. Goldberg tells Beck that Hillary Clinton is not literally a fascist, but then says that she has fascist tendencies and resumes listing ways that he thinks that liberals are like fascists. This subtle distinction is no doubt lost on most of Beck's audience and is ultimately meaningless even if it does stick since they will use it the same way that Goldberg does. But if Goldberg is worried about looking crazy, he might not want to write so many exclusive essays for Beck's paid subscribers.

[450] David Corn, "Cliven Bundy: I'm Just Like Rosa Parks," Apr. 28, 2014. http://www.motherjones.com/mojo/2014/04/cliven-bundy-statement-rosa-parks-slavery (accessed 05/08/14).

[451] Thomas Frank, *Pity the Billionaire* (London: Harvill Seckler, 2012), 131.

[452] I think that their highly defensive handling of racism exemplifies this. They grasp that being called a racist is a bad thing, yet they only partially register why. Racism is not simply impolite or politically incorrect, but fundamentally un-American. It is against our core egalitarian ethos. But bringing that up triggers multiple issues. For conservatives, patriotism is nothing but nostalgic tribalism. But when someone brings up principles, they bring up irksome responsibilities and unfinished business. One of these things is really thinking about America's identity. There is a meaning beyond "GO TEAM!" and romanticizing the past. Even if you are not a racist, the subject matter itself is loaded with all these awkward, unwelcome abstractions. You may not hate outsiders or the "Other," but you do not want to re-think patriotism either. And you sense that your belonging is somehow under assault even if nobody frames it that way because you have just been reminded that patriotism is a lot more complicated than you want it to be and that also means that it feels very different. The ground feels less certain beneath your feet and the result is a kind of "kill the messenger" hostility. Yes, some also lash back and project out of guilt because they really are racists and have been caught at it. Ted Nugent and his audience are an obvious example. But there are additional, invisible issues on the table, so the emotional stakes are higher than most people realize.

[453] Jonah Goldberg, *Liberal Fascism: The Secret History of the American Left from Mussolini to the Politics of Meaning* (New York: Doubleday, 2007), 15.

[454] Ibid.,175. The two lines immediately before this are hugely amusing and typical of the silliness you find on every page. "For more than sixty years, liberals have insisted that the bacillus of fascism lies semi-dormant in the bloodstream of the political right. And yet with the notable and complicated exceptions of Leo Strauss and Allan Bloom, no top-tier American conservative intellectual was a devotee of Nietzsche or a serious admirer of Heidegger." Apparently, Jonah Goldberg has never heard of Ayn Rand. She was a huge devotee of Nietzsche. Indeed, Nietzsche's superman was the template for all of her heroes. This is an interesting oversight, given Ayn Rand's hostile relationship with the *National Review*. The bad blood began with a negative review that Whittaker Chambers wrote about *Atlas Shrugged*. "From almost any page of *Atlas Shrugged*, a voice can be heard, from painful necessity, commanding: 'To the gas chambers – go!'" Once again, Jonah Goldberg seems "operationally uninterested in the intellectual history" of his own magazine. Maybe, I should edit it instead.

[455] Abigail Adams, *The Feminist Papers, From Adams to Beauvoir*, ed. Alice S. Rossi (Boston: Northeastern University Press, 1973), 10.

[456] Mary Wollstonecraft, *The Feminist Papers, From Adams to Beauvoir*, ed. Alice S. Rossi (Boston: Northeastern University Press, 1973), 55.

[457] William F. Buckley, "Our Mission Statement," *National Review*, November 19, 1955.

[458] John Blake, "Three ways MLK speaks to our time," CNN, updated 2:28 PM ET, Mon January 15, 2018. https://www.cnn.com/2018/01/12/us/mlk-relevance-

today/index.html (accessed 04/29/19).

[459] Michael Lind, *Up from Conservatism: Why the Right is Wrong for America* (New York: Free Press, 1996), 114.

[460] Ibid., 104.

[461] Thomas Frank, *Pity the Billionaire* (London: Harvill Seckler, 2012), 59.

[462] Elizabeth Dilling, *The Red Network: A "Who's Who" and Handbook of Radicalism for Patriots* (Kenilworth, IL: self-published 1935), 37.

[463] Glen Jeansonne, *Women of the Far Right: The Mothers' Movement and World War II* (Chicago: University of Chicago Press, 1996), 166-167.

[464] Jeffrey Kaplan, *Encyclopedia of White Power: A Sourcebook on the Radical Racist Right* (Walnut Creek, CA: Altamira Press, 2000), 97.

[465] Glen Jeansonne, *Women of the Far Right: The Mothers' Movement and World War II* (Chicago: University of Chicago Press, 1996), 10.

[466] Andrew Sullivan, "One Party is Unhinged," The Daily Beast, June 21, 2012. http://andrewsullivan.thedailybeast.com/2012/06/one-party-is-unhinged.html

[467] Lewis Black, "Glenn Beck's Nazi Tourette's," *Daily Show*, airdate May 12, 2010.

[468] "Rick Perry Partners With Pastor Who Thinks Oprah Is The Precursor To The Antichrist," Right Wing Watch (People for the American Way), July 8th, 2011. http://www.rightwingwatch.org/content/rick-perry-partners-pastor-who-thinks-oprah-precursor-antichrist. As my freind Rachel Rosen pointed out to me, "[T]he authors of Left Behind are all about the Antichrist working for the UN. There's a tendency in dispensational premillennialism to characterize the Antichrist as a man of peace; therefore, anyone talking about peace is suspect."

[469] Jonah Goldberg, *Liberal Fascism: The Secret History of the American Left from Mussolini to the Politics of Meaning* (New York: Doubleday, 2007), 395.

[470] Joshua A. Perper M.D., LL.B, M.Sc., Stephen J. Cina M.D., *When Doctors Kill: Who, Why, and How*, (New York: Copernicus, 2010) 57.

[471] Mary Wollstonecraft, *The Feminist Papers, From Adams to Beauvoir*, ed. Alice S. Rossi (Boston: Northeastern University Press, 1973), 58.

[472] John Adams, Article VII, Constitution of the Commonwealth of Massachusetts, 1780.

[473] "Food Stamps, The Struggle to Eat: As Congress wrangles over spending cuts, surging numbers of Americans are relying on the government just to put food on the table," *The Economist*, July 14, 2011.

[474] Department of Justice, Office of Public Affairs, "Justice and Education Departments Announce New Research Showing Prison Education Reduces Recidivism, Saves Money, Improves Employment," Thursday, August 22, 2013, http://www.justice.gov/opa/pr/2013/August/13-ag-948.html (accessed 05/11/14).

[475] Howard Zinn, *A People's History of the United States: 1492 – Present* (New York: Harper Collins, 2005), 10.

[476] Michelangelo Signorile, "Stacey Campfield, Tennessee Senator Behind 'Don't Say Gay' Bill, On Bullying, AIDS And Homosexual 'Glorification'"

http://www.huffingtonpost.com/2012/01/26/stacey-campfield-tennessee-senator-dont-say-gay-bill_n_1233697.html (accessed 1/29/14).

[477] "Rush: '[T]here is No Equality' Because '[S]ome People are Just Born to be Slaves,' While Others are 'Self-starters,'" http://mediamatters.org/video/2010/10/08/rush-there-is-no-equality-because-some-people-a/171719 (accessed December 17, 2012).

[478] Stephanie Coontz, *The Way We Never Were: American Families and the Nostalgia Trap* (New York: Basic Books, 1992), 96-97.

[479] Thomas Paine, *The Life and Major Writings of Thomas Paine: Includes Common Sense, The American Crisis, Rights of Man, The Age of Reason and Agrarian Justice*, ed. Phillip Sheldon Foner (New York: Carol Publishing Group, 1993, 1974) 369.

[480] Although the Founders might have added that the Tories of their day at least had some sense of nobless oblige. Baroness Thatcher did, after all, take her party in a new direction. No doubt conservatives will seize on this to argue that the label should no longer be applied. But the Tories remain pro-rich and anti-working class, so the fundamentals remain the same.

[481] Stephanie Coontz, *The Way We Never Were: American Families and the Nostalgia Trap* (New York: Basic Books, 1992), 99.

[482] Stephanie Coontz, *The Way We Never Were: American Families and the Nostalgia Trap* (New York: Basic Books, 1992), 102.

[483] Micaela von Marcard, trans. Stewart Spencer, "The Apotheosis of Despair," on page 13 of the liner notes for a 1992 Daniel Barenboim performance of Beethoven's Ninth Symphony, Erato records, disc D103194.

[484] I obtained these lines from the Schiller Institute's website.

[485] The Robeson version ends: "Build the road of peace before us/Build it wide and deep and long;/Speed the slow and check the eager/Help the weak and curb the strong./None shall push aside another/None shall let another fall./March beside me, Oh my Brother/All for one and one for all."

[486] Raw Story, "Hannity defends Rutgers coach: 'My father hit me with a belt, I turned out okay!'" http://www.rawstory.com/rs/2013/04/04/hannity-defends-rutgers-coach-my-father-hit-me-with-a-belt-i-turned-out-okay/ (accessed 04/21/13).

[487] As of this edition, his aides have already been found guilty of conspiracy, but the case against Christie himself is still in court.

[488] Crooks and Liars, "Allen West (R-FL) Brags about Torturing Iraqi Policeman," http://crooksandliars.com/blue-texan/allen-west-r-fl-brags-about-torturing-i (accessed 1/27/14).

[489] For a brief catalog of conservative pundits' Putin enthusiasm, see the *Daily Show* segment "Big Vladdy – Semi-Delusional Autocrats," http://www.thedailyshow.com/watch/thu-march-6-2014/big-vladdy---semi-delusional-autocrats (accessed 03/08/2014).

[490] The only time I am aware of the rank and file ever coming up is a 2018 NPR Morning Edition interview with Jonah Goldberg in which David Green mentions that a lot of Republicans support Trump's Russia policy. But he simultaneously says they are out of time, so we do not get Goldberg's answer. Green closes with: "And we should say, I mean, a lot of Republicans – we don't have time to actually dig into this,

maybe next time – but I mean, polls suggest that a lot of Republicans in the country support what [Trump] has done this week, whatever it is. Jonah Goldberg of the National Review, always great having you." And again, it does not address the fact that conservative enthusiasm for Putin predates Trump. ("Jonah Goldberg On Trump, Putin and the GOP, July 20, 2018).

[491] Tom Moran, "Chris Christie endorsement is regrettable: Moran," February 09, 2014 at 6:04 AM, updated February 10, 2014 at 11:24 AM, http://blog.nj.com/njv_tom_moran/2014/02/chris_christie_endorsement_is.html (accessed February 10, 2014).

[492] Chris Mooney, *The Republican Brain: The Science of Why They Deny Science – and Reality* (Hoboken, NJ: John Wiley & Sons, Inc.), 72.

[493] CBS News, "Rep. Joe Barton Apologizes to BP's Tony Hayward for White House 'Shakedown,'" http://www.cbsnews.com/8301-503544_162-20008020-503544/rep-joe-barton-apologizes-to-bps-tony-hayward-for-white-house-shakedown-video-/ (accessed 04/22/13).

[494] Annie Murphy Paul, "Reading Literature Makes Us Smarter and Nicer," *Time Magazine*, June 03, 2013.

[495] Mark Twain, *Innocents Abroad; Or the New Pilgrim's Progress* (Hartford, CT: American Publishing Co., 1869) 650.

[496] Kate Zernike and Megan Thee-Brenan. "Poll Finds Tea Party Backers Wealthier and More Educated," *New York Times*, 14 April 2010, https://www.nytimes.com/2010/04/15/us/politics/15poll.html (accessed May 8, 2019).

[497] Nicholas Carnes and Noam Lupu. "It's time to bust the myth: Most Trump voters were not working class," *Washington Post*, 5 June 2017, https://www.theguardian.com/commentisfree/2014/mar/26/caring-curse-working-class-austerity-solidarity-scourge (accessed May 8, 2019).

[498] David Graeber. "Caring too much. That's the curse of the working classes," The Guardian, 26 Mar 2014, https://www.theguardian.com/commentisfree/2014/mar/26/caring-curse-working-class-austerity-solidarity-scourge (accessed May 8, 2019).

[499] "Barbara Bush Calls Evacuees Better Off," *New York Times*, September 7, 2005.

[500] David C. Hammack, *Nonprofit and Voluntary Sector Quarterly*, 38 (2009):549.

[501] As noted in the *Chronicle of Philanthropy*, "Alan J. Abramson, director of the nonprofit-research program at the Aspen Institute, a Washington think tank, questions whether Mr. Brooks is putting too much stock in data on giving, which Mr. Abramson describes as 'mushy.' He notes that surveys on giving put the percentage of American households who give to charity at between 50 percent and 80 percent – an incredibly wide range. 'If somebody called you up and asked you how much you gave last year, God knows what number you would pull out of the air,' he says." Ben Gose, "Charity's Political Divide," *Chronicle of Philanthropy* 19, no. 4 (November 23, 2006): 3.

[502] *The Christian Century* wondered, "Do religious people have a tendency to overstate their participation in activities that they feel are virtuous?" (James Halterman, "Politics of Charity." *Christian Century*, June 12, 2007, 33.)

[503] Brooks thinks this is such a brilliant argument that he uses that Nader quote four times in a 183 page book (not including notes and appendixes). I feel so much better about my quote recycling now.

[504] Martin Luther King, *A Testament of Hope: The Essential Writings and Speeches of Martin Luther King* (San Francisco: Harper Collins, 1990), 241.

[505] James Halterman, "Politics of Charity," *Christian Century*, June 12, 2007, 34.

[506] Kris Hundley and Kendall Taggart, "America's 50 worst charities rake in nearly $1 billion for corporate fundraisers," *Tampa Bay Times*/CIR special report, June 6, 2013.

[507] Kris Hundley and Kendall Taggart, "Lack of regulation and meager penalties allow worst charities to thrive," *Tampa Bay Times*/CIR special report, June 7, 2013.

[508] Arthur C. Brooks, *Who Really Cares: The Surprising Truth about Compassionate Conservatism: America's Charity Divide--Who Gives, Who Doesn't, and Why it Matters* (New York: Basic Books, 2007), 4.

[509] Ben Gose, "Charity's Political Divide," *Chronicle of Philanthropy* 19, no. 4 (November 23, 2006): 3.

[510] *Maxed Out: Hard Times, Easy Credit and the Era of Predatory Lenders*, dir. James D. Scurlock, 87 min., Magnolia Home Entertainment, 2006, DVD. Scene @ 51:12.

[511] Arthur C. Brooks, *Who Really Cares: The Surprising Truth about Compassionate Conservatism: America's Charity Divide--Who Gives, Who Doesn't, and Why it Matters* (New York: Basic Books, 2007), 138.

[512] The closest Brooks gets to acknowledging any of Rockefeller's wrongdoing is on page 137. "To someone negatively disposed to Rockefeller – because of his business practices or wealth itself – 'God gave me my money' sounds like an outrageous justification ..." No dirty details there: Only the implication of petty jealousy.

[513] Mark Twain, *Mark Twain in Eruption: Hitherto Unpublished Pages about Men and Events*, ed. Bernard De Voto (New York: Harper & Brothers, 1940) 84.

[514] Arthur C. Brooks, *Who Really Cares: The Surprising Truth about Compassionate Conservatism: America's Charity Divide--Who Gives, Who Doesn't, and Why it Matters* (New York: Basic Books, 2007), 139. There is a speech in Lawrence of Arabia where a sheik boasts about all the money the Turks give him for his cooperation. In it, he concludes, "And yet, I am poor – because I am a river to my people," which is a pretty potent metaphor when you live in a desert. But I guess Rockefeller's Hypothesis does not apply out there.

[515] David Edwards, "Pat Robertson: Don't adopt sexually abused children that could grow up 'weird'," Raw Story, posted August 16th, 2012, http://www.rawstory.com/rs/2012/08/16/pat-robertson-dont-adopt-sexually-abused-children-that-could-grow-up-weird/ (accessed August 21st, 2012). I would like to thank Reverend Robertson for coming through for me at the last minute with a quote that was both timely and on point.

516 Marin Cogan, "Blowing Sunshine." *The New Republic*, April 15, 2009, 5.

517 Arthur C. Brooks, *Who Really Cares: The Surprising Truth about Compassionate Conservatism: America's Charity Divide--Who Gives, Who Doesn't, and Why it Matters* (New York: Basic Books, 2007), 154.

518 Peter Birkenhead, "Oprah's Ugly Secret," Salon, March 5, 2007. http://www.salon.com/2007/03/05/the_secret/

519 Lars-Erik Nelson, "Profits, politics, proselytizing: It's the Am-Way," *Daily News* (New York), October 28, 1998, p. 43. See also Gary Tippet, "Inside the cults of mind control," *Sunday Age* (Melbourne, Australia), April 3, 1994, p. 6.

520 My brush with these guys was in the early 1990s, when libertarian rhetoric, happy talk on the economy, and downsizing were all just revving up. The moment was both paradoxical and self-explanatory. Corporations were then exporting jobs and downgrading the pay and benefits of those that remained stateside, so staying put at your job did not look promising. Although, on the other hand, striking out on your own when Walmart was wiping out actual mom and pop stores should have seemed dubious too. This is why the network is there to hold your hand and show you how to get "independently" wealthy.

521 Blake E. Ashforth & Deepa Vaidyanath, "Work organizations as secular religions," *Journal of Management Inquiry*, December 2002, p. 366.

522 Thomas Frank, *One Market Under God: Extreme Capitalism, Market Populism and the End of Economic Democracy* (New York: Anchor Books, 2001), 59.

523 Tom Tomorrow (Dan Perkins), *Penguin Soup for the Soul* (New York: St. Martin's Griffin, 1998), 104.

524 Thomas Paine, *The Life and Major Writings of Thomas Paine: includes Common Sense, The American Crisis, Rights of man, The Age of Reason and Agrarian Justice*, ed. Phillip Sheldon Foner (New York: Carol Publishing Group, 1993), 620.

525 Abraham Lincoln, *The Complete Works of Abraham Lincoln*, ed. John G. Nicolay and John Hay (Harrogate, TN: Lincoln Memorial University, 1894), 1:307.

526 Marisol Bello, "Bridge collapse shines light on aging infrastructure," *USA Today*, May 24, 2013, http://www.usatoday.com/story/news/nation/2013/05/24/washington-bridge-collapse-nations-bridges-deficient/2358419/ (accessed 6/17/2013).

527 Paul Krugman, "Belt-tightening has proven to be disastrous in Europe," *Post Bulletin*, Jan 11, 2013. http://stories.postbulletin.com/news/stories/display.php?id=1520448 (accessed 12/16/13).

528 A.G. Sulzberger, "Facing Cuts, a City Repeals, Its Domestic Violence Law," *New York Times*, October 11, 2011.

529 Fredric Rolando, "The Postal Service is struggling, but not because of the mail" (op-ed), *Washington Post*, July 19, 2012.

530 Melanie Hicken. "Shutdown took $24 billion bite out of economy," CNN Business, 17 October 2013,

https://money.cnn.com/2013/10/16/news/economy/shutdown-economic-impact/index.html (accessed May 8, 2019).

[531] "Government Shutdown Cost Economy $11 Billion, C.B.O. Says," *New York Times*, January 28, 2019.

[532] Abraham Lincoln, *Collected Works of Abraham Lincoln*, ed. Roy P. Basler (New Brunswick, NJ: Rutgers University Press, 1953), 2:320.

[533] We will need another FDR or an LBJ without the albatross of Vietnam. But that is not to say that it is a "man's job" – a strong woman can do that. Although, I would prefer an honest consumer advocate like Senator Elizabeth Warren over an Iraq War-supporting former Walmart board like Secretary of State Hillary Clinton. From the grave, Molly Ivins, speaks for me on Hillary Clinton.

[534] David Jackson, "Obama finds big defender in Merle Haggard," *USA Today*, December 29, 2010.

[535] This was a sharp departure from the traditional British libel law which only focuses on whether the plaintiff's reputation is damaged. (Over two centuries later, McDonald's sued vegetarian activists in British courts for saying their food was unhealthy. It is unhealthy, but Mickey D's enjoyed a venue where that fact was beside the point.) Watergate was not mentioned in my textbook that I recall, but it was probably at the back of the authors' minds given the times and their emphasis on Zenger. I find it hard to imagine that such an insubordinate story would have made it into a textbook in, say, the conformist 1950s – or 1980s for that matter.

[536] Disappointingly, CBS's "60 Minutes" gave this nonsense a platform. Even more sadly, the host of the segment was Ed Bradley. To my knowledge, Molly Ivins was the only journalist who covered this panic with healthy skepticism (*New York Times*, 3 May 1980).

[537] Mark Twain, *A Connecticut Yankee in King Arthur's Court* (New York: Bantam Classic reissue edition, 2005) 77.

[538] Richard Locker, "Tea parties issue demands to Tennessee legislators: Among 5 priorities, state group wants kinder treatment of founding fathers in history courses," The Commercial Appeal, http://www.commercialappeal.com/news/2011/jan/13/tea-parties-cite-legislative-demands/ (accessed January 10, 2013).

[539] Valerie Strauss, "Texas GOP rejects 'critical thinking' skills. Really," *Washington Post*, http://www.washingtonpost.com/blogs/answer-sheet/post/texas-gop-rejects-critical-thinking-skills-really/2012/07/08/gJQAHNpFXW_blog.html (accessed January 10, 2013).

[540] Steven Rendall, Jim Naureckas, and Jeff Cohen, *The Way Things Aren't: Rush Limbaugh's Reign of Error* (New York: The New Press, 1995) 39.

[541] In the interests of full disclosure, I have, on rare occasion, forwarded a meme without double-checking it – but only when it fits a long-proven pattern. For example, when a widespread industry practice, like using child or prison labor, gets linked with a new brand it is easy to believe it. After all, they have to stay competitive in their industry. Moreover, the *Onion* is not the only parody news site out there. And, with insane newsmakers like Rev. Pat Robertson, parody is often difficult to detect. The larger claim is correct, even if the specific instance is not. Thus, I can understand the temptation to sigh and click "share." Everyone is more credulous when they have an established narrative. That is no excuse, but it is an explanation. But, what I do not

understand is doing the exact same thing when you think you have found something that is shiny and new. When you think you have found the Holy Grail of arguments, you want to *see* the Holy Grail and know as much about it as possible. This is particularly true if you think it is good news. Most people, understandably, do not look at depressing information too closely. After all, it's depressing. And they will probably look even less closely if they think that they already know the basic story. But something novel and positive should energize you with enthusiasm and curiosity. If I were a conservative Christian, I would have excitedly flipped to the story of Joseph as soon as Limbaugh's broadcast ended.

542 Shelia Marikar,"Experts Dispute Sarah Palin's Midnight Ride Account, Agree Paul Revere Did Not Warn the British" ABC News, http://abcnews.go.com/Politics/sarah-palins-account-paul-reveres-midnight-ride-shot/story?id=13773745#.UaLWilHKt8E (accessed 05/28/2013).

543 George R.R. Martin, "Where's the Beef?" Not A Blog, entry posted April 9, 2015, http://georgerrmartin.com/notablog/2015/04/09/wheres-the-beef/ (accessed May 8, 2019).

544 Only the Green Bay Packers can be said to represent anyplace since they are actually owned by the citizens of Green Bay, Wisconsin.

545 Look up two "That Mitchell and Webb Look" sketches on "football" (soccer) for a brilliant critique of spectator sports. You can easily find the videos online. There are two: One is set in a soccer stadium and the other is in an office and mentions *Raiders of the Lost Ark*. Watch them both.

546 Mark Steyn, "The Man Who Gave Us Newt," *National Review Online*, entry posted January 22, 2012, http://www.nationalreview.com/blogs/print/288873 (accessed August 24, 2012).

547 Charles Krauthammer, "The GOP's Suicide March," *Washington Post*, January 19, 2012.

548 Churchill did not claim authorship of the saying. "Many forms of Government have been tried, and will be tried in this world of sin and woe. No one pretends that democracy is perfect or all wise. Indeed, it has been said that democracy is the worst form of Government except all those other forms that have been tried from time to time." *Winston S. Churchill: His complete Speeches, 1897-1963*, ed. Robert Rhodes James, vol 7, p. 7566 (1974).

549 "Baracknophobia - Obey," *Daily Show*, airdate 04/07/09, http://www.thedailyshow.com/watch/tue-april-7-2009/baracknophobia---obey (accessed 1/02/14).

550 Rick Perlstein, "Exclusive: Lee Atwater's Infamous 1981 Interview on the Southern Strategy," *The Nation*, http://www.thenation.com/article/170841/exclusive-lee-atwaters-infamous-1981-interview-southern-strategy#axzz2b7u41H7l (accessed August 5, 2013).

551 *The Portable Curmudgeon*, ed. Jon Winokur (New York: Plume 1992), 169.

552 Yasmin Anwar, "Conservatives can be persuaded to care more about the environment, study finds," UC Berkeley Media Relations, December 10, 2012.

553 Regular Fox News commentator and former Cato Institute adjunct scholar Steven Milloy has a blog called junkscience.com. In addition to denying the threat DDT posed to the bald eagle, he is also skeptical of global warming, ozone depletion,

and the effects of secondhand smoke. Unsurprisingly, he has been a paid advocate for the tobacco and oil industries for many years.

[554] Yoel Inbar, David A. Pizarro, and Paul Bloom, "Conservatives are more easily disgusted than liberals," *Cognition and Emotion*, May 7th, 2008.

[555] Glenn Beck said, "Who are you to say, if I'm a devout Muslim and I come over here and have three wives ... that I can't have multiple marriages?" Paul replied, "I think it's a conundrum. If we have no laws on this, people take it to one extension further, does it have to be humans, you know?" A spokesman later said that Paul's sarcasm was not apparent over radio. I listened to the clip and he sounded nothing like the Sarcastic Guy in the "Kids in the Hall" sketch. Indeed, Paul's spokesman must not know the definition of sarcasm. It is saying the opposite of what you mean and Paul was agreeing with Beck. Whatever Paul's tone, the content makes it clear that he was not being sarcastic.

[556] There is a popular reality TV show called "Duck Dynasty" about a family of duck hunters. The "patriarch" of the family is deeply religious, racist, and homophobic. On top of this, he recommends marrying 15 and 16 year old girls because they are supposedly more subservient. Although, he does not mention any bride price so I suppose there is that technical distinction to consider.

[557] William Saletan, "The Party of Rape: Every time the GOP claims to have purged rape extremism, another Republican opens his mouth," Slate.com, http://www.slate.com/articles/health_and_science/human_nature/2013/01/phil_gingrey_todd_akin_and_richard_mourdock_the_gop_s_rape_problem_is_spreading.html (accessed 5/14/14).

[558] Mark Twain, *A Connecticut Yankee in King Arthur's Court* (New York: Bantam Classic reissue edition, 2005) 76-77.

[559] George Orwell, *George Orwell: A Life in Letters*, ed. Peter Davison (New York: Liveright, 2010) 232. Admittedly, Orwell is painting with a rather broad brush. I would probably not toss Mahatma Gandhi in the category of "superhuman fuhrer" even with the qualification of "varying examples."

[560] Klint Finley, "Geeks for Monarchy: The Rise of the Neoreactionaries," Tech Crunch, November 22, 2013, http://techcrunch.com/2013/11/22geeks-for-monarchy/ (accessed 12/2/2-13).

[561] Thomas Jefferson, *Writings of Thomas Jefferson*, ed. Andrew Adgate Lipscomb and Albert Ellery Bergh (Washington DC: Thomas Jefferson Memorial Association, 1905), 10:320-321.

[562] Ibid., 13:279-280.
[563] Ibid., 15:135.
[564] Ibid., 15:492.
[565] Ibid., 16:73.